D0712054

YOUR FRIEND FOREVER,
A. LINCOLN

Your Friend Forever,
A. Lincoln

THE ENDURING FRIENDSHIP
OF ABRAHAM LINCOLN
AND JOSHUA SPEED

Charles B. Strozier

with Wayne Soini

Columbia University Press
New York

Columbia University Press
Publishers Since 1893
New York   Chichester, West Sussex
cup.columbia.edu

Library of Congress Cataloging-in-Publication Data
Strozier, Charles B.
Your friend forever, A. Lincoln : the enduring friendship of Abraham Lincoln and
Joshua Speed / Charles B. Strozier.
     pages   cm
Includes bibliographical references and index.
ISBN 978-0-231-17132-8 (cloth : alk. paper) — ISBN 978-0-231-54130-5 (electronic)
1. Friendship. 2. Lincoln, Abraham, 1809-1865. 3. Speed, Joshua F. (Joshua Fry),
1814-1882. I. Title.

BF575.F66S77   2016
973.7092—dc23   2015022598

Columbia University Press books are printed on permanent and durable acid-
free paper.
This book is printed on paper with recycled content.
Printed in the United States of America

c 10 9 8 7 6 5 4 3 2 1

Cover design by Noah Arlow

References to websites (URLs) were accurate at the time of writing. Neither the
author nor Columbia University Press is responsible for URLs that may have
expired or changed since the manuscript was prepared.

CONTENTS

viii CONTENTS

PREFACE

I landed my first university teaching job at twenty-eight years of age in 1972 at what was then Sangamon State University in Springfield, Illinois (now a branch of the University of Illinois). With my family, I lived on an old, decidedly nonworking farm in the country. I did have chickens and horses in the barn, but otherwise things were a bit feral. My dogs fed on rabbits in the fields, there were lots of weeds, cars kept breaking down, and I never had enough money. I had a freshly minted PhD from the University of Chicago and was about to begin formal psychoanalytic training. I was young and ambitious, perhaps a bit brash, and committed to the serious study of history from a psychoanalytic point of view. As I had gotten my PhD in European history, under the direction of William McNeill, it was something of a treat to stumble onto Abraham Lincoln. Besides, what else can one do in Springfield, Illinois, but study Lincoln? I found the subject utterly engrossing and spent the next decade working on a psychoanalytic study of prepresidential Lincoln.

That book came out in 1982 (*Lincoln's Quest for Union*, Basic Books; rev. ed., 2001, Paul Dry Books) and caused quite a stir as the first serious psychological study of Lincoln. One chapter described Lincoln's friendship with Joshua Speed. I have watched now for decades, mostly from the perspective of my professorship at the City University of New York and from within my psychoanalytic practice in the city, at times with bemusement but also with some annoyance, at the way my work on the story of Lincoln's relationship with Speed has been so misunderstood. After much reflection, I decided to explore the subject of young Lincoln and his relationship with Joshua Speed in the depth it deserves. It seems that every forty years or so I write another book on Lincoln.

Speed was with Lincoln at every point in these years but mostly silent. He moved at the edges of politics, tentatively as Lincoln's friend. He ran a store in Springfield and dabbled in other business ventures. Historians have not known quite what to do with him. Why was he so important for Lincoln? Lincoln had a way of making everyone feel he was his best friend, but in fact only Speed really mattered. Everyone in Springfield knew Speed, and most liked him. He was often mentioned in the oral history that Lincoln's law partner, William Herndon, later gathered. Compared to Lincoln, Speed played only a small role in history (though after his election Lincoln tried to entice Speed to serve in his cabinet, and in the early part of the war he played a pivotal role keeping Kentucky in the Union). But for the most part, it is Lincoln we remember and seek to understand. Nevertheless, I argue Speed needs to be brought out of the shadows and his role in seeing Lincoln through the worst extended personal crisis of his life examined in detail; at the same time, we should not make Speed into more than he was in Lincoln's life. The book is mostly centered on understanding Abraham Lincoln; it is not a dual biography, but neither is Speed ignored. I seek to make him a three-dimensional figure, someone truly worthy of Lincoln's devoted friendship, even his love.

Nearly every detail of the narrative arc in Lincoln's life between 1837 and 1842 has been hotly debated; in fact, it is fair to say that, while books will undoubtedly continue to be written about all facets of Abraham Lincoln's life, the meaning of these years represents the last area of real disagreement about Lincoln's identity and character. Some see Lincoln's relationship with Speed as having been sexualized, thus turning Lincoln into a gay hero, which of course calls into question what has come down to us as the story of his early life, his identity, his marriage, his depressions, and much else. This line of thinking about

Lincoln as gay has a curious context in recent history, embedded as it has been in the age of AIDS from the early 1980s, a disease that has finally moved from the apocalyptic to the merely dreaded, along with all the recent legal, social, and political areas of acceptance of homosexuality. But the image of gay Lincoln, however, has occasioned a good deal of other books that portray him as vigorously heterosexual and pushes Speed into the background. In this version of the narrative, Lincoln litters the ground with broken hearts, prostitutes attract his eye, and the reason for the broken courtship with Mary Todd in late 1840 was his infatuation with another woman (and, it has been argued, Mary had gotten fat anyway). In these studies, Mary Todd Lincoln has been vilified, turned into a shrew in ways not seen in many years in the Lincoln literature, and the idea of Lincoln actually loving her dismissed as foolish. Mary's leading biographer (Jean Baker) further complicates the story by accepting the idea that Speed was Lincoln's lover but feels Lincoln was probably bisexual, and she argues that *Mary* broke the engagement. At least in that biography of Mary, as in some earlier ones, the storyline captures the texture of love in the Lincoln marriage, and the portrait of Mary is that of an interesting and complicated figure in her own right.

In all these tangled lines of argument, Lincoln's friendship with Speed is either made more of than it really was or unduly diminished in significance. Neither view is supported by a close read of the sources, especially Lincoln's own letters. A surprising number of extremely important and psychologically revealing such letters have survived. No other source trumps the significance of something Lincoln actually wrote, which is what this book most heavily relies on. But the letters themselves have long defied understanding. To grasp their deeper meaning, some theory matters. These letters—and much else—don't come to us naked. We can't settle contentious issues in the Lincoln story by a false positivism. My approach is avowedly psychohistorical. I apply concepts from psychoanalysis, hopefully critically and unobtrusively, to bring the evidence alive in new ways in order to appreciate the true role of Speed in the making of young man Lincoln. I do abandon tired Freudian ideas about sex and various complexes and instead draw on current notions of mutuality, empathy, and the self.

Besides Lincoln's letters, other sources of significance abound, including quite a lot of mostly unpublished material about Speed and his family members, including letters, wills, and other documents such as court records, as well as material that is more readily available, such as Speed's own *Reminiscences* and his many letters to and interviews with William Herndon about Lincoln after the war. Those letters and interviews are part of the trove of oral-history materials from all kinds of people who knew Lincoln, gathered mostly by Herndon and deposited in the Library of Congress, and recently published in a masterful (and massive) edition by Douglas Wilson and Rodney Davis. That book, *Herndon's Informants*, needs to be read along with a much earlier but crucial volume of Herndon's letters, *The Hidden Lincoln*, edited by Emmanuel Hertz, as well as other relevant memoirs and interviews, including in newspapers, often from many years later. In one sense, the sheer number of documents about young man Lincoln can be overwhelming. But one must read with caution and a critical eye. It is certainly not the case that merely stacking up endlessly derivative references in the oral history settles a given issue about Lincoln. Context is everything. Nothing that anyone wrote or said about Lincoln after 1865 is free from the shadow cast by a figure of mythic proportions in American memory. Nevertheless, oral history is invaluable, and much of what we know about Lincoln in this period is because of Herndon's work. But to draw intelligently on his research we need to keep in mind the dates of what people said to him and the all-important context in which they told Herndon things.

Herndon lacked good judgment in distinguishing what he knew firsthand and what he interpreted based on his understanding of what others told him. The record he collected about young Lincoln is invaluable (though itself inevitably filled with contradictions). But his interpretations of what it meant needs serious caution in accepting. Based on this criterion, anything Herndon writes about Lincoln before his direct experience with him is open to question. Some of the rest is equally problematic but for different reasons.

As Lincoln's friend after 1838, someone who lived in the same room with him and Speed for two years, and after 1844 his law partner, Herndon knew a great deal about young Lincoln, though he was prone to overstate his own significance. Herndon was an outgoing, flamboyant young man who intensely idealized Lincoln, something played out and reinforced by the way they addressed each other. He called him "Mr. Lincoln"; Herndon was "Billy." Herndon was well read and a

competent lawyer, but his mind was always rushing forward, franti-
cally searching for a new idea before digesting the last one. He wrote
with desperate dashes and piled on adjectives with breathless haste.
But he was devoted to the truth and, as best one can tell, never lied or
tried to skew his story to fit a predetermined view. Many scholars have
attacked Herndon's credibility. Full and uncritical acceptance of his
work as opposed to ready rejection of it because some of what he said
is fraudulent seems to me to be the wrong way of framing the issue.
Herndon sought to be utterly reliable, and as a researcher and oral
historian he mostly succeeded—except when his own psychological
conflicts clouded his vision. In his interviews, for example, he sought
to elicit full and complete accounts. The data from an interview, however, as in psychoanalysis, are shaped by the questions asked. Herndon was curiously intrigued by anything sexual about Lincoln, from
odd accounts of something off-kilter about his father's testicles to his
hero's seeming interest in prostitutes. Herndon also seems to have
nursed some fantasies—and grudges—in his account of Lincoln's
romances, struggles with intimacy, and sexuality. Herndon's "find-
ings" on such issues, even when grounded in the oral history, must be
taken with a grain of salt.

Most importantly, Herndon despised Mary Lincoln, and the feeling was mutual. Douglas Wilson has rightfully pointed out that the
enmity between Herndon and Mary Lincoln has been exaggerated,
that much of the bad blood between the two came from postwar writings of Herndon, and that Herndon went to some lengths to try to be
fair to Mary in his letters and biography of Lincoln. But Wilson may
go a bit too far in his efforts to correct the story. She certainly turned
her wrath on Herndon for his lectures about Ann Rutledge in 1866, for
which she never forgave him. He was, she wrote in 1867, a "miserable
man!" and a "dirty dog" who had been a "hopeless inebriate" saved
by her husband. That "wretched Herndon," she wrote later, with all
his "falsehoods, and villanies," deprived her of her "reason" (though
she quickly adds "*almost*"). But her enmity toward Herndon, though
mostly suppressed, had a long history. Mary thought Herndon was
coarse and a drunken lout. Once Herndon and some drunken cronies
broke a tavern window. Lincoln paid the fine to keep Herndon out of
jail, something undoubtedly noted by Mary. Herndon also had trouble
keeping afloat financially and, in at least one documented case, faced

charges from two local bankers, Jacob and John Bunn. As the scion of Southern plantation elegance and from her perch in the upper middle class in Springfield, Mary looked down on such indiscretions. She never once let him enter her house, despite the fact that her husband worked on a daily basis with Herndon for seventeen years not four blocks away. Herndon's revenge was to gather all the negative reports of her he could manage, to portray her in his letters and biography as crazy, and to describe Lincoln's life with her as a "domestic hell." He could not tolerate Lincoln's love for his wife, and she cherished an exclusive love for Lincoln that Herndon's abject devotion seemed to threaten. That triangle saw Mary Lincoln and Herndon in fierce competition for the attention of the man they both idealized, pitting them against each other like snarling dogs. Lincoln, in turn, probably played an unconscious role in setting up such a competition for his affections. One would think that all these years later observers need not get caught up in taking sides in the struggle between Mary Lincoln and William Herndon. Both were of value to Lincoln, if in different ways and for different reasons. But the sheer volume of material that Herndon left about Mary skews the record and influences the unwary. Some of it is undoubtedly authentic and valuable, but it is all secondhand and much of it tainted. Herndon had an axe to grind in anything touching Mary Todd Lincoln.[1]

***

Male friendship, especially its psychological texture, has evolved over time, and contemporary attitudes and values complicate our efforts to make sense of Lincoln's friendship with Speed. The first part of the nineteenth century was a time when young men could be, indeed were assumed to be, close, bonded, and intimate, even sleeping together, *without* being sexual partners. Some men, of course, were in fact lovers, and a number of good historians are just beginning to uncover a fascinating and ethically important history of male homosexuality in this period (the literature on female friendship and lesbianism, which mirrors that of men but is decisively different in some important ways, is quite well developed at this point). The reason the history of gay male love has been long dormant is its absolute suppression at the time, which meant it left scant evidence, and the belief until recently that it was not a story worthy of the telling. They didn't even have a term for same-sex love: "homosexuality" was not invented until later in the nineteenth century in Germany. Things are different now, which is good for society and all of us who live in it but actually clouds our vision of the past. One of the ironies of our general acceptance of homosexuality (except in the backwaters) in the present is that we assume men who are intimate friends, share their secrets, talk of their everlasting affection for each other, and sleep together are probably sexual partners. It takes a leap of imagination to enter into a time in American history when, on one hand, sex between men was regarded as loathsome and if known was severely punished and the basis for social ostracism while, on the other, intimacy—including sleeping together—and closeness, mutuality, and expressions of love were strongly encouraged and even regarded as desirable for men between mother and wife, men in that narrative space between family of origin and marriage with one's own children.

* * *

I was a young man in my early thirties when I wrote my first book about Lincoln. I was in psychoanalytic training but had not begun to see patients. But now all these decades later and after many years of psychoanalytic clinical work, one thing that I appreciate much more deeply is the distinction between moodiness, sadness, and garden-variety depression and *clinical* depression. The former is ubiquitous and protean. People struggle with depression in a myriad of ways and, like hitting mercury, it can disperse into pieces and surface in unlikely and disguised ways (including embedded in the body in physical symptoms). Such depression drags one down and can interrupt life's flow. But it also takes one into experience well below the surface. It is hard to imagine profundity without some melancholy, and no one in our historical experience better expresses that connection than Abraham Lincoln.

Clinical depression is another matter. It fragments the self and makes life hopeless. Eating, sleeping, and relating to others lose their value. One withdraws from life. Suicide is almost always imagined and sometimes carried out. Clinical depression takes one into a dark hole where creativity languishes along with the self. Nothing hopeful can emerge from such experience. It is toxic. This distinction in the forms of depression leads to an important feature in understanding Lincoln. He was clearly melancholy his whole life in a way that was not unconnected to his profundity. But in the years this book treats he was twice clinically depressed and suicidal in ways that did not again recur in his life. In the late 1830s up to 1842, Lincoln could easily have gone off the rails, and no one played a more important role in healing him than Joshua Speed.

Historians have broken apart the period from 1837 to 1842 to fit their interpretations of young Lincoln. But such fragmentation distorts the story and leads to deep confusion about the meaning of the evidence. In fact, those years from toward the end of Lincoln's life in New Salem and his arrival in Springfield up until his marriage only make sense if seen as of a piece, as one coherent psychological moment in the making of Abraham Lincoln. It was a time of crisis for him. Primarily through his friendship with Joshua Speed, which proved both therapeutic and redemptive, Lincoln vicariously resolved his uncertainties about love and intimacy and after a tortuous broken engagement found his way back to Mary Todd, who had graciously waited for him. In the process, Lincoln established a cohesive self that would never again risk clinical depression. After the early 1840s, he broke free to imagine a new future for himself and eventually, in the fires of war, foster what he called at Gettysburg "a new birth of freedom" for the country. Others have told that later story well. My task is the making of Lincoln. It is one of the more interesting personal stories of a young great man finding himself.

NOTE ON THE AUTHORSHIP OF THIS BOOK

I first met Wayne Soini in a workshop on historical narrative I taught in the summer of 2010 at the Norman Mailer Writers Colony in Provincetown, Massachusetts. Soini is a man of great intelligence and a prodigious researcher whose special interest is Anson G. Henry (Lincoln's doctor friend). Soini later enthusiastically became my research assistant for this book. As it moved forward, we exchanged a good two thousand e-mails on every conceivable aspect of young Lincoln, Speed, and the age and wrote notes to each other that sometimes drifted into arcane corners of scholarship. He was indefatigable in tracking down the answer to everything, and most especially obscure issues in the literature that he knows well, in the oral history, and in countless letters from the period relevant to the topic at hand. Soini also read and reread, edited, criticized, and made suggestions on everything I wrote this book. Although this book is in my voice, I could never have pulled it all together without Wayne Soini, and it is appropriate to note his role on the title page.

ACKNOWLEDGMENTS

As I describe in the preface, this book is the result of a long journey. Sadly, some friends to whom I am deeply thankful for helping me gain whatever insights I have into the themes of this book are deceased. I had many conversations with Roy Basler, the editor of Lincoln's *Collected Works*, in the 1970s about Speed and how to understand his friendship with Lincoln. Richard Current, who wrote a number of fundamental books about Lincoln, was equally helpful. John Y. Simon, the great Ulysses S. Grant editor and scholar who also knew Lincoln well, helped me understand the role of New Salem as a small stage on which an insecure Lincoln could practice his assigned roles. Later, the preeminent Lincoln biographer David Donald provided any number of valuable insights in my conversations and other communications with him. Probably more than any Lincoln scholar of the last generation, Donald agreed with the small—and large—pieces of the way I tell this tale of young Lincoln. I also learned much in the 1970s about contemporary psychoanalysis from my collaboration with Heinz Kohut, a man whose biography I also wrote.

My mentor/guru, Robert Jay Lifton, a research psychiatrist and one of the leading intellectuals in America for the last half-century, has heard me go on about Lincoln for many decades now. He patiently read the proposal and had much to contribute, then reviewed the draft manuscript and had many ideas on how to improve things. My old friend, Christopher N. Breiseth, a historian who also has written about Lincoln, saw things in the draft manuscript I would never have caught and generated an enthusiasm for the book I found infectious. My brother, Robert Strozier, has once again gone over a book of mine with his astute editor's eye and was especially helpful in shaping the last chapter. Geoffrey C. Ward, the noted writer and historian, as well as a family friend since childhood, a man who has helped me in my understanding of Lincoln for the last forty years, read the draft manuscript with care and attention. James Oakes, my colleague and friend at the Graduate Center of CUNY, made invaluable comments on the proposal at the start of things, made a running commentary in the margins of the draft manuscript, and was especially helpful in leading me to revise the way I discuss Lincoln and slavery. David Terman, a distinguished psychiatrist and psychoanalyst as well as an old and dear friend, encouraged me that I had the psychology right. Another old and dear friend in the psychoanalytic world, Tessa Philips, helped me, as always, get it right conceptually, especially the complicated meanings of what it meant for Lincoln to lose Speed as he found himself. David Traub, who has written a fine play about Lincoln's visit to Farmington in the late summer of 1841, read the draft manuscript with great care and attention to any phrasing that seemed too pedantic and/or unclear. We spent many hours in conversation going over the text, sharing stories of Speed and his friendship with Lincoln. Scott Knowles, a historian at Drexel University, saw some key things about the latter parts of the manuscript.

Three curators whom I got to know in the course of my work proved immeasurably helpful and saved me from any number of mistakes. Jennifer Cole, the associate curator of collections at the Filson Historical Society in Louisville, Kentucky, was invaluable in steering me to the excellent Speed collection in Filson, made sure my notes to their sources were accurate, and read the manuscript with an eagle eye. Erika Holst, the curator of collections at the Springfield Art Association, had all kinds of valuable comments, got into the weeds with the evidence, and made some astute conceptual observations that greatly improved things. And James Cornelius, the Lincoln curator in the Abraham Lincoln Presidential Library, truly a scholar and gentleman, proved thoughtful and insightful way beyond my expectations. He read every line, corrected mistakes, wrote "dubious" in the margin when he thought I needed to reconsider (and was always right), and in general brought his vast knowledge to bear on making the book better.

Many people helped me gather the photographs for this book over several years (besides those I took myself). Jennifer Cole assisted me with images at the Filson Historical Society in Louisville, Kentucky. Lisa Parott Rolf found images in the Speed Art Museum, including the color painting of young Joshua Speed. Michelle Ganz provided the image of Thomas Lincoln from the Abraham Lincoln Memorial Library and Museum in Harrogate, Tennessee. In the Abraham Lincoln Presidential Library in Springfield, Illinois, Robert Fairburn found images of the town and associates of Lincoln from the period; Jennifer Ericson provided the Lincoln images. I am grateful as well to the Meserve-Kunhardt Collection, which will soon be at Yale University.

Two anonymous outside readers of the manuscript for Columbia University Press (which is peer reviewed for all its publications), both of whom were clearly authorities in the Lincoln field, were both helpful with some criticisms but also encouraging in their praise.

Richard Morris, my wise and always helpful agent, had any number of ideas about this book as it evolved from something very different in its origins compared to where it ended up, steered me to Columbia University Press, and came up with the title for the book.

Many at the press played a crucial role in bringing this book to completion. My editor, Jennifer Perillo, ushered things along from my wobbly proposal to early drafts and what ended as a complete book. Her assistant, Stephen Wesley, proved helpful in guiding the complicated production of a book like this one. Robert Fellman brought an eagle eye to copy editing, and everyone in design and production at the press made a wonderful book out of my manuscript.

The credit to Wayne Soini on the title page and my comment about him in the preface only begins to express my appreciation for his role in coaxing this book out of me. There is not a word in it he has not reviewed several times, and his role as indefatigable researcher was unparalleled.

And thanks to my adorable Cathryn, who keeps me steady, which is no small task.

A NOTE ON SOURCES

In the field of Lincoln studies the source of unparalleled significance is the *Collected Works of Abraham Lincoln*, published in the 1950s (with some additional material published later). The *Collected Works* are now online, though in a format that is not very user friendly. The Library of Congress has a good deal of their collection of Lincolniana online, though there are holes, so one needs to consult the original sources for anything of significance. One very useful tool is Google Books, Google's massive project to digitize the world's knowledge. I doubt that grandiose scheme will be ultimately successful, but in the field covered by this study it has meant that many old books that are difficult to access are readily available online (for example, Speed's *Reminiscences*). Much else has been digitized and is available online, including Ida Tarbell's papers; the huge collection of Abraham Lincoln's legal papers, which are well indexed and searchable; and much from the collection of the Chicago Historical Museum (formerly the Chicago Historical Society).

The two main libraries with rich archival sources for my work have been the Abraham Lincoln Presidential Library in Springfield, Illinois, and the Filson Historical Society in Louisville, Kentucky. Once upon a time the archivists in Springfield were close colleagues and many of the researchers my former students, as I taught at Sangamon State University in Springfield from 1972 to 1986. It has been a pleasure with this book to make some new friends at the ALPL, especially the curator of the Lincoln Collection, James Cornelius. It was also a pleasure to conduct research at the Filson Historical Society in Louisville, Kentucky, on all their material. My work there would have taken much longer without the expert guidance of Jennifer Cole, the associate curator, Manuscript Division. She wrote her excellent MA thesis on James Speed, worked once at Farmington, and has all the relevant sources in the archives at her fingertips. She could not have been more helpful.

In recent decades many valuable publications have made some crucial primary sources available in book form, carefully edited, including the letters of Mary Todd Lincoln in 1972 (*Mary Todd Lincoln: Her Life and Letters*, edited by Justin G. Turner and Linda Levitt Turner); a new edition of Herndon's biography of Lincoln, edited by Douglas Wilson and Rodney Davis in 1998; and *An Oral History of Abraham Lincoln: John G. Nicolay's Interviews and Essays*, edited and published by Michael Burlingame in 1996. But for my work the essential text is *Herndon's Informants*, expertly edited by Douglas Wilson and Rodney Davis and published in 1998 (which is itself now online). This remarkable book makes available in a readable format with an excellent index the massive and chaotic records of Herndon's oral history housed in the Library of Congress. Before the publication of *Herndon's Informants* it was a nightmare to work with these materials, which constitute an entire archive in and of themselves. I once had the idea of doing this book myself, and in my 1982 study, *Lincoln's Quest for Union*, I was the first to characterize Herndon's research as the beginnings of oral history in America, perhaps in the discipline of history, but I also know I could never have had the patience to put together a volume as impressive as *Herndon's Informants*. One does need to read, however, as a companion to *Herndon's Informants*, the volume that Emanuel Hertz published in 1937, *The Hidden Lincoln*. Hertz's book makes available Herndon's extensive notes to himself, along with the voluminous correspondence between Herndon and his coauthor, Jesse Weik, in the 1880s as they prepared the manuscript of their invaluable, if flawed, biography of Lincoln, which was published in 1889 in what David Donald once characterized as "three ridiculous little volumes."

The many other sources that bear on my story are referenced in my notes. For a book that takes such a radically different position on the key issues from what exists in the literature, I am grateful for the rich scholarship that has preceded me. All that work saved me literally years of research, even if the ideas in this study have been rattling around in my brain for well over three decades.

YOUR FRIEND FOREVER,
A. LINCOLN

1

BEGINNINGS

On Saturday morning, April 15, 1837, with the sun shining on the dusty village of New Salem and the local white-throated sparrow singing its high whistling song, twenty-eight-year-old Abraham Lincoln said goodbye to Bennett and Elizabeth Abell, Kentucky emigrants who for years had hospitably opened their hilltop cabin to him. Lincoln was particularly fond of Mrs. Abell, who had once sewn and "foxed" his pants, as she put it later, and made him a buckskin outfit. He tossed his saddlebags, containing a change of underwear and his treasured copy of William Blackstone's *Commentaries on the Laws of England*, the core legal text of the era, over his shoulder and walked to the home of Bowling Green. This Virginia-born justice of the peace, whose courtroom dress consisted of a shirt and breeches "supported by one tow linen suspender over his shoulder," had served as a mentor and "allmost Second Farther," as one neighbor described the relationship, for young Lincoln. He set off on what Joshua Speed described as the fourteen-mile trip to Springfield, the new capital of Illinois. Lincoln had seven dollars in his pocket and carried a large debt from his failed business ventures of recent years.[1]

It was seven years since Lincoln, clad in buckskin and wearing moc-casins and a coonskin cap with a tail, had arrived in Illinois with his father, Thomas, his stepmother, Sarah, along with two families of his stepsisters and their husbands and children, a total party of thirteen people and a mutt dog. As he described later, they came on "waggons drawn by ox-teams," one of which was driven by Lincoln. They were then pioneers, which Sandburg describes as half-gypsy, whose "look-out is on the horizons from which at any time another and stranger wandersong may come calling and take the heart, to love or to kill, with gold or with ashes, with bluebirds burbling in ripe cornfields or with rheumatism or hog cholera or mortgages, rust and bugs eating crops and farms into ruin." Thomas Lincoln was constantly bothered by insecure titles to the lands he held first in Kentucky and then in southern Indiana. He disliked slavery, mostly because he felt—as did many white yeomen farmers—that slave owners threatened to take all the good land and undermine the livelihood of men like himself. As Lincoln put it in his autobiography: "This removal [from Ken-tucky to Indiana in 1818] was partly on account of slavery; but chiefly on account of the difficulty in land titles." Later, some of the same problems, along with fresh outbreaks of the milk sickness that had killed Lincoln's mother, Nancy Hanks Lincoln, and malaria, which had spread through the family, prompted Thomas and his clan to pull up stakes in the spring of 1830 and move to Illinois.[2]

The site where the family settled had been selected in advance by Lincoln's cousin John Hanks on the northern side of the Sangamon River, at the junction of the timberland and prairie ten miles west of Decatur. As John Hanks put it later, Thomas and the family built a log cabin "about 100 Steps from the N. F [north fork] of [the] Sangamon River & . . . on a Kind of bluff" and planted corn and vegetables for food and enough cotton to meet their clothing needs. Lincoln helped the family build a cabin and "made sufficient of rails to fence ten acres of ground, fenced and broke the ground, and raised a crop of sow[n] corn upon it the same year."[3]

The land on which the Lincolns had settled was not particularly pro-ductive, but even worse, the area turned out to be sickly. In the fall of 1830, as John Hanks put it, all the members of the family "were greatly afflicted with augue and fever," resulting in a general discouragement and a determination to leave. But they got caught in what Lincoln called the "very celebrated" deep snow of the winter of 1830–1831, the worst in recorded memory. On March 1, 1831, when those deep snows had melted, flooding central Illinois, Lincoln and his stepbrother, John D. Johnston, and John Hanks floated by canoe down the San-gamon River to Springfield, where one Denton Offutt hired them all for twelve dollars a month to build a barge, load it up with goods, and navigate it down the Sangamon, the Illinois, and eventually the Mis-sissippi to New Orleans. Lincoln never returned home after that trip, setting off, as he said, "the first time by himself." On the long journey south, Offutt recognized the talents of young Lincoln and offered to hire him as a hand in his New Salem store when he returned on his long journey of 1,273 miles upriver by flatboat from New Orleans. And so Lincoln arrived in New Salem in the late spring of 1831 "like a piece of floating driftwood," as he put it in his autobiography.[4]

New Salem proved to be an ideally sized small stage for a psycho-logically unsure young man with increasingly soaring ambitions; his many failures in love and work in this period could be forgiven and forgotten. Lincoln remained in this village of some twenty five homes and about one hundred people for a crucial six years, from twenty-two to twenty-eight years of age; a mark of its significance for him is that his description of his time there occupies over a quarter of his autobiography (written in 1860, before the presidency). New Salem was a bustling community founded with overoptimistic hopes that it would grow into a major commercial hub of river commerce along the river routes southwest from Cincinnati to St. Louis that led eventually to New Orleans. In this village on a hill overlooking a sharp curve in the Sangamon River lived artisans, a physician and graduate of Dart-mouth, a lawyer who served as justice of the peace, a Shakespeare-quoting businessman, and others with enough education, as William G. Greene put it later, to gather occasionally for "publick Discussions in which Mr. Lincoln participated."[5]

Lincoln, who was an impressive athlete, quickly asserted his manly credentials in this frontier community by outwrestling Jack Arm-strong of the nearby rowdy Clary Grove boys, joining in the rooster fights with the young men from the surrounding villages, participat-ing in the outrageous sport of "gander pulling" (a man riding on horse-back at a full gallop attempts to pull off the well-greased head of a live goose fastened to a rope or pole stretched across a road), and in fact chopping wood and splitting rails with a large axe. Ward Hill Lamon added later that Lincoln was "passionately fond of fine horses." That first summer in New Salem, along with a second stint in the fall, Lincoln volunteered in the Black Hawk War, which was fought mostly in Illinois when the Sauk Indian leader Black Hawk led a brief but ferocious war against the U.S. government. Lincoln never killed anyone and mocked himself later for his "charges against the wild onions" and "bloody struggles with the mosquitoes." His military service, however, was not without significance. He was elected captain of his company, "a success that gave me more pleasure than any I have had since," he wrote just before his election as president. He also made some important friends in the Black Hawk War, including Orville Hickman Browning, who would later become a political and legal colleague, and Major John Todd Stuart, who would serve as his first law partner.[6]

Other ventures in the New Salem years proved less successful. Along with William F. Berry, Lincoln purchased on credit the goods for a store that promptly "winked out," in part because Berry drank himself to death, leaving Lincoln with what he dubbed his "national debt." He tried surveying for a while, borrowing $57.86 from William F. Watkins to buy a horse, saddle, and bridle, but failed to make the payments, which led to a judgment against him in 1834. Lincoln worked fitfully as the postmaster of the village (mainly to be able to read the newspapers for free), served as the local agent for the *Sangamo Journal*, clerked during elections, worked in other stores, ground corn in the mill, harvested crops for local farmers, and spent the better part of one winter tending Isaac Burner's still.[7]

Lincoln put himself up for election to the state legislature soon after his arrival in New Salem. In a handbill he circulated and later published in the *Sangamo Journal*, Lincoln stoutly defends internal improvements, especially to the Sangamon River. A railroad from "some eligible point on the Illinois river" through Jacksonville to Springfield would be a "never failing source of communication" but would be prohibitive in its expense, which he estimated to be at least $290,000. Lincoln's much more limited and realistic proposal is to clear the timber out of the Sangamon River and dig out "the meandering of the channel" so that it could serve as a major source of commerce for all the local communities along its banks. In his handbill, debtor Lincoln also rails against usury in references to now-obscure local issues and strongly argues for support of public education ("For my part, I desire to see the time when education, and by its means, morality, sobriety, enterprise and industry, shall become much more general than at present"). He ends with a psychologically revealing note: "Every man is said to have his peculiar ambition. Whether it be true or not, I can say for one that I have no other so great as that of being truly esteemed of my fellow men, by rendering myself worthy of their esteem."[8]

Lincoln lost that election in what he says in his autobiography was the only time he was defeated by a direct vote of the people, but he won resoundingly (277 to 7) in his own precinct, where his neighbors knew him. At the next election in 1834, however, he won, as he did in the subsequent three elections of 1836, 1838, and 1840. Lincoln quickly drew the attention and respect of his peers, especially the established Whig leader John Todd Stuart, whom he knew and had served under in the Black Hawk War. Perhaps in Stuart, who served just above Captain Lincoln as a major, Lincoln found a role model, though later Lincoln was adamant that he read his law books "without an instructor." In any event, as early as 1832 and 1834, Lincoln often walked to Springfield to borrow books from Stuart, who noticed what Lincoln read—and did *not* read. Lincoln, he said later, was a "schollar from 1835—rather a hard student to 1845" who "read hard works— was philosophical—logical – mathematical" but didn't like history or biography." Stuart encouraged Lincoln to read law as early as 1832, an idea that interested him but became a project that moved slowly in the next few years, given his insecurities as mostly an autodidact who sought to overcome his lack of a formal education (Stuart said Lincoln at first was "sluggish—apathetic" and needed to be "driven").[9]

Lincoln began to dabble in legal affairs in New Salem. A good dozen legal documents in Abraham Lincoln's handwriting survive from the time before he became a sworn member of the Illinois bar. As law was practiced not only by lawyers but also by pettifoggers, as unlicensed practitioners were then known, documents drafted by Lincoln shaped, memorialized, and regulated transactions of importance in New Salem, including a realty appraisal, two realty penalty bonds, a bill of sale, a mortgage, three promissory notes, three receipts, and even a will for Joshua Short. Lincoln most likely drafted many other such documents; Abner Y. Ellis, for example, noted, "I remember he had an old form Book from which he used in writing Deeds, Wills & Letters when desired to do so by his friends and neighbours." Lincoln also represented litigants in the local court presided over by Bowling Green. Lincoln may have accepted neighbors' favors later for his legal work, but he always declined money; Jason Duncan, a New Salem neighbor, said, "As there were no Attorneys nearer than Springfield his services were sometimes sought in suits, at law, and he frequently consented to appear before Esq. Bowling Greens' court, to argue cases, but never charged his clients any fees so far as I Knew."[10]

Sitting on a wood pile, Lincoln read his Blackstone and other books he borrowed from Stuart's law library in Springfield, to the amazement of his neighbors, who thought he could be more profitably engaged in real work. But his years serving as a legal draftsman and as a trial advocate in Green's New Salem court, coaxed along with the indispensable and unflagging support of his mentor, Stuart, and the general esteem in which he was held, paid off. On March 24, 1836, Lincoln's name was entered into the record of Sangamon Circuit Court as a "person of good moral character," the first step toward becoming a lawyer. The following fall, on September 9, he was licensed to practice law in all courts of the state by two justices of the Supreme Court, and on March 1, 1837, six weeks before he moved to Springfield, he was sworn in as a member of the Illinois bar by the full bench of the Supreme Court. Stuart was the key figure in the background of this process and enlisted Lincoln to join him in a new law practice as soon as he was sworn into the bar. In anticipation of Lincoln's arrival, Stuart had some new business cards printed up that read: "J. T. Stuart and A. Lincoln, Attorneys and Counsellors at Law, will practice conjointly, in the Courts of this Judicial Circuit—Office N. 4 Hoffman's Row upstairs. Springfield, April 12, 1837." Lincoln had come a long way, though not in a short time. This card came into the new lawyer's hands some six years after he had first penned, on December 16, 1830, a notarized appraisal, filed with the Macon County clerk, for the farmer Jonathan B. Brown, of a thirty-dollar stray horse.[11]

The winter and spring of 1837 had also been a busy political season for Lincoln. One issue predominated, an issue in which Lincoln played a major role. When the legislature met in Vandalia on February 28, 1837, its main task was to decide the seat of the new capital. There was much grumbling at the poor and often unhealthy conditions in Vandalia, which was in any event too far south to be the capital of a state that was rapidly expanding in its central and northern sections. Still, Vandalia had able and self-interested champions, and there was much jostling for the prize. The best-organized group of legislators was from Sangamon County and was quickly dubbed the "Long Nine," since their collective height was fifty-four feet. Lincoln was the leader of this group of senators and representatives and had shrewdly laid the groundwork for the selection of Springfield as the new capital. He forged a strategy that swapped agreements on internal improvements with legislators from other counties for support in making Springfield the capital of the state. Lincoln managed to keep the Sangamon County group of nine focused on that single goal so that they eventually won the vote. On the first ballot, Springfield, though it led, received only 35 of the 123 votes, with the rest scattered among those for Jacksonville, Vandalia, Peoria, and Alton. By the fourth ballot Springfield gained a majority of 73 and became the selection.

Many in Vandalia, however, and most especially Speaker of the House William Lee D. Ewing, whom Lincoln said was not "worth a damn," were still politicking behind the scenes to reverse the vote. The economic, social, and political future of the town would be assured if selected, and Vandalia especially smarted at its loss. Lincoln, aware of the tentativeness of Springfield's new status, moved quickly after February to make it a fait accompli that it would remain as capital: he pushed an appropriation bill, which passed on March 3, to purchase 2.5 acres in the center of Springfield to create a town square for the new building and name a panel of three commissioners to oversee the project. The most active of those commissioners was Lincoln's close friend Dr. Anson G. Henry. In the next few months the city and the commissioners ceded the land to the state, prepared it for construction, selected an architect, laid the cornerstone with great fanfare, and began construction. Lincoln, in other words, was the local hero when he rode into town.[12]

* * *

Joshua Speed was the scion of a distinguished Kentucky clan that was spawned by the English historian John Speed in the early sixteenth century.[13] That Speed wrote tables of scriptural genealogy published in the very first edition of the King James Bible in 1611, a book that, along with Shakespeare, helped create modern English. John Speed also wrote a noteworthy history of England up to the reign of James I, the son of Mary, Queen of Scots. John's great-grandson, James, emigrated to Virginia in 1695, and his grandson in turn, another James Speed, married Mary Spencer in Charlotte County, Virginia, in 1767. This Captain James Speed fought in the Revolutionary War before receiving a crippling wound in 1781. To honor his service, the new American government, which had no money but lots of land, awarded him 7,500 acres in the newly formed territory of Kentucky. In 1782 Speed crossed the Alleghenies on the Wilderness Road, marked by Daniel Boone, with his wife, six children, and several slaves to settle on his new land. James Speed immediately assumed a public role in Kentucky, serving as a judge (though he had no legal training) and as a member of the Kentucky conventions of 1783, 1785, and 1787. He also began to acquire vast tracts of land. By the time Kentucky became a state in 1792 Speed possessed 45,000 acres mostly located in central Kentucky.

One of James's two sons was John Speed, who had "few opportunities for education," as a friend delicately put it later, but whose mind was "active, vigorous, and free, ever open to new truths." He was a "true and faithful friend" as well as a "wise and kind father." Some saw him as an infidel, but for Speed himself that merely meant he refused to believe uncritically in the absolute truth of every word in the Bible.[14] John Speed owned a store with his brother in the 1790s and also operated a salt works at Mann's Lick in southern Jefferson County. Speed operated the salt works with slaves hired from local plantations. The salt works gave him the means in 1800 to branch out into farming and plantation life after settling on a large tract of land near Louisville given to him by his father. After the death of his first wife, Abby, John Speed, a widower with two daughters and a son (who would soon die), married Lucy Gilmer Fry in 1808. Lucy Fry's family had emigrated from England to Virginia in the second half of the eighteenth century; they lived near Monticello and were close to Thomas Jefferson. Lucy was widely regarded as beautiful, dignified, intelligent, and a woman of sound judgment. She devoted herself to her family, which was to include eleven children, including James (Lincoln's future attorney general), born in 1812, and Joshua, born in 1814.

John Speed turned vigorously to farming after his marriage to Lucy in 1808. His main crop became hemp, a cash crop introduced early on by white settlers, who found it grew well in the rich soil of central Kentucky. Hemp was used on plantations throughout the South as rope to bale cotton and for general purposes in a farm's daily operations. Production of hemp was backbreaking, labor-intensive work. There were two distinct crops. The first, seed hemp, was planted in the spring in the best soil, which had to be carefully prepared. These seed plants were then harvested in early September, cut to the ground with hemp hooks, and hung to dry. The stalks were then flailed, the chaff dispersed, and the collected seeds stored for the next season's planting. Fiber hemp, on the other hand, was planted later and seeded more thickly to prevent the growth of weeds. After the plants reached six to ten feet in height, they were also harvested with hemp hooks. The plants were then left on the ground to rot so that the gum attaching the fiber in the stalks to the outer casing would dissolve. Sometime after Christmas these stalks were collected and put out to dry. "Hemp breaking" involved repeatedly bashing these stalks to gain access to the fiber within them. The fibers were gathered, weighed, and cleaned before being woven into a rough yarn and bagged.

The name of John Speed's plantation was Farmington, and many other things besides hemp were grown on this exceedingly large plantation, which functioned in many ways as a small village. Speed grew some tobacco and made cider from his large orchard. Butter came from cows overseen primarily by Lucy Speed. Corn, timothy, clover hay, and wheat were also grown at different times. In the large gardens, crops grown for consumption by the family and slaves included corn, potatoes, apples, cabbages, peas, beans, and sugar beets. Some fruits were also planted. Animals raised for consumption included pigs, cattle, turkey, chickens, and ducks. A grandson of James Speed later wrote rhapsodically about Farmington:

> Ample old-fashioned barns and outbuildings crowded close about
> a substantial country house, while in the hollow below a moss-
> covered rock spring house was the fountain head of a small, clear
> stream, whose steep banks and surface were green with young
> aromatic mint and tender pungent cress. Above the house, the
> fields, the orchard, and the murmuring stream curved the sky,
> washed tender blue by the soft spring rain.[15]

It took a lot of slave labor to make all this work. The hemp especially was grueling work and terrible for the lungs because of all the dust and pollen stirred by the flailing and hemp breaking. After he moved to Farmington in 1810, John Speed quickly began to buy slaves. He owned:

> 12 in 1811 (seven of whom were under 16 years of age and five over 16);
> 39 in 1812 (14 under 16 years of age and 25 over 16); and
> 55 in 1820, including 38 males (nine under 14 years of age) and 17 females (ten under 14 years of age)
> 62 in 1829

There was a rapid increase in the value of slaves in the 1830s, in part from a Kentucky law in 1833 that made it illegal to import slaves to sell in the state but also from broader economic forces. John, for example, bought a blacksmith in the early 1830s for three hundred dollars. In less than a decade the blacksmith was worth between $1,000 and $1,500. At John's death in 1840 he left fifty-four slaves valued at $19,000, or some three-quarters of a million dollars in today's money. The average Kentucky slave owner at the time owned five or fewer slaves, which made John Speed one of the largest slave owners in the state. But his operation at Farmington was even larger than suggested by the number of slaves he actually owned: as needed, John often leased slaves from his neighbors. There was not only the hemp to be planted, harvested, flailed or beaten, cleaned, and bagged, but all the other cash and consumption crops needed tending, not to mention the feeding and care (and slaughtering and butchering) of the animals. John Speed also at times hired out slaves to help pay for luxury goods and for the education of his children.[16]

John Speed was mostly noted as a humane slave owner who went out of his way to treat his workers well. He established an elaborate system for paying slaves a token amount of money for exceeding their quota of work. As James Speed later told the American Freedmen's Inquiry Commission:

> [My father] was a grower of hemp, and gave his negroes so many pounds of hemp to pick a day, and gave them so many cents a

pound for every pound they picked over their task, and entered it in a book; and at the end of the season, or whenever the negro required it, he made up the account, just as he would with anybody else and paid the negro the amount that was due him. Or if they were cording wood, they had a stated task for every day, and for all they did over that, they were paid.

James reported that his father also provided each slave and his wife a comfortable room in which to live. The room had a fireplace, a bed, clothes, chairs, tables, and cooking utensils. In their free time, they were allowed to keep a garden and raise chickens. John made a habit of giving his slaves "good wool hats," and with their earnings they would often buy better ones and "occasionally" shoes and coats. He gave a woman a month of rest after childbirth and generally did not work them in the fields raising hemp, though they did have to work "dropping corn," or hoeing, milking the cows and making the butter, sewing, and other tasks on this multifaceted plantation. James paints an idyllic picture of Farmington. The male slaves ate together in a large room in the winter and "under the trees or some cool place" when it was warm. The women ate on their own and fed the children separately. After dinner, the slaves' time was "generally spent as they pleased, in fiddling and dancing, laughing and talking."[17]

One important detail in James's 1863 interview with the American Freedmen's Inquiry Commission is that he and his brothers, until they were about seventeen or eighteen, worked five months or so in the fields with the slaves raising the hemp. "They were my associates. I swam with them, I wrestled with them, I did everything they did." Joshua Speed, in other words, not only benefited from the fruits of slave labor but was directly involved in the hard field work of Farmington. He seemed to detest it.

John Speed always spoke affectionately of his favorite slave on the plantation, Morocco, who could be trusted with cash when he traveled to fetch his sons James and Joshua from school. In one letter that John wrote Joshua, he sent thirty dollars with Morocco to give Joshua so that he could pay his debts and "rent at Mrs. McMecken," adding five dollars extra "for yourself and retinue for expences [sic]." It was not uncommon to give some trusted slaves such a status. James Speed reports that when he was young, "a gentleman would have a body slave that he would take round with him, and dress him up, but he rarely had any intercourse or consultation with him about anything; he was a machine."[18]

There was undoubtedly some truth to John Speed's self-conception as a humane slave owner. But one should be cautious about the idea of a good slave owner. In order to maintain slavery people like John Speed had to numb themselves to the gross injustice of owning other human beings and to ignore the harsh conditions of most slaves at Farmington, who engaged in backbreaking work planting and harvesting hemp and breathed dust-filled air that shortened their lives. From the perspective of 1863, James Speed recognizes that the servile status of a "body slave" was maintained by a "gentleman" rarely talking or consulting him, in fact, by treating him like a machine, a metaphor that robbed the slave of his humanity.

In the 1830s, John Speed once told a visitor from the North, "I do the best I can to make my slaves comfortable"—the best, that is, given severe limitations on their housing, health, and happiness. At some level, however, even John Speed recognizes the absurdity of his statement, for he adds, "I tell you, sir, you cannot make a slave *happy*, do what you will." John enslaves people and is then surprised he can't make them happy. His obtuseness went along with (and was perhaps in part sustained by) a marked condescension toward the slaves. In a long chatty letter that John wrote to Joshua Speed in 1836, he reports on life at Farmington, the children in the family, their health, and activities. He adds: "the negroes . . . are all well and behaving themselves as they should do."[19]

Southerners like John Speed and his sons failed to see the violence and terror that maintaining slavery required. John Speed, who claimed to be humane, had no intention of extricating himself from the lavish lifestyle slavery provided. He not only purchased a large number of slaves but was known to broker their sale, which put him perilously close to the vile traders who gathered up slaves in places such as Kentucky and took them to the markets in New Orleans. John Speed was also harsh if he felt the need. In December 1818 he wrote his sister-in-law, Mary, who lived forty miles south of Louisville in Bardstown, Kentucky, about her slave Henry, who "does not behave himself as he ought." John tells Mary to send Henry to Farmington in exchange for another slave because Henry "could not be broke at a better time." John clearly knows how to "break" a slave. In 1840, just before his death, a slave named Bartlett set a fire in Farmington's hemp factory. John immediately sold Barlett to W. H. Pope for $575, "to be taken from the state" on the grounds that it was his "duty to dispose of Bartlett." We don't know if John Speed whipped his slaves, but we do know he had no patience with slaves who tried to escape. He once placed an ad in a local newspaper offering a significant reward for recovering his runaway slave Charles Harrison. Speed describes Harrison as a man of "common size" with yellowish skin, eyes "showing a good deal of white," and about twenty-eight or thirty. Charles, as he was called in block letters in the advertisement, was highly valued by Speed, as he was a "very intelligent fellow," handy, a good shoemaker, gardener, butcher, and bricklayer, among other things. Speed assumed Harrison would make for the free states of Ohio or Indiana and probably try to become a stowaway on one of the Ohio River's many commercial boats, which often employed free or enslaved African Americans. Speed offered fifty dollars for Harrison if found in Kentucky (a considerable sum at the time) but one hundred if recovered on the north side of the Ohio River, that is, free territory, as that would require the labors of loathsome slave runners.[20]

Thomas Jefferson figured closely in the Speed family. He had been a neighbor of the Frys in Virginia, and in 1810 John and Lucy Speed drew on the inspiration of Monticello as they planned their own plantation. It is an urban myth in Louisville that Jefferson actually drew up the plans for the house at Farmington. In fact, a local Kentucky architect designed the project, which took several years to build, required the labor of many slaves, and cost a small fortune. But by 1816 this Federal-style home, one of the first brick buildings in Kentucky, was completed and instantly became one of the more remarkable mansions on any plantation in the state. The home (where Lincoln stayed in the summer of 1841) had imposing columns, a pond out front, many spacious rooms inside, and was surrounded by hemp works, a salt-production facility, a granary, slave quarters, and other outbuildings.[21]

Joshua was born on November 14, 1814, into this busy plantation life of wealth and elegance. The family bustled with children (besides Joshua, there was Mary, Eliza, Lucy, James, Peachy, William, Susan, Philip, John, Martha, and Ann, not counting Thomas and two other boys named James who died in infancy). Joshua grew up with a

perennially pregnant mother until he was eight and a gaggle of tod-
dlers underfoot until he left for school at fifteen. Joshua, who was
never close to his father but devoted to his mother, Lucy, was reticent
to talk or write about his early experiences and relationships, either
in his many communications with Herndon after the war, in which
he focused on his friendship with Lincoln, or in two public lectures he
gave a number of times in the 1870s (one lecture dealt with Lincoln),
which were published first in 1884 and again in 1896.[22]

It would seem, however, that something of a mild depressive shadow
hung over many of the Speeds. Joshua's uncle wrote his brother John
Speed of his "anxiety of mind for your unsettled situation" caused by
his "melancholy or hypochondriacal complaints to various somatic
issues," a typical formulation of the time that reversed the actual
sequence, making the depression a function of bodily ailments, of
nerves, or of an improper balance of humors. Among Joshua's siblings,
there is evidence that at least two suffered from depression, and his
brother James demonstrated something approaching clinical depression. James Speed thus wrote in his diary on March 11, 1844, that "I
am harassed out of my life with the phantoms of my own imagination,
a morbid sensibility is killing me inch by inch." William Speed, for his
part, was deeply disturbed when his wife, Ann, died. And most importantly for our story Joshua himself suffered from depression, along
with his friend Lincoln. In a crucial letter much later, Lincoln writes to
Speed that "you are *naturally of a nervous temperament.*"[23]

Joshua had contrasting relationships with his parents. He seemed
deeply resentful of his father and had trouble being around him. Their
struggles were elemental and elusive. John had once noted, albeit
ironically, the sibling rivalry between James and Joshua, but that was
minor compared to the tension between Joshua and his father. In 1829
on the day before Christmas, John Speed wrote to Joshua in stilted
prose expressing his concern for his son's health, but in the course of
his letter he makes a telling reference to the tension between father
and son:

> The time I have spent with you, & the deep interest excited for
> your safety, will, in spite of all your abuse of me, continue to
> render your father anxiously solicitous for your final recovery of
> health and for the development of those faculty elicited, whilst

your frail vessal [*sic*] was at sea, without rudder or ballast. Be firm and be prudent, and have patience—

He hopes God will "preserve you, & so guide your path in life, as to be an honor to yourself & family."[24]

Joshua's affection for his mother, on the other hand, was deep and abiding. On a trip in 1839, Speed's carriage overturned and nearly threw him into the Mississippi River. "Like a poor fellow who has been jolted almost to death & finally upset," Speed wrote Lucy about the accident, "the first thing I thought of was my mother since when I have thought of you oftener than any one of the family." He escaped serious injury, he tells her, except for some "severe bruises upon my head." He minimizes his injuries: "Thanks to my blood, though I will not say from which side it comes, for a thick scull [*sic*]—or is it so light that coming in contact with a harder substance it only rebounds as a trapball?" He notes, in an interesting aside about his vanity, that the doctor doesn't think his injuries will leave scars. "God forbid they should—I believe, I would rather loose [*sic*] a limb." One man in the carriage seemed near death and asked Speed to write his will and handle his money. Not long after that the man recovered, much to Speed's delight. Speed concludes with a telling comment about money that is probably an unsubtle request that his parents send him some: "Owing to this accident & my consequent dentintion [*sic*] I shall not have more than half as much money in pocket as I expected on my arrival at Springfield, counting upon no other accident."[25]

Four years later, in a stray letter that has survived, Speed writes his mother in what was his habit on Christmas day ("On the annual recurrence of this day I have made it a rule ever since I left Kentucky to write to you"). Writing is the next best thing to seeing her and "claiming and receiving from you your kiss, and your blessing." The day stirs in Speed "fond recollections of pleasures past and brighter hopes for the future." He hopes sincerely that he has done nothing to "forfeit the love or esteem of my parents," even though he has not done enough to "improve my mind." Though his heart may be "vitiated and probably debased in many respects," still, "when I approach my mother either in thought or person," he adds in a rather pretentious note, his heart "beats as fondly and is as free from blemish or disgrace as it was at its first pulsation." Then he speaks more directly: "That I may continue to have your love for the future is my fondest hope, and to merit it will be my highest aim." He then apologizes for the inadequacy of his letter writing. "I do not pretend to be accomplished."[26]

Joshua was educated in the public schools of Jefferson County, for a while under the tutelage of his maternal grandfather and namesake, Joshua Fry. In 1829 he then went to St. Joseph's College in Bardstown, founded a little over a decade earlier by local Catholic clergy and highly regarded for its academic excellence. He was just shy of his fifteenth birthday when he was sent away by his fifty-seven-year-old father and forty-one-year-old mother. Perhaps standing on the portico of the house at Farmington bidding him farewell were some of his ten siblings, then including five other teenagers and three younger children, along with various house and field slaves. Joshua followed his older brother James to St. Joseph's College. James, who enjoyed college life, wrote cleverly once from school to his father about getting rid of some old cravats and shoes and buying new ones in Lexington, including a coat of "black bumbizeene," the "pantaloons yellow nankeen and white drilling," and the "waistcoats all kinds and colors." He also noted how pleased he was with the "ladies of Lexington."[27]

Joshua was a sickly child, something that certainly was not helped by working in the fields with his brothers next to the slaves five months of the year harvesting hemp. At least twice Joshua had to leave school and return to Farmington to be cared for at home. Once in November 1829, Joshua got a serious intestinal bug of some kind that also included worms. His father, John, assumed responsibility for his care while his mother was away from the plantation. John dutifully reports to his wife that the doctor is going to add "pink root" to his medicines for the worms. John gets involved in the gory details of his son's illness. "Joshua's bowels are much mended," he says, and has had "no discharge" for fourteen hours. Still, the "discharges" are "too loose though they are of good color. Every day he is getting better, and was even able the day before to eat some potatoes."[28]

In the fall of 1830, at sixteen years of age and having recovered physically, Joshua returned to school. Once again, however, well before the end of the school year, Joshua got sick and had to withdraw from college and return to Farmington to recuperate; his illness followed immediately on one of equal gravity for James (perhaps the same illness), who also withdrew from school and returned home.

Once Joshua was well, however, and unlike his brother, Joshua was reluctant to return to St. Joseph's. His father wanted him to go back to college and perhaps follow his older brother to law school, but Joshua held his ground and decided not to return.[29]

It was a transformative moment in the life of Joshua Speed. He was just a teenager but a self-willed one. To become himself he felt he needed to get away from his father, to escape from under the shadow of the powerful and domineering John Speed. Joshua needed to follow his own path, which at that point meant leaving school, Farmington, and his family. He had no particular road he wanted to follow, no known worlds to conquer. He didn't want to go to sea, travel west, or become something completely different professionally from his upbringing. He only knew that he had to be separate from his father and make the decisions about his life for himself and by himself.

Joshua chose to move about seven miles away and get a job clerking for William H. Pope, who owned a wholesale store in Louisville on the south side of Main Street, one door below Second Street. Joshua worked for Pope for the next two and a half years, almost certainly sleeping above the store, as he would later in Springfield and as was common for young men breaking into business. Farmington lay close enough from downtown Louisville so that he could occasionally visit his family—though there is nothing specific in the record to indicate he made such visits—but far enough away so that he had to sleep and live in the store.[30]

Louisville had a population of seven thousand in 1828, which made it larger than Lexington. Located on the banks of the Ohio River where the falls occur, the area of what became the city had been occupied by Native Americans for centuries, given its strategic significance. But the Louisville that Joshua encountered in the spring of 1831 was a thriving city of some renown in the West. A traveler that year reported the displays of "wealth and grandeur" and hundreds of houses on stone foundations that exceeded anything found in the Western states. The stores were filled with commodities that "dazzle the eye," and the sounds of bells from the steamboats on the river as well as the "cracking of the coachmen's whip" and the "stage driver's horn" all "salute the ear." Everyone is well dressed and bustling about. Some famous hotels served well-heeled travelers, especially the grand Louisville Hotel. Galt House was famous for its fine Southern cooking.

A Galt House Christmas menu card from a few years later included venison with currant jelly, rib of bear with Poivard's sauce, wild turkey with cranberry jelly, wild goose, buffalo tongue a la Godar—and all for fifty cents. Charles Dickens stayed in Galt House once and reported it was a "splendid hotel" where he felt "as handsomely lodged as though we had been in Paris." A more jaundiced traveler, however, James Freeman Clarke, from Boston, experienced Louisville as "one of the ugliest" cities in America. It had "plain brick shops and houses," the streets never cleaned, and the "flat expanse of the city" very "tiresome" and "hard to be borne." Yet another traveler at the time found Louisville "very green and raw" and the character of its people "manly, intelligent, generous, fresh; natural refinement."[31]

Hard economic times, however, were soon to fall on the city. An important part of the local economy had been portaging boats around the falls. The Ohio River was the main artery connecting goods flowing from the mid-Atlantic states to New Orleans and the West. The minor obstacle of the falls at the bend in the river where Louisville grew—the only site of falls on the Ohio River—was easily overcome by portage, and the city offered an elegant respite from travel while the boats were being transported. But the completion of the Louisville and Portland Canal in 1831 ended the portage business overnight, eroding as well its extensive hospitality infrastructure, along with supporting businesses like the wholesale store where Joshua Speed worked. The suddenness of the change ushered in a local depression that was in turn complicated that year by the outbreak of a cholera epidemic. Louisville had never really recovered from the depression of 1831 when the panic of 1837 hit the state. By then, however, Joshua Speed had left the city.

The economic downturn, and perhaps Joshua's desire to get even further away from his dominating father, led him to relocate to Springfield in 1834. It is not entirely clear whether Speed came to Springfield in 1834 or 1835. In 2002 Allen C. Guelzo discovered a previously unknown Speed letter in the papers of Josiah G. Holland, written on June 22, 1865. In it Speed says his "acquaintance with Mr. Lincoln" began in 1834. Speed also wrote a "statement" for Herndon in 1882, copied by someone else, just before Speed's own death, that begins, "In 1834, I was a citizen of Springfield." On the other hand, in the lectures that form his *Reminiscences*, Speed says on the first page of his Lincoln lecture that he arrived in Springfield in 1835. In the absence of any corroborating evidence, it seems best to use the memory of the younger Speed in 1865 that he repeats just before his death. Speed was also completely settled in Springfield as a merchant and had lots of friends by 1835, which additionally supports the earlier date.[32]

The only roads leading to Springfield, Speed later wrote, were those carved out by the constant flow of immigrants, "then coming from the States south and east, principally Kentucky, Tennessee, Ohio, and New York." These settlers came with "long trains of wagons covered with white sheets, filled with women and children, beds, bedding, and light furniture, all bound westward." They were of all "grades and classes of society, from the cultivated ladies and gentlemen with ample means to the poor man who owns not more than his clothes, and who chopped wood and did work in the camp and drove the oxen as compensation for the privilege of moving with the train." The sight of the prairie that surrounded Springfield grabbed Speed's attention. It was "covered with grass as high as our wheat, waving in the breeze and resembling the billows of the ocean as the shadows of the fleeting clouds passed over it." The prairie was a particularly gripping sight when it caught fire. "Sometimes the prairie was lit up by the burning grass, and as the flames were seen in the distance, like a ribbon of fire belting the horizon, it would almost seem that the distant clouds were on fire."[33]

Springfield was then a "village" (as Speed referred to it) of approximately twelve hundred. The town had developed rapidly after Robert Pulliam first stumbled on the site in 1817.[34] It might well have petered out, as happened so often on this leading edge of America. But one early settler, the enterprising young Elijah Iles, set up business for himself, laid out the streets, and managed to negotiate with the legislature to secure land titles for himself and his neighbors. Iles loved Springfield, and from the beginning he wanted to make it a major city. He was expansive about the game so readily available in central Illinois, the "Venison, Turkey, Prairie Chickens, Quail, Squirrel, beef and enough pork to season," not to mention the "honey and the best of milk and butter, and the never-to-be-forgotten corn dodger, and the hoe cake." Some of the richest soil in America, abundant game, plenty of water, and virtually free land (at least at first) made Springfield a very appealing potential metropolis on the prairie. Commerce, however, developed slowly. Money, for one thing, was scarce and often of dubious value, depending on what was often the perilous condition of the bank that issued it. Even specie was often counterfeit or "shaved." As a result, barter was the norm in most Springfield stores for much of that first decade and continued less commonly after that. In the first store on the square, thirty bushels of oats secured eight yards of calico; a bag of raccoon skins bought two hundred pounds of salt. The next place of business to be opened was the tavern. Exchange of money there replaced barter. Brandy and wine cost 25¢ per half pint, gin for 18¾¢ and whiskey for 12½¢. After about 1822 craftsmen arrived in Springfield in a steady stream, including saddlers, blacksmiths, shoemakers, and cobblers. By the end of that first decade, Springfield had five dry-goods stores, a post office, a printing company, and three cabinet shops that employed carpenters, joiners, and other mechanics. There were problems. The town's mud was ubiquitous, and one could get stuck in it up to the knees. The stables and privies stank in the summer, everything was dirty, and the market swarmed with flies. But, of course, such drawbacks characterized most other towns in what was, after all, the urban *frontier* of America.

Springfield attracted professionals at a surprisingly rapid rate. The first physician was Gershom Jayne, who settled in Springfield in 1823. He built a cabin on Jefferson Street between Second and Third Streets, later moving to Fourth and Jefferson, and practiced medicine in town for the next forty-seven years. Within ten years seven other physicians (Garrett Elkin, John Todd, E. H. Merryman, Ephraim Darling, Jacob Early, James Gray, and Lincoln's friend A. G. Henry) and one dentist (James Spence) joined Jayne in providing medical services to the citizens of Springfield and its surrounding lands, dispensing calomel, castor oil, blue-mass pills, and sage tea, along with occasional doses of quinine. Lawyers as well flocked to the new community, beginning with James Adams in 1821. All were "men of intelligence," wrote John Todd Stuart, who arrived in 1828 to find five other lawyers in town. The Sangamon County court met only twice a year in Springfield, so only by riding the circuit, which constituted a quarter of the state, could a lawyer make a living in Springfield. Along with doctors and lawyers came the preachers. By 1830 there was a Methodist church and an even more imposing brick Presbyterian church. The first newspaper was the *Sangamo Spectator* in 1826, which failed within a few years, along with two other papers, but in 1831 Simeon Francis started the *Sangamo Journal*, the Whig paper, which was followed by the *Illinois*

Republican (between 1835 and 1839) and the more durable *Illinois State Register*, the Democratic paper, in 1837. Lincoln wrote frequently for the *Journal*—James Matheny said Lincoln wrote "hundreds of such Editorials"—as did Stephen Douglas for the *Register*. The later rivalry between Lincoln and Douglas began in the late 1830s in their respective warring political mouthpieces. And between 1828 and 1837 there was the official whipping post on the northeast corner of the town square. A large number of citizens gathered in 1828 for the first public whipping, administered by Sheriff James D. Henry, of a (white) man named Robinson for stealing a bar of iron. In 1837, when it was learned that Lincoln and his colleagues had successfully maneuvered to make Springfield the capital of the state, a rowdy crowd of men and boys, in joyous celebration and many probably full of liquor, piled boxes and other goods at the base of the whipping post, poured a barrel of tar on top, and lit the post, which went up in a "blaze of glory." That was the end of the whipping post, which, in any event, had by then been replaced by a jail.

While Springfield itself was a small town, it supported economically and culturally nearly eighteen thousand people in Sangamon County. That explains why this town of barely fifteen hundred by 1837 could support nineteen dry-goods stores, six retail groceries, one wholesale grocery, four hotels, four coffee houses, four drug stores, two clothing stores, and two shoe stores. Craftsmen included cabinetmakers, hatters, and mechanics. All of that economic activity created a more culturally sophisticated citizenry than such a relatively small population would suggest. It had an educated and refined elite social circle. Many came from well-placed families in Kentucky, some owning slaves (like the Speeds and the Todds), where they had been accustomed to the refinements of middle- and upper-middle-class life. The members of this elite were drawn to Springfield because it was relatively close geographically, the land was cheap, they could readily establish themselves in business or the professions, and some, like Ninian Wirt Edwards, married to one of Mary Todd's sisters, could play a major role in state and local politics and achieve a prominence far greater than what he might have expected in Kentucky. Most were also Whigs, and Lincoln fitted well into their values and outlook on life.

The elite could also be pretentious. Carl Sandburg was the first historian to note the significance of the class distinctions in Springfield.

The farm women who came to town wore shoes where they used to go barefooted; the men had changed from moccasins to rawhide boots and shoes. Farmers no longer spent time killing deer, tanning the hide and making leather breeches to tie at the ankles: it was cheaper and quicker to raise corn and buy pantaloons which had come from Massachusetts over the Ohio or the Mississippi river or the Great Lakes. . . . Carriages held men riding in top-hats and ruffled silk shirts, and women in silks and laces. . . . Its people were mostly from Kentucky, coming by horse, wagon, and boat across country not yet cleared of wolves, wildcats, and horse thieves.

One Springfield man who wrote a piece in 1904 for the *Saturday Evening Post* related an anecdote of members of the town's elite going on a sleigh ride but excluding Lincoln. He said he knew it "sounds queer enough," but we "considered ourselves a 'tony' crowd," and Lincoln, "although an extremely clever and well-liked fellow, was hardly up to our standard of gentility." The Edwardses, who hosted their salon with lively banter, well-dressed men and women, and violins, lived on what they called "Quality Hill" to the southwest of the town center.[35]

Speed's store fitted snugly into this economic and cultural life of Springfield. It was located on the west side of the town square in a row of three two-story brick stores built on Fifth Street south from the corner of Washington Street in 1831. Speed's store was on the southwest corner of Fifth and Washington Streets. When Speed arrived in town in 1834 he immediately joined his cousin James Bell (his mother's sister's son) in a partnership to run the store on the square. It may be that Speed's specific choice of Springfield was because Bell was in a position to help him get established. In any event, "I was a merchant at Springfield," Speed wrote later, "and kept a large country store, embracing dry goods, groceries, hardware, books, medicines, bed-clothes, mattresses, in fact every thing that the country needed." It was never the same store twice, because "dry goods" as a category described happenstance items that Speed stumbled on in this or that deal. The store, Bell & Co., opened on March 26, 1835, with an inventory valued at $12,000. Did John Speed extend some credit to launch his son Joshua in business? If so, it would explain why Joshua chose Bell as his business partner. Such partnerships, in any event, were common at the time. There was not much specie in the West in these days, and any paper money circulating was from local banks that often went belly-up in the constant swirl of economic panics, downturns from bad crops, and cholera and other epidemics that disrupted life in general. Agriculture, which dominated the economy, was also by definition seasonal, so the only way a merchant could make money was to offer goods for credit and then try to unload those goods for cash (though stores sometimes accepted produce in lieu of payment). Often promissory notes served as a form of commercial credit, but, given the difficulty one could face in collection, most merchants preferred transactions that could lead to payment in specie at some not-too-distant point. But one needed to start with inventory, and somehow Bell and Speed were able to establish their store with quite a valuable stock.[36]

Speed, like other merchants, established other partnerships for short periods to handle a specific load of goods, delve into a new economic niche, or simply to expand and diversify his operations. One such partner we know about was A. Y. Ellis, but few records survive of that partnership. Charles Hurst also figured in Speed's life as a clerk; he became a merchant and was to play an important role in Speed's unloading of his obligations when he left Springfield in the spring of 1841. But Lincoln also came to have a stake in Speed's store. While not an investor—perhaps because he was gun-shy of such endeavors after his disastrous experience with William Berry in New Salem—Lincoln handled his friend's law cases, those testy suits against late or nonpayment of debts, of deadbeats fleeing town, or sorting out estates of the dead who left obligations. There were relatively few cases until the late 1830s, but as Susan Krause, in an excellent examination of the legal relationship between Lincoln and Speed (that extended well into the 1840s), shows, Lincoln handled five cases for Bell & Co. in the late 1830s, cases he carried over and expanded into his law partnership with Stephen Logan and then again when he took on Herndon as his partner in 1844. Lincoln did a good job for his friend Speed. He won 67 percent of the twenty-two identifiable cases he handled: four cases were dismissed by the plaintiff's attorney and probably were negotiated out of court in Speed's favor, the results of two cases are obscure and another that involved Lincoln representing a litigant against Speed may not have been adversarial, and only one was decided against Speed. Of course, Speed's shrewdness in business must have made Lincoln's work as a lawyer easier.[37]

Speed was quite aware of Abraham Lincoln, who was well known by then as a rising Whig who in 1836 gave a memorable speech that was part of his campaign for reelection to the state legislature. The speech was part of a debate between Lincoln and his Democratic opponent, George Forquer. It seems from his account later of the event that Speed simply remained in the crowd listening and taking it in. Forquer, a scheming former Whig who turned Democrat to obtain a political position from the Jacksonians, rose to speak first. Noted as someone with a reputation for being sarcastic but effective, Forquer said he would have to "take down" Lincoln. There was in fact some bad blood between the two men, as Forquer had represented a plaintiff who sued Lincoln in 1833 and successfully collected on an IOU that contributed to the huge debt Lincoln carried for the rest of the decade. Forquer gave a "slasher-gaff" speech, as Speed puts it, "dealing much in ridicule and sarcasm." Lincoln listened carefully, then stood up to answer. "It seemed to me then," Speed wrote later, "as it seems to me now, that I never heard a more effective speaker. He carried the crowd with him and swayed them as he pleased." Speed even committed to memory much of the speech, especially Lincoln's humorous reference to the first lightning rod in Springfield, which Forquer had erected on his house. Lincoln had seen the rod the day before giving the speech and, not understanding its purpose but intrigued by it, bought a book specifically to figure it out. He then worked in a reference to the rod in mocking Forquer's opportunistic switch in party loyalties.

> I am not so young in years as I am in the tricks and trades of a politician; but, live long, or die young, I would rather die now, than, like the gentleman, change my politics, and simultaneous with the change receive an office worth $3,000 per year, and then have to erect a lightning-rod over my house to protect a guilty conscience from an offended God.[38]

* * *

In 1872 John Nicolay, as part of the massive biography of Lincoln he had undertaken with John Hay, came to Springfield to interview people who had known Lincoln in his early Springfield years. One such conversation was with William Butler, one of Lincoln's close friends, who began his interview by noting how gloomy Lincoln was in the spring of 1837. At some point after the legislative term ended in Vandalia, probably in early April, Lincoln traveled to Springfield with Butler and two colleagues. When the party stopped overnight along the way, Butler noticed that Lincoln tossed and turned all night, enough to keep him awake. Butler asked Lincoln what was wrong. He said:

> I will tell you. All the rest of you have something to look forward to, and all are glad to get home, and will have something to do when you get there. But it isn't so with me. I am going home, Butler, without a thing in the world. I have drawn all my pay I got at Vandalia, and have spent it all. I am in debt—I am owing Van Bergen, and he has levied on my horse and my compass, and I have nothing to pay the debt with, and no way to make any money. I don't know what to do.[39]

The generous and voluble Butler was moved to help Lincoln. Without asking him, after they arrived in Springfield Butler sold the horse and used the proceeds, plus a substantial but unspecified extra amount from his own pocket, to pay off Van Bergen *and* another debt to the bank. He then gave Lincoln's saddlebags to his wife, who unpacked some of the clothes into a drawer and washed the rest. They were a mess, as Lincoln was always "careless about his clothes." He never bought a hat or pair of socks. Then, and later, whenever he needed an item, Mrs. Butler went out and bought the necessary items and put them in the drawer. When Lincoln discovered what had happened to the horse and clothes he was "very much mortified," though it wasn't for another year that he learned just how much money Butler had put up to pay off the debts. Butler refused then or later to let Lincoln pay him back and made clear he expected Lincoln to board free at his home, an offer Lincoln could hardly turn down. Lincoln did, however, need to wind things up in New Salem, so he borrowed Butler's horse and rode to the village, where he stayed for a week until April 15.

Lincoln then rode back to Springfield on Butler's horse, with "no earthly goods but a pair of saddle-bags, two or three law books, and some clothing which he had in the saddle-bags," as Speed later wrote to Herndon. Lincoln first "took an office," which meant arranging to set up quarters with his new law partner, John Todd Stuart, and found a cabinetmaker, who agreed to build him a bedstead. He then walked to Speed's store, tossed his saddlebags on the counter, and asked how much it would cost to buy materials for a bed. Speed calculated the price of the mattress, the blankets, and other needed materials as Lincoln browsed the store, noting the cost of each item. As he walked around, Lincoln told Speed he had just been admitted to the bar and was joining John Todd Stuart as his partner. His also told him of his plan to turn a small room adjacent to Stuart's office into a sleeping room and that he had in fact already hired a local carpenter to build the bedstead. Speed calculated it would cost him seventeen dollars (though in another account Speed said the figure was thirty dollars). He offered to grant him credit for the cost of the materials, which at first Lincoln refused, and he nearly left the store, as he was still heavily indebted from his failed store partnership in New Salem and had only some seven dollars in his pocket. But Lincoln finally replied: "It is probably cheap enough, but I want to say that cheap as it is I have not the money to pay. But if you will credit me until Christmas, and my experiment here as a lawyer is a success, I will pay you then. If I fail in that I will probably never be able to pay you at all." Speed was struck by Lincoln's sad tone: "I never saw so gloomy, and melancholy a face." He told Lincoln that since the "contraction of so small debt" affected him so deeply, he offered another plan. "I have a very large room, and a very large double-bed in it; which you are perfectly welcome to share with me if you choose." Lincoln asked where the room was, and after Speed told him, without saying a word, he walked upstairs and deposited his meager belongings. He came downstairs and with his face "beaming with pleasure and smiles" announced, "Well Speed I'm moved."[40]

2

TWO FRIENDS, ONE BED

No two men were ever more intimate.
—Joshua Speed to William Herndon, June 22, 1865

Abraham Lincoln at twenty-eight years of age in 1837 was still rough around the edges but also on the way up in the world. As befit a figure well known in the state legislature, his pants no longer hung well above his boots; he even had a black suit and had begun to sport what became his distinctive top hat. He was a fully certified lawyer now and the junior partner of an old acquaintance and fellow Whig legislator, Springfield's leading lawyer, John Todd Stuart.

Lincoln wore his thick black hair parted on the right, bracketing his large ears and accentuating his long face. His strong mouth often broke into a wide smile when he told jokes, which was frequently, and dimples appeared in his cheeks, especially on the right side. His sparkling grey eyes were round and deep and suggested mystery and a haunting tension. They evoked a perennial sadness that few friends or colleagues fully understood. A decade after arriving in Springfield, Lincoln once referred to "my old, withered, dry eyes" that "are full of tears yet," and in the 1850s, well before the war, he said his "own poor eyes" might not last to see the end of slavery. The eyes suggest a kind of premature insight that carried its burdens and took its toll. Profundity was a part of Lincoln's earliest style.[1]

Lincoln, Joshua Speed said once when he first saw him, was "ungainly" and, at another time, "a long, gawky, ugly, shapeless, man." Lincoln, Speed continued, was six feet, four inches tall, "a little stooped in the shoulders," with "long arms and legs, large feet and hands, a high forehead," and a head that was "over the average size" (which had the subtextual meaning in the nineteenth century that its owner possessed unusual intelligence). Speed's physical description of Lincoln sets up his observation that "He never lost the mobility of his nature, nor the kindness of his heart." Speed also noticed Lincoln's grey eyes and the wrinkles in his face and forehead that deepened with age, the way channels dig into streams. Lincoln was a "very sad man," but when he warmed up "all sadness vanished, his face, his face was radiant and glowing, and almost gave expression to his thoughts before his tongue could utter them." Speed often pondered what it was that "threw such charm around him" and concluded "it was his perfect naturalness. He could act no part but his own. He copied no one either in manner or style."[2]

Joshua Speed, who turned twenty-three in November 1837, was a strikingly handsome young man. He spoke in a Southern drawl and wore his curling dark hair long, nearly reaching his ear lobes and just above his collar in the back, lending him the appearance of the contemporary romantic English poet Lord Byron. Speed's thick eyebrows framed wide blue eyes that were set apart evenly in his long but proportioned face. His nose reached to thick lips that in turn framed a sharply defined, angular chin. He was smoothly shaven. He was of average height and thus dwarfed by his friend Lincoln. Robert Kincaid describes Speed as "friendly, handsome, blue-eyed, medium-sized." In the earliest surviving image of Speed, a small oval painting typical of the time, he looks confidently out from the canvas, a man ready to run a store and invest wisely. He seems intelligent, friendly, warm, and gentle. "He took a lively interest in public affairs," his nephew wrote later, and "his personal friends and associates were in all parties." His friendships, however, were "never affected by political or religious views differing from his own."[3]

Speed was prepared psychologically to idealize Lincoln. He was younger, more uncertain about himself, more vulnerable, softer. Lincoln was physically impressive and bore himself with the assurance of the fine athlete he was, his height exaggerated by his tall hat. Speed speaks with awe of Lincoln's involvement in the "manly sports" in New

Salem in which he either engaged or helped judge. Lincoln's physical presence and athleticism drew Speed into his orbit. One expression of Speed's instant attraction was that he spontaneously refused to charge Lincoln rent. It is commonly assumed now by scholars that the transaction nevertheless carried an implicit financial obligation and that there was an unspoken agreement that Lincoln would handle Speed's legal matters for free. While that may have been true later (though then also open to question), this interpretation ignores that Speed himself makes no mention of such an arrangement in his account of welcoming Lincoln into his home and bed. Speed is otherwise quite detailed about the sequence of events leading up to and involving Lincoln in these years. In fact, Speed seemed instinctively motivated at the outset *not* to complicate his relationship with Lincoln by tethering it to financial obligations and placing it on a formal, business basis. He wanted their relationship to mature into a real friendship.[4]

At the same time, it is worth noting that the way Speed tells the (retrospective) story of inviting Lincoln into his bed free of charge makes him the savior, someone who rescued Lincoln from destitution at a moment of great need in his life. It put Speed in charge of the relationship, at least for the moment. Unlike his childhood, when John Speed ruled the house and everything that happened in it, Speed was now master in his own home, no longer under the thumb of his oppressive father or overwhelmed by all his annoying siblings. He was the one with agency by inviting his appealing new friend to share his bed.

Lincoln's self-presentation was as someone older than his age, in contrast to Speed, who appeared younger, thus lengthening psychologically the five actual years that separated them. Speed was not unaware of this dimension of their friendship. In describing Lincoln in New Salem, he notes Lincoln gained the sobriquet "Honest Abe," but once in Springfield, "as he grew older," Lincoln came to be called affectionately "Honest Old Abe" as early as his mid-thirties. The introduction to Speed's *Reminiscences*, written by his nephew John Gilmer Speed, adds that Speed "regarded life with a serious business-like gravity, which led him to seek the companionship of young men of like disposition, or of persons older than himself."[5]

Speed seemed to bask in Lincoln's easy assumption of superiority in his self-presentation, which was joined to a ceaseless ambition. Lincoln reached for the stars. Orville Browning said of Lincoln in this period that he was "always a most ambitious man." Herndon agreed. His ambition, said Herndon, was a "little engine that knew no rest." The "sober truth" is that Lincoln was "inordinately ambitious," which became manifest "in the year 1840 *exactly*." Herndon's precise dating of the beginning of something so much a part of one's character as ambition is overly precise, but it also reflects his keen awareness of Lincoln's early sense of his own potential greatness. There was at this point in Lincoln's life a gap between his ambition to be a well-known lawyer and leading Whig politician (his dream was probably to be a senator in the mold of his hero, Henry Clay) and his actual existence as a small-town lawyer at the far edge of a large country. In a typically ironic and self-deprecatory line in an 1838 letter that speaks to his keen awareness of this chasm at this point in his life between actuality and ambition, Lincoln refers to "all my fancied greatness." Those closest to him saw the potential greatness but didn't feel it was all that fancied.[6]

Curiously, given the difference in their social status before the mid-1830s, Lincoln was actually more worldly than Speed. By 1837 he had lived in three states; taken two flatboat trips to New Orleans; had all kinds of personal and business experiences in New Salem; served two stints in the Black Hawk War, in which he chased Indians to the border of Wisconsin; and had become a leading Whig in state politics and lived in Vandalia. Speed, to the manor born, knew luxury but little more than life at Farmington and two years of service in a store in Louisville before coming to Springfield in 1834. His life had been privileged but circumscribed.

Lincoln stood apart from Speed in his intellectuality. Both men were highly intelligent. Speed had a more formal education, including his incomplete stint at St. Joseph's College. He probably studied some Latin, perhaps a bit of Greek, and was exposed to readings in the humanities, mathematics, some limited science, and religion. But he was not intellectually inclined. In his many letters to his father and brother, along with the large number of letters he wrote Herndon after the war, Speed is clear, direct, and articulate but never makes literary allusions that suggest deep learning. He is passionate about the major political issues of the day and would play an important role for Lincoln in the early stages of the war, but nothing he writes is original or even provocative. He was shrewd but not profound, honest, moral, and engaging without possessing the qualities of mind that would set him apart from other respectable young men in Springfield.[7]

Lincoln, though mostly an autodidact, read more widely and deeply than his friend. Lincoln was unchurched (though to keep his wife happy he later paid for a pew in her church) but had absorbed the Bible into the very fabric of his soul, especially the book of Matthew, references to which are everywhere in his writings, though he also evokes directly or indirectly any number of Old Testament stories in his writings and speeches throughout his life, including Genesis, Psalms, Isaiah, and Ecclesiastes, for example, as well as subtle references to less well-known books like Samuel and Hebrews. One of Lincoln's uses of the Bible was to make covert allusions to it in his speeches (as opposed to his more direct quotations, as in the "Discoveries and Inventions" speech or "House Divided"). One very good example of a covert allusion occurs in the Lyceum speech in 1838. His point about mob rule is that it comes from within and is not imposed by an outside tyrant. "If destruction be our lot," he says, "we must ourselves be its author and finisher." The covert reference here is to Hebrews 12:2: "Looking unto Jesus, the author and finisher of our faith." That kind of reference surely resonated with his audience without Lincoln having to play a religious card. "Lincoln got the preacher's points," Robert Bray astutely puts it, "without acting the preacher."[8]

Lincoln knew most of the great soliloquies in Shakespeare by heart and warmed to long discussions of the plays themselves, especially the tragedies, and the intricacies of plot and character development. Lincoln came to know some contemporary poets through Speed, especially Lord Byron (Speed said later, "I don't think he [Lincoln] had ever read much of Byron previous to my acquaintance with him"), but Lincoln never read anything as closely and deeply as Shakespeare. He now knew the law well, including what was then the fundamental legal text in the Anglo-American world, Blackstone's *Commentaries on the Laws of England*. And no one reveled in the daily paper more than Abraham Lincoln. He read it with the passion of a writer and politician. He was a powerful and effective speaker in that era before microphones and teleprompters. He knew how to project his high-pitched but resonant voice to an audience that might be in a church hall, a meeting room of an inn, or outside at a fairgrounds. He was a master of mood. He often joked with folksy charm to large and small groups of mostly uneducated people, putting them at ease but also never talking down to them about the complicated and contentious political issues of the day. He honed all of these skills on a daily basis in his law practice and frequently gave political speeches and at times major speeches on topics of interest to him.[9]

No one was more appreciative of Lincoln's intellect than Joshua Speed. He almost gushes. "No truth was too small to escape his observation," Speed wrote later, "and no problem too intricate to escape a solution,—if it was capable of being solved. Thought, hard, patient, laborious thought; these were the tributaries that made the bold, strong, irresistible current of his life." Describing a speech Lincoln gave in 1840, Speed stressed his "wonderful faculty" to deliver long and complicated speeches without notes. He remembered everything. "He might be writing an important document, be interrupted in the midst of a sentence, turn his attention to other matters entirely foreign to the subject on which he was engaged, and take up his pen and begin where he left off without reading the previous part of the sentence. He could grasp, exhaust, and quit any subject with more facility than any man I have ever seen or heard of." His mind, Speed felt, "was like polished steel." If you made a mark on it, "it was never erased. His memory of events, of facts, dates, faces, and names, surprised everyone."[10]

Speed was ready in 1837 to connect with such an outsized figure. But there was as well a practical side to Speed's spontaneous invitation to have Lincoln live with him. The two were linked politically. On the very day Speed invited Lincoln into his bed—April 15, 1837—the local paper noted that Speed had been selected secretary of a public meeting to boost the chances of a railroad coming through Springfield. But also as a shrewd businessman who later would become hugely rich, Speed must have recognized there was an advantage to hitching himself to this newly arrived lawyer in town. Lincoln was a rising star and already a powerful young man, largely responsible, because of his political skills in the legislature, for moving the capital to Springfield. He was immensely appealing as a man and was connected with the Todd-Edwards clan through his new law partner, John Stuart. Everyone felt Lincoln was marked for leadership of the Whig party and eventually for some kind of higher office. He was known as a good writer and close to Simeon Francis, the editor of the Whig paper in town, the *Sangamo Journal*. He penned an untold number of stories and editorials then and later for the paper, writing that influenced local and state politics and the economic health of Illinois. A close connection with Abraham Lincoln, in other words, was good for business.

On several levels, therefore, it was not surprising that Speed invited Lincoln to share his bed in the large room on the second floor above the store. On the face of it there was nothing unusual in this arrangement. The living and sleeping arrangements Lincoln and Speed worked out were quite typical of this period and place in American history. Inns at that time, with few rooms, simply separated the men from the women. Inns were often only slightly larger than residential cabins. To make some money, an owner might even enlarge his loft, which could only be reached by a ladder. The shared room would then have a fireplace where food and liquor could be served. Everyone crowded into all available space—for warmth as much as anything else. Both before and after Lincoln met Speed it was a common experience for Lincoln to share a bed with other males. Richard Lawrence Miller has put together a list of all the males Lincoln slept with before he arrived in Springfield: a hired hand in 1830 with whom Lincoln was working; McGrady Rutledge, Stephen Perkins, Daniel Burner, Slicky Bill Greene, and Abner Lewis during his years living in New Salem; John Stuart in Vandalia during the legislative session of 1834–1835; and after Speed left Springfield, Milton Hay for a time, as well as William Herndon and Leonard Swett when they were out on the circuit together, though that could mean sleeping in more communal quarters with several men huddled under shared blankets to keep warm, waking to drink what his colleague, Henry C. Whitney, called "tough" coffee.[11]

Domestic architecture at the time, as well, forced a sharing of beds for the typical family, especially as one moved west from the major coastal cities on the eastern seaboard. Speed, for example, was raised on a wealthy Kentucky plantation, but by today's standards the house at Farmington is hardly imposing, and there were two adults and many children living in it. He certainly paired up with his male siblings to sleep, even though we don't know from available evidence which ones, where, or when. Later, in boarding school, Speed undoubtedly shared a room and perhaps a bed with a schoolmate, something common to the era.

On the frontier as Lincoln experienced it there was never any measure of private space. As a young boy, he slept on a cot in the same room with his parents and one older sister in a tight log cabin in Kentucky.[12] It had an earthen floor with a roof made of slabs held in place by poles and stones. The "windows" were mere holes in the wood covered with greased paper. At one end of the room stood a stone fireplace with a chimney. The beds and cots were pushed against the wall during the day and then pulled out at night, huddled near the fire in winter. Everyone dressed—and undressed—in the common space. When the family first moved to southern Indiana (Lincoln was seven), joined by some of Nancy Lincoln's relatives, the Sparrows, and an illegitimate cousin, Dennis Hanks (then eighteen), they lived for a year in the lean-to, fighting off the snow and cold, in a home not much of an improvement over camping outdoors. The next year Thomas enclosed the cabin but never put in windows, and he had not yet finished the roof before winter. It was only after 1819 when Lincoln's new stepmother, Sarah Bush Johnston, a widow, arrived with three children from a previous marriage that Thomas added a loft to the log cabin. It was quite a crowd for one room: Thomas and Sarah, three boys ranging in age from ten to twenty-one, and three girls ranging in age from twelve to fourteen. The boys (Lincoln, Dennis Hanks, and Sarah's son, John D. Johnston) slept in that loft one step away from the girls. There is some suggestion of sexual tension in the air: within a year Dennis Hanks married the teenaged Elizabeth Johnston and built his own cabin a short distance away.

There were also some particular reasons for men in Springfield, Illinois, in the late 1830s to be close and live and sleep together. For one thing, the panic of 1837, which is better described as an economic depression that swept the land, created severe pressures on young people setting out in business or in the professions at the very moment that there developed a shortage of housing after the influx of people following Springfield becoming the state capital. There was also a distinct shortage of eligible women for men to marry. The Illinois state census of 1840 reported that for Sangamon County (that of course included Springfield as its major urban center) there were 2,515 men and 2,037 women between the ages of twenty and forty, which is approximately a ratio of men to women of 5:4.[13] In the case of Springfield, many young men in the business and political elite came from Kentucky, including those in the Stuart and Todd clans, and of course Joshua Speed; Lincoln was also from Kentucky, even though he came to Springfield more indirectly, via Indiana and New Salem.

Because of his childhood and experiences in New Salem, Lincoln was entirely at ease living in crowded rooms of men sleeping together. In such a context and because of his appealing personality, he could be very playful. The young Leonard Swett sought out Lincoln once in Danville (he does not give a date for the story but from the context it was probably in the early 1850s). He was advised he would find Lincoln in the hotel room of Judge David Davis, a rotund man who engineered Lincoln's nomination in 1860 and later became associate justice of the U.S. Supreme Court. Swett timidly knocked at the door and heard two voices say, "Come in." There he found "two men undressed, or rather dressed for bed, engaged in a lively battle with pillows, tossing them at each other's heads." One was Davis, who stopped the fight for the moment and leaned against the bed, exhausted, puffing "like a lizard." The other man was Lincoln, dressed in a "long, indescribable garment, yellow as saffron, which reached to his heels." This "immense shirt," carved out of a bolt of flannel, was held up by one flimsy button at the throat. Swett confesses to a "succession of shudders when I thought of what might happen should that button by any mischance lose its hold." Lincoln strode across the room to shake Swett's trembling hand and announce himself. "I will not say he reminded me of Satan, but he was certainly the ungodliest figure I had ever seen."[14]

So there was nothing unusual in the culture or in the historical moment in the mere fact that Lincoln and Speed slept together. Custom and individual experience, however, are not always congruent. The experience of a sensitive or talented few may depart sharply from that of the many. Social history provides necessary context for biography but cannot fully explain individual psychological experience at any given moment of time. Just because it was common in nineteenth-century America that men slept together does not mean it was of no significance that young Lincoln, at a critical moment in his development, made the most important friendship of his life with another young man with whom he was to sleep for the next three and a half years, one very tall man, the other of ordinary size, in a double bed, probably stuffed with corn husks, hair, or feathers, each perhaps loosely draped in a bolt of linen, as described by Swett, or, as noted by Whitney, sometimes Lincoln on the circuit wore a "short home made yellow flannel undershirt & had nothing else on," tossing and turning in their dreamscapes. The question is, what does it mean?[15]

In recent years, a number of historians have assumed that Lincoln and Speed had sex and were homosexual lovers. Larry Kramer, the playwright and AIDS activist, even once claimed a source of his found a secret diary of Joshua Speed, along with prurient letters, hidden in the floorboards of the old building that housed Speed's store, documents that detail his sexual relationship with Lincoln. Since Kramer has failed to produce the diary, most agree it is a hoax. Furthermore, the find would be quite remarkable since the building with Speed's store in it underwent a bad fire in 1855 and basically burned to the ground. In his long-awaited magnum opus, *The American People: Volume 1: Search for My Heart*, which came out in 2015—and which he conveniently calls a *novel*—Kramer sidesteps the diary issue but writes a four-page account of the Speed and Lincoln friendship in the first-person voice of Speed, as though he were writing such a diary or reminiscences:

> From the first night we met I held him my arms, each night for going on four years. And he held me in his arms even tighter. . . .
> No two men were ever so intimate. I can say that now. I knew it then, for a few years. He knew it until the day he died. I did not. I did not. Now I wish I had . . . He fucked me immediately. And I immediately invited him to live with me.

And so on. Kramer follows this imagined first-person account with a seemingly more historical description of the friendship, speaking in the third-person omniscient self:

> Surely their relationship must have been known, witnessed, talked about. How could it have escaped the notice of customers, women coming in to do the cleaning and laundry, to wash the sheets? Such a deep friendship must indeed have been known, and even accepted, by many a friend and neighbor and fellow citizen.[16]

Kramer aside, there is no direct evidence to prove that the Lincoln-Speed relationship was sexualized, or was known as sexualized, witnessed as such, or talked about as homosexual by any contemporary friend, neighbor, or citizen in Springfield, then or later in the oral history. Writers as varied as Jonathan Ned Katz, Charles Shively, John

Stauffer, and Clarence A. Tripp, among others, have fallen back on the tendentious argument that two young men sleeping together who were so closely bonded and who wrote such intimate letters to each other must have sexualized their relationship.[17] One needs to consider such an argument rather closely. Its main flaw is that it imposes twentieth- and twenty-first-century assumptions on nineteenth-century customs and attitudes. We live in an era in which attitudes toward homosexuality have radically altered. While there is still resistance in some social sectors to gay marriage, for example, and many young men who present as gay are unfortunately still bullied in the backwaters, for the most part Americans (especially those under forty or so) are increasingly at ease with all forms of homosexuality, feel gay marriage should be legalized everywhere (as the U.S. Supreme Court recently held), gay adoption made legal, etc.

This change in attitude, however, has had the curious collateral effect of creating cultural assumptions that overt expressions of love and intimacy between two young men probably mean their relationship is, or has the potential, to be sexualized. Today in the United States, generally speaking, young men are mostly cautious about expressions of tenderness for each other, of holding hands or other forms of touching, unless, of course, they *want* to convey to each other and to the world that they are in love and openly gay. Heterosexual men readily hug in greeting and parting, and young men might high-five each other (often with elaborate rituals), but in general such men avoid expressions of real tenderness and would never sleep together—unless, again, they were sexual partners and comfortable with conveying that to themselves and to the world. Heterosexual young men, in other words, understand there is a boundary between expressions of fondness in friendship and anything that might suggest to themselves or the world that their relationship is sexualized.

The social context of nineteenth-century friendship presents a picture so different from the present in so many particulars that it can be hard to fathom. It was a social reality then that homosexuality was wrong and should be condemned—though the term itself only came into use in the latter part of the nineteenth century in Germany and then gradually spread to the rest of the West. Sodomy (which literally means anal intercourse and is hardly an unknown practice between men and women but in social context meant sex between men) was illegal. When it became manifest, sodomy, along with some instances of bestiality (or, as it was called, buggery), were punished quite severely. The best historian of the subject is Jonathan Ned Katz, who found, for example, the case of William S. Davis, who was indicted in Baltimore in 1810 for attempting to commit sodomy on William Carpenter. Davis was convicted and sent to jail for three months, forced to "stand in the pillory" for an hour, and pay a fine of five hundred dollars, a very large sum. On an appeal that was denied, one judge declared: "The crime of sodomy is too well known to be misunderstood, and too disgusting to be defined farther than by merely naming it." Katz found 105 such cases in the United States during the nineteenth century (two in Illinois). As he says, prosecution of "sodomy," "buggery," or "crimes against nature" moved west with the expansion of the country, though some of the cases deal with libel suits in which a man or woman fights back against charges of such sexual practices. Katz's careful research clearly reveals that the attitude in nineteenth-century America was that homosexuality was wrong, disgusting, and when made manifest should be punished severely. Someone like Walt Whitman, who was homosexual, necessarily remained in the closet. At the same time, Katz and a number of other researchers have found extensive and well-documented examples of what are obviously nineteenth-century homosexual relationships, along with a trove of previously suppressed photographs of men tenderly holding hands, embracing each other, and engaging in other displays of affection that are clearly indicative of a sexual relationship between them. There was, in other words, a rich subculture of homosexuality in the nineteenth century. Its history has been mostly ignored or suppressed until recently, and to have that dimension of social life brought into the open has deepened our understanding of nineteenth-century America *and* shown how embedded same-sex love is in the American experience.[18]

The condemnation of homosexuality, however, joined the culturally sanctioned belief that young men could, even should, be close and loving with each other—as long as the boundary against sexualization was rigidly maintained. Psychologically speaking, the culture privileged expressive intimacy but punished homosexuality, and the boundary between sensuality and sexuality was clear. Expressions of love and affection between young men, often in florid literary terms, were encouraged, along with some restricted touching, but eroticism of any kind and especially sexuality that involved the genitals or orgasm was strictly forbidden. Very commonly young middle-class men had an intimate but not sexual male friendship in their twenties and into their thirties that bridged the world of playmates as a child and the families that they then created with a female sexual partner. The friendships served as the vehicle for the uneasy transition from the comforts of childhood into a world of dreaded intimacy with idealized but remote, heavily garbed, and sexually guarded women. Loving and intimate male friendships during a specific phase of the life cycle were one of the many psychological byproducts of the way Western culture sharply divided the two worlds that men and women inhabited into gendered separateness.

The broader context of such friendships is important. The best historian of this subject is E. Anthony Rotundo, who discovered all kinds of interesting examples of close male friendships that were almost certainly not sexualized. In college in the early part of the nineteenth century, Daniel Webster began his letters to his friend James Hervey Bingham with greetings like "Lovely Boy" or "Dearly Beloved" and signed off with "Accept all the tenderness I have, D. Webster." In between were many terms of endearment: "You are the only friend of my heart, the partner of my joys, griefs, and affections, the only participator of my most secret thoughts." The most common topic of concern in their correspondence was, as with Lincoln and Speed, women. Webster and Bingham constantly wrote each other about "the Misses." They exchanged advice, fell into romantic language about female beauty while cursing their wiles, and consoled each other when courtships went awry. After college, as Webster got discouraged in his quest for a wife, he wrote Bingham of his need to have him near him and said, jokingly, but of course with meaning, that Bingham and he should "yoke" themselves together (as in marriage), that "your little bed is just wide enough; we will practice at the same bar, and be as friendly a pair of single fellows as ever cracked a nut." By the time they would turn thirty, Webster fantasized "we will put on the dress of old bachelors, a mourning suit, and having sown all our wild oats, with a round hat and a hickory staff we will march on to the end of life, whistling as merry as robins."[19]

James Blake and Wyek Vanderhoef met in 1848 when they were both in their twenties. Blake confided to his diary his joy at finding

Wyek as a friend. "Long have I desired a friend, one whom I could trust myself with upon this journey of life." It was "a beautiful thing" to retire from the "cold, selfish arms of the world" into the "pure embrace of friendship." After their last night together before a separation, they embraced each other in their common bed and sank "peacefully to sleep." Blake wrote in his diary: "We laid our heads upon each other's bosom and wept, it may be unmanly to weep, but I care not, the spirit was touched." It is striking that Blake feels some anxiety about acting like a woman by weeping but sees nothing unusual about laying his head on his friend's bosom and experiences the embrace of his friend as exalted and touching his spirit.[20]

Nor should one forget Herman Melville's *Moby-Dick*, published in 1851. When Ishmael first meets the harpooner Queequeg, the two are accidentally thrown together in a common bed in an inn. Ishmael wakes the next morning to find Queequeg's arm "thrown over me in the most loving and affectionate manner. You had almost thought I had been his wife." The next night, after getting to know and like the harpooner, Ishmael says, "there is no place like a bed for confidential disclosures between friends." As with a man and his wife, who open the "very bottom of their souls to each other," so "lay I and Queequeg—a cozy, loving pair."[21]

***

The key question, of course, is not whether Lincoln and Speed were close and intimate—that is well documented—but whether their relationship was sexualized, that is, was both erotic and sexual and involved the genitals and orgasm. This is not an issue that can be airily dismissed as irrelevant. It matters if a relationship is sexualized, and it is certainly something we would like to know about Lincoln and Speed, not to condemn but to understand them. It is important to keep in mind that the context is the absolute contemporary condemnation of homosexuality, so any hint of Lincoln's relationship with Speed as sexualized would have raised all kinds of red flags among those close to one or both of the young men. The key issue is shame. Sex among men, because it was so strongly condemned, inevitably—and one can add unfortunately—would generate a pervasive shame among those who crossed that line, with implications for attitudes and behavior.

The ways in which shame from participating in transgressive sexuality, as defined in this particular cultural and historical moment, would get handled could vary widely. Springfield, Illinois, around 1840, was a small town with a gossipy elite, such that a sexualization of the friendship between Lincoln and Speed, two prominent local men, would have changed both men. And, even more significantly, their newly intense and sexualized love likely somehow would have revealed itself, then or later.

In fact, not a single contemporary acquaintance, relative, neighbor, or nosy observer *ever* found anything unusual in the friendship of Lincoln and Speed. In the debates of 1858, Stephen Douglas, who knew Lincoln well from this period, said he once ran a grocery (that is, a saloon) in New Salem and made many other untrue charges that he was a drunkard, ruffian, gambler, and traitor (for not supporting the Mexican War). The slur Douglas especially hoped to make stick was that of Lincoln as a man who ran a saloon in New Salem. Douglas said in the Ottawa debates in 1858 that "I was a school-teacher in the town of Winchester, and he a flourishing grocery-keeper in the town of Salem." Lincoln replied that he decidedly did not keep a grocery but did work the "latter part of one winter in a small still house, up at the head of a hollow." Lincoln's reply was perhaps a bit coy, for the store he briefly owned in New Salem with William Berry probably had on its porch a barrel of whiskey from which customers could drink; at least Berry himself certainly dipped into such a barrel, since he drank himself to death. But in all of this, Douglas, who could be unscrupulous and was quite willing to stretch the truth to gain a debating advantage, never hinted at a sexual transgression on Lincoln's part.[22]

Furthermore, Lincoln himself spoke of his friendship and time spent sleeping with Speed without any hint of shame or embarrassment. In talking about his appointment of James Speed as attorney general in 1864, for example, Lincoln commented, "I will offer it [the cabinet post] to James Speed, of Louisville, a man I know well, though not so well as I know his brother Joshua. That, however, is not strange, for I slept with Joshua for four years, and I suppose I ought to know him well."[23] After Lincoln's death, no one in all the vast trove of oral-history materials about his childhood and youth gathered by William Herndon reported anything odd or unusual about their relationship. Herndon himself, one should note, who *lived in the same room* with

Lincoln and Speed for over two years, thought nothing of their relationship (except, perhaps, some jealousy that he was not as important in Lincoln's life as Speed). Herndon also had a keen eye for the
salacious. He was endlessly interested in all kinds of supposed details
about Lincoln's sexual life, warmed to tall tales of his encounters with
prostitutes, and in his interviewing was alert to anything sexually off-
kilter in Lincoln's family, reporting on the "evidence" from testimony
half a century later of Thomas Lincoln's emasculation, or castration, or
dwarf-size testicles, or wondering if the mumps "went down on him."[24]

The first historian to hint at something more than a close platonic
friendship between Lincoln and Speed was Carl Sandburg in 1926, in
the flush of Freud's theories about homosexuality:

> Joshua Speed was a deep-chested man of large sockets, with
> broad measurement between the ears. A streak of lavender ran
> through him; he had spots soft as May violets. And he and Abra-
> ham Lincoln told each other their secrets about women. Lincoln
> too had tough physical shanks and large sockets, also a streak of
> lavender, and spots soft as May violets.[25]

Some have said Sandburg's terms, "streak of lavender" and "spots soft
as May violets," were his way of calling Lincoln gay without having to
say it. I think that is unlikely. Sandburg was not a prig. If after a life-
time of research he had come to believe Lincoln was a homosexual, he
would have said so. His terms were less coded to hint the men were gay
than a way of describing both Speed's and Lincoln's softer, more vulnerable sides, which shielded their vigorous masculinity (those deep
chests, physical shanks, and large sockets). It seems, instead, that
Sandburg was confused by the intimacy of the friendship in the context of what were then changing views of the subject. It didn't seem
to fit. Sandburg's friend Roy Basler, the editor of Lincoln's *Collected
Works* (published in the 1950s), furthermore assured me in the 1970s
that Sandburg told him he intentionally pulled back from interpreting
the relationship because he felt he lacked the requisite psychological
skills to make sense of it.

Implying that he never found another such soul mate, Speed said
in a letter to Josiah Holland: "No two men were ever more intimate."
What may be the best characterization of the Lincoln-Speed relation-

ship comes from John Gilmer Speed, Joshua Speed's nephew, with whom he was close and shared much, who wrote later that when Speed and Lincoln lived together,

> there existed an intimate friendship singular in the lives of both men, for neither of them in after life was unreservedly intimate with any other man. They appear to have had no concealments from one another and to have discussed affairs of the most sacredly personal matters. . . . They confessed to each other their sentimental perplexities and of these, as is well known, Lincoln had more than a full share.[26]

3

FRIENDSHIP

Real intimacy between Lincoln and Speed was not immediate. Lincoln's caution about letting anyone in on his feelings and Speed's youthful admiration for a man he seemed to consider great from the outset created space between them. Their friendship evolved. It was to Mary Owens that Lincoln confided, three weeks after his arrival in Springfield, that "I am quite as lonesome here as [I] ever was anywhere in my life." Lincoln, in fact, did not mention to Speed his troubled courtship of Mary Owens, which ended in the second half of 1837. Lincoln also refused to show Speed a crucial passage in an important letter he wrote later to a Dr. Drake of Cincinnati (see chapter 7). Furthermore, a close read of Speed's many interviews with and letters to Herndon, as well as his *Reminiscences*, suggests he and Lincoln at first circled each other's emotional orbit. In his quasi memoir, Speed lingers on Lincoln's 1836 Forquer speech that so attracted his attention and of course describes in detail their initial meeting, but otherwise he says nothing specific about their years sleeping together. That comes out in Speed's various communications with Herndon, and the stories relate mostly to the period beginning about 1839 (though the dating here is inevitably approximate). For the next two years, Speed has much to say about Lincoln, when they became the truest of friends. The arc of friendship, in other words, took about a year and a half for real closeness to develop. Then nothing could break the bond.[1]

Joshua Speed too often vanishes into the shadows of the Lincoln story. In the literature, he has no texture as a human being, and certainly his profound role in Lincoln's life has never been appreciated. In fact, Joshua Speed was at the center of Lincoln's emotional well-being during this critical period of his self-development. The rhythms of their daily existence were ultimately completely intertwined. They parted each morning after drinking undoubtedly "tough" coffee and a light breakfast (Lincoln never ate much). Once ready for the day, Speed only needed to move behind the counter and tend his store on the southwestern side of the square, while Lincoln walked north across the square to his law offices at 4 Hoffman's Row. In the early afternoon, Lincoln would rejoin Speed, and they would walk a few blocks south to the large home maintained by William Butler and his bustling and warm family. There they ate dinner. After a meal and friendly conversation, Speed and Lincoln returned to work for the rest of the day, then reconnected and perhaps read, making lively conversation or discussing literature or politics, often with good friends. As the evening waned, Speed probably climbed into bed first, joined in the dorm room by his clerk, Charles R. Hurst, and somewhat later by William Herndon (until he got married at twenty-one to a seventeen-year-old girl on March 26, 1840). Speed, who knew more about Lincoln's daily rituals than any other male friend or acquaintance, later told Herndon that Lincoln was "irregular in his habits of eating and Sleeping," and having asked him once when he slept, he answered, "just when every body else is tired out." But at some point Lincoln climbed into bed with Speed, quietly so as not to wake him, and they slept until the morning, an arrangement that lasted generally and continuously—with breaks when Lincoln was out on the circuit or Speed was out of town on business—from April 1837 until the beginning of January 1841.[2]

In these years, Speed is involved in nearly every activity of Lincoln's: sharing a bed; working with Lincoln in Whig politics and on civic activities; lending him books, including his own favorite, Lord Byron; eating together; exchanging confidences; walking with Lincoln to the grove of the Edwards mansion on "Quality Hill"; attending dances and flirting; taking part in Lincoln's Whig Party work; even following

Lincoln occasionally on the circuit. The record of their shared life is well documented but widely scattered in diverse sources that no one before has bothered to pull together in one place. Before 1842 there are no letters between them because they were virtually never separated, and the oral history that Herndon gathered later was all about Lincoln and only incidentally about Speed. But, in fact, their relationship became the emotional lodestone for each man, who experienced the other as not really separate and independent but as another who completed himself, someone necessary for a cohesive sense of well-being. Everything about their feelings and dreams and abiding fears was talked about, especially as their friendship deepened in the conversations that Lincoln and Speed had with no one else.[3]

**

Speed's store—and the imposing presence of Lincoln, who was increasingly valued by his friends for his astonishing humor and ability to tell tall tales, as well as his charisma in general—became the center of adult male interaction in Springfield in the late 1830s. A "throng of loungers," as Herndon put it, gathered regularly there in the evenings to talk about everything under the sun. At the epicenter of any group that regularly gathered in the store, Speed makes quite clear, was Abraham Lincoln.

> Mr. Lincoln was a social man, though he did not seek company; it sought him. After he made his home with me, on every winter's night at my store, by a big wood fire, no matter how inclement the weather, eight or ten choice spirits assembled, without distinction of party. . . . They came there because they were sure to find Lincoln.[4]

The context for the group that came to meet in Speed's store was the proliferation of diverse and ephemeral literary clubs and debating societies that swept over Illinois (and the nation) like a prairie fire in the 1830s. "Americans of all ages, all conditions, and all dispositions," noted Alexis de Tocqueville, who traveled around America in the 1830s, "constantly form associations." Some of these associations, he noted, were "commercial and manufacturing companies, but the most interesting were the thousands of other kinds of groups, "religious, moral, serious, futile, general or restricted, enormous or diminutive." Tocqueville saw these associations as uniquely American, groups that brought men together—and, sometimes, as with the lyceums, men and women together—and kept them from being isolated. Nothing, he felt, in trying to understand America is "more deserving of our attention than the intellectual and moral associations of America."[5]

Even New Salem formed a debating society, which had attracted Lincoln's attention while he lived there. Thomas J. Nance arrived in central Illinois from Kentucky in October 1832, promptly established a subscription school at Farmer's Point, two miles south of New Salem, and formed a debating society in January 1833 with the august title of "The Tyro Polemic and Literary Club." He signed up thirty-seven members and wrote a constitution that included provisions that "No member shall leave the room during business without a permit from the President" and "No member shall speak longer than fifteen minutes at a time, without a permit from the Prest." He was elected president, not surprisingly, and in his inaugural address urged his listeners to be "studious in your conduct, and thoughtful about your mental improvement." And he continued.

> Remember that this is the morning of life in which pursuit is ardent and obstacles readily give way to vigor and perseverance. It is in your power to convert this season of learning into a source of satisfaction if you will but employ your time in continuous and useful reflections. While we thus employ our time we should carefully avoid those frivolous and uninstructive amusements which ruin and debase the mind of many an inconsiderate youth. The principal difference between man and man is chiefly owing to the cultivation of the mind. Anticipating the pleasures that are to be derived from an educated mind, may each of you pursue the path that leads to honor, usefulness and true enjoyment.[6]

In Springfield, a good deal more uninhibitedly bawdy "Poetical Society" (as James H. Matheny put it) took shape before Lincoln's arrival but gained new momentum after 1837. Milton Hay, the clerk of Lincoln's firm, confirmed his own frequent presence and the group's existence before Lincoln. "Jim and I with other boys had been cronies," Hay told John Nicolay when Nicolay, Lincoln's wartime secretary, was interviewing him for a biography of Lincoln. "We were in the habit of running about together as boys do nights and Sundays, and we made the Clerks office a sort of headquarters" to which Lincoln often came to treat them to stories. At the cyclically slow clerk's office in the same building and on the same floor as the Stuart and Lincoln law office, Evan Butler, Newton Francis, Matheny, and other young men (including Milton Hay) hung out together, chatting and writing, and they welcomed it when "Lincoln would Come into the clerk's office." Speed noted how Lincoln never hesitated to ask questions, even if they touched on subjects he knew little about, for example, geology or topics of scientific interest. But as to religion, "always open & avowed—fair & honest" before these "close and bosom" friends, Lincoln, Bible in hand, would "read a Chapter—argue against it" from the "inherent or apparent contradiction under its lids."[7]

This mostly literary group continued to meet until sometime in 1839. Under the guidance of the group's secretary and apparent original organizer, James Matheny, a court clerk then, later a lawyer and a judge, Springfield's literate young bachelors amused one another with a combination of high and low poetry. The key figures in the poetry group were Matheny, Noah Rickard (Sarah's brother and William Butler's brother-in-law), Evan Butler, Milton Hay, Newton Francis (Simeon Francis's *Sangamon Journal* coeditor beginning in 1838), Lincoln, Herndon, and Speed on the sidelines. Lincoln must have thoroughly enjoyed this audience, an attentive roomful over whom he held sway in experience, eloquence, and anecdotes. Not only did Lincoln share, reciting at length, his beloved Burns's "Holy Willie's Prayer," new poetry of Byron and much Shakespeare; he also debuted original doggerel of his own. The smutty nature of some of the group's "poetry" may be judged from the sole surviving sample fragment of Lincoln's contributions, as recalled by Matheny:

> Whatever spiteful fools may say,
> Each jealous, ranting yelper,
> No woman ever went astray
> Without a man to help her.

In his old age, Herndon wrung his hands over his rakish little group. "I am free to admit I would not encourage a similar thing nowadays."[8]

In late 1839, a more serious and less literary but still informal group began to take shape in the store on many evenings. As Herndon described in his biography, "The store had a large fire-place in the rear, and around it the lights of the town collected every evening. As the sparks flew from the crackling logs, another and more brilliant fire flashed when these great minds came into collision." It was "Lincoln's headquarters." Speed himself later said the gatherings were "a social club without organization." It was a group distinctively of the era, intellectual, literary, and passionate while at the same time decidedly male and rather rough and tumble.[9]

To call the conversations in the back of Speed's store a "salon" would be a misnomer, as it had no name, and that term implies an effete character from another era. The group was also not a lyceum. Those forums for lecture and discussion, performance, and debate, much like the "Tyro Polemic and Literary Club" in New Salem, were open to anyone, including women, and had their own familiar rituals on the landscape of nineteenth-century America. Lyceums, which were basically settings for adult public lectures, sprang up in New England beginning 1826 and quickly snowballed: thousands of local lyceums existed by 1840, mostly in small towns. Dues of a dollar or two annually underwrote this form of adult education in scientific, historical, and cultural subjects by local volunteer speakers and itinerant professional lecturers. Any expenses not covered by dues were paid via admission charges at the door, a standard twenty-five cents per lecture (although some lyceums managed to rake in a dollar at a time by bundling five or six tickets into a package).[10]

What formed in the Speed store was something different and unique to its time and place. The process of the group's creation was undoubtedly gradual and never institutionalized as something a certain crowd of men did. By 1839, of course, Speed's store—with the presence of Lincoln—already had a sound reputation as a good place for male conversation in the evening. It is probably the case that the formation of the group coincided with the beginnings of when, in 1839, Springfield became the working capital of Illinois, the actual seat of government offices and the place where the legislature began to convene that December. The accounts of the gatherings from the oral history stress sitting around the fire in the back of Speed's store, which would suggest it was a winter activity. Because the group apparently formed around the first legislative session to meet in Springfield, it attracted people like Orville Browning, who lived in Quincy, Illinois. But the group also reached far beyond legislators. William Herndon later said the "lights" of the town—meaning the leading male intellectuals—met "every evening" in Speed's store. That is surely an exaggeration but may express something about the frequency with which like-minded men gathered in Speed's store in the evenings to talk and share ideas. While Lincoln was always at the center of the group, Speed was there by his side. Speed's admiration of his friend was such that he welcomed the modest, even subservient, role of host to those who gathered to talk with each other but most of all to be part of the circle around Lincoln.[11]

In advance of such gatherings, Speed must have arranged the kindling, probably with his clerk, Billy Herndon, and lighted the wood in his fireplace, prepared the coffee and cider, and perhaps added something sweet or savory for his guests. Speed never expected to take full part in the discussions, competing against experienced politicians for attention when they got together, along with some well-read and articulate men. Besides, that was not Speed's character. But he could—and did, as his list of memories reveals—enjoy watching and listening, seeing faces gleaming in the fires he made, hearing appreciative laughter in response to Lincoln's stories. Significantly, Speed made no claim to have spoken at these caucuses, nor did Herndon, a college dropout who gratefully sat at the feet of brilliant and educated high-minded men speaking on "politics, religion and all other subjects." There in the room, Herndon says, "public sentiment was made." The same dry-goods store in which Herndon measured and cut ribbon in daylight was a different and magical place by night.

Among those who came to Speed's store in the evening were Whig friends and legislators (Edward D. Baker, Orville Browning, John J. Hardin, and others); Democratic figures (Stephen A. Douglas, John Calhoun, Archer Herndon, and Josiah Lamborn); a politician-turned-judge like Jesse B. Thomas; others like William Butler, the court clerk and entrepreneur; and whoever else might fit cozily in back of the store by the fireplace and be able to contribute to the conversations. As mere clerk of the store, Herndon felt greatly privileged to attend these sessions and spoke of being dazzled by these orators' "brilliant thoughts and youthful enthusiasm." Although Herndon vouched personally that

"politics" and shaping of "public Sentiment" was done at these meetings, it was an outwardly apolitical and nonpartisan forum.

But not entirely. Given the passions of the day, political disagreements inevitably arose, especially since the group included the leading
Whigs and Democrats in the state, each with their own local newspaper, in which scorching attacks of opponents were part of the regular
journalistic fare. It would be hard to imagine keeping politics out of
the room with both Lincoln and Stephen Douglas sitting around a
fire on a cold winter evening in the 1830s, in Springfield, Illinois. In
what was likely one of the politicians' group's first meetings held at
the store, in December 1839, Speed witnessed what he later described
to Herndon: "They got to talking politics—got warm—hot—angry.
Douglas Sprang up and Said—Gentlemen, this is no place to talk
politics—We will discuss the questions &c publicly with you." That
debate, in January 1840, was held in the Presbyterian church in town,
involved eight speakers, and lasted eight days. Each speaker had a
night to himself. "Like true knights they came to fight in intellectual armor clad," Speed wrote in his *Reminiscences*, describing the
eight-day debate. "They all stood high, and each had his followers,
adherents, and admirers." Lincoln's speech was especially noted and
published in the local Whig paper, the *Sangamo Journal*, filling seven
columns, as Speed proudly recalled later. Speed even committed to
memory the closing of the speech:

> If ever I feel the soul within me elevate and expand to those
> dimensions not wholly unworthy of its Divine Architect, it is
> when I contemplate the cause of my country, deserted by all the
> world beside, and I standing up boldly and alone, hurling defi-
> ance at her victorious oppressors. Here, without contemplating
> consequences, before heaven and in the face of the world, I swear
> eternal fealty to the just cause, as I deem it, of the land of my life,
> my liberty, and my love. And who, that thinks with me, will not
> fearlessly adopt the oath I take! Let none falter who thinks he is
> right, and we may succeed. But if, after all, we shall fail, be it so;
> we still have the proud consolation of saying to our consciences,
> and to the departed shade of our country's freedom, that the
> cause approved of our judgments and adored of our hearts we
> never faltered in defending.[12]

Speed was clearly greatly impressed with his friend. But he also remembered others in the store fondly and once in later life reminisced about the old days in a letter to Joseph Gillespie: "The usual thoughtful cast-iron face of Lincoln, animated and excited with humor which soon was to be uttered in his inimatible [*sic*] style, very illustrative of an argument which he was making or a moral he was endeavoring to enforce." And the others around the stove: "The manly beautiful face of Baker, the merry laugh of Hardin, the strong mind of old Arch Herndon, the taciturn but thoughtful countenance of Bill Butler and though differing with all politically, the genial little giant, Douglas." All are now gone, he says, clearly with a sad sigh. "All of these or most of them usually assembled around my fireside in the old store at night. Rain or hail or shine there was always present a goodly number. It was not then as now. There were no gas lights. Many of them living full half a mile away . . . it was Lincoln's home and mine. They came because they were sure to find him there."[13]

Given that a "full half a mile" was walking distance, through unlit streets or not, Speed was crediting Lincoln with being a magnet drawing any man, after his supper, who could get to the store. While Arch Herndon might have also wanted to visit his son, Billy, the others Speed named were, indeed, in his store by night only because they wanted to see and hear Lincoln. Baker, an immigrant born in London and whose father taught him to speak the King's English, spoke like an orator; Douglas, born in Vermont, conversed genially, his Yankee twang never completely extinct; and the Kentucky drawl of Butler, Speed, and the others would have been both unmistakable and familiar from infancy to Lincoln. What Lincoln, along with Speed, created and maintained nightly for whole weeks at a time was a social life for men, married and unmarried, besides the barroom. Although Speed tagged Butler as "taciturn" and referred to the "strong mind" of Arch Herndon (who owned a tavern, after all) without characterizing them very clearly as particularly vocal, the men Lincoln invited were primarily speakers, articulate, professional gentlemen making their livings as lawyers, legislators, and judges. At the gatherings, the speakers chased after the same game, sharing their best thoughts aloud and engaging in intelligent conversations all more widely ranging *perhaps* because it was less partisan (or seemingly less partisan) than anywhere else in town.

Edward D. Baker, whose "manly beautiful face" appealed to Speed, was born in London in 1811, but his family soon settled in Philadelphia. He ended up in Illinois as a teenager, and his lively mind soon attracted Governor Ninian Edwards, who loaned him books and mentored him. He read voraciously, especially in history, biography, and poetry; was passionate about his Whig politics; and was greatly admired for his articulate, if somewhat florid, speeches. David Donald says he was so popular that he might have aspired to the presidency himself but for his British birth. Baker was spiritual and briefly considered becoming a preacher, in part because he gave such captivating sermons, but he was better suited for law and politics, which is where his heart was when he arrived in Springfield in 1835 with a wife and growing family. Herndon later characterized him in dramatic form during a lecture he gave in Springfield on December 26, 1865:

> One of these men [in Lincoln's life] was somewhat heavy built—about the average height of the American People: his face was round and somewhat florid-smooth and clear: he had large danc-ing blue eyes. His head was round—his hair fine—having a tall broad forehead and what is called ball headed. He was squarely—rather roundly built: he was quick—active & full of energy—, having great fancy—more of fancy than imagination. He was lively—spontaneous—generous-profuse—careless—had an exquisite sense of the Beautiful. He was bold brave—chival-rous—restless uneasy. He is—was not a native of America. This man cut and carved his own way through life—coming among us a poor lad—leaving us a famous one. He was social, leading the boys—here and there—in their love for him. This man was all action—all motion—all freedom & generosity. He possessed an unequal power over the young. They loved this man and followed with cheers & vim where he led, asking no questions. This man was the gallant Col. Baker—once our townsman and dear friend.

Lincoln in the 1840s became Baker's rival in some political battles within the Illinois Whig party, but he remained close to him person-ally, even naming his second son, "Eddy," born in 1846, after him.[14]

John J. Hardin, whose "merry laugh" stuck in Speed's memory, was a handsome young man from Lexington, Kentucky, who had been educated in classical studies at Transylvania University. He was well connected socially, as he was a relative of Elizabeth Edwards and Mary Todd, and he had gotten to know Lincoln well, first during the Black Hawk War, in which they both served, and later in the Illinois state legislature. Hardin was tall and imposing, with the manners of a soldier (he became a general in the state militia). Paul Simon, a shrewd observer of Lincoln in the state legislature (where Simon himself, roughly a century and a half later, served), argues that Hardin and Lincoln were close but not particularly warm. Hardin did play a crucial role in Lincoln's life in these years, however. He assumed leadership of the Whigs in the legislature when Lincoln got very depressed in early 1841 and the next year forcibly intervened to prevent Lincoln's near-duel with James Shields, seizing the duelists' swords and keeping them.[15]

Archer Herndon, of "strong mind," according to Speed, was born in 1795 and was the father of William Herndon, which made him older than most of the others who came to gather in the store to talk. He was one of the early settlers in Springfield, having arrived in 1821, and was to become a successful merchant in town, opening the first tavern, or hotel, in the city. He was a Democrat who served in the legislature during the same terms as Lincoln and joined him as one of the Long Nine who engineered moving the capital from Vandalia to Springfield in 1837. William Herndon, leaving no stone unturned in gathering his oral history of Lincoln after 1865, interviewed his father once on September 28, 1866. Archer Herndon, then infirm and only able to talk for a brief period, wove a few tales of his youth in Virginia playing "fives" with an iron ball, enjoying cock fights, playing cards, hunting, singing songs during the communal shucking of corn, and whipsawing planks. He also read "the best British literature of the day" and studied philosophy. "Old Virginia boasted then as now of her integrity—honor—valor—power to rule [or] reign," he adds in the immediate wake of the Civil War, as Virginia lay in ruins and the humiliation of total military defeat.[16]

William Butler, the "Bill Butler" of "taciturn but thoughtful countenance," was the clerk of the Sangamon County Court, James H. Matheny's boss, and a savvy politician who had come to know Lincoln during the Black Hawk War and in the state legislature. Quickly drawn to Lincoln when he arrived in town, Butler played two important roles in Lincoln's life: he offered to feed him free of charge (Speed also ate at Butler's, but he had to pay), and he assumed Lincoln's debt so that he could begin his career without that great burden. When Lincoln offered to repay the debt, Butler would have none of it. Butler had told him: "I want you to come down here, and board here and make my house your home." After Speed left Springfield in May 1841, Lincoln also slept in the Butler home and knew his family well. Butler's wife did Lincoln's laundry and would buy him new socks, which she placed in his drawer; the absentminded Lincoln never seemed to notice. In the summer of 1842 Butler also served as Lincoln's second in his aborted duel with James Shields. It was in the Butler home in November 1842 that Lincoln dressed for his wedding to Mary Todd. [17]

The extraordinary participant in the informal gatherings in the large back room of Speed's store, given later history, was Stephen Douglas. He had come to live in Springfield by then and was already a well-worn political opponent of Lincoln's in state politics. The image of young Lincoln and Douglas sitting in front of that fire with Speed lounging nearby on a cold winter night talking about everything under the sun is quite compelling. By the time Lincoln and Douglas squared off for their debates in 1858—certainly the most famous in American history and rivaling the greatest of debates anywhere—both men knew the other's strengths, vulnerabilities, and commitments well. In 1858 Lincoln never underestimated his opponent, and Douglas was well aware of the great skill of the man he faced. That intimate knowledge came from those long nights in the back of Speed's store.

Others dropped by at times to join the discussions. James H. Matheny grew up in Springfield and was a clerk of the court. He became a close friend of Lincoln's and served as his best man at his wedding. Anson G. Henry (who will be discussed at greater length in chapter 7), a doctor and beloved and trusted friend of Lincoln, must have come at times to join the conversation. John Calhoun was an important local Democrat whom Lincoln knew since his New Salem days. Once described as a man of "first class ability but too indolent to be a leader," Calhoun often joined in "courteous" debate with Lincoln.[18] Orville Hickman Browning, three years older than Lincoln, was a lawyer who also served in the Black Hawk War. While Browning was an important ally in Whig politics, it was Browning's wife, Eliza, who was a particularly close friend of Lincoln. Josiah Lamborn, almost exactly Lincoln's age, was nearly as tall and picturesque, dramatic, and eloquent; as attorney general, he relentlessly pursued cases. He was a

Democrat who served as a foil for Stephen Douglas but fell into hard times and died penniless at thirty-eight. Jesse B. Thomas Jr. was a lawyer who served as a circuit court judge in the late 1830s. As a Democrat who opposed Lincoln, he was once humiliated in debate by Lincoln in what became known as the "skinning of Thomas," an event that left Lincoln feeling deeply regretful for hurting his old colleague. Along with these men, those in the poetical society often met in the store but sometimes gathered in an available lawyer's office. This group, whose membership overlapped those Speed mentions who met more informally in the store, seemed more bent on discussing literature and included Lincoln; James Matheny, who served as secretary; Noah Rickard, a young lawyer who once helped Lincoln and some other friends tie up a wife beater, strip him to the waist, and summon his wife, who "wailed him tremendously"; and Evan Butler, Milton Hay, and Newton Francis, all literate young lawyers in Springfield drawn to Lincoln's mighty intellect.[19]

✳ ✳ ✳

Sometimes Speed traveled on business, especially to St. Louis but at least once all the way to Pittsburgh, where he complained to his sister Mary that he had a cold because of the "irregularity of my habits, in traveling night and day." Occasionally, members of Speed's family visited him in Springfield, as when another sister, Lucy, came to stay in November 1839 (one wonders where she slept). While Lucy was in Springfield, Speed's father wrote her—it is telling that he didn't write Joshua—a chatty and affectionate letter that noted this was the first time he had been separated from her. Mother and Peach, he reports, have gone to the city (Louisville) to make "sundry calls" in a new carriage. Someone on the plantation is in bed sick; another is working in his place. The work "spreading hemp" should finish by Tuesday. "Your poultry stock" is increased. His disagreements with Rev. Clarke remain as they were, and "we agree to differ" on matters of faith. He plans over the weekend to hear a lecture in Louisville. And so on. John is especially pleased to report the production recently of five hundred barrels of cider. He tells Lucy to ask Joshua whether he wants a barrel. John Speed says that he hopes his daughter will return soon and bring Joshua with her, though he understands she will remain "until Joshua's business admits of his coming with you."[20]

Joshua Speed, meanwhile, seems quite well situated in Springfield, secure in his home with Lincoln, and moving forward with his life. With Lucy still with him, he wrote one of his regular Christmas letters to his beloved mother on December 25, 1839. These letters were never addressed to both his parents. The slight of his father seems deliberate, for Joshua not only fails to include John in the letter but on its envelope writes "care of John Speed, Esq.," which meant it would pass through his father's hands but was not addressed to him. He does avoid open conflict ("Up to this time of my life nothing gives me more pleasure than a consciousness that I have done nothing to forfeit the love or esteem of my parents") and is eager for their approval and recognition that his character is "free from blemish or disgrace." But Speed is especially effusive in his affection for his mother. "Next to seeing you and claiming and receiving from you your kiss, and your blessing," writing you is the "most pleasant way to me of spending this day."[21]

At the center of Speed's life was Abraham Lincoln, with whom he spent virtually every waking moment when they were not working in their separate offices. The only consistent separation between Lincoln and Speed occurred when Lincoln rode the circuit in the fall and spring (and in the summer of 1840, when Lincoln spent a good deal of time away from Springfield in political work leading up to the presidential election). Adding up those days riding the circuit from the multivolume book that tracks Lincoln's whereabouts throughout his life, between April 1837 and January 1841 Lincoln was apart from Speed about a total of about nine months in the three and a half years they lived together (Lincoln's circuit riding lengthened in later years).[22]

But even that seemingly precise calculation ignores some interesting and relevant evidence for time spent together. Speed worked with Lincoln on many Whig committees and schemed with him on all manner of political developments; he also seemed always to be in the audience when his friend gave a speech. That is why he could give a detailed account of the Forquer speech in 1835 (before he knew Lincoln) and of Lincoln's extended speech in the eight-day debate in the Presbyterian church in early 1840. But Speed also took the trouble to sit patiently in court when Lincoln spoke. He said to Herndon: "I have heard him

often since [the Forquer Speech]—in Court and before the people."
Court days were exciting times. People came in from the countryside
in droves with complaints of neighbors' pigs breaking down fences,
land disputes, debt settlements, and occasional divorces. Often lawyers were matched to clients in the moment, after a quick consultation
on the square. Lincoln was readily available as he gathered clients and
headed into court. And there "often," it seems, was Speed sitting on
the hard bench, watching in wonder at the skilled arguing of Lincoln.[23]

Speed also at times traveled with Lincoln on the circuit. In 1839
Speed was once with Lincoln in a small town about thirty miles away
from Springfield. The court broke up, and the retinue of lawyers,
judges, and other officials began to ride home. Passing through a
"thicket of wild plum, and crab-apple trees," they decided to stop and
water the horses. Lincoln, however, who had been at the rear of the
retinue, was nowhere to be found. John J. Hardin, who had been with
him, rode up and explained that a severe wind had blown two little
birds out of their nest. Lincoln had picked them up gingerly and then
spent some time locating their nest to return them to it and safety.
He told Hardin that he felt the need to return the birds to "the home
provided for them by their mother." Then, when Lincoln finally joined
the group of lawyers and others by the water, his friends laughed at
him for his concern about two little birds in the wild. But Lincoln said
earnestly, "I could not have slept tonight if I had not given those two
little birds to their mother." It is a charming anecdote about Lincoln,
but the more interesting question is why Speed was with Lincoln in
this out-of-the-way place. Perhaps he had business there. It is far more
likely Speed simply had some free time on his hands and wanted to be
with his friend.[24]

4

DEPRESSION

With Speed and largely through Speed Lincoln found his bearings. On the surface, Lincoln presented as a well-put-together young man of great talent and potential. He was one of the leading citizens in town and had begun his practice with its most prominent lawyer, John Todd Stuart, someone so politically shrewd that in August 1838 he would narrowly defeat Stephen A. Douglas for the congressional seat from central Illinois. Lincoln was rapidly gaining a reputation for dealing effectively with the juries of common people (to whom he never spoke down and with whom he could be riotously funny) and then arguing more elegantly the legal issues on appeal to the Illinois Supreme Court. In politics, as well, Lincoln was recognized as an able orator who could articulate Whig positions with effectiveness. And he was well liked by everyone. His humorous stories were already legion, but that aspect of Lincoln can be overemphasized. Lincoln, simply put, was a warm and generous human being. J. Rowan Herndon, a cousin of William Herndon who knew Lincoln in New Salem, said of him then that he was "the favorite of all" and "he Loved all of them as they Loved him."[1]

People were drawn to him, and when he got in trouble they wanted to help him. Then and later Lincoln felt most comfortable in the company of women who were older (even if by only a few years), married, and had children: Elizabeth Abell, Eliza Caldwell Browning, Elizabeth Rickard Butler, Eliza Rumsey Francis, and even Elizabeth Edwards, for example. Once he was married himself and a father, he called Mary Lincoln "Mother" (though that was also a convention). Men were equally drawn to help Lincoln. In New Salem, he had sunk into serious debt because his business partner, William Berry, with whom he tried to run a store, drank himself to death. In a complicated exchange of goods and notes—Reuben Radford transferred some goods to William G. Greene, who sold them to Lincoln and Berry for four hundred dollars, who in turn assigned it back to Radford, who then assigned it to the wily Peter Van Bergen—Lincoln ended up holding the bag when his store with Berry went bankrupt. Van Bergen then sued Lincoln and Greene, and Lincoln was suddenly faced with a judgment against him for his horse, saddle, bridle, compass, chain, and other surveyor's instruments, which at the moment were crucial for his livelihood. At an auction that Lincoln did not attend, a local farmer, James Short, a great admirer of Lincoln, bought all the items for $120 and gave them back to his friend. Short later told Herndon that after Lincoln moved to Springfield he paid him back.[2]

Lincoln also, of course, drew on the financial help of William Butler and secured free rent from Speed. With Speed, a small-business owner with a limited inventory, his offer of a bed simultaneously saved him from potentially losing valuable merchandise. Perhaps Speed felt it was better to bring Lincoln into his bed than lend him seventeen dollars because he might not repay it. Lincoln for his part was being a bit coy with Speed about his finances. He was not, in fact, flat broke. On April 20, 1837, Lincoln sold a lot of land in Springfield he owned for $75, and a month later, on May 9, sold another for $30. Those sums equal about $2,000 in today's dollars. Neither Lincoln nor Speed, in other words, dealt with the other as either totally candid or fully self-sacrificing friends when they met. Rather, they approached the other somewhat warily, at the traditional "arm's length" of people doing business.[3]

While he was insecure financially, what Lincoln mostly struggled with was his depression, which led him at times to make some bad judgments. At least once he got into a questionable political fight. The most noteworthy was a vicious and personal encounter with

James Adams in 1837. His struggle with Adams began as a legal case, when Lincoln represented a family that felt Adams had defrauded them. Lincoln, it seems, had little respect for Adams as a lawyer, politician, or man. Things got complicated when Adams, a Democrat, decided to run for an office also sought by Lincoln's close friend Anson G. Henry. Between June and the election in August, Lincoln published a series of increasingly intemperate anonymous letters, signed "Sampson's Ghost," in Simeon Francis's Whig paper, *The Journal*. In fact, they were so out of order that the letters actually hurt Henry, who lost the election handily, and Lincoln's reputation as a man of integrity was tarnished.[4]

The shadow of depression followed Lincoln and haunted his every move. Few would question that Lincoln was melancholy, as they called it, though he preferred to use what was then the more technical term "hypochondria," which he dubbed, almost affectionately, his "hypo." Friends and colleagues were all aware Lincoln, as an adult in Springfield and on the circuit, and most noticeably in the White House, frequently fell into dark moods. But those close to Lincoln much earlier also noted his pervasive sadness. John Hanks, his cousin, others in the family, and many neighbors commented on his melancholy as an important part of Lincoln's character as a child. Later, in New Salem, a neighbor, Robert Wilson, who knew him well, described how Lincoln "appeared to enjoy life rapturously" but was the "victim of terrible melancholy" at a crucial moment of loss and when by himself could get "so overcome with mental depression, that he never dare carry a knife in his pocket." Douglas Wilson is skeptical of this evidence of Lincoln's suicidality in this period, "the pocketknife," he says, "hardly being a notorious means of self-destruction." In fact, a small, sharp knife serves the purpose well, which is also why on psychiatric wards in hospitals there are no sharp instruments of any kind allowed. With almost any such item, you can slit your wrists deeply along the vertical line of the arm and bleed to death.[5]

What caused Lincoln's depression? One answer that seemed to appeal to Lincoln and certainly was widespread in the culture was the idea that the liver was somehow of special significance as a mediating organ between the intestines and the brain in causing hypochondriasis. The leading psychiatrist of the era, Benjamin Rush, felt there was such a connection, as did most medical textbooks at the time. given

the state of medical knowledge, Lincoln probably believed the constipation he struggled with was correlated with, if not a causal agent of,
his depression. He therefore eagerly sought out any cure for evacuat-
ing his sticky bowels. Lincoln's first law partner, John Stuart, equally
persuaded by the explanations for disease and the cures available to
him, brooded over the state of his afflicted friend's irregularity. Stuart
wrote to Herndon in 1865 that "Lincoln is—was a kind of vegetable—
that the pores of his flesh acted as an appropriate organ for such Evac-
uation &c—differed with other men about this—Lincoln was a torpid
man gloomy . . ." Henry C. Whitney, who later knew Lincoln well on
the circuit, explained more clearly Stuart's murky point:

> What Stuart said was this[:] "Lincoln's digestion was organically
> defective so that the excreta escaped through the skin pores
> instead of the bowels": and I "advised him to take Blue Mass [pills
> that were a mercury-based medicine] and he did take it before he
> went to Washington & for five months while he was President
> but when I went to Congress he told me he had quit because it
> made him cross."

It was undoubtedly painful for Lincoln that the blue-mass pills failed
to relieve his depression and only aggravated his mood.[6]

Despite all these struggles, in typical fashion, Lincoln found much
humor in his intestinal distress and often told off-color jokes about
farting, shitting, and related topics. Herndon related a story he heard
Lincoln tell "often and often." In his notes, Herndon headed the story
"The Man of Audacity." In the story, which Lincoln undoubtedly embellished, once at a large party with many ladies and gentlemen present
a man of audacity was placed at the head of the table to carve the turkeys, chickens, and pigs. He whetted his carving knife, set to work
on the turkeys, but expended too much energy and farted. A silence
reigned. Everyone was embarrassed. The man of audacity, however,
was unmoved. He made a show of taking off his coat and rolling up his
sleeves, whetting the knife again, squaring his shoulders, said: "Now,
by God, I'll see if I can't cut up this turkey without farting." At another
time, Herndon, who fancied himself an intellectual, once asked Lincoln in great seriousness if he believed in heredity. Lincoln thought
for a few minutes and replied that, yes, he had no doubt personality

traits passed from one generation to another. Old so-and-so from New Salem, for example, had fathered five boys. "I know that —— suffered terribly in the old days from chronic diarrhea, and you know for a fact that every one of the boys has turned out to be a perfect shitass!"[7]

A different kind of theory of origins about his depression had Lincoln ruminating on his mother's emotional state during her pregnancy with him. Henry C. Whitney wrote Herndon in 1887 a letter with important passages that were crossed out (probably by Herndon), though they remain sufficiently legible to decipher. In the crossed-out part of the letter, Whitney reports Lincoln told him that his mother, Nancy, while pregnant with Lincoln, was in a state of "constant trepidation and frequent affrights." As Whitney reported it, Lincoln seemed to feel these "affrights & trepidations made a maternal *ante natal* impression on our hero." His melancholy, in other words, Whitney concluded, "was stamped on him while in the period of gestation. it [*sic*] was part of his nature and could no more be shaken off than he could part with his brains."[8]

This rather wild theory that seemed to have meaning for Lincoln himself could have sprung from his private reflections, though we can't dismiss the possibility that he heard some story of distress during Nancy's pregnancy from his mother or later from another relative. But there is another way to approach this problem of origins. Was it in his genes? Evidence exists that depression and other mental illness ran through the history of the Lincoln family. His father, Thomas, was erratic and perhaps disturbed; his uncle Mordecai suffered mood swings (but was also an alcoholic); several cousins seemed bipolar, and one first cousin, Mary Jane Lincoln, was admitted to the Illinois state insane asylum after thirteen years of suffering. But many people on the nineteenth-century rural and urban frontier were "sad," for survival itself posed huge challenges, and death often visited families. Furthermore, as with Mordecai, it is always risky to assume mental illness when alcoholism is present; one cannot distinguish symptom from etiology. As for this Mary Jane Lincoln, a forlorn figure lost in the currents of nineteenth-century life, what family doesn't have such a relative somewhere on its family tree?[9]

Furthermore, the single most important figure in Lincoln's life, his biological mother, seemed psychologically mature and decidedly not depressed. The best witness is Lincoln himself, who described his mother, Nancy, to Herndon as "an intellectual woman, sensitive and somewhat sad." That "somewhat" is an important qualifier for a man who used words carefully. Lincoln definitely idealized Nancy, whom Speed said he "always" referred to in conversation as his *angel mother.*" Lincoln once told Herndon in a confessional buggy ride: "God bless my mother. All that I am or ever hope to be I owe to her." She was by all accounts a remarkable woman, tall and slender, wrote John Hanks, "beyond all doubts an intellectual woman, rather extraordinary if anything." According to Dennis Hanks, she was "the most affectionate [woman] I ever saw," "never knew her to be out of temper," was "immovably calm," "keen, shrewd, smart, and I do say highly intellectual," "perception was quick, judgment was acute almost," and "not heavy in thought, feeling, or action." (When Hanks calls Nancy "intellectual," he probably means she was smart, for she was illiterate.) These detailed assessments do not add up to a description of a depressed woman. It would seem that Nancy Lincoln, a highly intelligent and appealing woman, responded warmly, affectionately, and appropriately to her gifted son, nourishing him with rich emotional supplies into his late infancy. Such a solid maternal relationship begins to explain from a theoretical point of view Lincoln's marked adult characteristics of flexibility, empathy, humor, creativity, and ultimately profound wisdom. What mattered for Lincoln in terms of the making of his later depression was the sudden trauma of her death when he was nine. That left him with the awful task, suddenly thrust on his shoulders, of trying to figure out his place in the world without her.[10]

Life was rough in the log cabins of Lincoln's youth, especially after Thomas moved his family from Kentucky to southern Indiana when Abraham was seven. After a cold winter in what may have been a makeshift cabin, things settled and seemed on a good path. But without warning, the "milk sickness" from cows eating poisonous white snakeroot descended on the family. Lincoln had to watch helplessly as Nancy Lincoln got sick from infected milk. This "milk sickness" ran its deadly course in a matter of days, causing loss of appetite, listlessness, weakness, vague pains, muscle stiffness, vomiting, abdominal discomfort, severe constipation, bad breath, and, finally, coma and death. Nancy Lincoln died in a matter of days, as did Abraham's aunt and uncle Sparrow.[11]

In less than a year, Thomas left him and his sister alone under the hapless care of Dennis Hanks for several months to go off and find another wife. The children were bereft, barely able to survive. When Thomas returned with the new stepmother and her two daughters and a son, Abraham and Sarah, according to Dennis Hanks, "were wild, ragged and dirty . . . she [Sarah, the new stepmother] soaped, rubbed and washed the children clean, so that they looked pretty, neat, well, and clear. She sewed and mended their clothes, and the children once more looked human as their own good mother left them." Lincoln came to love his stepmother, and, as Speed wrote later, based on the kind of private feelings that Lincoln shared with no one else, "His fondness for his step-mother and his watchful care over her after the death of his father deserves notice. He could not bear to have any thing said by any one against her." Sarah Johnston Lincoln herself told Herndon he was "the best boy I ever saw," and with him she was uniquely attuned: "His mind and mine—what little I had—seemed to run together." Her kindness undoubtedly helped mitigate the loss of Nancy, but it also surely took many years to adjust to losing his mother at such a young age and the radical changes in family life that descended on him as a result of Nancy's death.[12]

At eighteen years of age, Lincoln then lost his adored sister, Sarah, with whom he had weathered the storms of their childhood and with whom he was by all accounts extremely close. Sarah, according to John Hanks, was a "good woman—Kind, tender, & good natured and is Said to have been a smart woman." Sarah had married Aaron Grigsby, a member of the clan Herndon called the "leading family" in nearby Gentryville, in 1826, but Grigsby's "cruel treatment" of her, as a neighbor later noted, enraged young Lincoln. Matters went from bad to worse. Sarah quickly got pregnant after her marriage but then gave birth to a stillborn child and herself died in the process because the doctor was drunk and unavailable, which in Lincoln's view was part of the general failure of the family to care for his sister properly. When Sarah died, in the words of a Grigsby relative, Lincoln "sat down on a log and hid his face in his hands while the tears rolled down through his long bony fingers. Those present turned away in pity and left him to his grief." Both deaths that Lincoln suffered as a child and as a late adolescent were sudden and shocking. Those he most loved died, leaving him vulnerable to loss, without good coping skills in mourning, and prone to depression at actual or symbolic evocations of death.[13]

Lincoln was also effectively fatherless. Thomas Lincoln spent his life on a steady descent down the social ladder. Herndon gathered from the old farmers in Kentucky and Indiana all kinds of toxic views of Thomas, especially about his supposed sexual inadequacy or sterility. For Herndon, Thomas's sterility served to bolster his (highly unlikely) theory of Abraham's own illegitimacy but also to explain Thomas's "utter laziness and want of energy." The problem, Herndon wrote, "is due to the fact of fixing." Thomas was, in the opinion of one typical neighbor, Nat Grigsby, "a lazy man, but . . . a piddler, always doing but doing nothing great, was happy, lived easy and contented." Herndon and Weik concluded Thomas was in general "roving and shiftless," "proverbially slow of movement, mentally and physically," "careless, inert and dull."[14]

That exceedingly harsh view of Thomas reflects more of Herndon's skewed perceptions than historical actuality. Thomas Lincoln was in fact a perfectly good human being, a hard-working farmer with some skills as a carpenter, a sense of humor, and sufficiently interesting to attract two impressive women to marry him. An Indiana tax book for 1814 ranked him fifteenth out of ninety-eight in terms of property values for those listed in the local county records. He was generally respected in the various communities in which he lived. He helped build some churches and joined social activities. He seemed not to be a drinker—something that distinguished him from others on the frontier—and, according to Dennis Hanks, didn't "cuss none." He was a good father, and Sarah (Lincoln's stepmother) said Thomas was determined to see his talented son acquire skills he himself lacked.[15]

Some aspects of young Abraham's character seemed molded in identification with Thomas. Both were noted for their sense of humor, they were upright and trustworthy, and they were strong and good wrestlers. They were noted for their kindliness and sense of fun. And it may be that part of what drew Lincoln to the law, especially his handling of land cases, lay in Thomas's struggles with gaining clear title to land in his forced migration west.

Yet a profound distance defined Lincoln's relationship with his father. It is not that Lincoln hated him. There were some whippings when he was a boy, but that was hardly remarkable on the frontier—

or elsewhere in the nineteenth century—and there is no sense that Thomas's occasional whippings left a lasting impact on Lincoln's character. Hatred is the wrong construct to define Lincoln's feelings toward his father. The issue was rather that Lincoln felt that Thomas was inadequate to the task of serving as the fatherly source of greatness for his soaring ambitions. Lincoln even seemed to have developed an elaborate myth of his own beginnings that hovered on the margins of his unconscious. As Lincoln told Herndon in a dreamy state once on a buggy ride, he thought his "angel mother" was the illegitimate daughter of "some Virginia planter" and that bastards were stronger and smarter for the experience. Thomas was thus incidental to Lincoln's imagined true heritage back to the founders, those real fathers.[16]

Lincoln felt distain for Thomas and treated him as a shameful figure, which may tell us more about Lincoln than about his father. He regarded Thomas as dull and something of a fool for being illiterate; he, Lincoln wrote in his 1860 autobiography, was a "wandering laboring boy" who grew up "literally without education." Lincoln seldom visited him in Charleston, Illinois, a mere ninety miles from Springfield, and then, it seems, he stopped by more to see his stepmother, Sarah, than Thomas and his other relatives. He did not invite him to his wedding, never invited him into his home, which, once enlarged, became a striking upper-middle-class house complete with horsehair couches, never introduced him to his wife or children, and was increasingly annoyed at having to give Thomas money in the 1840s. Lincoln did regularly send his father and the clan of seventeen people Thomas helped support small amounts of money and assign an occasional note to him. Herndon and others have taken that as proof of Lincoln's "parental love and duty," but it is more likely he just wanted to get Thomas and the rough-hewn Charleston clan off his back (except for his stepmother). He seemed to feel it was his duty not to let them suffer, but he didn't have to like it. On Christmas Eve, 1848, Lincoln replied sarcastically to yet another request from Thomas through John D. Johnston for twenty dollars because Thomas faced losing his home because of forgotten judgment against him.

> Your letter of the 7th was received night before last. I very cheerfully send you the twenty dollars, which sum you say is necessary to save your land from sale. It is singular that you should have

forgotten a judgment against you; and it is more singular that the plaintiff should have let you forget it so long, particularly as I suppose you have always had property enough to satisfy a judgment of that amount.

Lincoln helps his father not lose his house, but he does so without generosity of spirit. It is not Lincoln's finest hour.[17]

The following May Lincoln took the trouble to visit his father when word came from Augustus Chapman, the husband of Lincoln's cousin Harriet Hanks, that Thomas was dying of heart disease and hoped to see Lincoln. Chapman laid it on thick: "He [Thomas] is very anxious to see you before he dies," and his "cries for you" are "truly heart rendering." Thomas also invited Mary and the boys to come visit as well, as "we are very comfortably fixed" (it is doubtful Mary would have agreed how comfortably fixed their log cabin was). The next day Lincoln's stepbrother John D. Johnston added his own pressure, saying that Thomas has "all most Despared of see ing you" and wants to be sure Johnston adds that he wants to tell Mary that he "loves hure."[18]

Despite being busy, Lincoln went to see Thomas. He discovered that Thomas was not dying at all. He had had some lung congestion and was recovering. Lincoln stayed only briefly and quickly returned to Springfield. It left a bad taste, as he probably felt it was all a ruse to get money out of him. It drove Lincoln to distraction. The false alarm and manipulations around Thomas's illness in 1849 clearly influenced Lincoln's refusal to visit Thomas two years later in 1851 when his father was in fact on his deathbed. The request to visit again came through letters from John D. Johnston and Harriet Hanks Chapman. Lincoln wrote a letter to Johnston full of excuses (he was busy, and Mary was sick) and platitudes ("He notes the fall of a sparrow," referring to Matthew 10:29–30 and Hamlet 5.2.231, "and numbers the hairs of our heads; and He will not forget the dying man, who puts his trust in Him"), whereas the real feeling comes later in the letter: "Say to him that if we could meet now, it is doubtful whether it would not be more painful than pleasant." Painful for whom? Lincoln then failed to attend his father's funeral and spent the rest of his life muttering occasionally about buying a grave marker. He never managed to find time for that task. Local Coles County residents erected a marker in 1880.[19]

Joshua Speed's conflicted relationship with his father, John, while different in particulars, paralleled that of Lincoln in terms of emotional texture. John could be overbearing toward his sensitive son. John was the grand Southern planter who ran a small village and was the master of many children and even more slaves. Joshua seemed to feel the weight of his father's presence and basically removed himself from his home at sixteen. It was undoubtedly welcome for Speed to leave Louisville altogether at twenty and live a two-day journey away in Springfield. John Speed may well have helped fund his son's first business venture but otherwise hardly saw him after 1834. And when John got sick in 1840 Joshua did not visit and made no effort to attend his funeral (though this is less remarkable given the distance). In fact, the arc of Joshua's life took him away from Louisville and his father from sixteen to twenty-eight years of age, but once John was dead and out of the picture Joshua returned home to Kentucky, where he led the rest of his life as a leading citizen.

Their troubled relationships with their fathers, though different in form, served as yet another source of a deep and perhaps mostly unspoken bond between Lincoln and Speed. And one can speculate more deeply. Abraham Lincoln and Joshua Speed were sensitive souls who struggled with depression and complex issues of intimacy. Erik Erikson has noted that to make sexuality available for mastery, "a man must confront his childhood and, above all, give an account of his conflicts with his father." It could be said, reasonably, that both Lincoln and Speed retreated as young men from giving such an account. It was too painful. They departed from that emotional playing field, and as a result spent much of their youth in a confused state of psychological disarray, unable to love, uncertain about intimacy, and only able to find comfort and security in their friendship with each other.[20]

✳ ✳ ✳

Lincoln's yearning for a close connection with a woman he could love and trust not to die came to a head as a young man living in New Salem in the 1830s. At about twenty-five years of age—late, developmentally, it should be noted—he fell in love for what seems to have been the first time in his life with Ann Rutledge in New Salem. As Isaac Cogdal reported, Lincoln told him in 1860 that "I did honestly—& truly love the girl & think often—often of her now." She was eighteen years old when Lincoln arrived in town in 1831 after taking Offutt's flatboat to New Orleans. Ann was the daughter of James Rutledge, a prolific father of ten children who had helped establish the town and owned a tavern (or hotel) where Lincoln boarded for his first year in New Salem. William Greene, Lincoln's good friend and a man who could be equally florid and astute, was ecstatic about Ann. Herndon gathered all kinds of reports from other New Salem inhabitants about Ann's beauty, good character, and high intelligence. She was a woman of "Exquisite beauty" matched by an intellect that was "quick—Sharp—deep & philosophic as well as brilliant." She was "gentle & kind a heart as an angl—full of love—kindness—sympathy." Mentor Graham said that they studied together under his tutelage. "Lincoln & her both were staying at My house . . . tolerably good Schollar in all the Common branchs including grammar . . . Lincoln and she was Engaged." Everyone adored and respected her. While Greene may have gushed, the problem Lincoln faced in courting Ann is that she was engaged to John McNamar, who had left for New York after a falling out with his business partner (which may have been related to jealousy over Ann) and had not returned after several years. For a long time it seems Ann Rutledge told Lincoln she could not marry him until she had freed herself from McNamar.[21]

Lincoln courted Ann regularly and respectfully between 1832 (when he returned from the Black Hawk War, which was when McNamar left for the East) and 1835, visiting her on the farm several miles north of New Salem, where she and her family had moved by then. That distance made it easier to be discreet and develop their relationship but maintain the fiction of her continued engagement with McNamar. In the spring of 1835, according to her brother and cousin, Ann abandoned any hope of ever seeing McNamar (whom she knew as McNeil because as a young man he changed his name to avoid assuming his father's debts in New York) and became formally betrothed to Lincoln.[22]

Then suddenly Ann Rutledge died on August 25. The summer of 1835 was hot in central Illinois, and many caught what was probably typhoid fever but was locally called "brain fever." Ann suffered from the fever for several weeks before succumbing. As her brother told Herndon: "The effect on Mr Lincoln's mind was terrible; he became plunged in despair, and many of his friends feared that reason would desert her throne. His extraordinary emotions were regarded as strong evidence of the existence of the tenderest relations between himself and the deceased." Mentor Graham told Herndon that Lincoln said he "felt like Committing Suicide often" after Ann died. Hardin Bale reported Lincoln was "locked up by his friends" to "prevent derangement or suicide." And so on. All these reports to Herndon that Lincoln went insane in his grief would later turn off some historians as a mere tale of nineteenth-century romantic tragedy. But none of the many witnesses to Lincoln's grief among those in Herndon's oral history denied it, and the only difference in their accounts is how they characterized its intensity.[23]

Lincoln was distraught over losing Ann Rutledge and, it seems pretty clear, became clinically depressed after her death, poised near suicide. The sheer number of his friends and neighbors who recalled how extreme his reaction was to Ann's death should be taken seriously. It is a telling detail in the report of Hardin Bale that Lincoln had to be "locked up by his friends" so that he would not commit suicide. Did they create something of a suicide watch through the first crucial few days after his betrothed's death? That seems to be what Bale is suggesting, since none of the twenty-five or 30 log cabins strung out along New Salem's single dirt path had actual locks. But the closeness of the quarters would have allowed Lincoln's friends to stay with him in his grief, perhaps take away his pocketknife and any razors he owned, and try to talk him back from the edge.

One should not minimize the deep sadness Lincoln felt over his loss of this beautiful and remarkable woman, even if later romantic embellishments, some in paintings, stories, and poetry, have a delirious Lincoln beating his chest on her grave in the driving rain. By all accounts, it was the first time he was in love, and his extended courtship bound him to this most impressive young woman. He fell in love with Ann Rutledge and seemed ready to take on a wife in his quest for a coherent identity. Her sudden death was tragic, and, to use a term of great importance in contemporary psychoanalysis, it was also traumatic. Two factors contributed to Lincoln's traumatic reaction to her death. First, it came without warning and was extremely painful to witness. Typhoid is a bacterial disease that runs its course in three to four weeks and brings a rising temperature (to 104 degrees), diarrhea, intestinal hemorrhaging, encephalitis, delirium, and, if untreated, as of course it was in New Salem in the mid-1830s, often death.

But second, the extremity of Lincoln's reaction to the death of Ann Rutledge, especially the testimony of his suicidal inclinations at her loss, suggests he had a fragile self that was extremely vulnerable to loss. In this, Lincoln seemed *re*traumatized by Ann's death. His wild despair and depression, in other words, because it reached such extreme lengths, leads one to suspect that it evoked the earlier losses of his mother and sister, losses never fully worked through, leaving him vulnerable to fragmentation as an adult when faced with events that directly or symbolically evoked the childhood trauma of his mother's death and to a lesser degree that of his sister. Lincoln knew intimately of the "death scenes of those we love," as he later wrote to Joshua Speed.[24]

***

With the support of his friends, and in time, Lincoln came back from the precipice. The following year he attempted to engage, however fitfully, in another courtship, even though his heart was never really in it. He was still much too depressed over Ann's death. In 1833 Mary Owens, a well-educated woman of means from Kentucky, had visited her New Salem sister, Elizabeth, who was married to Bennett Abell. During that visit, Mary briefly made an acquaintance with Lincoln. Mary returned three years later at the urging of Mrs. Abell, who wanted to fix her up with her good friend Lincoln. Although he had courted a teenager in Ann Rutledge, Lincoln seemed to feel most comfortable at this stage of his life with older, married women, who in turn nurtured him as surrogate mothers. Elizabeth Abell might also have been a bit worried about the prospects of her sister in marriage. Both Owens and Lincoln were twenty-eight years of age in 1836, which was precariously close to what was then the socially tainted status of spinsterhood for a woman. Mary Owens was impressive in many ways. She was not only rich and formally educated but was very intelligent. A number of respondents told Herndon how "intellectual" she was, that is, not just smart (Lincoln was that) but apart from them in her knowledge of things, wide reading, and general sophistication. Mary Owens, however, was not beautiful. She was five feet, seven inches tall, muscular, with blue eyes and brown hair, and she weighed 160 pounds. Her forehead, reported Johnson Gaines Greene, was "massive & angular—Square, prominent & broad."[25]

Lincoln, it seems, tried hard to court Mary Owens over the next year or so. He must have enjoyed talking with a woman of such intelligence, hanging out at the Abells or taking jaunts in the countryside. His first surviving letter to Owens is from the end of 1836. Lincoln writes from Vandalia (still the state capital), where he has gone for the legislative session. He reports on various political things, including his efforts at moving the capital to Springfield, and ends with a comment that his letter is so "dry and [stupid] that I am ashamed to send it." But very shortly, if not already in 1836 (Elizabeth Abell palpable, if not vocal, in the background), he and Mary were talking about marriage. On May 7, 1837, a few weeks after his move to Springfield, Lincoln reports to Owens on his loneliness ("I am quite as lonesome here as [I] ever was anywhere in my life") and his distaste for the pretensions of the elite ("There is a great deal of flourishing about in carriages here") before addressing the serious issue of their marriage. He dwells on the problems. She would be poor living with him in Springfield, "without the means of hiding your poverty," the subtext of which is Owens's privileged upbringing. Lincoln wants to do the right thing: "Whatever woman may cast her lot with mine, should any ever do so, it is my intention to do all in my power to make her happy and contented; and there is nothing I can imagine, that would make me more unhappy then to fail in the effort." But he cannot tell her he loves her. All he can do is put the decision about marriage back in her lap: "I know I should be much happier with you than the way I am, provided I saw no signs of discontent in you." He tells her he will abide by his previous commitments to her, but he doesn't really think she wants him or would like living in Springfield. Therefore: "My opinion is that you had better not do it."[26]

It seems she turned down this highly ambivalent offer of marriage. Three months later, after parting from her for what would be the last time, he writes, "I can not see you, or think of you, with entire indifference," a phrasing cast in a double negative that skirts any suggestion of affection. The most he can say with certainty is that "I want in all cases to do right, and most particularly so in all cases with women." What seems the right thing to do is leave her alone because that is what she wants. Feel free not to answer the letter, he urges her, and it will not call forth "one accusing murmur from me." Beating a dead horse, he adds: "Do not understand by this, that I wish to cut your

acquaintance. I mean no such thing. What I do wish is, that our further acquaintance shall depend upon yourself."[27]

Mary Owens later married Jesse Vineyard and settled in Missouri.
Herndon, once he learned of the relationship from his New Salem
informants and that she was alive, tracked her down and relentlessly
hounded her with questions about her courtship with Lincoln. He
especially wanted her to send him Lincoln's letters, which she consented to on May 1, 1866, after "quite a struggle with my feelings."
He then wrote her with many questions, which she answered on May
23, though she made fun of the way he catechized her in "true lawyer
style." She explained that her sister, Elizabeth Abell, had been "very
anxious" to see her and Lincoln get married, but she had come to feel
Lincoln was "deficient in those little links which make up the chain
of woman's happiness,—at least, it was so in my case." He had a good
heart, she says, but "his training had been different from mine" and
"that congeniality which would otherwise have existed" was missing in
their relationship. Elizabeth Abell later wrote Jesse Weik (Herndon's
coauthor) that Mary "received him [Lincoln] as a man of fine intellect and (although crude) energetic and aspiring." He was lacking in
"smaller attentions," Mary added in a letter to Herndon on July 22,
and was "sensitive almost to a fault."[28]

That is from Mary's perspective. Lincoln's experience of the courtship varied significantly. Another of his matronly friends was Eliza
Browning, the wife of Orville Browning, his political and legal colleague.
Browning was from a slave-owning Kentucky family and was always
well dressed and dashing, full of old-school politeness. He was devoted
to his wife, the former Eliza Caldwell, who was also from a good Kentucky family. They lived in Quincy, Illinois, over one hundred miles from
Springfield, but Lincoln's circuit riding took him near enough to Quincy
so that he was able to visit with them fairly often. He was not particularly close to Orville, who would later become a senator from Illinois,
but he was especially fond of the unconventional Eliza, who had a warm
and generous heart, was smart, a habitual smoker of cigars, and had a
great sense of humor that included mocking her own ungainliness. On
April 1, 1838, he wrote Eliza a long narrative of his courtship with Mary.
On this traditional fool's day—Falstaff also appears in the letter—
Lincoln wove a tale about an early relationship with an unnamed woman
that Eliza only much later came to learn was more than a mere joke.[29]

His "great friend" Elizabeth Abell, Lincoln reports, told him she would bring back her sister from Kentucky, where she planned to visit in 1836, "upon condition that I would engage to become her brother-in-law with all convenient dispatch." He had seen the woman three years earlier, and she seemed "intelligent and agreeable." He saw no reason not to "plod through life" with her "hand in hand." He was concerned, however, for she seemed a "trifle too willing," but nothing prepared him for what he saw when they met. She was not just "over-size" but "a fair match for Falstaff." She was not just an "old maid" but reminded him of his mother, "and this, not from withered features, for her skin was too full of fat, to permit its contracting in to wrinkles; but from her want of teeth, weather-beaten appearance in general, and from a kind of notion that ran in my head, that *nothing* could have commenced at the size of infancy, and reached her present bulk in less than thirtyfive or forty years." Perhaps this is how Lincoln remembered his mother Nancy on her deathbed. But since he had to hold to his bargain with Elizabeth Abell, he tried to find good things about her. It was not easy. After much delay, he finally felt duty bound to propose, to meet the terms of his agreement. And then she rejected him. He was astonished. He, with all his "fancied greatness," had been rejected. And in that curious moment, he "began to suspect that I was really a little in love with her." Others have been made fools of "by the girls." In this instance, he "made a fool of himself." The only answer is for him never to marry, he concludes, for he could never be satisfied with anyone who would be "block-head enough to have me."

The historian Richard Current wrote many years ago that "Lincoln emerges from the Owen affair as cautious, half-hearted, a little crude, and even self-centered in the role of suitor."[30] That may not go quite far enough. Beyond boasting to Eliza about how cleverly he had avoided both matrimony and dishonor, Lincoln was cruel and snide about Mary's appearance by emphasizing her bulky physicality and simultaneously ignoring her intelligence and learning. The only redeeming human aspect of the letter is that Lincoln mocks his own pretensions and acknowledges a twinge of love for her after she rejected him. What one can say emphatically is that young man Lincoln remained confused about issues of love and intimacy.

***

Despite Lincoln's mental breakdown after the death of Ann Rutledge, which seems to have contributed to his inability to connect with Mary Owens, Lincoln for the most part did not otherwise appear to his neighbors in New Salem as chronically melancholy, and at least one, James Matheny, even claimed Lincoln was never depressed. Some thought he was a bit lazy, or odd for reading all the time, but he was also greatly admired. No one remembered him in their accounts to Herndon as sad and gloomy, wandering aimlessly along the dusty street or in the surrounding fields, except after the death of Ann, which stood out by comparison. It may have been the case that Lincoln was better adjusted to life in this rough setting that closely approximated his childhood experience. He lived in log cabins, occasionally split rails, and developed his mind and professional skills slowly and without much competition. He was also glad to be apart from his father and his uneducated extended clan of step-relations, not to mention the tedium of farming.[31]

But a dark despair of uncertain childhood origins lingered in young Lincoln. For the moment, his depression was relatively quiescent, just below the surface. He was in a state of what the psychoanalyst Erik Erikson called a moratorium, that moment in youth when a troubled, and often talented, young person holds at bay peremptory developmental demands, keeping them dormant and suppressed without being resolved, waiting for a kind of inner transformation that will permit the construction of a usable identity. Erikson stresses that someone in such a developmentally delayed state of tension slows things down, easily slips into "tortuous self-consciousness," and most of all recoils from intimacy. The danger in closeness with another is the potential loss of self. For Lincoln, the unconsummated love for Ann Rutledge and then her sudden, tragic death brought back in full force the earlier trauma of his mother's death. A suffering young Lincoln fell back on a cover of blandness that allowed some expression of his depression only to those few he trusted. He thus wrote Mary Owens in 1836 from Vandalia that things "have conspired and have gotten my spirits so low, that I feel that I would rather be any place in the world than here." He also told his friend William Butler, around the same time, of his despair at not having a home, of being in debt, and of having nothing to look forward to.[32]

That sense of ingrained depression became more outwardly noticeable after his arrival in Springfield. He was less able to mask his moods, or less motivated, or perhaps more troubled in ways that he could no longer suppress. He became visibly distracted, quick to withdraw into himself, and most witnesses remembered him as usually sad. Speed, who said in his *Reminiscences* that "Generally, Lincoln was a very sad man," reported that he offered his room to Lincoln because the "tone of his voice was so melancholy." Elizabeth Edwards said he was "not Social—was abstracted—thoughtful" and added later in her interview with Herndon that Lincoln was a "peculiar man." And Herndon himself wrote of his law partner that "his melancholy dripped from him as he walked." Lincoln's depression was manifest as well in the poetry that drew his attention in these years. He had a special attraction for the gloomy poems of Lord Byron, who wrote of sleep residing at the boundary of death and existence, of tears and tortures, and of divided souls. Speed, who wrestled with his own depression, said he introduced Lincoln to the poetry of Byron, but in fact many in the Speed circle read and talked about Byron. Lincoln was especially fond of the apocalyptic themes in Byron's "Darkness," which James Matheny reported was one of Lincoln's favorites. In it the sun is extinguished and the stars wander in eternal space. Earth has only one thought, "and that was Death / Immediate and inglorious." The rivers, lakes, and oceans stand still, as ships rot in the sea. The waves are dead, the moon expires, the air becomes stagnant. It is an unrelenting image of the death of death itself as the earth comes to a grinding halt.[33]

No one understood Lincoln's depression better than Joshua Speed. Lincoln did mention feeling blue to Mary Owens in 1836, told William Butler of his loneliness around the same time, and shared with Robert Wilson his thoughts of suicide. But in general Lincoln, whom David Davis said was "the most reticent—Secretive man I Ever Saw—or Expect to See" and whom Herndon described as "terribly reticent, secretive" and the "most shut-mouthed man I ever met," kept a tight rein on his feelings. Except to Speed, who saw at firsthand both his moments of joy (when he warmed up, Speed said, "all sadness vanished," his face "radiant and glowing") and sorrow. Speed heard and witnessed everything. Lincoln told Speed about his mother and his feelings for her, about his adored stepmother, and about his feelings of death and apocalyptic dread. To Speed, likewise inclined to obsess, who dreamed of his lost youngest sister as if she were alive and woke up gloomy, Lincoln shared his dread of death and the sadness of life. Their minds ran in the same deep channel.[34]

5

SEX AND PROSTITUTION

There is nothing like stories of sex, especially its transgressive forms, to elicit the fantasies of friends, neighbors, acquaintances—and historians. The greater the figure, the more cautious one must be in assessing reports of experiences that are illicit. Nowhere is that need for caution greater than with Abraham Lincoln. For one thing, Herndon's oral history—conducted in the wake of Lincoln's apotheosis after his death—unearthed some extraordinary tales from the old days. Some of those (previously ignored or dismissed) stories have become newly salient in the more current debate about Lincoln's sexual identity. Second, Herndon himself as he aged contributed mightily to what has come down to us about Lincoln, sex, and prostitution, which itself has a context. In the latter part of the nineteenth century men feared appearing unmanly and emasculated from "nerve disease" or, as they preferred, the more technical term neurasthenia. Herndon, ever the chest beater, had a personal stake in his portrait of Lincoln as virile and actively heterosexual.[1]

The most unlikely story of all is that Lincoln fathered a child in New Salem and forced the mother's marriage to another man in the village whom he then dispatched out of town. The story as reported to

Herndon is that Lincoln was the father of a child by Jane Burner, who was to marry Jason Duncan. Johnson Gaines Greene reported to Herndon that sometime in 1835 or 1836 (though Johnson's brother, William G. Greene, dated the same story from "1833—possibly in 1832") Jane had a child of "uncertain fatherhood" after she married Duncan. It was "supposed to be Duncan's—or Lincoln's." Red flags went up for Herndon, who was then furiously conducting interviews throughout Kentucky and Indiana on a research trip in the fall of 1866. Four days later, Herndon tracked down William G. Greene and asked him about the charge that Lincoln might have fathered Jane's child. William replied with certainty that "Lincoln never touched her [Jane Burner] in his life" and that she was a "good [clean?] girl . . . a clever girl—a handsome girl—not brilliant, but good." Lincoln apparently did know and like Jane—Lincoln liked nearly everyone in New Salem—and, with William, encouraged Jason Duncan, a physician, to marry her and "go off," or move, to Macomb, Illinois. Herndon, always eager for sexual gossip, the next day reinterviewed Johnson about Jane Burner and Lincoln. This time around Johnson Greene hedged his story: "I really do not Know who was the father" of Jane Burner's child, he says categorically. But he could not help making trouble by adding that his brother and Lincoln used to "run the machine" (be highly sexual) and implies that because Jane Burner was a woman of "Strong passions—weak will—Strong desire to please & gratify friends," even though also "a good woman," William Greene and Lincoln persuaded Duncan to marry her and get her away from them.[2]

There are a number of discrepancies in this evidence. For one thing, Johnson Gaines Greene told Herndon of *Jane* Burner, whom Lincoln supposedly got pregnant and had Jason Duncan marry. Johnson's brother, William G. Greene, told Herndon four days later (and presumably independently of what his brother had said) about *Nancy* Burner, whom Lincoln "never touched" but with Greene "urged Duncan to Mary her & go off." They can't even agree on the first name of the Burner girl. Second, Johnson Gaines Greene seems a busybody, for after he is confronted with what his brother told Herndon, he retracts his story about Jane Burner bearing Lincoln's child. But William Greene's word is also suspect. He asserts flatly that Lincoln never touched this Miss Burner—whatever her first name—so why then say she needed to be married and sent off from the village?

The only certain conclusion one can draw from Herndon's notes of his three interviews with the Greene brothers in the fall of 1866 is that Lincoln was not the father of Jane (or Nancy) Burner's child. Was he flirtatious with her? Possibly, though Johnson Gaines Greene's colorful phrase that Lincoln and his brother "ran the machine" suggests nothing specific, and the idea that Lincoln and Greene encouraged Duncan to marry Jane to get her away from them is so odd and out of context from all else that we know about Lincoln in New Salem as not to be believable. Johnson Gaines Greene's story about Jane Burner stands out for its uniqueness. No one else reported to Herndon that Lincoln ever did or said anything inappropriate with the young women of New Salem or the surrounding towns. There were lots of stories about Lincoln—spending too much time reading, working fitfully at many tasks, being distracted, etc.—but never that he took advantage of young women within his world, including in some of the homes where he boarded.[3]

The evidence becomes trickier with prostitution, which thrived in Springfield at the time. A number of law cases attest to what Erika Holst has called this "wicked" side of a community of 1,500 at the edge of America. Sometimes the evidence is merely suggestive. A slander suit in 1840 began with a charge that a local minister was keeping a woman in the woods (*Ellison v. Bohannan*). Two decades later, Nancy Clarkson sued her husband James in 1860 in Sangamon County for divorce on the grounds of his activities with "lewd women" (*Clarkson v. Clarkson*). But many of the cases that have been uncovered in the remarkable work of the Lincoln Legals project and published in the huge documentary record prepared by Martha Benner and Cullom Davis provide more direct evidence of prostitution in Springfield. In 1859 Sherman Harrington charged his wife, Hepsiba, with prostitution, among other things, and won a divorce (*Harrington v. Harrington*). In 1851 Milden and Elizabeth Kitchell accused a woman named Jacobus of obtaining "her fine clothes by whoring," though the case was dismissed and the Kitchells agreed not to make any further charges regarding the chastity of Jacobus (*Jacobus v. Kitchell et ux.*). In 1854 a Mr. Brenner was found guilty of keeping "a common ill-governed and disorderly house to the encouragement of fornication" and fined twenty dollars (*People v. Brenner*). In the late 1840s Jesse Rawls left for Oregon for a few years and when he returned charged his wife, Lavinia, with being a prostitute, though he later dismissed the charge (*Rawls v. Rawls*). And in 1850 a complicated slander case began with a charge against John Allsop that he kept a whorehouse in town (*Tennery et ux. v. Sturgeon*).[4]

The most remarkable case, however, handled by none other than the firm of Lincoln and Herndon in 1859, refers to multiple whorehouses in Springfield at the time. A mother of four, Cynthia Klein, sought divorce as a battered wife from her husband, John. Lincoln or Herndon added to her petition that John spent time in "every house of ill fame in Springfield." That was all John needed to answer the charge by admitting he had gone to brothels—but only after she deserted him. Furthermore, John claimed to have witnesses who saw Cynthia in brothels with prostitutes (presumably acting as one herself) and bringing their thirteen-year-old daughter with her. After trial, the judge denied Cynthia's petition and granted John's, who got his divorce as well as custody of the children. John, however, was required to pay Cynthia alimony of four hundred dollars, presumably to keep her off the streets.[5] Cynthia did not have Lincoln and Herndon file an appeal. This case and the others mentioned do not provide evidence for how many whorehouses there were in Springfield at the time, but it is clear from this evidence that there were several.[6]

The question, however, is not whether prostitutes were available for Lincoln and Speed but whether either man, or both, took advantage of the opportunities to visit and have sex with them. One stray piece of evidence suggests that Lincoln went to prostitutes as early as during his service in the Black Hawk War in 1832. It comes from an interview Herndon later conducted with John Todd Stuart, Lincoln's mentor in the law and first partner after he arrived in Springfield. Herndon's notes are frustratingly incomplete and make firm conclusions risky. Stuart told Herndon: "Lincoln & myself were in Iles—Spy Battalion—Got to Galena—went to the hoar houses—Gen Henry went—his magnetism drew all the women to himself—All went purely for fun—devilment— nothing Else." Herndon's ears undoubtedly perked up at the mention of the "hoar houses." But the notes are ambiguous. The only certain pieces of information that one can extract from this quote are that General James D. Henry's charisma made him the center of attention for the prostitutes the soldiers visited and that Stuart also participated in the visits. He suggests Lincoln went as well ("All went"), but there is an important gap in Herndon's highly elliptical notes from Stuart and Lincoln's service in the spy battalion of Captain Elijah Iles and the arrival of the troops in Galena, Illinois, after which they then visited the whorehouses. Stuart does not say in so many words that Lincoln visited the prostitutes, which as long as he was bothering to tell the story in the first place to Herndon after the Civil War, one would think he would make clear. The reference thus could be read several ways and on its own is nothing more than merely suggestive of whether (or not) Lincoln was a regular of, or went at all to, prostitutes.[7]

In a widely quoted line from a letter a year before he died, Herndon said of Lincoln that he had "terribly strong passions for woman, could scarcely keep his hands off them." Most quote only this first part of the sentence as evidence that Lincoln was robustly active sexually as a young man. The end of the sentence about Lincoln's strong passions for women, however, is telling: "and yet he had honor and a strong will, and these enabled him to put out the fires of his terrible passion." David Davis, the judge who was close to Lincoln, said of his friend that he was "a Man of strong passion for woman—his Conscience Kept him from seduction—this saved many—many a woman." What Herndon and Davis testify to, in other words, is that Lincoln was a man of sexual passion but of an even stronger will that he drew on to keep himself under control. Control of one's passions—which meant suppressing everything from masturbation to intercourse—was highly prized by nineteenth-century middle-class men (and women) in that era before good contraception, illegal and dangerous methods of abortion, and when virtue was associated with virginity.[8]

Other evidence from the oral history supports this same image of a Lincoln in strong control of his world of sexual desire but add to it that he was generally a highly moral man who was also shy around women. William Greene told Herndon that Lincoln in New Salem was "entirely *free* from the vices [of] running after Women Drinking whiskey or playing Cards for Money." Another old New Salem character, Abner Y. Ellis, told Herndon that Lincoln was a "verry shy Man of Ladies" and "had no desire for strange woman [i.e., prostitutes] I never heard him speak of any *particular woman* with disrespect though he had Many opportunities for doing so while in the Company with J.F.S. [Joshua Speed] and Wm B [William Butler] two old rats in that way."[9]

So the "old rat" Speed seems the culprit. In 1885 Herndon wrote to his coauthor, Jesse Weik:

Lincoln came to this city in 1837 and from that time to 1843–44 he and Speed were quite familiar, to go no further, with the women. I cannot tell you what I know, especially in ink. Speed was a lady's man in a good and true sense. Lincoln only went to see a few women of the first class, women of sense. Fools ridiculed him; he was on this point tender-footed.

Herndon is clearly suggesting Lincoln and Speed had a number of sexual experiences before their marriages with women, presumably prostitutes, because Lincoln was shy with "women of the first class." The most suggestive line in the passage is when Herndon says, "I cannot tell you what I know [about Lincoln and Speed with women], especially in ink." It reads as if Herndon is holding onto a salacious secret. And in fact he was. A few years later in a document among the Herndon papers labeled as "Joshua F. Speed" and in Herndon's writing, dated "Jany 5th '89," Herndon wrote up the remarkable story of Lincoln going to a prostitute. Herndon tells the story, which he says he heard directly from Speed, who was apparently "keeping a pretty woman in this City." Lincoln said (to Speed, who in turn told Herndon) he was "desirous to have *a little*" and asked Speed where he could "get *some*." Speed tells Lincoln he will gladly send him to a place with a required note. Lincoln took the note and gave it to the "girl," who "after some protestations, agreed to satisfy him." And then, as reported by Herndon:

> Things went on right—Lincoln and the girl stript off and went to bed. Before any thing was done Lincoln said to the girl—"How much do you charge." "Five dollars, Mr. Lincoln." Mr. Lincoln said—"I've only got $3." "Well said the girl—"I'll trust you, Mr. Lincoln, for $2." Lincoln thought a moment or so and said—"I do not wish to go on credit—I'm poor & I don't know where my next dollar will come from and I cannot afford to Cheat you." Lincoln after some words of encouragement from the girl got up out of bed,—buttoned up his pants and offered the girl the $3, which she would not take, saying—Mr. Lincoln—"You are the most Conscientious man I ever saw."[10]

Until the last couple of decades, Lincoln scholars tended either to dismiss the story as unlikely or chuckle about it to themselves without caring much about its meaning. More recent observers, however, have lent Herndon's account of Lincoln and Speed visiting prostitutes more credence to bolster their image of Lincoln as a high-testosterone and decidedly heterosexual young man (which subtextually counters the picture of Lincoln as homosexual). Richard Lawrence Miller, for example, uncritically swallows whole Herndon's report of the "girl" who would give Lincoln "a little" as proof positive of his sexual identity. On the face of it, such an argument makes eminently good sense. It would hardly be surprising that young bachelors in Springfield in their late twenties and early thirties would be having sex with prostitutes. Middle-class mores at the time placed strict taboos on sex before marriage with respectable women—the prevailing "Cult of True Womanhood" forbade it—and if liaisons did develop, and especially if the woman became pregnant, immediate marriage was assumed. That intertwined web of taboos and social customs carved out a clear niche for prostitutes to meet the needs of young unmarried men.[11]

But there is room to doubt this report from Herndon. For one thing, the date of the document that contains the story (January 5, 1889) and its source as Speed is misleading. The date refers to when Herndon wrote down the story from memory. It could not be that Herndon interviewed Speed in 1889 because the latter died in 1882. Speed also became rather formal and was increasingly influenced by his wife's deep religiosity as he aged (he formally converted to Christianity shortly before his death), and it contradicts all we know of his character to believe he would have told Herndon that story in an interview after 1865, and certainly not in his later years. Besides, Speed wrote all kinds of letters to Herndon after 1865, sent him other materials, and sat for several interviews with Herndon. In none of those communications did Speed ever write about or tell Herndon the prostitute story, perhaps because he was never asked, but more importantly because the story may have had a very different meaning for Speed than for Herndon.

So where did the story come from? It is reasonable to believe that Herndon heard it from Speed (Herndon was always meticulous not to lie). But when did he hear it? The most likely explanation is that Speed told him the story at some point before he left Springfield, that is, probably in the late 1830s up to 1841, and that Herndon then wrote it down for himself (and perhaps Weik) near the end of his own life. The story is thus located in the far mists of time nearly half a century earlier.

The murkiness of Herndon's memory and the vast time between hearing it originally and writing it down (in two stages, first in the cryptic 1885 letter to Weik and four years later as a note to himself) explains the serious errors of dating in the story. By 1842 both Lincoln and Speed were married—and Speed, as of the spring of 1841, was not even living in Springfield any longer (though he returned for a few months in the fall of 1841). Herndon clearly got confused in his dating, as he was not suggesting Lincoln and Speed were going to prostitutes in 1843 or 1844, well after man each was married. Second, Herndon's claim that "Speed was a lady's man in a good and true sense" is exceedingly vague. Speed was comfortable with women in social situations. He seemed to have flirted with any number of them at the "Coterie," the group of local elites and professionals that met at the Edwards home. All that, however, says nothing about prostitutes and even less about sexual encounters. Furthermore, Herndon distinguishes Speed as a "lady's man" from a much more naïve Lincoln, who only visited with "women of the first class," with whom he was so insecure he was mocked by some—perhaps women *and* men—which hurt his feelings ("he was on this point tender-footed").

The language is also stilted though not unimaginable as something Lincoln would say. Lincoln told dirty jokes, but it stretches credulity that he would ask his friend Speed where he "could get a *little*." The scene itself with the woman to whom Speed introduces Lincoln is also odd, even comical. Few men get their clothes off and into bed with a naked prostitute before calling it off, especially if she is willing to grant credit for the deed. It is also not unimportant that in this seemingly documented case of Lincoln going to a prostitute it ends with him *not* consummating the act for whatever reason.

It all seems a Lincoln joke lost in translation, perhaps related by Speed and believed as real by the exceedingly earnest Herndon. It is less likely that Herndon fabricated the story than that he never got it right in the first place hearing it in front of that fire in the back of the store or late at night in the dorm room. Any number of possibilities could explain the confusion. Speed may have been teasing Herndon. Lincoln may have been teasing him as well or joining Speed in teasing Herndon. One must also understand how slippery Herndon was when dealing with anything concerning Lincoln's sexuality or the sexuality of his parents or other members of his family. Herndon tended to take in and remember anything he heard that was salacious without considering what could be called formally the provenance of a story.[12]

In the same 1889 letter to Weik in which Herndon reported the prostitute story, he tells another tale of Lincoln and a farmer's daughter. Lincoln, Herndon says, was in Bloomington for court about 1850 or 1851. On the way home he stayed the night with an old friend, a Mr. Cottenbarger. There were three beds in the one room, with curtains between the beds. The bedsteads were arranged so that the "foot of one bed was close up against the head of the other." The farmer and Lincoln were in the two outside beds and in the middle was the grown daughter of Cottenbarger. During the night the girl's feet fell on Lincoln's pillow, which "put the *devil*" in him. He reached up his hand and "put it where it ought not to be." The girl woke up and went to her mother's bed to report what had happened. She told her, "For God's sake, say no more and go to bed, the man means nothing. If the old man hears of this, the deuce will be to pay." Lincoln heard the conversation but was fairly sure the father had been awake the whole time. Cottenbarger was a "great big burly strong man with great courage," and Lincoln began to figure out a way of defending himself. But nothing happened until the morning, when he saw the farmer whet the blade of a butcher knife and whisper with his wife before going off into the woods. The woman made a fire and breakfast before hustling Lincoln off. He jumped into his buggy and rode off for home, "a deeply and thoroughly mortified man."[13]

A farmer's daughter? One can only imagine how many dirty tales from the nineteenth century on are placed in such a setting, one made for a tall tale with a crusty theme. And no one could spin such a story better than Lincoln, especially when he was telling it to the world's most gullible listener. The only real surprise is how many historians have let themselves be equally gullible. In the circle around Lincoln in those days, Herndon was the outsider. He was not privileged in friendship by anyone. He also completely lacked a sense of humor, a defining aspect of Lincoln's identity. Herndon rushed about, reading everything in haste, urgently filling his writing with dashes and breathless asides. He seldom stopped to reflect. When he drank it was often to excess and caused behaviors that led to great shame in a small town;

he sometimes was even tossed in jail overnight. In the early period, Lincoln kept Herndon at arm's length; later he was decidedly Lincoln's *junior* partner. Lincoln never revealed to Herndon any of his deeper feelings about anything. There is no question he kept to himself truly private matters about sex and intimacy. But Lincoln's reserve carried over as well to other kinds of issues. In 1848 Lincoln visited Niagara Falls. He wrote up a quite remarkable fragment for himself about how moved he was by the sight. "It calls up the indefinite past. When Columbus first sought this continent—when Christ suffered on the cross—when Moses led Israel through the Red Sea—nay, even, when Adam first came from the hand of his Maker—then as now, Niagara was roaring here." And so on. When Herndon asked him, however, what he felt when he saw Niagara Falls (not knowing of the fragment), Lincoln replied: "The thing that struck me most forcibly when I saw the Falls was, where in the world did all that water come from?"[14]

So the stories of Lincoln leaving the prostitute or putting his hand where he shouldn't with the farmer's daughter, as processed in distant memory by Herndon over half a century, are problematic at best and deserve to be treated as Lincoln jokes that Herndon didn't get. It is also easy to imagine Lincoln told the story in a way to make it seem real for the very reason that he could tell Herndon would believe it. As with the report about Niagara Falls, Lincoln often mocked Herndon. He hardly feared exposure from his law partner about transgressions, but he did enjoy telling off-color stories that would be believed by his earnest law partner.

But there is more. Herndon also reports a tale about Lincoln and prostitutes from his days in New Salem. Herndon wrote Jesse Weik in 1891, two months before Herndon's death and two years after the appearance of their biography of Lincoln, a long letter that detailed Lincoln's "devilish passion" that drew him to a "girl" in Beardstown in 1835 or 1836 from whom he contracted syphilis (in his old age Herndon seemed to equate sex with the devil). Herndon remembers Lincoln telling him of the encounter and his concerns about having syphilis, which led him to consult by mail with a Dr. Drake of Cincinnati. Herndon wrote all this down in a "little memorandum book" buried in his notes that ended up in the hands of Ward Hill Lamon in 1872 and was then lost. Herndon presumably wanted Weik to know of the episode before he died.[15]

It is not surprising that Lincoln, if he were concerned about having syphilis, would seek out advice from a renowned doctor well out of town. But, again, did Herndon have the story correct? Speed also knew about the Drake letter. He reported to Herndon in 1866 that Lincoln wrote Drake a long letter "descriptive of his case" over the break with Mary Todd. Lincoln even took the trouble to read the letter out loud to Speed, who was of course in the thicket of Lincoln's emotional turmoil over the breakup. There was, however, one section of the letter that Lincoln kept to himself. Speed assumed in 1866 that that part of the letter had to do with his tortured response to the death of Ann Rutledge; Herndon, writing to Weik twenty-three years later, believes the unread section of the letter dealt with Lincoln's apparent belief he had caught syphilis. In making that assertion, however, Herndon moved from reporting, which he did (reasonably) well, to interpretation, something he almost always botched. The context of the letter strongly supports Speed's interpretation that Lincoln wrote Drake about his depression and suicidality in connection with the broken engagement with Mary Todd.[16]

This Dr. Daniel Drake of Cincinnati specialized in psychiatry, not general medicine or anything having to do with infectious disease. Drake lived from 1785 until 1852 and became a leading authority on "dyspeptics, hypochondriacs . . . and other unhappy souls," as he put it in one article he wrote for the *Journal of Medical and Physical Sciences*. A Princeton graduate, Drake was the founder of the Medical College of Ohio in Cincinnati in 1819 (which early on had something of a checkered history) and was closely associated with the founding two years later of the Commercial Hospital and Lunatic Asylum. Drake went on to lecture widely and write seven scientific texts and one memoir. Lampooned once in a local paper as "Dr. Pompous," Drake was associated as well with Rev. Dr. James Elijah Slack, who was the first president of the medical school. Among their many interests, Drake and Slack worked at the Cincinnati Natural Museum and seem to have been part of a circle of lively medical intellectuals in Cincinnati who had connections with John James Audubon.[17]

Lincoln undoubtedly got the idea of writing Drake from his close friend Anson G. Henry, a doctor in Springfield who had himself graduated from the medical school in Cincinnati in 1827. In early 1841 Henry was playing an important role tending to his friend Lincoln in his depression, trying anything and everything to help him get rid of his "hypo." Speed was certainly right about Lincoln's motivation in writing Drake, though whether the private part of the letter dealt with Ann Rutledge cannot be known. What matters is that Lincoln felt scared enough himself about his depression and his suicidality to reach out to a national expert for help (and some medicine) on the advice of Henry. It is also relevant that Lincoln brought Speed intimately into this narrative, reading the letter aloud to him and apparently only to him; had others known of the letter, it certainly would have been reported later to Herndon in his earnest research into the full story of the broken engagement with Mary Todd.[18]

But what about the supposed syphilis? As Milton Shutes, an astute medical doctor himself, carefully argued in 1957, there is absolutely no evidence that Lincoln had syphilis. This sexually transmitted, bacterial disease, so dreaded before antibiotics, moves through the body in relentless stages, the third of which, after between four and fifteen years, ends in tumors, cardiovascular complications, or dementia (and sometimes all of these symptoms). Shutes wisely guesses, assuming that it is true Lincoln told Herndon he thought he had syphilis, that Lincoln suffered from syphiliphobia, a widespread fear at the time. Lincoln's letter to Dr. Drake, however, had nothing to do with fears of syphilis or whores from Beardstown.[19]

And finally, where was Speed in all this? Was the Springfield entrepreneur and later Kentucky slave owner "keeping a pretty woman" on the side, as Herndon reports? It is hard to tell for sure. Because Speed was so close to Lincoln in these years, in fact sleeping in the same bed with him, there are no contemporary letters, and his relative historical insignificance did not occasion many later stories in the oral history Herndon diligently gathered. It is best for the moment to suspend judgment about Speed, sex, and women.

6

BROKEN ENGAGEMENT

The story of Abraham Lincoln and Mary Todd's broken engagement in late 1840 has been the focus of much disagreement in recent years. The oldest interpretation (Herndon) is that Lincoln was hoodwinked into the engagement by an assertive and difficult Mary Todd, withdrew into himself at the last minute, and simply failed to show up at the actual wedding. That line of argument gave way (Ruth Painter Randall) to the idea that Lincoln loved Mary but got cold feet leading up to the wedding, perhaps because he felt unable to match Mary's social status or properly take care of her. In the end, however, love triumphed, though not without some delays. Mary's more recent biographer (Jean Baker) makes Mary herself the key actor in the drama and argues she got jealous and was flirting with others (including Edwin Webb and Stephen Douglas) to annoy him. In a climactic scene, she stamped her feet and threw him out on his ear. The most important recent revision of the story, however, comes from several authors (Douglas Wilson most of all, who has influenced Michael Burlingame and Richard Lawrence Miller, among others), who place Matilda Edwards at the center of the drama. They argue that Lincoln was never more than half-interested in Mary Todd to begin with but felt an almost perverse need to be honorable about his apparent commitment to her, which went out the window temporarily when the beautiful teenaged Matilda suddenly showed up in Springfield in November 1840. Lincoln fell madly in love with her and inevitably broke off his engagement.[1]

Historians' and biographers' views of the broken engagement have been further complicated (and influenced) by their feelings about Mary Todd herself as a person and, by extension, her marriage to Lincoln. On the one hand, for example, is Ruth Painter Randall's story line, who portrays Mary as a smart, witty, attractive woman deeply devoted to her husband despite some of her own troubles and whose love is returned in kind. Randall's version of the broken engagement tells of "a great American love story, whose dramatic elements— broken engagement, family opposition, secret meetings of the lovers, and a challenge to a duel—outstrip most works of fiction." Others, in what is something of a general theme in the literature, one that revives Herndon's views, interpret the marriage as "woe-filled" and quotes Herndon about the "domestic hell" Lincoln had to endure, truly a "burning, scorching hell." As Herndon put it in his biography: "To me it has always seemed plain that Mr. L married Mary Todd to save his honor, and in doing so he sacrificed his domestic peace." One needs caution to navigate these rocky shoals.[2]

The varied interpretations of the broken engagement are not entirely mutually exclusive, though they move on separate tracks. Each narrative draws on specific evidence, and most make important arguments that fill in gaps and need thoughtful consideration. But examined closely it is clear that no explanation of the broken engagement to date deals adequately with the contradictions in the evidence. One can only believe that Lincoln felt intimidated by the lordly Todds, for example, if one ignores his self-confidence and even touch of arrogance (God only needed one "D," he is said to have quipped, while the Todds required two). Or, even more importantly in terms of recent arguments, the supposed significance of Lincoln's attraction for Matilda requires an observer to ignore her statement to a family member (Elizabeth Edwards) that Lincoln never "stooped" to pay her a compliment. And so it goes. The evidence surrounding the broken engagement is often spurious. Just as one line of argument seems convincing, it comes up against evidence that calls it into question. We need to take in all the evidence, including the confusions, and recognize that the story is actually more interesting for its nonlinearity and seeming contradictions.

***

Mary Todd's father, Robert, was the major figure in a distinguished Kentucky family. He was educated at Transylvania University and was admitted to the bar when he was just twenty years of age. He soon excelled in business, politics, and Lexington civic life. He ran various retail businesses and expanded into cotton manufacturing, owning a large packaging plant and wholesale outlet. In the 1830s he became the first president of the new Branch Bank of Kentucky. He played a key role in political affairs as well, socialized with the likes of Henry Clay, and helped shape Whig ideas in the state. He could be high strung and impetuous, but he was widely admired for his wealth, power, and family connections. Robert's first marriage was to his second cousin, Eliza Parker, by whom he had seven children (including the eldest, Elizabeth, born in 1813, and Mary, born in 1818). Eliza died in childbirth in 1825, leaving the thirty-four-year-old Robert in despair with a household of children. In less than a year and a half later, he married Elizabeth Humphreys, who began producing a second batch of eight more children in thirteen years. There were tensions between the first set of Todd children and their stepmother. The house was crowded, and she seemed hateful.[3]

In Springfield, meanwhile, the "Coterie," as mentioned in the previous chapter, was the name given to the social circle that assembled in the home of Ninian and Elizabeth Edwards. Ninian, born in 1809, the same year as Lincoln, was the son of Ninian Edwards, the territorial governor of Illinois (later governor and U.S. senator). The boy had politics in his veins. Ninian had been educated at Transylvania University, where he excelled, was first in his class, and gave his graduation speech in Latin. Undoubtedly, Ninian came into contact with Robert Todd early on, as he began to court his oldest daughter, Elizabeth, when she was barely of age and married her when she was nineteen. Elizabeth, well educated herself, especially for a girl in that period (she was fluent in French, for example), was quite comfortable moving to Springfield with her new husband. It meant escape from her stepmother in Lexington, and Springfield itself had become something of a Todd enclave. There were cousins, including John J. Hardin, and Uncle John Todd Stuart, and soon other sisters and brothers-in-laws. Erika Holst has shown convincingly how wide a kinship net the Todds actually cast. Beside Elizabeth and Ninian, John J. Hardin, and John Todd Stuart, the clan included Dr. William Wallace and his wife, Frances Todd (Mary's sister); the dry-goods merchant Clark Moulton Smith and his wife, Ann Todd (another sister); a host of children that extended the kinship networks; and the many relatives and in-laws of Ninian Edwards (Benjamin Edwards, Nicholas Ridgely, John Cook, James Lamb, and Ann and Antrim Campbell).[4]

At their home on "Quality Hill," sometimes dubbed "Aristocracy Hill," just to the southwest of the square on Second and Jackson Streets, Elizabeth and Ninian greeted guests in French, hosted frequent parties with dancing and violins, and set a standard for social elegance unmatched in Springfield or, indeed, in any of the surrounding towns of central Illinois. The house itself was two stories and large enough to hold within it "a dozen prairie-farmer cabins," as Sandburg colorfully puts it. Elegant brocade embellished the eaves, along with ornamental railings, engraved doors, and a long driveway that deposited visitors at the front veranda. At the north end was the large parlor where the Edwardses hosted their parties and soirees. A reporter once somehow got invited to one of these parties in 1840. He spoke with pedantic enthusiasm of the women in "degrees of fashion and beauty" but none a true "*belle*," a contemporary term reserved for a woman of true elegance and high fashion. There were "tasty and tidy decorations," but what really caught his attention was "Mrs. Edwards's supper table" in its elegant simplicity. He "half inclined to believe" that "Mrs. Edwards is in practice one of those very unfashionable modern ladies, who consider a personal attention to housewifery, a *duty*, and not a disgrace." Those in the Coterie mostly spoke in such stuffy language. James C. Conkling wrote his fiancée, Mercy Levering (a good friend of Mary Todd) about a sleigh ride he took in 1841. "We have had a fine fall of snow" for the last three weeks, but during it, "The merry sound of the bells was constantly ringing in our ears. Day and night the sleighs were continually in motion and a few of our choice bloods seemed to vie with each other in the rapidity of their motion[,] the gaiety of their equipage and a continued display of their gallantry." He himself took one trip of nearly 170 miles across the prairie and found it "exhilarating."[5]

The Todd sisters, though often at odds with one another, bonded in their intense dislike of their stepmother and desire to escape Lexington. Elizabeth became a beacon of hope in that regard. She first brought Frances to live with her and Ninian in Springfield in 1836 and invited Mary Todd to visit in the spring and summer of 1837. But the house was crowded, Elizabeth about to give birth, and, besides, Mary had promised her father she would return to Lexington at the end of the summer. In May 1839, however, Frances married William Wallace and moved out of the Edwards home. Now that there was space, Elizabeth invited Mary to come live with her. And so in June 1839, Mary moved to the town she would call home until 1861.[6]

Mary was a striking young woman at twenty-one years of age. Her earliest photograph from seven years later shows an attractive woman gazing expectantly at the camera. Full cheeks suggesting a tendency toward plumpness accentuate the softness of her face. Light brown hair pulled back from a high forehead frames wide eyes and a petite nose. The mouth is a straight line standing over a rounded chin. A long graceful neck plunges into folds of obscuring Victorian fabric. Short arms are propped uneasily, one against a chair, as she waits through the long exposure. Her long-fingered hands rest in her lap. This is Mary Lincoln, then a young wife and mother of a toddler.

She was never seen as beautiful, but one childhood friend accurately described her as "certainly very pretty with her clear blue eyes, lovely complexion, and soft brown hair," a bright and intelligent face, and a "perfect arm and hand." Ruth Painter Randall describes her as a "bright-faced, eager girl, impulsive, quick-tongued, warmhearted, affectionate, mercurial, interested in everything, joyous with life." James Conkling said Mary was the "very creature of excitement you know and never enjoys herself more than when in society and surrounded by a company of merry friends." Mary was only five feet, two inches tall but carried herself gracefully. As none other than Herndon put it, she was, when young, "pleasant, polite, civil, rather graceful in her movements, intelligent, witty." She was "polished, very well educated, and a good linguist" (which was hard not to notice since she spoke, like her sister Elizabeth, fluent French) as well as a "fine conversationalist" with her pronounced Southern accent. For four years in her adolescence she had attended Madame Mentelle's boarding school, where she learned "breeding and manners from the point of view of feudal Europe," as

Sandburg puts it. Some of what she was taught by this émigré socialite included cotillions, waltzes, hornpipes, galopades, Mohawks, as well as Spanish, Scottish, Polish, and Tyrolienne dances. Herndon, after his generous description of her intelligence and wit, goes on gratuitously to talk about how she "became soured, got gross" after her marriage, but that may reflect his bitterness at her dislike of his drunkenness and complete exclusion of him from her home more than a really accurate observation. In any event, Herndon was not alone in noting Mary as vivacious, infectiously enthusiastic, and delightfully witty. Ninian Edwards said she could "make a Bishop forget his prayers."[7]

Mary's letters from this period burst from the page. The sentences run on with few paragraph breaks but with occasional dashes. Indiscriminate underlinings give a feeling of exaggerated drama. She covers a wide range of topics. She also has a capacity for self-reflection and ironic humor that give depth to her somewhat superficial concerns with the swirl of social life around her. Would her real nature be satisfied with the excitement of the continued parties? She doubts it. "I would such were not my nature, for mine I fancy is to be a quiet lot, and happy indeed will I be, if it is, only cast near those, I so *dearly love*, my feelings & hopes are all so sanguine that in this dull world of reality tis best to dispel our delusive day dreams so soon as possible." She laughs at her own frailties and at her plumpness. In the fall of 1840 she describes herself as the "same ruddy *pineknot*" but without quite the "exuberance of flesh" she previously carried. Alas, "quite a sufficiency" remains. There is a certain reflective detachment in her descriptions of the most trivial occurrences. She provides concrete information (for example, how many guests were at the ball), describes the courtships of others as an outside observer might, and easily separates her own fantasies and dreams from the lives of those around her.[8]

The age difference of nine years separating Lincoln and Mary was not that remarkable in central Illinois at that time. There were far more eligible middle-class men than women in Sangamon County, resulting from the character of westward urban movement. It was not remarkable for a man to wait to marry until settled in his career (though Lincoln's delay exceeded the norm). Custom, however, dictated that attractive late-adolescent girls were expected to find mates before too far into their twenties. Elizabeth Edwards, for example, married

Ninian at nineteen; her sister Frances married William Wallace at twenty-four. Very few women married later than that.

It is imaginable, though not documented, that Lincoln met Mary that summer of 1837, but he certainly became acquainted with her after she arrived in 1839. Interestingly, it was Speed who was the intermediary. "Through the influence of Joshua F. Speed, who was a warm friend of the Edwardses," Herndon wrote in his biography based on his personal knowledge of both Lincoln and Speed at the time, "Lincoln was led to call on Miss Todd." Elizabeth Edwards emphasized that once Lincoln was "led to call" on Mary he quickly became utterly enthralled with her: "He was charmed with Mary's wit and fascinated with her quick sagacity—her will, her nature—and Culture—I have happened in the room where they were sitting often and often, and Mary led the conversation. Lincoln would listen and gaze on her as if drawn by some Superior power, irresistibly So."[9]

What Elizabeth noticed, Mary surely did as well. But what was she to do with her admirer? Mary, while certainly eligible for marriage at twenty-one years old, had good reasons to be cautious. She understood keenly that it would radically change her life, and not necessarily for the better. Marriage, especially for a woman, as Jean Baker has wisely noted, was not something entered into lightly. Before the Civil War in America, love might not be eternal, but marriage was definitely forever. Divorce was not an option, except in unusual circumstances that seldom freed a woman as we might think of it and usually merely cut her loose from a social or economic support system. Marriage was not the mutual legal partnership it came to be later. In marriage, under the domestic-relations laws of all states at the time, a woman lost her civil and legal rights as she became one with her husband. The results could be disastrous. "In Mary's Springfield," Baker notes, "there were plenty of wives whose lives had been blighted by syphilitic, drunken, nonproviding husbands."[10]

Lincoln himself could be awkward around women. He had, after all, grown up in log cabins and was mostly self-taught, and the only women he knew labored over household chores, dealt with animals, churned butter, did their washing by hand, and cooked in an open fire. He wasn't dancing the polonaise on the prairie. In his courtship of women, he also knew only tragedy (with Ann Rutledge) or disappointment (with Mary Owens).

But Lincoln was not a naïf, and he was both intensely ambitious and upwardly mobile. He moved away physically and mentally from the log cabins of his childhood and youth in New Salem as soon as he could. His economic philosophy, grounded in Whig politics but equally built into his personal ideals, centered on his belief in the "right to rise." That he did. Once financially secure, he became a successful lawyer, moved into a home that he soon doubled in size, and entered the upper middle class in Illinois. He also adopted the attire of a gentleman, including his distinctive top hat. Part of the appeal of Mary Todd for him was undoubtedly her distinguished lineage and the magical, if somewhat scary, world of femininity she inhabited. One can also exaggerate Lincoln's unease around women. He was able to draw on his humor in nearly all situations. In a contemporary letter in 1839, Mary Hedges Hubbard wrote Ellen S. Hubbard: "I stayed at the same table that Mr. Lincoln did. He is the most amusing man I ever did know almost. He kept us laughing all the time."[11]

Lincoln and Mary actually shared some important interests, despite the differences in their backgrounds. Both loved poetry and could recite long passages from memory, though her interests in literature ran more to the lighthearted than his fascination with Byron's gloomy apocalyptic images and Burns's folk and peasant settings. Both were witty and sharp tongued and, something seldom noted, shared a sense of humor. She got his irony. When he once told her he wanted to dance with her "in the worst way," she said later he was right. Both also were interested in Whig politics, and though Mary as a woman could not enter politics, she warmed to the debates and issues of the day. As a child, Mary had even known Henry Clay, who was Lincoln's great hero and made Mary something of a link to his ideals. Elizabeth testified that Mary was "frivolous" and loved "Show & pomp" but was drawn to power and was an "Extremely Ambitious woman and in Ky often & often Contended that She was destined to be the wife of some future President." A number of young and politically active and ambitious men courted her, including Stephen Douglas, a grandson of Patrick Henry, and the widower of "modest merit" Edwin Webb. But it surely did not escape Mary's notice that Lincoln was, as Elizabeth Edwards put it, a "great man" and a "rising Man" in Springfield. The same charisma Lincoln exuded in Speed's store with his male friends carried over to his budding relationship with Mary on the elegant horsehair couch in the Edwards home.[12]

It is unclear at what point Lincoln and Mary began to talk about marriage. Elizabeth Edwards, who with Ninian encouraged the courtship, says Lincoln "Commenced Seeing Mary" in the winter of 1839–1840. What does that mean? What it was *not* was a declaration to the world of their engagement. There was definitely not an exchange of rings, as there might be today, and no announcement that would have attracted a lot of attention. But to have "Commenced seeing" each other, in the words of Mary's sister and confidante, means their relationship was in some state of courtship, and possibly an advanced one, by the early months of 1840. Whatever understanding existed between Lincoln and Mary, however, was relatively private and remains unclear. The private character of their relationship and when it was actually an engagement has prompted some recent theorizing that because their courtship lurked in the shadows perhaps it never occurred. But whatever actually caused the breakup, it seems that Lincoln and Mary considered themselves engaged to be married by some point in the fall and brought at least two people into full knowledge of their intentions toward each other: Elizabeth Edwards, who uses the word "engagement" to describe the obligations he broke later in the year, and Joshua Speed, who described Lincoln's awkward moves with Mary that fall. Furthermore, everyone, from Ninian Edwards, to Orville Browning, to James Matheny, to Jane D. Bell, and many others who commented on Lincoln's depression in 1841, noted it came because he broke off his "engagement" with Mary.[13]

It is an open question, however, whether that business of having "Commenced Seeing" each other, as Elizabeth put it, in the winter of 1839–1840 involved mutual talk of marriage. Most historians have argued it did and that Lincoln and Mary were most likely engaged by the summer of 1840. Mary took a trip to Missouri that summer and wrote a long, chatty letter to Mercy Levering, one with a detailed description of a ball with a Virginia reel that was "poetry in motion," though it left her exhausted, in which she also mentions *"some letters"* that were "entirely *unlooked for*. This is between ourselves, my dearest, but of this more anon." Most have argued those letters were from Lincoln, and the assumption is that they were basically engaged by then.

There is a counterargument. Douglas Wilson (and a number of others in recent years) is struck by the absence of testimony about the supposed engagement from friends and acquaintances, including James Conkling and Mercy Levering, as well as Mary's failure to note it specifically in her letter in July, and he concludes it therefore probably didn't happen. That may be a bit like Sherlock Holmes finding the major clue to the crime in the dog that didn't bark in the night. Another way of approaching this question is not to dismiss that *something* in the way of courtship was happening between Lincoln and Mary well before the summer of 1840 but to ask why it was kept so relatively private. One can imagine Lincoln was cautious about a love attachment after his experience with Ann Rutledge, but the ever-voluble Mary had no such constraints. Perhaps she simply didn't really have anything to broadcast, at least not yet. Their relationship, which was a simmering courtship, existed in a murky space between a "Commenced Seeing" each other and actual engagement. Too much talk could poison things.[14]

Besides, Mary was a social butterfly in general and exuberant with life in the fall of 1840. In her long and chatty letter to her best friend, Mercy Levering, in mid-December 1840, Mary gossips about Speed's affection for Matilda Edwards and describes her sister's recent party for nearly one hundred guests. Mary notes that the widower Edwin Webb has tried to court her (he is "our *principal lion*") and is at most of the parties (he "dances attendance very frequently"), but she also airily dismisses him as unworthy of her attention, in large part because of what she says in another letter were his "two *sweet little objections.*" Both Speed, and especially Lincoln, have a place in Mary's letter in December. She says, referring to Mercy's apparent line that "time has borne changes on its wing," that Speed's "'*grey suit*' has gone the way of *all flesh*"—presumably a reference to his leave taking of Springfield that was then intentional but in process—and "*Lincoln's lincoln green* have gone to dust." What does she mean? It is much too lighthearted, though obscure, to suggest she means the relationship is dead. It could well be a private reference to something Mercy and she had shared with each other. The one thing that is clear in the letter is that Mary has marriage on her mind, for she says, in a phrase that is joking but may carry deeper feelings: "Why is it that married folks always become so serious?"[15]

At some point, Lincoln and Mary began to talk about an actual wedding date. It seems that the date they set was January 1, 1841 (which is why after the breakup Lincoln dubbed it the "fatal first"). Lincoln was cautious about marriage. He was still not fully stable financially in 1840. He had an income of about a thousand dollars annually from his practice, plus his salary as a state legislator, but neither was secure. He was about to dissolve his law partnership with John T. Stuart, who had been in Washington for much of the previous two years and was virtually certain to be reelected. Stuart was absent, for all intents and purposes. Even more importantly, the collapse of the internal improvements program, much heralded by Lincoln and his Whig colleagues, in the wake of the economic depression after 1837, made his financial future unreliable. Lincoln had not yet even completely paid off his debts from his New Salem days. He had barely any savings, still lived with Speed, and boarded with the Butlers. Lincoln in his early thirties was moving forward with his life, but he still faced uncertainties that might have caused him to question whether he was ready to marry and make a family.[16]

Lincoln was also very busy that year campaigning for William Henry Harrison's presidential campaign. The Illinois Whig convention, controlled by Stuart, nominated Lincoln as one of Illinois's Harrison and Tyler electors. He stumped central and southern Illinois at his own expense, except where fellow Whigs offered him a meal or a bed, giving pretty much the same speech every time, with modifications for local audiences. It was a raucous campaign, with barrels of free whiskey at state fairs and plenty of outrageous charges on all sides. But there were also serious issues at stake in a country reeling from the depression. The campaign was absorbing for Lincoln. For about half the time from April to November he was gone from Springfield lawyering and giving political speeches. Mary also left that summer for an extended trip to Missouri. A myth later developed that he visited her there, but it was debunked as long ago as 1953. After they "Commenced Seeing" each other in the winter of 1839–1840, in other words, they were mostly apart until the fall, though their separation for much of 1840 in and of itself proves nothing, occasioned as it was by Mary's travels and Lincoln's work and political commitments. Why assume that they grew apart during these months just because they were physically separated? One could just as easily argue that absence made their hearts grow fonder. The evidence is admittedly thin, but we do have the suggestive references by Mary in her letter from Missouri that most feel refers fondly to Lincoln. It is worth noting as well that nothing has ever surfaced indicating there was a cooling of their ardor over that period.[17]

In late October, Lincoln, perhaps exhausted by the campaign, got himself embroiled in a dispute with a William G. Anderson that came perilously close to a duel. Lincoln would come even closer to an actual fight in a couple of years, but his near-duel with Anderson is often overlooked as background in understanding the broken engagement, suggesting how exhausted and emotionally distraught he was. At a political rally in southern Illinois (nicknamed Little Egypt, since the southernmost town in the state is named Cairo), Anderson, a Democrat and former legislator, apparently criticized Harrison's record in the War of 1812. Lincoln responded in a sharp and sarcastic way that mocked Anderson, or at least that is how the latter experienced it. Anderson wrote Lincoln a note on October 30 in which he called him "the aggressor" and said, "Your words imported insult." He said Lincoln should inform him if in fact he "designed to offend me," all of which were code words in the elaborate dance leading to a duel (which was by then illegal in Illinois and would have destroyed his political and even legal career). Lincoln wrote back immediately to defuse the situation, said he entertained no unkind feelings toward Anderson, and expressed regret that he permitted himself "to get into such an altercation."[18] That apology satisfied Anderson and allowed Lincoln to walk away from the dangerous possibility of fighting a duel.

By September Mary was back in Springfield and, according to James Conkling in a letter to Mercy Levering on September 21, seemed not as "merry and joyous" as usual. Lincoln, meanwhile, was in town briefly but again basically out on the circuit and doing some final politicking until the election on November 2. Within a span of about a month after that, when both Lincoln and Mary were finally consistently in the same place, he proposed, and they set the date of their wedding for January 1, 1841. Soon afterward—probably in late December—Lincoln broke off the engagement. What happened?[19]

Some have argued that Mary got fat during her trip to Missouri based on two pieces of evidence. One is the September 21 letter of Conkling, in which he reports to Mercy Levering in his stilted way that "if she [Mary] should visit Missouri [again] she will soon grow out of our recollection," and the other is Mary's letter in December, also to Mercy Levering, in which she mocks herself as a "ruddy *pineknot*" with an "exuberance of flesh." But Conkling's letter is hardly definitive and could be simply a joke about Mary, whom he liked and whom he knew Mercy loved. To read it as decisive proof that Mary had gotten so fat as to disgust Lincoln stretches its potential meaning. And Mary's letter actually indicates, if anything, that she has *lost* weight, if one reads the whole passage. She is indeed the "same ruddy *pineknot*," she says, but now *not* with an "exuberance of flesh, as it once was my lot to contend with," although, she adds, in a note of self-honesty, "quite a sufficiency." If anything, in other words, Mary lost weight in the fall. Lincoln had long since fallen in love with a short woman who tended to be plump and who worried about her weight. That would not seem to have changed in the fall of 1840.[20]

More significantly, many have argued, was the presence of Matilda Edwards. This beautiful, eighteen-year-old cousin of Ninian Edwards left her father's home in Alton to come visit Springfield in November, just in time for the swirl of parties associated with the meeting of the legislature in special session in early December and in regular session in January. The adorable Matilda, with long, golden locks, even pinned up as a respectable woman would have worn them, turned the heads of many men and reputedly received twenty-two offers of marriage. She was pious and earnest, and she firmly rejected the advances of Stephen Douglas because she felt he had bad morals. In the end, she married the older and financially secure Newton D. Strong in 1843. Elizabeth Edwards, who was at first baffled by this choice, reported that, "Miss Edwards one dy [sic] was asked why she married such an old dried up husband—such a withered up old Buck: She replied: 'He had lots of houses & gold[.]' "[21]

But Matilda has come to occupy the central role in the reinterpretation of the broken engagement in recent years. The argument is forceful in its simplicity: Lincoln fell in love with Matilda soon after her arrival in Springfield, and that precipitated the break with Mary. Four important witnesses support this story line.

The first was Ninian Edwards in his interview with Herndon on September 22, 1865. In Herndon's shorthand, Ninian said, "That Lincoln's Courtship with Miss Todd—afterwards Lincoln's wife—that he, Lincoln, fell in Love with a Miss Edwards . . ." She "became aware" of his feelings, and "the Lincoln and Todd engagement was broken off in consequence of it." Ninian, of course, was not only Matilda's cousin; he was her protector and the master of the house in which she lived and where all her suitors sought her out.[22]

The second witness is Orville Browning, Lincoln's friend and political ally. Browning, who was reasonably close to Mary, lived quite far from Springfield but stayed with the Butlers when the legislature was in session. On Lincoln's relationship throughout 1840, he says, "she did most of the courting until they became engaged," presumably at some point in the fall. Then Matilda Edwards came to town, and Lincoln "fell desperately in love with her, and proposed to her, but she rejected him." His "aberration of mind resulted entirely from the situation he thus got himself into—he was engaged to Miss Todd, and in love with Miss Edwards, and his conscience troubled him dreadfully for the supposed injustice he had done, and the supposed violation of his word which he had committed."[23]

Browning is clear that he believed Lincoln felt he had made a mistake in getting engaged to Mary Todd, and if "circumstances had left him entirely free to act upon his own impulses" he would not have proposed. But having done so, he felt "honor bound to act in perfect good faith towards her." Browning says he used to spend a good deal of time at the Edwards home, where he often talked with Mary. "In these conversations I think it came out, that Mr. Lincoln had perhaps on one occasion told Miss Todd that he loved Matilda Edwards, and no doubt his conscience was greatly worked up by the supposed pain and injury which this avowal had inflicted upon her." Browning says Mary "made no concealment that she had very bitter feelings towards her rival Matilda Edwards." Mary was "thoroughly in earnest" in her effort to secure Lincoln's affections. Matilda, for her part, was "something of a coquette."

The third witness is none other than Joshua Speed. Some very cryptic notes that Herndon took in a conversation with Speed can be read as supporting the Matilda theory: "In 1840 Lincoln went into the Southern part of the State as Elector Canvasser debator Speaker— Here first wrote his *Mary*—She darted after him—wrote him—Lincoln—seeing an other girl—& finding he did not love his wife wrote a leter saying he did not love her." It is not unreasonable, though hardly conclusive, to guess that this "other girl" Speed mentions is Matilda.[24]

Finally, Jane D. Bell wrote Ann Bell on January 27, 1841, reporting that Lincoln had been engaged to Mary for "some time":

> when a Miss Edwards of Alton came here, and he fell desperately in love with her and found he was not so much attached to Mary as he thought. He says that if he had it in his power he would not have one feature in her face altered, he thinks she is so perfect (that is, Miss E.) He [probably Speed] and Mr. Lincoln could never bear to leave Miss Edward's side in company. Some of his friends thought he was acting very wrong and very imprudently and told him so and he went crazy on the strength of it so the story goes and that is all I know . . . torn off No one but Speed . . . torn off[25]

One wonders, however, about these four witnesses to the Matilda theory. First, Ninian Edwards is actually quite unclear about what he told Herndon. After reporting Lincoln's love for Matilda, Ninian adds: "Lincoln did not ever by act or deed directly or indirectly hint or speak of it [his love] to Miss Edwards: she became aware of this—Lincoln's affections—the Lincoln and Todd engagement was broken off in consequence of it." So Ninian's story is that Matilda somehow sensed Lincoln's love for her that was otherwise *never* communicated to her directly or indirectly and that somehow was the cause of the broken engagement. Whom did Matilda tell? Could it have been Mary? If so, why not say it? The suggestion is that Ninian wasn't really clear at all as to what went on and was making some, perhaps wild, guesses. Besides, it is worth noting that his wife, Elizabeth, who was closer to the key players in the drama, dismissed the Matilda theory out of hand. It was for her a fantasy born of insanity. "In his [Lincoln's] lunacy"—that is *after* the breakup—"he declared he hated Mary and loved Miss Edwds."[26]

Browning, for his part, hedges his bets as he recounts his version of the story to Herndon. "I think it came out," he says, that "perhaps on one occasion" Lincoln had told Mary he loved Matilda. Browning clearly believed Matilda was the key factor in the broken engagement but acknowledges he is not at all certain. That "I think" and his "perhaps" should be noted carefully. Browning, in other words, is a second-hand witness and could have been merely influenced by the rumor mill (though it is significant that he remembered, however vaguely, Mary telling him about Matilda).

Speed's interview with Herndon is the most confusing of all. In the first part, he fails even to mention the name of the supposed woman who interfered with Lincoln's move toward marriage. But then he says that Lincoln told him in no uncertain terms that he did not love Mary anymore and was determined to write her a letter to that effect, which he wanted Speed to deliver. It is impossible to know exactly when Lincoln wrote the letter, but it seemed to have been in the late fall of 1840, perhaps even during the special session of the legislature that ended December 5. Speed tried to convince his friend not to put his feelings into writing but to go see her directly. Lincoln got annoyed and said Speed was obstinate and that he would find someone else to deliver the letter, at which point Speed said if Lincoln had "Manhood Enough" he would go talk with her and dispense with the letter (a phrase that sounds more like Herndon than Speed). Lincoln reluctantly took Speed's advice and went himself to tell Mary he did not love her and wanted to break off the engagement. Herndon's notes on Speed's testimony, however, are hard to figure out.

> [Lincoln] Went to see "Mary"—told her that he did not love her—She rose—and Said "The deceiver shall be deceived wo is me."; alluding to a young man She fooled—Lincoln drew her down on his Knee—Kissed her—& parted—He going one way & She an other—Lincoln did Love Miss Edwards—"Mary" Saw it— told Lincoln the reason of his Change of mind—heart & soul— released him—[27]

There seems little doubt from Speed's testimony that Lincoln told Mary he didn't love her anymore, that what followed was an emotional scene in which Mary said something about her own revengeful deception of him, and that in the turmoil of the moment he drew her to his knee and they kissed. The role of Matilda Edwards in the breakup, however, is not so clear from this account. Herndon writes, "Lincoln did Love Miss Edwards," which seems unequivocal, except that it is followed by the note that Mary "Saw it" and that she was the one who "told Lincoln the reason of his Change of mind—heart & soul," which led to her releasing him from any obligation to marry her. The sentence about Matilda, in other words, a sentence that seems clear in its meaning, becomes decidedly obscure by the very next sentence, which suggests Mary told Lincoln what he felt (she "told Lincoln the reason of his Change of mind"). She is telling him why he doesn't love her anymore. She tells him his feelings.

Perhaps in the moment Lincoln simply let Mary have her way in explaining to him his motivations. It gave Mary some agency in the breakup. Certainly, nowhere else did Speed ever mention Matilda as a factor in the breakup, and these confusing notes by Herndon can be read several ways. Mary, furthermore, continued to live with Matilda in the same household for another year. Elizabeth Edwards told Herndon: "The whole of the year [of] the Crazy Spell Miss Edwards was at our house." Mary and Matilda got along quite well and maintained a friendship after Matilda moved to Pennsylvania with her husband, Newton D. Strong, in 1843. It is not likely that Mary, who readily nursed grievances, would have remained consistently warm and friendly with Matilda if she really believed that Lincoln had fallen in love with her and that is why he broke off the engagement. And Mary's (and Lincoln's) friendship with Matilda continued well into the future. In 1848, Lincoln (then in Washington serving a term as a congressman) wrote Mary back in Lexington: "A day or two ago Mr. Strong, here in Congress [also a congressman], said to me that Matilda would visit here within two or three weeks. Suppose you write her a letter, and enclose it in one of mine, and if she comes I will deliver it to her, and if she does not, I will send it to her."[28]

Finally, we have the Jane Bell letter, which only exists in copies and could even be a forgery. Besides, Jane Bell, while contemporary and independent, is hardly a sterling witness, as she was not living in the Edwards home and not close to any of the key players as the engagement drama unfolded. What she absolutely documents in her letter in late January 1841 is the *story* of Matilda's role in the breakup that came to circulate in Springfield. There is no question that the story of Matilda's role became prime gossip that gained a robust life of its own for many decades. In later years, neighbors and friends in Springfield tried to explain the story of the broken engagement with Mary Todd in an atmosphere in which Lincoln himself had already become a saintly and heroic figure while Mary, never much liked in Springfield before the Civil War, became a paranoid recluse (she died in the home of

Ninian and Elizabeth Edwards in 1882). To give just one example, John J. Hardin reportedly said that Lincoln confided in him, "that he thought he did not love" Mary Todd "as he should and that he would do her a great wrong if he married her," which may, or may not, have anything to do with Matilda Edwards. The source for the Hardin quote is from a newspaper interview with Hardin's sister in 1896, no less, which has been quoted along with a similar story in a newspaper interview with the son-in-law of another sister in 1891. That puts us at least three degrees of separation from the actual events, well over half a century later, and, perhaps most significantly, after the publication of Herndon's biography in 1889. Elizabeth Grimsley, a cousin of Mary Todd, has also been quoted from another 1895 interview, arguing that Lincoln "doubted whether he was responding as fully as a manly generous nature" should to Mary and that he "had not the overmastering depth of an early love," statements that may, or may not, have been true but that offer no proof of Lincoln's supposed love for Matilda Edwards.[29]

The main problem with the Matilda theory, however, far more than the provenance of the evidence, is the fact that she herself categorically refuted it. Elizabeth Edwards specifically says she asked Matilda after all the drama surrounding the broken engagement unfolded, "if Mr. Lincoln Ever Mentioned the subject of his love to her." Matilda's answer was that, "On my word he never mentioned Such a Subject to me: he never even Stooped to pay me a Compliment." Unfortunately, Matilda died at twenty-nine in 1850, so Herndon could not track her down for an interview, but her statement to Elizabeth, a reliable witness present through all the drama and in direct contact with all the players, is without qualification.[30]

The person who did matter in relation to Matilda and whose case was pushed by the Edwardses was Joshua Speed. Mary wrote Mercy Levering in mid-December 1840, praising Matilda Edwards as a "lovelier girl" than anyone she had ever known and adds: "*Mr. Speed's* ever changing heart I suspect is about offering *its young* affections at her shrine." Ninian Edwards, the protector of Matilda in the absence of her father, felt that the appropriate match for his cousin was his good friend Speed, which he told Herndon clearly and directly in 1865 (though Herndon's notes on the interview add some confusing, if tantalizing, details): "Edwards Admits that he wanted Speed to marry Miss Edwards & Lincoln Miss Todd: he gave me policy reasons for it—

the substance of which I give in an other place." Unfortunately, those notes that might explain Herndon's reference to "policy reasons" and what they could possibly mean in this context have since been lost. Ninian Edwards's wife, Elizabeth, however, adds a telling detail to the story. In her (often quoted) interview with Herndon some months after he talked with her husband, Elizabeth provides a rather complete narrative about Lincoln's courtship of her sister Mary Todd in her home. In the middle of her story, as a kind of insertion, she tells Herndon: "Mr Speed Came to See Miss Matilda Edwards—left & went to Ky—Miss Edwards Staying." Elizabeth immediately returns to the story of Lincoln and Mary and their troubled courtship and addresses whether Matilda had any role in the breakup. The implication of all this evidence about Speed and Matilda is that Speed came along with Lincoln while he courted Mary. Speed, it seems, was interested in Matilda and courted her.[31]

In a letter to his sister Mary somewhat later, Speed describes (in February 1841) a beautiful woman whose blond hair swished "like the wind at play with sunbeams":

> Two clear blue eyes, a brow as fair as Palmyra marble touched by the chisel of Praxalites. Lips so fresh, fair and lovely that I am jealous even of the minds that kiss them. A form as perfect as that of the Venus de Medicis. A mind clear as a bell, a voice bewitchingly soft and sonorous, and a smile so sweet, lovely, and playful, and countenance and soul shining through it. . . . All these charms combined in one young lady, if nothing else interposed, would be enough to keep me here. Would they not?[32]

The next month Speed wrote to another sister (Eliza) again of his fascination with a young woman who seems very much like Matilda. He writes:

> Her hair hands loosely or in curls about her much like the wind at play with sunbeams—Three dimples she has upon her face one upon each of her rosy cheeks and one upon her chin each the grave of some unfortunate lover—and your poor ill-fated and susceptible brother lies entombed in the one that is darkest and deepest—

I never expect to see the light of the sun again or any other light than that of the two stars that ever beam just over the dimple in which my heart lies buried—She is gone—I never expect to see her more—Could I be otherwise than melancholy! If I smile at all it is but a cheat—Like a rose blooming over a sepulcher would be a smile playing upon a face like mine when all feeling is dead and dust beneath it—

In neither letter does Speed specifically mention Matilda's name, so it is only a guess that he is describing her. But if it is Matilda, she seemed uninterested and not the one whose "possession" Speed could "hardly ever hope to realize."

* * *

Other, less likely, explanations have been offered to explain why Lincoln broke his engagement with Mary. Jean Baker turns things upside down and makes Mary the initiator of the breakup. She argues that Mary was fed up with Lincoln's hesitation and uncertainties and had come to feel he might not be right for her. The climactic moment came at a party in late December, perhaps even New Year's Eve, to which Lincoln had promised to escort her. He was late, and to punish him she was ostentatiously flirting with Edwin Webb. Lincoln was uncertain of her commitment in any event, and they quarreled. "Go," she cried with a stamp of her little foot, "and never, never come back."[33]

There are any number of problems with this story. First, there is no evidence for a New Year's Eve party, though it would not be surprising for the Edwardses to host such an event. More to the point, there is no evidence that Lincoln was committed to escort Mary to a dance that may, or may not, have been taking place, nor that he was late, nor that Mary was flirting with Webb. Lincoln furthermore was hardly threatened by Edwin Webb, whom he instead consistently regarded as a close colleague. A little over a month after these supposed events transpired, Lincoln wrote John Todd Stuart on February 5, recommending Webb to be appointed district attorney: "I really have my heart set upon Webb's appointment to this place; and that I believe the whole party would be gratified with it." Finally, Baker is the first to report this angry, foot-stamping scene. Contemporary documentation omits it. James Conkling wrote Mercy Levering of the breakup but only said, in his pretentious and formal way, that poor Lincoln was experiencing the "worst of pain, to love and not be loved at all." Conkling's letter in late January furthermore spoke to the events that unfolded *after* the breakup but says nothing about a dramatic scene that might have caused it. There is, in fact, only one piece of secondhand gossip provided by only one informant that Mary broke things off. Abner Y. Ellis told Herndon in 1866, fully a quarter of a century later, that "I had it from good authority" that Mary initiated the breakup.[34]

Then there is Sarah Rickard. Sarah, who was born in 1824 in Virginia, was the younger sister of Eliza Butler and at some point when she was ten or eleven came to live in Springfield with the Butlers. Sarah was lively and cute, though only thirteen in 1837. As she later wrote Herndon, Lincoln apparently joked in future years that when he first met Sarah, she was a "little Girl wearing these Pantletts." Lincoln's comment is slightly suggestive, for "pantalettes" (the French invented them) were basically part of the underwear girls and women wore well into the nineteenth century. They were cotton pants or leggings attached at the waist. For women pantalettes were knee length and could provide tantalizing glimpses of covered legs when sitting. Girls wore pantalettes that reached to mid-calf or to the ankles and were meant to be visible underneath their shorter and more flexible skirts. Lincoln's joking comment emphasized Sarah's youth when he met her in 1837, a very young girl not yet garbed as a woman, perhaps prepubertal or just beginning menarche, on the cusp of womanhood but not yet fully possessing the body of mature woman.[35]

Both Lincoln and Speed, who took their meals with the Butlers, socialized and joked with Sarah and the rest of the family on a frequent basis as Sarah aged from thirteen to seventeen and Speed from twenty-three to twenty-seven (Lincoln from twenty-eight to thirty-two). According to Sarah, Lincoln memorably brought her to see her first play, *Babes in the Woods*. Further, when she turned sixteen, Lincoln "became more attentive." In the winter of 1840–1841, Lincoln, according to Sarah's account forty-eight years later, proposed marriage and told her, "Sarah will become Abraham's wife." Whether he was joking or in earnest (and during this particular winter of 1840–1841 Lincoln was not himself by anyone's accounts), Sarah was her own person and regarded Lincoln, who she said had a "peculiar manner," as a friend or, at best, an older brother. "His General deportment," she said, "would not be likely to fascinate a young girl just entering the society world."[36]

Sarah, however, seemed much more interested in Speed as a potential husband. He was closer to her in age, handsome, had a bright future in business, and was not "peculiar." Before leaving for Kentucky, Speed obliged Lincoln to speak to her in his absence if Sarah was distressed. Reporting to him, Lincoln wrote Speed on February 3, 1842, that "I have seen Sarah [Rickard] but once. She seemed verry cheerful, and so, I said nothing to her about what we spoke of." It is also telling that Speed in his later communications with Herndon was intent on deleting any reference to Sarah. He wrote Herndon on November 30, 1866, "I have erraced a name which I do not wish published—If I have failed to it any where strike it out when you come to it—That is the word Sarah—" Why would he care? Perhaps it was because of some link between Sarah Rickard and Lincoln, but why would that matter in 1866? Speed had no trouble telling Herndon all he knew about Lincoln's troubled courtship of Mary Todd and other personal matters. Lincoln was very much dead in 1866 and his widow a remote presence. But Speed was alive and devoted to his wife, Fanny Henning Speed. It is not unreasonable to suppose he cared about Fanny learning of anything about an earlier romance he had had with or feelings for Sarah Rickard.[37]

***

All we know for sure is that Lincoln early on became infatuated with Mary Todd, who in turn came to love him, despite their differences; that they courted and drew close in 1840 and set their wedding date for January 1, 1841; that Lincoln became deeply confused about his love for reasons that are unclear and broke off the engagement in two steps; and that Mary explained to herself his otherwise contradictory behavior in terms of his love for Matilda Edwards. Perhaps Lincoln even told Mary that he loved Matilda, and maybe he did; maybe he loved both Mary and Matilda, or maybe not. Perhaps Lincoln had a crush on young Sarah Rickard, or maybe not. Or, least likely, was it that he was put off by a fat Mary? Maybe all these conflicting accounts capture a piece of the truth. Or maybe the most likely explanation for the broken engagement is one no one saw because it didn't make a lot of rational sense. That explanation brings Joshua Speed into the story.

7

THE WINTER OF
DISCONTENT

None of the psychological subtext of the events surrounding Lincoln's broken engagement with Mary Todd was fully conscious for either Lincoln or Speed. Desire lurked in forbidden realms. Both men reached out to women to find love, but those efforts were thwarted by their much deeper connections to each other. Those ties had long given solace. The safe haven they felt was in the confidence, trust, and security of their relationship with each other. It was a balm that banished the terrors of depression, especially for Lincoln, though they shared equally in their self-doubts about love, sex, and intimacy. Lincoln wore his confusions on his sleeve. But Speed shared the same doubts. Despite how he portrayed himself to people like the Edwardses, or Orville Browning, or any number of others in town, Speed was candid with Herndon about his own engagement the summer after Lincoln's own broken one: "Strange to say something of the same feeling which I regarded as so foolish in him—took possession of me—and kept me very unhappy from the time of my ingagement until I was married—"[1]

Joshua Speed had a reputation as a handsome young man who was something of a flirt. Lincoln in a letter alluded to his friend's many courtships ("Ann Todd [Mary's sister, later married to Charles M.

Smith], and at least twenty others of whom you can think"). Mary Todd talked about his "ever changing heart." Unlike his socially awkward and introspective friend, there was nothing "peculiar" about Speed, whose even features and handsome face, modesty, intelligence, and solid business sense drew people to him. Speed, raised in luxury on a Southern plantation and having enjoyed the benefits of some formal boarding-school education, was at ease in social situations, able to mingle, make small talk, dance, and enjoy good company. Ninian and Elizabeth Edwards were both fond of Speed (he was their "warm friend," as Herndon puts it), and, as Ninian told Herndon, he was especially eager for Speed to marry Matilda Edwards after her arrival in November 1840.[2]

Matilda could not have been unaware of Speed's advances (and Ninian's wishes for her to marry him), just as word of Lincoln's seeming love for Matilda, communicated to everybody except Matilda herself, must have reached her ears. And Lincoln's odd proposal to Sarah was in the context of her much greater interest in the younger and more stable Speed, with whom she had grown up. It is important to remember in this regard that Speed arrived in Springfield in 1834 and became so close to the Butler family that Mrs. Butler named her baby, born in the second part of 1835, "Speed." Sarah, Mrs. Butler's sister, was then but eleven years old and being raised by her and her husband. Speed ate dinner with the family, as Lincoln would after his arrival in Springfield in 1837, and thus Speed watched Sarah grow from a girl to a cute teenager. Lincoln's allusion to Sarah in an 1842 letter ("I have seen Sarah but once. She seemed verry cheerful, and so, I said nothing to her about what we spoke of") suggests Speed's serious attraction for her at one time.[3]

These overlapping courtships, sexually unconsummated and full of ambiguity, had one very important meaning missed by all observers: they indirectly joined Lincoln and Speed. Both men, it seems, were inclined to love women, but at this moment in their lives their most intense and meaningful emotional connection was with each other. That grounded them and bound them tightly together. They spent much of their time with each other and most nights tumbled side by side into that creaking bed. Each knew the other's deepest feelings, feelings otherwise kept private and apart from others. Each found reflection of self in the other, a kind of mirroring that silenced doubt and confusion. Even Herndon, who idealized Lincoln, liked Speed, and slept in the same room (but in a different bed) for two years, could only guess at the depth of their friendship and the intensity of their connection.

The courtships of Lincoln and Speed, as a result, were uneven, confused, and conflicted. Lincoln may have been attracted to Matilda but afraid, or at least hesitant, even to pay her the slightest compliment at exactly the time Ninian Edwards was pushing forward Speed, who was surely better trained in social manners, to flirt with Matilda at the Coterie soirees. And within weeks Lincoln apparently made an ill-timed marriage proposal to Sarah, one in which he invoked the Bible, even though he must have known of her feelings for Speed and of his attraction for her. All of this courtship activity with women was confused because it was incidental to the much more profound, if partially unconscious, connection between the two men. Lincoln developed some kind of fantasied ideas about Matilda because he knew she was reserved for Speed, just as he reached out to Sarah, who he knew cared for Speed. None of this overlap divided the two men. There is no indication of jealousy or bad feeling at all, probably because it was understood at some level by each that the women they were either flirting with or developing fantasies about were emotionally incidental to them. And thus this psychological subtext complicated and undermined the courtships. Given Lincoln's apparent love for Matilda, for example, it is striking he never told her of his affections (assuming he had them). Though less noted by historians, the dual courtships of Sarah seem equally odd (though we know much less about the details than we do about Matilda). Both men, and especially Lincoln, placed their shared women on idealized pedestals that made them unreachable, which was the point. Not a single observer—Elizabeth and Ninian Edwards, Orville Browning, A. Y. Ellis, Herndon himself, and on and on—who commented on some aspect of the overlapping courtships of Lincoln and Speed, especially with Matilda Edwards and Sarah Rickard, ever noted any rivalry, competition, or tension between the two men. Its absence is telling.

This context of courtship confusion also explains much about Lincoln's break with Mary. There is no reason to doubt he loved her as best he could at this stage of his life, which is to say he loved with great ambivalence. But at some point Lincoln and Mary were engaged, with their wedding planned for January 1, 1841. He broke it off—when, exactly, is not clear—without a good explanation, something that confused her and compounded her hurt. She retaliated with anger, sputtering about how the deceiver shall be deceived, whatever that meant to her in the moment, and he tried to convince himself he broke the engagement because he loved Matilda. At the time, he probably thought that was true, or he may simply have been allowing Mary to have this explanation, which at least lent the broken engagement a measure of rationality least wounding to sensitive Mary's self-esteem.

The insult of the broken engagement also reverberated in the family. Elizabeth Edwards would say later: "Mr. Edwards & myself after the first Crush of things told Mary & Lincoln that they had better not Ever marry—that their natures, mind—Education—raising & were So different they Could not live happy as husband & wife—had better never think of the Subject again." The context here is important. It was no small thing to break off an engagement in the nineteenth century. Middle-class young people in general lived under attentive eyes. They were allowed "ever-changing" hearts (as Mary wrote about Speed) in dances, sleigh rides, and parties, but pairing off was a matter fraught with high seriousness. An engagement was not without consequences. An engaged couple was subject to enormous pressures, both external and internal, to follow through on their mutual commitment. Women, especially, were at risk of loss. Whether rejecting or being rejected by a chosen lover, a woman whose engagement ended short of marriage, her virtue suspect, became a doubtful secondhand choice as anybody else's wife. Such wounded or stigmatized women grieved through "breach-of-promise" lawsuits that, borrowed from English common law, had been incorporated into American law beginning in the early nineteenth century. Men, although not immune from hurt in the wake of a failed pairing, were expected to tough it out.[4]

The net effect of Lincoln's self-imposed misery is that it left him with the awful quandary of losing everything and everybody and having deeply hurt Mary in ways that were unfair to her, made her vulnerable, and compromised his own sense of honor.

***

Lincoln, in other words, went a little crazy in this winter of his discontent. The issue was not Mary or Matilda, though the noise of his confusion played out on a stage of courtship and broken engagement. What mattered to Lincoln was the imminent departure of Joshua Speed. That threatened the ground of his being.

Lincoln and Speed had long found a recognition of self in the other and established the kind of empathic bond that gives meaning to life and wards off despair. Lincoln, about whom we know more, was especially vulnerable at this stage of his life. He met Speed when he was just coming off his suicidal depression after the death of Ann Rutledge and was still finding his way in his new professional identity. At first, it seems, he was cautious with his new friend. But in time and within the frame of their constant interactions Lincoln came to experience a deep trust in Speed, a trust that calmed Lincoln. He seemed to experience his friend as soothing, engaging, warm, supportive, and unchallenging.

The safety of the friendship created a haven from the dangers posed by the uncertain world of women toward which both Lincoln and Speed moved but in which they stumbled about. During this troubled winter, Lincoln became betrothed to and then broke off his engagement with Mary Todd, simultaneously moved toward and away from Matilda Edwards, and reached out in an almost bizarre way to Sarah Rickard, a teenage girl half his age he couldn't have seriously wanted to marry. The context was his terror at losing Speed.

When Speed first came to Springfield in 1835, his cousin James Bell set him up in business (and it may have been that John Speed, Joshua's father, secured the credit that Bell extended to Joshua). As a partner of James Bell & Company, a business relationship that continued as long as Speed remained in town, Speed was then able to use that credit (or actual loan) from Bell to stock his store on the square. This cousin Bell was one of the most active businessmen in Springfield, advertising often in the *Journal* and enlisting the legal assistance of Lincoln and others over many years as he bought and sold goods and sometimes skirted the edge of insolvency. Bell and others, including Speed, often established a number of complicated business relationships as they sought to spread the risk in purchasing supplies for their stores from far-off cities like St. Louis or even New Orleans. The arrival by wagon of a new load of supplies—fur hats, fancy silks, and fine dresses, along with hoes, rakes, metal for fences, nails, and other things—were then divided proportionately according to their share of the investment by the wholesale merchants who then in turn stocked them on the shelves of their dry-goods stores.

Speed proved adept at business and never apparently suffered any major reverses. He did need assistance in running the store. One early employee (whom he paid the substantial sum of seven hundred dollars a year) was William Herndon, who worked for Speed until Herndon's marriage in March 1840. Herndon's fellow clerk, one who stayed on, was Charles R. Hurst, a humorless, tight-lipped man whom Herndon seemed never to like. At least one can infer that dislike, for Herndon barely mentions him in his book and never interviewed him after the war, although Hurst continued to live in Springfield and operate a dry-goods store. Hurst, as a result, has passed into obscurity. Both Herndon and Hurst slept in the spacious room upstairs the entire time Herndon worked in the store.[5]

John Speed had died in March 1840, and, while Joshua didn't attend the funeral (the distance made that impossible), he was under pressure to return to Kentucky to help his family keep Farmington productive (see chapter 8). What seemed more important to Speed's determination to leave Springfield was the worsening economic climate. As a shrewd merchant, Speed adapted to the unfolding disaster better than others. The country as a whole was hit hard by the "panic" of 1837—more accurately described as a roiling economic depression—which hit Illinois with unusual severity because of a number of unwise state investments in internal improvements. Credit all but disappeared for many ventures. The danger to merchants like Speed was particularly great because bankruptcy was not allowed. If a note was called, you had to pay or suffer a judgment. But, ironically, another even greater danger that Speed foresaw lurked on the horizon: a long-delayed bankruptcy law.

There had been such a law in 1800, but it lasted only three years. Capitalism in general privileges those who control money and credit, rather than debtors, but such attitudes were particularly strong in early America. Whigs moved in a somewhat different direction, and the newly elected Congress in 1840 managed to pass a bankruptcy law on April 19, 1841, though this one too lasted only two years. That immediately gave relief to all those citizens owing money to merchants like Speed for those fur hats and hoes they had bought on credit. A scan of Simeon Francis's *Journal* in early 1842, that is, roughly a year after

Speed left Springfield, makes clear the effects of opening the debtor floodgates. The issue of the paper on January 28, 1842, lists over thirty names in three columns of petitioners seeking to make their debts uncollectible after payments of fractional or total discount. By March 11 that list reached two whole pages and six full columns of such notices, and by April 15 the front page was given over in its entirety to six columns of bankruptcy notices, printed in reduced type to fit them all. In the same issue, two lawyers advertised their bankruptcy expertise "to such persons as may desire to obtain the benefit" of the new bankruptcy laws.

Anticipating economic uncertainty, Speed decided to sell his store to his long-term clerk Charles Hurst sometime in the late summer of 1840 and probably around August. It did not happen overnight. Speed began putting ads in the paper calling for his customers to settle up as early as September 1840, even though, as Speed told Herndon, "I sold out to Hurst 1 Jany 1841," the very day the notice of the sale appeared in the *Sangamo Journal*. Speed thus decided to leave Springfield by the late summer or early fall of 1840. The point of the ads was to give Speed the chance to collect on as much of the money owed him as possible before he left. The sale of the store to his clerk was conditional upon some money down, some future payments, and a complicated division of assets. Hurst may have felt he had gotten a bad deal, for he stopped speaking with any of those with whom he once had bunked at the old store. But Hurst continued to enjoy the goodwill of Speed's uncle James Bell, an aging but still active Springfield merchant. Just around the point that Speed was leaving, Hurst and Bell engaged in at least one large transaction together. That known and documented but vague transaction, by which Bell & Company received at least eight hundred dollars' worth of goods from one Nelson Fry on their promissory note, encumbered Bell, but Hurst, as his guarantor, was secondarily liable to pay Fry.[6]

Throughout the fall of 1840, in other words, the shadow of emotional doubt that hung over Lincoln was Speed's imminent departure from Springfield. A little over a year later, Lincoln wrote Speed that since "that fatal first of Jany. '41" he should have been "entirely happy" but for the "never-absent idea" that there is "*one* still unhappy whom I have contributed still to make so. That still kills my soul." The context suggests that the image of the "fatal first" was a well-worn phrase between the two friends, though the term had a political meaning as well. As Paul Simon has pointed out, January 1, 1841, was when the state technically went bankrupt. Newspapers often referred to that first day of January 1841 as the "fatal first." Lincoln thus adopted something that was in the air for his own uses. It marked the terrible guilt he felt at hurting Mary but subtextually (and more unconsciously) captured his doomed sense at losing Speed. As a phrase, the alliterative "fatal first" succinctly captures the way in which Lincoln so tightly joined ideas of love and loss, hope and death.[7]

The world closed in. Lincoln moved to the Butlers' home, where he would now both sleep and board; Speed, it seems probable, worked out an arrangement with Hurst that allowed him to stay above the store until he actually left town later that spring. It is possible Speed boarded with the Butlers in their large house, but, beside the family and now Lincoln, both Browning and Thornton were there while the legislature met. It is more likely that Speed continued to sleep above the store until he left for Kentucky, though he still took his meals with the Butlers and remained around the busy Butler home often in the coming days.

***

If one examines the events that unfolded around the broken engagement entirely from the point of view of Lincoln's relationship with Speed and from within the multiple accounts of those events by Speed, one can gain much traction in understanding them. Some of the mystery that has encrusted the narrative with myths melts away. Speed frames the story of the broken engagement in his several communications to and interviews with Herndon in the context of Lincoln's special relationship with him. "He disclosed his whole heart to me," Speed says, affirming the significance of their relationship and its centrality in the emotional life of both men. Mary was merely the vicarious screen on which Lincoln's desire was projected. She seemed to him the object of his desire. It was she who drew his conscious attentions. But what lurked in other realms that even he didn't grasp was his terror at losing his friend Speed, whose presence provided the only solace he could find in his ungrounded state.

"In the winter of 40 & 41," Speed says, "he [Lincoln] was very unhappy about his engagement to his wife" (which, incidentally puts to rest any doubts about the engagement itself). "Not being entirely satisfied that his *heart* was going with his hand—How much he suffered then on that account none Know so well as myself—" Only Speed had that special knowledge of what Lincoln was feeling. He notes that Mary "darted after" Lincoln at one point, but the heart of his knowledge came to center on the troubled letter Lincoln wrote Mary to break off the engagement. "Seeing an other girl," Speed says in an oddly stilted and ambiguous phrasing, he decided he could only make himself clear, including to himself, by writing a letter to Mary breaking off the engagement. Lincoln once before with Mary Owens had basically ended an engagement with two tortured letters. He seemed to need that protection against directly expressing his feelings. But with Mary Todd it was especially painful for him. Having drafted the letter, long since lost, Lincoln seemed then to collapse in terror at the thought of actually handing it over to Mary and asked Speed to be his messenger and deliver it.[8]

Speed was appalled. He strongly advised his friend that you don't break off an engagement by letter. "Words are forgotten," Speed told him, "Misunderstood—passed by—not noticed in a private Conversation." Besides, it was cowardly, especially not even for him to deliver it, which he told Lincoln in no uncertain terms. He said: "If you think you have *will* & Manhood enough to go and see her and Speak to her what you say in that letter, you may do that." Apparently, that reference to a lack of "manhood" got through to Lincoln, and he realized he alone had to face Mary and tell her he wanted to break the engagement. Things didn't go well. The issue of Matilda may have entered into their conversation, though Speed is not at all clear on this issue, but there is no question she got angry at what she felt was Lincoln's act of betrayal in breaking the engagement: this is where she uttered her exclamation about the deceiver being deceived (which probably confused Lincoln as much as it does us all these years later). He was moved and, full of his own doubts, "drew her down on his Knee," kissing her before parting. It left him distraught.[9]

The sequence seems to be that Speed at this point in his life was still in relatively better shape psychologically as Lincoln fell apart, which allowed Speed to be the voice of reason and comfort for Lincoln. As Speed planned the sale of his store and his departure from Springfield, Lincoln fell into a confused state in which he said all manner of crazy things to and about the women in his life. He was in a panic. The mostly unconscious and certainly unacknowledged dread at the thought of losing Speed unhinged him. The commitments involved in marriage—and perhaps the act of sexual consummation—seemed overwhelming. He had moved toward love the previous winter, as he and Mary talked of their future together (even if not a formal engagement announced to the world). But with Speed's decision to leave Springfield, made around August 1840 (when he began to collect on his debts in preparation for the sale of the store to Hurst), Lincoln suddenly felt overwhelmed and uncertain. The onset of his depression was not something that happened overnight, and it seemed to surprise him in its intensity. But by late in the fall he only knew he had to extricate himself from his approaching marriage to Mary.[10]

Douglas Wilson, in *Honor's Voice*, seeking to minimize the significance of Lincoln's depression (and to claim it had nothing to do with Mary Todd or Joshua Speed), argues that the key issue was the famous defenestration during the special session of the legislature that ended on December 5. The Whigs were intent on not allowing a vote on an antibank measure the last day of the session and purposely absented themselves from the deliberations to prevent a quorum. Lincoln and two colleagues, however, attended the session to be sure no vote was taken. A shrewd Democrat, spotting who was in the room, called for a roll call, and suddenly there were enough members present for a quorum. Someone locked the door to prevent the Whigs from leaving, so Lincoln and his two colleagues opened a window and jumped out. Wilson concludes, "The humiliation of this inglorious escapade was painful and immediate" and led to his depression, even though Lincoln himself *never* referred to the defenestration with shame or in any context in which he discussed his "hypo" or the pain of his courtship. David Donald, a very good historian, even reads the defenestration as evidence of Lincoln's giddy new love for Mary, which influenced his "boisterous conduct toward his fellow legislators" and his "much publicized leap" from the window during the legislative debate.[11]

✳ ✳ ✳

Once he broke his engagement with Mary, Lincoln acted with the kind of eternal negative so characteristic of someone in crisis, withdrawing from all commitments and turning on the world and its dangers. He fell into a suicidal depression, which may not have occurred immediately. Psychologically, it is worth noting that depression follows no preordained course (unlike, say, a cold or stomach virus), and it is entirely possible that Lincoln began to fall into a depression in December, even early in the month, in conjunction with a host of events but especially with the broken engagement, but that his depression only reached clinical proportions after the charged first of January, when he had been scheduled to be married. Even then, he did not immediately take to his bed. Depression, especially a serious episode, is not a linear thing. The depression was accompanied by what others reported (though in different language) as hallucinations, delirium, cognitive confusions, and clear intentions to take his life. It was not unlike what he seemed to go through after the death of Ann Rutledge and probably evoked his experience at the death of his mother. But the intensity of his depression in January 1841 was truly surprising, both for him and for those who cared about him. Lincoln's friend Orville Browning, who was then staying with the Butlers where Lincoln moved after the first of January, reported in an interview with John Hay that Lincoln's "aberration of mind" and "derange[ment]" lasted a week or so. He was so affected, however, "as to talk incoherently, and to be dilirious to the extent of not knowing what he was doing." Browning in turn told Herndon that Lincoln that month was "Crazy as a *loon*." Jane D. Bell said in a contemporary letter that Lincoln "came within an inch of being a perfect lunatic for life."[12]

Speed was one of only two people allowed to tend to Lincoln (though Elizabeth Butler, who had long darned his socks and made his meals, hovered nearby and reportedly urged Lincoln to recover). A. Y. Ellis, in business with Speed and close to Lincoln, wrote Herndon later that after Lincoln took to his bed, "no one was allowed to see him but his friend Josh Speed & his friend *the doctor* I think Henry." Speed said Lincoln went "Crazy," adding important details about Lincoln's suicidality. They "had to remove razors from his room—take away all Knives and other such dangerous things—&c—it was terrible." Speed wrote, "In the winter of 1841 a gloom came over him till his friends were alarmed for his life."[13]

As the gloom overtook him, Lincoln's law practice ground to a halt by the middle of the month, and he stopped attending the legislature, then meeting in the state house, for about a week. It is worth noting that Lincoln regretted not securing a government position for all the political work he had done to get William Henry Harrison elected president, though he was respected for making the loss less calamitous than expected. He also must have felt some responsibility for the state's formal declaration of bankruptcy on January 1, 1841, given his support for internal improvements that went sour after the panic of 1837. But neither his failure to win office nor the continuing political battles with the Democrats over the economic crisis can begin to explain his depression in January 1841. He never talked of office or bankruptcy either with shame or in any terms that would suggest he was emotionally distraught because Stuart—known as "Jerry Sly" for his deviousness—was unable or unwilling to secure him a post in Washington or because he thought his political career was somehow jeopardized by the swirl of events. If anything, Lincoln's professional star in this period was steadily rising.[14]

But his soul was another matter. Nor was he unaware how mad he had become. In two revealing letters, written on January 20 and January 23 to his law partner John Stuart, then serving in Washington as a congressman, Lincoln acknowledged the shame he felt at his collapse ("I have, within the last few days, been making a most discreditable exhibition of myself in the way of hypochondriasm") and three days later bemoaned his "deplorable state" of mind, expressing what is best described as the negative grandiosity so typical of clinical depression: "I am now the most miserable man living. If what I feel were equally distributed to the whole human family, there would not be one cheerful face on the earth. Whether I shall ever be better I can not tell; I awfully forebode I shall not. To remain as I am is impossible; I must die or be better, it appears to me."[15]

Of course, at some rational level, he knew others had suffered equal, if not greater, levels of torment, but in the moment Lincoln's experience of his suffering was that no one anywhere, no human being alive on the earth, was as miserable as he felt. That actually placed him in a special rung of hell and distinguished him as unique. If everyone felt as he did, no one would be cheerful.

Yet in the extremity of these statements lies a hidden, if largely unacknowledged and mostly unconscious, pleasure. Lincoln wallows in his misery in a way that makes him special indeed as he imagines himself more unhappy than anyone else alive. Deep depression does this. Freud noted that "The self-tormenting in melancholia . . . is without a doubt enjoyable." The "disturbance of self-regard" in depression, as Freud put it, is the heart of the matter. In depression, Freud continues, there is "a profoundly painful dejection, cessation of interest in the outside world, loss of the capacity to love, inhibition of all activity and a lowering of self-regarding feelings to a degree that finds utterance in self-reproaches and self-revilings."[16]

Lincoln, however, was wise—and desperate—enough to seek expert help for his depression from Dr. Drake in Cincinnati, a man noted for his treatment of hypochondriasim, as Speed recounted (and discussed in chapter 3), but Drake wrote back that he could hardly prescribe anything without meeting with Lincoln. What Lincoln could do, however, was to keep those dear to him close at hand. That meant Speed for sure, who may well have delayed his departure from Springfield after the sale of the store to Hurst in order to help care for his friend (though there is no direct evidence for that). Speed, however, played a role in the Drake letter, as Lincoln read it aloud to him, presumably to be sure it was an accurate description of what he was suffering. But Lincoln refused to read part of the letter, something that mystified Speed in the moment but was clarified when he learned later from Herndon about how unhinged Lincoln had gotten after the death of Ann Rutledge. Speed assumed when he learned about Ann that the unread part of the Drake letter dealt with his suicidal depression over her death, something he still felt so much shame over that he couldn't even let Speed know about it.[17]

But Lincoln also turned in his despair to the ministrations of his old friend Doctor Anson G. Henry. Lincoln had a longstanding friendship with Henry that dated from even before his move to Springfield in April 1837. "Doc" Henry, as he was called, was a New York–born, Ohio-trained physician who moved into politics out of inclination and to make more money than the meager earnings he managed from medicine on the urban frontier. In early 1837 Henry became the Whig Party's proposed commissioner for construction of the new State House, a part-time position for which he was then appointed by the legislature and paid three dollars a day. The first note Lincoln wrote after arriving in Springfield that April was to vouch for Henry to the state auditor to get that project rolling. But Lincoln knew and had already decided to help Henry with another idea: securing for him a term as probate court judge, an elected office in those days. Lincoln served as Henry's campaign manager, pumping out pseudonymous "negative campaign-ing" letters to the editor against the incumbent, Judge James Adams. Lincoln seemed to go too far, and Henry not only lost the election but stirred up vocal partisan criticism for squandering public mon-ies. Hapless as a public official, Henry's lack of routine and inherent carelessness when it came to paperwork made it impossible later for Henry to account for his expenditures on the new State House. Seven years later, three arbitrators had to be appointed, one of them Lincoln, who ultimately found that Henry owed $271 to the state.[18]

When Lincoln took to his bed at the Butlers' home in January 1841, his old friend and physician, Doc Henry, came to his side to tend him. Witnesses agree that Henry saw his patient daily. One witness, Hiram Thornton, a legislator who also lodged at the Butler home during the session, said that Lincoln went to Henry's office each day, and Abner Y. Ellis claimed "on good authority" that Lincoln drank shots of "strong Brandy" as prescribed by Henry. Joshua Wolf Shenk, in some very good research, has suggested as well that Henry, who had been a stu-dent of Dr. Daniel Drake and admired Dr. Benjamin Rush, the father of American psychiatry, might have followed a much more rigorous course of treatment. Rush's classic text on the subject was published in 1812 and assumed that a psychotic patient (as was his oldest son, John Rush) needed to be assaulted in a way that reinvigorated the body and psyche. For Rush that included bleeding, swallowing a wide range of tonics, including mercury to purge the stomach, using pain-ful mustard rubs, and so on. Drake, for his part, suffered depression and prescribed and used on himself bleeding; forced vomiting from strong emetics; the drinking of various tonics, including quinine sul-fate, sulfuric ether, ammoniated alcohol, and piperine (derived from black pepper); and the copious use of opium and morphine. There is, however, no direct evidence that Henry used such radical treatments on Lincoln, and one would think that had Lincoln been bled, for exam-ple, someone would have mentioned it.[19]

Doc Henry and Speed, apparently in rotation, spent time at Lincoln's bedside. According to Speed, they mainly kept him company, talked with him, and watched against the presence of any knives or sharp instruments. But whether Lincoln was ambulatory, Henry was certainly a familiar and friendly face near Lincoln during his breakdown. Much later Henry wrote his wife that Lincoln "told me things which he has never yet named to anybody else." Presumably in his confused state Lincoln let slip some confidential feelings about things to his attending doctor, who was otherwise discreet. But even without knowing what Lincoln confided in his doctor, there is no question that Lincoln in this period became quite dependent on Henry. On January 20, Lincoln, fearing that Henry might leave town because of his insecure finances, wrote his law partner, Stuart, that he had come to "an impression that Dr. Henry is necessary to my existence" and begged Stuart to secure a patronage plum for Henry as the postmaster of Springfield (which he never got).[20]

***

Most accounts of Lincoln's depression center on the worst period of his breakdown: January 1841. That was undoubtedly when he was most troubled and close to suicide. In time he came back from the edge, again attending the legislature, aggressively resuming his law practice, and more or less slowly reentering the world as a normal human being. At some point, as Speed specifically wrote Herndon, Lincoln wrote a poem about suicide that was published in the *Sangamo Journal*, but it has never been found. Such a creative effort was undoubtedly part of his gradual recovery. But what mostly kept Lincoln together emotionally is that he remained tethered to Speed for the rest of 1841. That connection and the balm it gave him saved Lincoln from further disarray.[21]

Thomas Lincoln. Lincoln had a troubled relationship with him. Lincoln felt ashamed of his father, seldom visited once he left home, and later kept Thomas away from Mary, himself, and their children in Springfield.

Image courtesy of the Abraham Lincoln Library and Museum of Lincoln Memorial University, Harrogate, Tennessee

Joshua's father, John Speed, courtly and remote, built up Farmington, just outside Louisville, into one of Kentucky's largest plantations. Joshua Speed didn't get along with his father, and left home at 16 to work in Louisville. This miniature painting of John Speed was done by Thomas Seir Cummings close to the time of Speed's death in 1840. It is a watercolor on paper.

Collection of the Speed Art Museum, Louisville, Kentucky

Joshua Speed adored his mother, Lucy Fry Speed, who lived until 1874. She was kind and motherly to Lincoln when he visited Farmington in the late summer of 1841 and gave him a Bible that he always cherished. This miniature painting of Lucy Fry Speed, probably from 1840, was done by Thomas Seir Cummings. It is a watercolor on paper.

Collection of the Speed Art Museum, Louisville, Kentucky

The elegant and sculpted approach to the colonnaded home at Farmington. The home housed a gaggle of 13 children, and the plantation itself was worked by as many as 62 slaves in 1829. Lincoln visited here in late summer 1841.

Photograph by the author

This tiny, rustic cabin in which Lincoln may have been born is certainly like the site of his birth, just 55 miles from Farmington, and could not have been more different from Speed's elegant birthplace.

Courtesy of the Abraham Lincoln Presidential Library & Museum (ALPLM)

Speed's store was located in Springfield, Illinois, on the southwest corner of Fifth and Washington streets, on the west side of the square—about three-quarters of the way up in this picture. Here Lincoln lived with his friend, Speed, for nearly four years from 1837 to 1841, sleeping in the same bed, except when business took one or both away for brief periods.

Courtesy of the Abraham Lincoln Presidential Library & Museum (ALPLM)

The large and elegant Edwards house in Springfield could fit a "dozen prairie-farmer cabins" in it, as Carl Sandburg put it. The house was on "quality hill," sometimes called "aristocracy hill," southwest of the square. Mary Todd lived here with her sister, Elizabeth, from 1840 until she and Lincoln married in its parlor room on November 4, 1842.

Courtesy of the Abraham Lincoln Presidential Library & Museum (ALPLM)

Elizabeth Edwards, Mary's older sister, thrived in the elite social circle of Springfield. She was a masterful hostess who greeted her guests in French and held forth at soirees in the parlor of her large home. This portrait hung in their mansion.

Courtesy of the Abraham Lincoln Presidential Library & Museum (ALPLM)

Ninian Wirt Edwards, the son of the first territorial governor of Illinois (later governor and senator), greatly admired Speed but doubted whether Lincoln was socially acceptable to be the husband of Mary Todd. This portrait also hung in the Edwardses' mansion.

Courtesy of the Abraham Lincoln Presidential Library & Museum (ALPLM)

The first photograph of Mary Todd Lincoln shows her in 1846, after her marriage and already a mother. She was fiercely loyal to Lincoln during the long months of their broken engagement.

Courtesy of the Abraham Lincoln Presidential Library & Museum (ALPLM)

William Herndon when he was a young man, probably from the 1840s when he became Lincoln's junior partner. Herndon later compiled a massive oral history of Lincoln that was the first of its kind in American history, and wrote an important biography of Lincoln with Jesse Weik in 1889.

Courtesy of the Abraham Lincoln Presidential Library & Museum (ALPLM)

LEFT: Stephen A. Douglas, one of the leading Democrats in central Illinois by 1840, knew Lincoln and Speed well. Douglas sometimes visited Speed's store in the evenings to talk for long hours before the fire with the leading young men in town.

Courtesy of the Abraham Lincoln Presidential Library & Museum (ALPLM)

BELOW: This color print from circa 1850 shows the Louisville waterfront. Lincoln worked alongside slaves building the locks on this waterfront as a young man in 1827.

The Filson Historical Society, Louisville, Kentucky

LOUISVILLE
(Kentucky)

This small oval painting of Fanny Henning at 16 years of age in a white dress, never before published, shows her fair complexion and brown hair.

The Filson Historical Society, Louisville, Kentucky

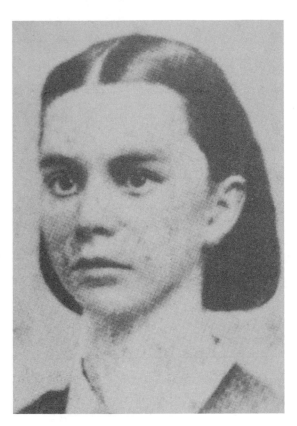

LEFT: Young Fanny Henning in her early twenties, when she was courted by a hesitant Joshua Speed. Lincoln wrote Speed that Fanny was "one of sweetest girls in the world" and that it was her "heavenly *black eyes*" that originally captured Speed's heart.

Courtesy of the Meserve-Kunhardt Collection

BELOW: Here Joshua and Fanny Speed pose with her younger sister, probably in the mid-1850s, after they had moved into Louisville from Pond Settlement.

Courtesy of the Meserve-Kunhardt Collection

Lincoln stands with his son, Willie, in front of his stately home at Eighth and Jackson streets in Springfield (an unseen Tad is hiding behind the post). The house showed Lincoln had arrived in the middle class.

ABRAHAM LINCOLN.
FROM AN AMBROTYPE TAKEN IN 1858
AT PITTSFIELD, ILL, BY C. JACKSON,
TAKEN DURING THE LINCOLN-DOUGLAS
CAMPAIGN.

Lincoln in 1858. Three years earlier he had reiterated to his slave-owning friend, Joshua Speed, his absolute belief that slavery was wrong. He also expressed annoyance that (relatively) enlightened people like Speed in the South failed to speak out against the spread of slavery into the territories.

Mary Lincoln, in the gown she wore to the first inaugural ball, liked to flatten her hair and cover her head with fresh flowers. She had trouble dealing with the constant criticism she and her husband received and would be devastated by the death of their son Willie in 1862.

LEFT: Lincoln in the spring of 1862, in a photograph taken by Matthew Brady. Lincoln, who often allowed himself to be photographed, was keenly aware of the political uses of this new medium. In this picture, one can sense the pressures of the war weighing on him.

Courtesy of the Abraham Lincoln Presidential Library & Museum (ALPLM)

BELOW: Joshua Speed often visited Lincoln in the White House. He posed for this picture by Matthew Brady in about 1862, in the same (or an identical) chair as Lincoln had used for his picture. Speed played an important role keeping Kentucky in the Union and helped run guns for Kentucky loyalists in the early months of the conflict.

Courtesy of the Meserve-Kunhardt Collection

ABOVE: Joshua and Fanny Speed in the 1860s. Joshua by then was a leading citizen in Louisville, rich and greatly admired. He and Fanny never had children but nourished close relations with their many nieces and nephews in the extended Speed clan.

The Filson Historical Society, Louisville, Kentucky

RIGHT: This yellowing photograph shows Speed not too long before his death in 1882. Speed wrote many letters to, and sat for interviews with, William Herndon about Lincoln in the years after the Civil War. Speed also wrote up his own reminiscences of his friendship with Lincoln.

The Filson Historical Society, Louisville, Kentucky

Alexander Gardner's photograph of Lincoln on February 5, 1865, was the last picture taken of him before he died. The slight smile evokes a president of great wisdom and humanity at the end of an awful war, but one that brought a new birth of freedom to America.

8

KENTUCKY BLUEGRASS

Speed, like Lincoln, suffered from the "hypo." And, like Lincoln, he was shaken by their separation. Speed wrote his sister Mary on February 2, 1841, to tell her how pleased he was to hear from her, especially since her letter arrived "unlooked for and unexpected." That made the letter all the "more gratefull" because it arrived "like an absent but not forgotten friend" whose sudden appearance is "welcome, *most welcome*." Speed confided in Mary how terrible he felt. Mary's letter came "just at a time when I needed something to brace me." He had been suffering, he said, "so much of late from sick head aches and hypo, that I am almost unmanned." Speed's reference to feeling "unmanned" is a curious nineteenth-century male association with depression: to suffer from it risks emasculation, even symbolic castration. Speed continued to suffer bouts of depression for the next several months. He complained to another sister, Eliza, on March 12, of time hanging heavily "upon my hands," even though he also reported he was trying to court someone (who is unnamed in the letter). Like Lincoln in these same months, Speed struggled back from the abyss.[1]

For several weeks, neither Speed nor Lincoln wrote to the other. This one can surmise from a surviving letter from Speed to their mutual friend William Butler. Not long after Speed's arrival back in Kentucky, he wrote Butler on May 18 that he was glad to hear from Mrs. Butler that Lincoln by then was "on the mend." Speed urges Butler to tell Lincoln that he (Speed) was much better and had had only one "attack" since he left Springfield, on the river during his journey. He remained unsettled, however, reporting to Butler, "I am not as happy as I could be and yet so much happier than I deserve to be that I think I ought to be satisfied."[2]

This curious wording reflects Speed's modesty and self-deprecation, traits that drew people to him, but the idea that only some relief from misery was all he deserved suggests as well that he struggled with issues of self-esteem. We should not be too quick to psychologize here, as he may have been ironic in his letter to Butler, making fun of his own suffering with a very good friend. But there is something actually sad about Speed's apparent feeling that he didn't deserve real happiness and should in fact accept a state of being that was only somewhat less than terrible. Depression and self-esteem are generally linked in this way. Esteem plummets in depression in ways that further aggravates the depression itself, contributing to a sense of hopelessness and unworthiness. We have no indication of the childhood sources of Speed's tendency toward depression, but it is not unreasonable to guess that he had, as Lincoln, long struggled with such issues.

Speed wrote Lincoln directly on June 13 (a letter not preserved but referred to by Lincoln), and Lincoln wrote Speed a long letter in a largely comic vein on June 19, presumably to cheer him up. Lincoln habitually wore a mask and told funny stories to ward off the blues. True to form, he seems to have held back on writing Speed until he had a hilarious story to share with his ailing friend. Speed in his note may have intimated missing Lincoln and even being sick absent his friend's comforting presence. In any case, at the end of his exuberant letter, Lincoln renewed his promise to visit Speed.[3]

Both men were walking wounded. Issues of self-esteem can range from feelings of inadequacy about appearance, intelligence, or a sense of worthiness to subtle feelings about not quite matching up, of being unable to love on terms appropriate to one's ideals, or any number of other possibilities. Such sensibilities that get etched onto the motherboard of the self make one especially vulnerable to real and imagined injuries. Often depression and despair are the consequence of such experiences. Such a complicated process is not one that can easily be observed by someone outside of the direct experience of the one suffering depression. At best one can empathically enter into another's experience of hurt and shame, which form the context for depression. That is exactly the role Speed played for Lincoln. In a broader sense, it is only through the empathic investigation of another, for example, that we can begin to understand why the raised eyebrow of a critic will be dismissed as obnoxious by one person but throw someone else into a state of hopeless despair. That said, certain kinds of human experiences have the tendency to create vulnerabilities in the self that make one open to injury and result in depression. Among these experiences are death and its equivalents. In that regard Speed seemed very much like Lincoln.

Speed lingered on death, dreams, and the supernatural in ways quite similar to Lincoln. One suspects their ruminations, which they undoubtedly shared with each other at great length over their years together, both expressed their moodiness and encouraged it to fester. Speed, for example, tells Mary on February 2 of his "apprehension for the future" and that the only way to "direct my mind from such unpleasant thoughts" was to turn to the past and "exert" its memory. He forces himself into a quasi dreamscape, where he sees "friends and kindred come before me" as "travellers do a clear stream, in a common ferry boat." While thus dwelling on the past, his mind conjures up "the forms, faces, and features, of those who pass over it, as the clear stream would the figures of those who were crossing it." Lincoln, too, often spoke in a kind of dreamscape, as when he told his neighbors and friends on his departure from Springfield: "All the strange, chequered past seems to crowd now upon my mind."[4]

In Speed's letter to his sister, he reports an actual dream from the previous night of "poor little Ann," his sister who died at eight years of age in 1838 and whose death brought Speed back to visit Farmington (something he did not do when his father died). In the dream Speed saw Mary "in your sweetest tone" singing "Angels Whisper," a popular ballad from the *Songs of the Superstitions of Ireland*, composed by Samuel Lover. Mary, the most musical of all the Speeds, might well have been at the piano while she sang this wildly sentimental popular song of the time. In it a mother weeps by the side of her baby for her fisherman husband far out on the "wild, raging sea." The mother prays with her beads while the baby slumbers, knowing that "the angels are whispering with thee." The mother tells the sleeping baby to pray with her to the angels to keep watch over the father, and, sure enough, in the morning the husband, Dermot, returns. The mother caresses the child with a blessing, for she knows "the angels were whispering with thee." Speed could easily imagine Ann sitting next to Mary in the dream. Ann was "more beautiful if possible in death than she was when living." Ann conveyed to Mary her "thanks to you, for the song you sang" and seemed to convey to Speed that she, in her "pea green silk," would sing of the coming of spring.

As Ann started singing in his dream he half woke up and "saw her form vanishing from my sight." The fleeting little girl in his dream pointed to "some flowers that bedecked her forehead in the shape of a wreath" and said to Speed: "This is the only part of my dress they buried me in that I have kept." Speed begs Mary *not* to tell him if in fact Ann was buried with such a wreath, as it would be too confirming of his fears. "I am forever," he says, "though reluctantly, a believer in ghosts." And he tells Mary a story. On his trip back to Louisville in 1838, not knowing at the time that in fact Ann had just died, he lay down on his bed, exhausted from travel. He thought of all the friends he was about to visit and was happy. Little Ann was there with him, kissing him "more tenderly than she was wont to do." He felt her spirit with him, an idea he dismissed at the time, but then found upon his arrival home that she was dead. Speed was left believing Ann's ghost had visited him during his journey.

Joshua Speed had decided to return to Kentucky, having made the final decision around August 1840. "To place myself in a situation to go if necessary," he tells Mary he had sold his stock, "which took effect the 1st of January last." He has no regrets about making such preparations to move, as it was "long meditated," but he felt suddenly overcome by self-doubts. "My determination then, to go to Ky to live only furnished me without good protest for putting in execution that which my inclination prompted me to do," he says, in complicated phrasing that makes him the passive agent of the process. He wonders whether he should leave. "I am as yet very undetermined as to what I shall do or even where I shall go." He has many friends in Springfield, "of whom I may justly and hope ever shall be proud." He has done well and managed to succeed both in friendship and business up to the level of his abilities. "While I have not done anything to rank me among the first men here, either for mind or money, I feel confident that I have credit for as much talent as I deserve and I think have made as much money [as] I could have expected for one with as little age, experience, credit, or capital as I had to start upon."

Speed's main problem with returning to Kentucky was that he had no interest in running the plantation that all members of the family euphemistically called the "farm." Speed notes in his February 2, 1841, letter to Mary that during his visit to Farmington the previous spring, after his father died, he was attentive to the "earnest solicitation" of his siblings Mary, Eliza, and Philip to return to Kentucky and do what he could to "prop up a tottering concern." He is especially glad at least that Philip has agreed for now to take over Farmington, as he is "much better calculated to manage it, and govern the negroes than I could be." And he adds, tellingly: "Whenever I have thought seriously of leading the life of a farmer, it has always seemed tasteless to me."[5]

But Speed is also not entirely consistent about this business of "farming" and governing the slaves. He had no trouble owning slaves for his household service even long past the Emancipation Proclamation and would benefit financially from his share of the profits from the continued operation of the plantation (though the details here are not available). Within a year of his return to Louisville, Speed, while not the principal operator of Farmington (that task went to Philip), seemed to have embraced aspects of running the plantation with relish. Lincoln's letter to Speed on March 27, 1842, is partly in response to his friend's clearly very positive account of his life running and perhaps working on the plantation. "As to your farm matter," Lincoln says, adopting the euphemism to avoid hurting his friend's feelings, "I have no sympathy with you. *I* have no farm," Lincoln says with emphasis, "nor ever expect to have; and, consequently, have not studied the subject enough to be much interested with it. I can only say that I am glad *you* are satisfied and pleased with it."[6]

In Speed's letter to his sister Mary, he leaves his final decision about returning in question. At most he commits himself to visit. He has some debts to pay, but more importantly he has to collect on money owed him. Once he has that money in hand, he says, and "conscious I am not doing wrong, I will snatch as much time from my business as I can and visit you."

There is another possible reason Speed stayed in Springfield in the spring of 1841. He wrote Butler on April 3, 1842: "I received a letter from Evan a few days ago, in which much to my gratification he informed me, that it was Susan instead of Mary Ann who had given birth to the little one." Given the inevitable delays in communication, as well as the intervening role of this unknown Evan, the baby could have been born in February and conceived the previous May, or just before Speed left Springfield. This mysterious Mary Ann—thankfully, it seems, for Speed—did not give birth to a baby. It is imaginable Speed stayed in Springfield because of his relationship with this unknown Mary (and then left quickly). It is unlikely, however, that Speed feared he had conceived a baby with this Mary Ann. One is that Speed was always naïve about love and sex, something that comes through in his courtship of and marriage to Fanny Henning (discussed in chapter 10). But the other difficulty in imagining that Speed feared that a former girlfriend might have given birth to his baby in early 1842 is that Speed was in Springfield from September to early January 1842, having accompanied Lincoln back from Kentucky. Any lingering paternity issues from a pregnant Mary Ann would have presented themselves to him in those months. He hardly needed Butler in April 1842 to reassure him of the paternity of a baby born to this Susan.'

So Speed hesitated about moving back permanently to Kentucky. He had returned briefly well after his father died in March 1840, but that was clearly to help settle the estate, not a final move. Speed had roots now in Springfield. He had played any number of civic and political roles, was a booster for the town itself, and was constantly among those building up the Whig party in Illinois. He had well-developed business connections, having figured out the complicated (and often risky) tasks of buying goods on credit and selling them before notes were due. Speed was also greatly admired as a person. Men as diverse as Ninian Edwards, William Butler, and Stephen Douglas held him in high esteem. They, and many others, came to Speed's store at night because they felt comfortable in his presence.

But what probably weighed Speed down more than anything was the tormenting thought of his friend tossing and turning in the room at the Butlers', filled with suicidal thoughts, literally out of his mind for the moment. Speed would never be as close to any other man as he was just then with Lincoln. And that friend was in crisis as he wrote his sister, which may well have led him suddenly to develop doubts about leaving Lincoln to return home, despite his earlier decision. At least that seems to be the most likely explanation of what is left out of Speed's letter to Mary. It would have been nearly impossible for him to explain to her the Sturm und Drang of events with Lincoln over the last couple of months.

But the ever-reliable and compassionate young man also worried about the needs of his mother and siblings. His concerns for the care of his mother trumped other issues. Mary Todd heard from Speed shortly after his return to Kentucky in late May or June 1841 and reported to her friend Mercy Levering that Speed's "mother is anxious he should superintend her affairs." In the family discussions following the death of John Speed, decisions that deeply influenced Joshua as he prepared to leave Springfield, brother Philip took on the responsibility of running the plantation. Philip lived in the house with his wife and two half-sisters, Mary and Eliza. Peachey Peay, another sister with her husband (who died in 1849) and children, also apparently lived in the house. Lucy Gilmer Fry Speed, the mother, was generously provided for in John's will. She received fifteen slaves of her choice, presumably to help her run her household or lease out to give her financial support, as well as the elderly Peggy, an attendant slave who probably had come along with her when she married John. Lucy lived with her daughter Susan Speed Davis, though it is not clear from the records whether she was actually living at Farmington or nearby, as the census records are unclear about residence. Philip eventually moved to a nearby tract of land on the estate, as did another brother, Smith Speed.[8]

This large family, in other words, struggled to figure out how to keep things going after the death of John Speed. It was definitely not, however, a "tottering concern," as Joshua wrote Mary Speed in early 1841, at least not economically. What was tottering was Joshua's commitment to the operation. John Speed had grown his "farm" from a small operation to one of the largest and most prosperous plantations in Kentucky. It was also well positioned to benefit from the great explosion of wealth in the South in the 1840s and 1850s, before everything came crashing down in the fires of war. The price of hemp, for example, Farmington's principal crop, had increased by 150 percent since the panic of 1837, when it hit $70 a ton, rising to $100 a ton in 1838, and reaching $180 in June 1841 as Joshua returned home. The price of slaves was also increasing at a furious pace. In James Speed's later testimony to the American Freedman's Inquiry Commission after the war, he notes that the value of John Speed's slaves was already high upon his death in 1840 but would triple in value over the course of the next two decades.[9]

John Speed's will documents the extent of his holdings. As inventoried by his lawyer son James, of John Speed's slaves (all with first names, some, like "Morocco" or "Cato," rather exotic, others, like "Julia Ann" or "Mary," the way whites would name their children, others distinctly black, like "Sary" or "Buck," or just spelled uncommonly, like "Sinderella" or "Winney") somewhat less than half were "prime" farmhands, or skilled men and women, twenty-five were children under age fourteen (two of them less than a year old), and five, who were probably old or disabled, were valued as "zero." The inventory did not assign any value for the house itself and other buildings or improvements on the judge's considerable real-estate holdings of some five hundred acres. In his will, however, John did linger on his household furnishings, including a "piana [sic] and stool," which the judge made out specially by belated codicil to go to the musically talented elder daughter, Mary, along with its sheet music; his library, described as one "case of old books generally broken Sets also 5 maps"; a gold watch; fine china, kitchen utensils, and even a novel form of "refrigerator" (by that name); all the farm equipment of hand tools, twenty-one hemp rakes, twenty hemp hooks, and one hemp roller, along with a valuable crop of "hemp on the ground" ready to be harvested the spring he died; an ox wagon with yokes, bows, and "false tongue"; two horse wagons with gear; ploughs and harrows; a buggy and harness, along with a pair of fit carriage horses; one "Old blind horse," two "Old Brood mares," four colts, two riding horses, and eleven "Old work horses"; some seventeen milk cows and one bull, nine heifers, three of which were still "sucking calves"; five work oxen, along with one "Beef"; forty-seven "fat hogs," twelve sows, twenty-five pigs, and one "Irish Grazier boar"; "Turkies chickens & ducks"; two thousand bushels of cribbed corn, with another thirty acres on stalks in the fields; 225 bushels of "Irish potatoes"; sixteen bushels of dried beans and peas; thirty bushels of sugar beets; sixteen barrels of apples; a thousand cabbages; seventy barrels plus ten casks of cider "being made into vinegar"; salt pork; timothy hay and clover for the livestock; tallow and forty dozens of tallow candles; a half-barrel of currant wine; a half-barrel of sugar and twenty pounds of coffee; a thousand bushels of coal for the fireplace, along with prepaid certificates for two thousand bushels each year deliverable in 1840, 1841, 1842, and 1843 from McKee's coal yard in Louisville; and substantial interest payments due annually from six people to whom he had lent money *and* a two-hundred-dollar note due on or about July 25, 1846, from the city of Louisville. It is always difficult to assess currency value over time, but, as a conservative estimate, John Speed's estate at his death was worth well over a million dollars.[10]

✳ ✳ ✳

In Mary Todd's chatty June 1841 letter to Mercy Levering, she notes that Lincoln "deems me unworthy of notice," since she has not seen him "in the gay world for months." It was out of character for Lincoln to be so absent from the Edwards home. Ninian Edwards later told Herndon that Lincoln came by his house every Sunday for four years (clearly meaning when Lincoln was in town and not out on the circuit or giving political speeches elsewhere in the state). In her letter to Mercy, Mary keeps her tone light, something she strived for in letters in this period, but she cannot help conveying to her friend her real feelings: "I would that the case were different, that he [Lincoln] would once more resume his Station in Society." Mary adds a comment about her warm feelings for Speed, "our former most constant guest," who left Springfield for Kentucky "some weeks past," as he has "some idea of deserting Illinois" but "will be here next month." These cryptic comments make several things quite clear: Lincoln had not been visiting the Edwards home or attending any parties since the broken engagement with Mary; she retained her feelings for him and hoped he would rejoin her company; and, most interestingly, Speed left for Kentucky seemingly for good in late May or early June and at least intended to return within a month, probably to visit Lincoln to see how he was (though he also might have had business to attend to); and possibly she was hoping her comments to Mercy about Lincoln would get back to him in gossipy Springfield.[11]

Though the absence of evidence is not the same as evidence of absence, it would seem that in fact Speed did not return to Springfield.

He may have gotten caught up in family affairs at home in Kentucky upon his arrival, though he had not yet begun to court Fanny Henning, the woman he later married. The more important question by far is why he is writing Mary Todd within days of his return to Kentucky. Her reference to him clearly indicates she saw him as a friend, and she knew well how close he was to Lincoln himself. Perhaps for Mary, Speed served as a stand-in for Lincoln and a continuing link in the triangular set of relationships. From the moment of the broken engagement, Lincoln (as he put it later) felt tormented with guilt "for the never-absent idea, that there is *one* still unhappy whom I have contributed to make so." Lincoln may have been glad for his best friend's ongoing friendship with Mary Todd. There is no indication Lincoln asked Speed to keep up the relationship, but neither did he interfere. It was solely Speed who thus kept Lincoln vicariously connected with Mary, and, as we shall see, Lincoln would continue to use Speed vicariously to work through the most important emotional issues of his life. And for Speed, his continued friendship with Mary helped maintain contact with the woman he knew his friend loved but could not then reach out to. Finally, for Mary her active friendship with Speed kept her connected with Lincoln's other half. She seemed to be actively waiting, though quietly, for the man she loved.[12]

Although not in the "gay world" of parties at the Coterie, Lincoln was able to resume his law practice, perhaps by February and certainly in March. The worst of his disoriented emotional state was behind him. One should not imagine, however, that such depression suddenly melts away like a cured infection or the way sunburned skin becomes entirely normal after a few days. Lincoln remained deeply troubled, aloof, and apart from society, but at least he was no longer suicidal and was able to throw himself into his legal work, which itself probably was partly healing in its ability to distract and occupy his attention. He believed it was important not to be idle as a way of staving off depression.[13]

Lincoln avoided idleness that late winter and spring of 1841. When the legislature adjourned on March 1, he got very busy very quickly by establishing a new law partnership. John Stuart was away in Washington now most of the time, and he and Lincoln had never really become close (Stuart's interviews with Herndon are surprisingly harsh in some of the things he says about Lincoln, whom he notes never invited him to dinner despite being in his house "a hundred times"). So Lincoln turned to Stephen T. Logan, whom Lincoln later described as "one of my most distinguished, and most highly valued friends." Logan was nine years older than Lincoln. Shortly after his arrival from Kentucky he was elected circuit court judge and in that capacity certified Lincoln's enrollment in the Sangamon County bar in 1837. But he wanted to earn more money and soon went into private practice, first with the eloquent Edward D. Baker but then with Lincoln, beginning on March 1, 1841, because he felt the much more folksy Lincoln could help him with juries. Logan, as David Donald put it, had a "harsh, cracked voice" that made him ineffective as a speaker, and "juries were often put off by his wizened figure and his wrinkled countenance, topped by a mass of frowzy hair."[14]

Lincoln jumped into the fray as he wound up his cases with Stuart and took on ones from Logan. In March Lincoln dealt with thirty-eight cases, mopping up his old Stuart and Lincoln cases and working on some that fell into his lap after he joined Logan. In April he handled eleven cases, in May another seventeen, and so on for the rest of the year. He was, in other words, busy again, though entirely with the law and not at all with politics. In that he had been disappointed. He had not been able to get a federal office through Stuart in the new administration, and William Henry Harrison himself was a nonstarter as president. On March 4 the sixty-eight-year-old Harrison was sworn in, delivered the longest inaugural address in history in the rain, caught pneumonia, and served the shortest presidency on record when he died on April 4. The new president, John Tyler, an anti-Jackson Democrat and a slave owner from Virginia, was not someone who would throw any crumbs to a hard-working Whig in Illinois. Lincoln, who had reached out to Stuart for a patronage appointment in January, now ceased looking to Washington for work. He accepted that he had to make a living in the law, which meant having a new partner and rededicating himself to his practice.[15]

The best-documented case Lincoln handled in this period—because he described it in great detail in a letter of close to two thousand words to Speed and then, five years later, in a not entirely professional newspaper article—was the astonishing murder trial of the Trailor brothers (though technically it was an examination by the justice of peace and the mayor whether to proceed to trial).[16] Lincoln loved the case because it so aptly caught the spirit of human folly. It formed the story that he sent to cheer up his friend Speed. The case had aroused the "highest state of excitement here for a week past," Lincoln wrote Speed on June 19, 1841, "that our community has ever witnessed." The three Trailor brothers, Archibald, Henry, and William, lived, respectively, in Springfield, Clary's Grove, and Warren County, and were suspected of bludgeoning Archibald Fisher to death. At first when Fisher went missing it was not much noted until the postmaster in Springfield heard from his counterpart in Warren County suspicions that Fisher had been "disposed of unfairly." That greatly aroused everyone to conduct a mass search for the body, probing privies, digging up fresh graves, but to no avail. When the brothers were also arrested, Henry cooperated with the prosecutor and accused William and Archibald of throwing the body into the "Spring Creek between the Beardstown road bridge and Hickoxes mill." The furious mob sped off to the mill dam "like a herd of buffaloes" and destroyed it to draw the water out of the pond. No body was found. Then they "went up and down, and down and up the creek, fishing and raking, and ducking and diving for two days, and after all, no dead body found."

Still no body had been found when the dramatic examining trial began with Lincoln, his partner Stephen Logan, and Edward D. Baker in defense of the two remaining accused Trailor brothers.[17] Lincoln took great pleasure in reporting some of the absurd details. Nothing amused him more than the testimony of Dr. Elias Merryman about his discovery on the trail leading to Spring Creek. Merryman said he found two hairs, which, after "a long scientific examination," he reported were "triangular human hairs," which can grow as whiskers, hair under the arms, "and on other parts of the body." These two hairs Merryman judged were whiskers "because the ends were cut, showing that they had flourished in the neighbourhood of the razor's operations." But everything went haywire when a Doctor Gilmore, who knew Fisher, said he had long been somewhat addled in mind from an accident and that the doctor had in fact seen Fisher the day before, confused, as was his wont, but very much alive. The brothers were released, even though Henry Trailor kept insisting "no power on earth could ever show Fisher alive." Those who had searched so furiously for the body were perplexed. "Some looked quizzical, some melancholy, and some furiously angry," Lincoln wrote. James R. Langford, a carpenter and joiner who had taken the lead in destroying the mill dam and wanted to hang Hickox for his objections, "looked most awfully wo-begone; he seemed the '*wictim of hunrequited haffection*,' as represented in the comic almanac we used to laugh over." Lincoln concludes his tall tale of the trial by noting that Elias Hart, who had famously hauled Mary Todd home once in his bray, said "it was too *damned* bad, to have so much trouble, and no hanging after all."

A public meeting promptly convened to reclaim the reputation of the local defendant, Archie Trailor (the brother who lived in Springfield). The *Sangamo Journal* did not state where the meeting was held, but it was probably in the back of Speed's store, since in the report that came out of the meeting it was Charles R. Hurst who moved that a committee—consisting of Hurst, defense attorney Edward Baker, Dr. Merryman the whisker witness, and James Gourley, Lincoln's cobbler and long-time friend—be formed to draft resolutions. The committee offered a resolution of deep regret that Archibald Trailor had been "suspected of so foul a crime" while praising him for "integrity and upright deportment."[18]

At the close of his letter to Speed, Lincoln adds two personal notes: "I stick to my promise to come to Louisville" and "I have not seen Sarah [Rickard] since my long trip." He further suggests that the only real relationship in the apparent swirl of those around Lincoln and Speed in the winter of 1840–1841—other than that between Lincoln and Mary Todd—was that between Speed and Sarah.

＊＊＊

Lincoln was unsteady emotionally when he arrived in Kentucky to visit with Speed on August 18, 1841. He was "moody and hypochondriac," as Speed wrote Herndon on January 12, 1866, and "at times very melancholy," clearly manifesting a "deep depression" that pained Speed's mother. But his sadness, his regret over hurting Mary, and his continuing despair over whether he would ever resolve the issues of intimacy in his life continued to lurk in his soul. Perhaps the relaxed atmosphere in the loving Speed family helped, as did the freedom from his law practice, which had been intense that spring and early summer. Most of all, however, Lincoln was now reunited with Joshua himself, who was clearly the one who persuaded Lincoln to come for a visit.

Ninian Edwards later said that Lincoln "was taken to Kentucky—by Speed—or went to Speed's—was Kept there till he recovered finally." Having pressured his friend to visit for some months, Speed's presence now created the safety in which Lincoln could honor his melancholy feelings. He was able to shed his mask.[19]

Lincoln was welcomed by the friendly Speed family and for the next three weeks, until September 7, lived the genteel life of a white man on a Southern plantation in antebellum America. "Lincoln came to see me," Speed later wrote to Herndon, "& staid sometime at my mothers in the Summer & fall of 1841." At Farmington he was completely immersed in aristocratic Southern life supported by a large number of slaves. He was assigned a slave as his personal servant, though one supposes that Lincoln did not make many, if any, demands. House slaves kept the house clean; prepared, cooked, and served the food; carried out tasks like doing the laundry, chopping wood, and churning butter; and at the end of the day quietly removed themselves from the house and retired to their separate quarters. In the meanwhile, the bulk of the slaves trudged out to the fields each morning to work in the hot August sun as the dust stirred from toiling in the fields of hemp. It was an experience for Lincoln quite unlike what he had known from his childhood in dirt-floored cabins, where his mother and sister carried out all of the household tasks while his father labored in the fields to turn the rich but clotted soil with a horse-drawn plow. A mere twenty-five years and some fifty-five miles separated Lincoln's childhood experience on the rough frontier near Hodgenville, Kentucky, from his brief stint as a gentleman on the Speed plantation just outside Louisville.[20]

In the house at Farmington, Lincoln stayed in the big front room on the left of the wide hall (at least by oral tradition; there is no other evidence to support where he slept). He connected immediately with Joshua's siblings, especially his half-sister Mary (from John's first marriage), now forty-two and single. Mary, who was musical, smart, and close to Joshua, became Lincoln's favorite. In a letter to her just after he left, Lincoln told Mary she was his "devoted one" and that they were "cronies." The two seemed to joust playfully, and Lincoln referred to how, once, he was "under the necessity of shutting you up in a room to prevent your committing an assault and battery upon me." Lincoln also played with the two-year-old Eliza Davis, the daughter of Joshua's sister Susan Fry Speed Davis, and told Mary in his letter to kiss her "o'er and o'er again" for him, sent his respects to "all your sisters (including 'Aunt Emma') and brothers," and asked Mary to tell "Mrs. Peay [Joshua's older sister], of whose happy face I shall long retain a pleasant remembrance, that I have been trying to think of a name for her homestead, but as yet, can not satisfy myself with one."[21]

No one in Farmington came to matter more to Lincoln than Joshua's mother, Lucy Fry Speed. She sensed his depression as only a tender-hearted mother figure could, and, as with other matronly women in his life, Lincoln was drawn to her. She doted on him and often served him "delicious dishes of peaches and cream," especially after he developed a toothache and an incompetent dentist in Louisville unsuccessfully tried to pull the tooth. Lucy also connected with Lincoln psychologically. Noting how melancholy he was, Speed later reported:

> My Mother observed it [his melancholy]—and one morning when he was alone—she with a womans instinct being much pained at his deep depression—which she had observed—presented him a bible—advising him to read it—to adopt its precepts and pray for its promises—
>
>   It made a deep impression upon him—I often heard him allude to it—even after he was President—As an evidence of the impression made upon him—Soon after his election he sent her a photographic likeness of himself—with this inscription in his own handwriting
>
>   "To my very good friend Mrs. Lucy G. Speed from whose pious hands I received an Oxford Bible Twenty years ago."

More immediately, just after leaving Farmington, Lincoln wrote Mary Speed to tell Lucy that he intends to read the Bible she gave him regularly "when I return home." And he adds: "I doubt not that it is really, as she says, the best cure for the 'Blues' could one but take it according to the truth."[22]

One would not want to be cloying about Lincoln's Bible reference in his 1841 letter to Mary Speed or Joshua's account of his mother's gift in his 1866 letter to Herndon. Both reek of nineteenth-century sentimentality, especially Joshua's description of his mother and Lincoln in the immediate wake of the war. It is a story that evokes the image of a good Christian woman tending to a future American political saint in his time of trouble, giving him a Bible that cures him of his melancholy, and setting him on a path of righteousness that of course ends with his saving the nation and freeing the slaves.

On the other hand, there is some suggestive indirect evidence that Lincoln changed spiritually in 1841, perhaps under the influence of his depression and the tender ministrations of Lucy Speed. For one thing, it was only after 1841 that Lincoln began to mention God. He had scrupulously avoided such references in his letters and speeches, but after 1841 it became commonplace for him to bring God into his discourse. For example, in a 1846 handbill, Lincoln said he was not a formal member of a church but never "denied the truth of the Scriptures," never disrespected religion, that while he inclined toward the "Doctrine of Necessity" as a young man he no longer held those beliefs, and that he had held onto his new attitudes about religion and spirituality "for more than five years."[23]

There was a context for Lincoln's apparent new sense of belief after 1841, however important Lucy Speed seemed as a catalyst. Lincoln had always been unchurched but deeply spiritual, and he had grown up on the Bible, knew its stories in both the Old and New Testaments by heart, and was including subtle biblical allusions in his speeches as early as his "Young Men Lyceum Speech" of 1838. Furthermore, his comment to Mary Speed in his 1841 letter is coy in its suggestion that he lacks a basic familiarity with the Bible that he will now turn to as soon as he can because Lucy Speed says reading it will cure him of his blues. That does not mean Lucy was unimportant. The truer meaning of the story is that Lincoln felt touched by Lucy's warmth in giving him the Bible. He was in fact very melancholy while at Farmington. Lucy's maternal care and understanding became an important source of healing for him. That is what he responded to. It mattered to *her* immensely that he take the Bible as a gift and believe her that reading it would cure him. The book he knew. It was the mother he lacked, and Lucy was about as good a surrogate as he ever found. But in the process Lincoln perhaps (re)discovered spiritual meanings in the Bible that found a deeper resonance.

Lincoln's most politically consequential new friend during his stay at Farmington was Joshua's brother James Speed, who would become his attorney general in Lincoln's second administration and then for a while under President Johnson. James Speed was then a practicing lawyer in Louisville. Lincoln often borrowed a horse and rode the seven miles or so into Louisville to visit with James, talk about "slavery and the questions of the day," and peruse James's law library. Sometimes Lincoln walked to and from Louisville for these visits, and on one of them he had a scary incident. Late one evening, three thugs sprang from a dark alley. One brandished a long knife that he waved ominously close to his neck, demanding a "loan" of five dollars. Lincoln said all he had was a ten-dollar bill, which he handed over. "There's $10.00 neighbor. Now put up your scythe."[24]

James was considerably more progressive about the "questions of the day" than the rest of the Speeds, but one can easily gloss over the easy acceptance of slavery by the family. They justified their comfortable life in several ways. It was familiar, of course, and something of a family myth that life at Farmington was notably less violent than in the areas further south that were newly developing to take advantage of the huge rise in cotton prices after the 1820s; the system that produced that wealth was far away, which insulated the Speeds from it psychologically, even though their rising wealth came from the hemp they grew, which was used to produce the rope that wrapped those ever-increasing bales of cotton produced on the plantations that stretched from Louisiana to Georgia. We can't be absolutely sure, but it is probably the case that neither Joshua nor James were personally capable of whipping anyone for anything (or directing an overseer to carry out beatings), though throughout the 1840s and 1850s Joshua especially leased slaves out for hire and could not know how they were treated by others. They did assume the inferiority of blacks, which they seemed to feel at this point and until much later justified their enslavement. Joshua wrote his brother as late as September 1865 of the politics of enforcing the Emancipation Proclamation: "We who know & feel the deeper prejudices against this race, [know] how incompetent they are to protect themselves from gross injustice and imposition." The brothers nourished a kind and protective but ultimately condescending attitude toward blacks.[25]

✳ ✳ ✳

Then there was Fanny Henning, who captured the heart of Joshua Speed. As Lincoln wrote to Mary Speed, Fanny was "one of the sweetest girls in the world." There was nothing about her, he continued, "that I would have otherwise than as it is." His only concern is her "tendency to melancholy," though he adds immediately, "This, let it be observed, is a misfortune not a fault." So Fanny joined the magic circle of depressed friends. It was hardly something Lincoln held against her. He is clearly fond of Fanny and feels she is wonderful for his best friend. Her melancholy, which he must have immediately spotted, is her misfortune. The mistake, he advises Speed, would be to blame her for her depression. In contemporary terms, the advice is not to confuse the girl for the symptom.[26]

Beautiful Fanny Henning with those "heavenly *black eyes*," as Lincoln put it later in a letter to Speed, was a scion of the Henning family that came to Kentucky from Virginia at the beginning of the nineteenth century. Her father, Samuel Henning, after his first wife's death in 1810, married Elizabeth Williamson, whose brother John owned a large tract of land in Jefferson County east of Goose Creek. Samuel Henning bought some of his brother-in-law's land after his marriage, and it would appear that is where Fanny was born on September 12, 1820. She attended the Science Hill Female Academy in Shelbyville, Kentucky, as did her sister, but at twenty-one years of age, in the summer of 1841, she was long since finished with her education.[27]

There are conflicting accounts of where Speed met and courted Fanny. The lawyer who probated Fanny's will in 1902 wrote that they met in the Louisville home of Fanny's brother, James W. Henning, who later became Speed's business partner. In a letter Lincoln wrote a few months later, he reminds Speed how they made not one but two trips to Lexington, Kentucky—some seventy-five miles away— specifically for the purpose of visiting Fanny (though he doesn't explain why or for how long she was in Lexington). Peyton Hoge in the local Louisville paper in 1938 and Robert L. Kincaid in a more scholarly article a few years later (though without footnotes) spun a more exotic tale. Fanny was staying with an uncle, John Williamson, on his home not far from Farmington. Lincoln accompanied Joshua on his visits to court Fanny, but this uncle John was too much in the way. Lincoln therefore took it upon himself to distract John's attention by engaging him in a lively conversation about politics. Lincoln pretended to be a Democrat, knowing that Williamson was a staunch Whig and could be led easily into an intense argument. Williamson forgot all about his niece, whom Speed proposed to on that very night. Fanny Henning warmly accepted, and she and Joshua Speed were formally engaged.[28]

9

HOMEWARD BOUND

Though there is no certain path to healing depression, and one is always subject to renewal of the suffering, Lincoln was getting better, and he knew it. Lincoln wrote Speed early in 1842, "I have been quite clear of the hypo . . . even better than I was in the fall." Lincoln's visit to Farmington set him on a path toward recovery. The relaxed family setting at Farmington with Speed's loving and nurturing mother and Joshua's friendly siblings all helped improve Lincoln's state of mind. What mattered most of all, however, was the presence of Speed himself. Besides their daily interactions, long walks, and the opportunity simply again to be at his side, Lincoln's presence coincided with Speed falling in love. Speed had found his soulmate in young Fanny Henning, just twenty-one years old. Although Speed got engaged just before Lincoln was scheduled to leave Farmington, the two men decided they couldn't separate again immediately. There is no direct documentary evidence of their conversation or of the basis for Speed's decision to return to Springfield with Lincoln. One has to infer his motivation, but some very good hints about it arise from his behavior and from a careful reading of some critical sources.[1]

There was much to keep Speed in Louisville. It was home and where his large and extended family lived. That loving family drew Speed to it, and now that his father, John, was no longer alive nothing stood between his natural inclinations to be close to his mother, siblings, and in-laws. Second, if not more significantly, Speed was engaged to Fanny Henning. Speed could, of course, marry and take Fanny back to Springfield, something he may have considered, though this devout and upright young woman seemed tethered to Louisville. Speed also immediately connected with his future brother-in-law, James W. Henning, and, as was his wont, may have even already begun business deals with him in Louisville while he continued to keep tabs on his remaining investments in Springfield. Finally, Speed was settling down in Louisville, perhaps more than he consciously realized. It was a year since he had begun to wind down his business affairs in Springfield and nine months since he had sold his inventory and turned things largely over to Hurst. Speed's personal identification with Springfield was clearly fading. Seven months earlier he had expressed doubts to his sister about the wisdom of leaving Springfield but then never acted on those doubts. And the trip back to Springfield that he wrote about to Mary Todd in June almost certainly never happened.[2]

It seems obvious that as the lure of Springfield faded and the reasons to stay in Louisville increased, Speed's need for and connection to Lincoln intensified. The sudden engagement itself during Lincoln's visit was the psychological byproduct of their renewed friendship. With Lincoln at his side, Speed gained the confidence and grounding to commit himself formally to marry Fanny. Then, as had happened to Lincoln, Speed was soon filled with doubts, confusions, even despair. He got sick, miserably sick, with Lincoln's affliction. Speed's family was vocal in their "uneasiness about Joshua's health," presumably wanting him to delay his departure. But Speed pushed on to be reunited with his friend, despite what Lincoln ambiguously called Speed's "little disposition." Indeed, it "turned out to be nothing serious" and was "pretty nearly forgotten" by the time they reached Springfield. Since Speed later told Herndon specifically that he got depressed after his engagement, his "little disposition" on the trip with Lincoln could well have been emotional rather than physical: he got better because he was back in close communion with his friend. Speed's crisis paralleled Lincoln's turmoil after his engagement to Mary Todd a little less than a year earlier, though apparently not quite as severe (it was "something of the same feeling"). Speed, of course, had borrowed support from Lincoln earlier, when he took Lincoln with him to court Fanny on two long trips to Lexington and then to help him propose by distracting Fanny's uncle, John Williamson, while he visited with her in another part of the house. Speed, as Lincoln had done with Mary, needed his friend by his side before reaching out to love a woman. That moment of engagement, however, with its fearsome prospect of intimacy with a woman that *simultaneously* meant the loss of Lincoln, threw Speed into a panic that he likened to his friend's suicidal depression the previous January.[3]

Not surprisingly, Speed therefore dreaded Lincoln's return to Springfield after what was, for the times, a relatively short visit of twenty-one days. Everything had happened too quickly. Lincoln had arrived to his great pleasure, and he and his family threw themselves into welcoming him and resuming their friendship. Then Speed caught the eye of Fanny Henning and in a matter of days proposed to her—and then promptly got confused and depressed. It is imaginable that Speed knew Fanny Henning before Lincoln arrived and might have socialized and even flirted with her, but he is clear in what he wrote Herndon that he only "courted" Fanny after Lincoln arrived. The two events in Speed's life—Lincoln's arrival and his engagement to Fanny—got compressed both in time and in psychological space. Speed now needed Lincoln to help soothe him, just as Speed himself had played that role for Lincoln in the past. Lincoln, of course, himself still only on the road to recovery, was glad to have Speed at his side. Moreover, Lincoln, to an extent greater than Speed, nourished the fantasy that Speed and Fanny would marry and make Springfield their home ("I regret to learn that you have resolved not to return to Illinois," Lincoln wrote Speed a few months later). In the meantime, Lincoln tended his friend, an example of mutuality that took him out of his own self-absorption and had the added advantage of soothing himself. They decided to return together to Springfield.[4]

* * *

On Tuesday, September 7, at noon, Lincoln and Speed boarded the steamboat *Lebanon* in the locks of Louisville's port on the Ohio River for their trip. The Ohio River was the major transportation artery for moving goods—and slaves—from east to west and eventually south. The Ohio River moves westward from Pittsburgh and soon forms the eastern and southern borders of Ohio, thus marking the northern boundary of Kentucky as the river moves southwest, along the way marking the boundary of Indiana and Illinois as it flows toward Cairo at the southern tip of Illinois. At that point it becomes the major contributory to the Mississippi River, which of course flows directly to New Orleans. That bustling city, with its major port on the Gulf of Mexico, was the most important contemporary center in the country for the sale and trading of slaves. Its open markets and frenetic activity were legendary. Many African Americans being sold in these markets were undoubtedly local, and some were perhaps smuggled in from the Caribbean, given the immense and increasing value of slaves, but most of those on the block in New Orleans had been brought there from the upper south, especially from states like Virginia and Kentucky, by the water route.[5]

Not unexpectedly, Lincoln encountered just such a cargo on the *Lebanon*. As he wrote Mary Speed on September 27—his letter to her is the earliest surviving document of Lincoln's direct impressions of slavery—he saw on board the steamboat a "gentleman" (Lincoln says sarcastically) who had purchased "twelve negroes in different parts of Kentucky" and was transporting them to a "farm" in the South. The scene is thus of a slave trader, generally a reviled figure, who had traveled throughout Kentucky to buy the slaves. He then boarded the *Lebanon* along with the regular passengers to transport the slaves, undoubtedly to New Orleans, where he would be able to sell them for a handsome profit. Lincoln softens the scene in its telling from the very beginning by referring to the trader as a "gentleman" and the brutal plantation where he knows the slaves will end up as a "farm." Lincoln is writing his friend Mary Speed a kind of thank-you note for his stay at Farmington. He adopts these euphemisms as part of the discourse that he knows fits the mask of gentility around the issue of slavery worn by most Kentuckians.[6]

The scene of the twelve slaves on board the *Lebanon* startled Lincoln. As he tells Mary, the slaves were chained "six and six together." Attached to the left wrist of each slave was a small iron clevis that was in turn fastened to a main chain by a shorter link of chain, "so that the negroes were strung together precisely like so many fish upon a trot-line." In this dreadful state, "separated forever from the scenes of their childhood, their friends, their fathers and mothers, and brothers and sisters, and many of them, from their wives and children," they were being sent into "perpetual slavery where the lash of the master is proverbially more ruthless and unrelenting than any other where." The scene as Lincoln narrates it deliberately distinguishes the relatively good life for slaves in Kentucky, where they live with friends and fathers and mothers and brothers and sisters and wives and children, from the deep South, with its "perpetual slavery," "the lash of the master," and its "ruthless and unrelenting" system.

Here Lincoln was trying not to offend his good friend and recent hostess by setting up this image of a dreadful and cruel form of slavery in the deep South, which implicitly affirms the myth of a more humane slavery in Kentucky. In fact, as he knew well from both personal experience and his reading, slavery in places like Kentucky was as brutal as it was anywhere. Slaves were worked mercilessly, fed inadequately, whipped on the plantations and at special posts in towns if they dared to appear on the street after 7:00 pm, and ripped from families if it proved profitable to sell them. In fact, many whites in Kentucky in this period were getting rich by deliberately breeding slaves like cattle, then breaking up families and selling the prime hands to dealers—like the one aboard the *Lebanon*—who then transported them to New Orleans for the larger market. It was a convenient part of the myth to vilify the slave traders, as Lincoln does in his letter to Mary Speed, though of course the dealers were merely serving to keep the market functioning, which met the economic needs of slave owners. By the 1850s, Kentucky was annually exporting between 2,500 and four thousand of its slaves for sale in New Orleans. To prevent runaways, as a poignant historical marker in Louisville notes, "traders operating near the Ohio River kept slaves shackled together in pens when not being displayed to buyers."[7]

The point of the story about the slaves on board the *Lebanon*, however, was not simply to provide Lincoln an opportunity to spin a tale for Mary about slaves on transport to New Orleans. She was familiar with that. On the contrary, Lincoln's purpose was to draw a lesson from a scene that was of great personal meaning for him, one that he could share with Mary and expect her to grasp. For he adds to his description that "amid all these distressing circumstances" this group of slaves were the "most cheerful and apparently happy creatures on board." One man who had been sold because of an "over-fondness for his wife"—suggesting Lincoln talked directly with the slaves to inquire about their experience and feelings—"played the fiddle almost continually." Others "danced, sung, cracked jokes, and played various games with cards from day to day." How true it is, he says portentously, that "God tempers the wind to the shorn lamb." This well-known saying, which is not biblical but from Laurence Sterne's 1768 novel *A Sentimental Journey*, means that God treats the weak with greater kindness than those better able to care for themselves. Lincoln's explanation of the quote to Mary, however, tellingly just misses the mark. He says: "He [God] renders the worst of human conditions tolerable, while He permits the best, to be nothing better than tolerable." The first part is an accurate interpretation of the saying. The second part of Lincoln's sentence, however, is more a projection of his miserable state. The slaves on the *Lebanon* somehow turned the tragedy of their condition into a bearable experience. Lincoln, however, who has so much to be thankful for cannot but feel miserable. The wind beats down on his shorn back.

Lincoln thus turns the condition of the slaves on board the *Lebanon* into a parable about his own suffering. Those who were truly oppressed were playing the fiddle, singing and dancing, and cracking jokes. He is privileged but unable to be happy. He does feel their suffering and is appalled at their condition, but he is greatly impressed at their seeming ability to transcend their fate and enjoy some song and dance in the moment. Lincoln, for all his freedom and security, mopes. In this, he appropriates the scene to serve his own psychological needs. There may perhaps be another theme embedded in Lincoln's story of the condition of the slaves on board the Lebanon, as well. The key is the central image of the twelve slaves strung up on the chain "like so many fish upon a trot-line." That image accurately reflects the reality that slaves were property. It is even possible Lincoln was subtly criticizing Mary with this metaphor, which turns the people he is looking at into so many caught fish flopping about as they hang, dying, on a string.

* * *

Lincoln was consistently antislavery. He said in 1864: "If slavery is not wrong, nothing is wrong. I can not remember when I did not so think, and feel." That statement, made over a year after issuing the Emancipation Proclamation and in the context of building political support for racial equality in America, to which he was then committed, may gloss over his ambivalence about race as it inevitably related to slavery. He said in a debate with Douglas in 1858:

> I am not, nor ever have been in favor of bringing about in any way the social and political equality of the white and black races,—that I am not nor ever have been in the favor of making voters or jurors of negroes, nor of qualifying them to hold office, nor to intermarry with white people; and I will say in addition to this that there is a physical difference between the white and black races which I believe will for ever forbid the two races living together on terms of social and political equality. And inasmuch as they cannot so live, while they do remain together there must be the position of superior and inferior, and I as much as any other man am in favor of having the superior position assigned to the white race. . . . I do not understand that because I do not want a negro woman for a slave I must necessarily want her for a wife. My understanding is that I can just let her alone.[8]

Until the war he had trouble imagining racial equality, even as he disliked, even detested, slavery itself. What young man Lincoln most hoped for was to see slavery simply disappear. In a speech he gave on temperance in 1842, he ended with a vision of a time when there would be "neither a slave nor a drunkard on the earth." Around the same time Lincoln wrote a colleague that he wished slavery would die "a natural death," which he believed should be the logical fate of something he believed was intrinsically evil.[9]

The increasing political ferment over slavery in the 1830s, including the beginnings of the abolition movement, which led to a number of riots, posed challenges for young Lincoln. The first time he had to grapple formally and politically with the issue of slavery came in the legislature a month before he moved to Springfield in 1837.[10]

Abolitionists, although comprising only a tiny minority of voters and an even smaller number of nonvoting female supporters, were effectively drawing attention to the cruelty and essential evil of slavery. Most of those in state legislatures wanted the issue to go away, but while they detested the abolitionists, they wanted slavery dealt with, if at all, at the state level. The various states' concerted move to stifle abolitionists began after March 16, 1836, when John Calhoun, the high-strung firebrand senator from South Carolina who considered slavery a positive good, stormed out of the Senate when a petition was presented to end slavery in the District of Columbia. After Calhoun's protest, the Senate adopted a gag rule forbidding the presentation of petitions about slavery, and a number of states both in the North and South passed resolutions going on record condemning abolitionist agitation and declaring slavery to be none of the federal government's business.

Illinois received these resolutions in its 1837 session, and in its debate nearly every legislator voted in agreement. Not Lincoln. Along with only one colleague, Dan Stone, Lincoln made five attempts to amend the original harsh condemnation of abolitionists. After failing to amend the resolution that passed the legislature, Lincoln and Stone filed a protest in March 1837, which they handed to the clerk just before adjournment, taking advantage of a rarely used parliamentary loophole. That way there was no debate on or changes made to the statement, but it was duly filed and therefore formally noted. That protest, undoubtedly written by Lincoln, allowed him to go on record about slavery and abolition in carefully crafted terms that he felt could be useful in the future. His statement dances away from the extreme abolitionist position of people like William Lloyd Garrison toward a complicated middle ground, one that in fact increasingly characterized the position of many at the time who detested slavery and sought ways to limit it and eventually put it on a road to abolition. Lincoln thus condemns the evils of slavery, which is "founded on injustice and bad policy," but equally criticizes abolition doctrine that "tends rather to increase than to abate its evils." Lincoln concedes that Congress has no power to "interfere with the institution of slavery in the different states," but he makes one exception: the District of Columbia. There Congress could regulate or abolish slavery.

Abolishing slavery in the District of Columbia remained a key goal for Lincoln, who favored gradual emancipation and specific and narrow action. Of three proposals considered viable by those opposing slavery—repealing or modifying the fugitive slave laws, prohibiting slavery in the territories, and abolishing slavery in the District of Columbia—Lincoln took a public stand only on the last. It was the most conservative action of the three viable political approaches to ending slavery, but it became one he never backed away from. When Lincoln was in Congress in the late 1840s, he drafted a bill to do exactly that. However, lacking support from *any* colleagues, the freshman congressman ultimately did not file his draft. In the 1840s, Lincoln was not a spokesman for prohibiting slavery in the territories nor of slaves being "men" under the Declaration of Independence's truth that "all men are created equal." After 1854, however, in the words of James Oakes, "Lincoln came out of semiretirement and redefined himself as an antislavery politician."[11]

* * *

For someone not directly involved with slavery as he grew up, Lincoln actually knew quite a lot about it and had had a good deal of personal experience with blacks. The Kentucky into which he was born had about 20 percent of its population as slaves. In Hardin County, near his actual birthplace and where he spent the first seven years of his life, there were 7,500 whites and some one thousand slaves in 1811. On the road from Louisville to Nashville, as Foner puts it, "settlers, peddlers, and groups of shackled slaves regularly passed." Thomas Lincoln left Kentucky over disputed land titles, but he also disliked slavery and wanted to settle in the free state of Indiana. That meant Lincoln in his adolescence seldom had any encounters with slavery, but it may be that his relation to his father influenced his evolving attitudes toward the institution.[12]

A curious indirect experience Lincoln had with slavery as a child occurred in his reading. John Locke Scripps wrote an approved campaign biography of Lincoln in 1860 (*Life of Abraham Lincoln: The Only Biography of Himself That Abraham Lincoln Ever Authorized, Revised, and Endorsed*) in which he includes among the books that most influenced Lincoln one by James Riley, *An Authentic Narrative of the Loss of the American Brig* Commerce. Riley, the captain of a ship that crashed off the west coast of Africa, was taken into slavery by some Arabs who sought to make money by selling him and his crew in Morocco.

Riley describes in great and evocative detail the harrowing trip across the Sahara Desert, starved for food (in a few months he went from between 230 and 240 pounds to ninety pounds), forced to drink camel urine and eat the boiled blood of slaughtered camels to survive, and he also tells of the beatings and whippings he suffered at the hands of his owners. It would be hard for anyone reading the book in America after it was published in 1817 not to connect Riley's dramatic experiences with the institution that was in front of their noses.[13]

One reasonably well-documented, almost always overlooked, yet early encounter Lincoln had with slavery and blacks was when he worked on the locks in Louisville building the canal. A. H. Chapman, a relative from Kentucky, wrote Herndon that "In the year 1827 A Lincoln & his Step Brother John D Johnston went together to Louisvill Ky to try & get work & earn some money, thy obtained work on their arrivall there on the Louisville & Portland Canall." It was lucrative work for the eighteen-year-old Lincoln. The pay for skilled labor was at least thirteen dollars a month, along with free food and luxuries like coffee, sugar, whiskey (for those who wanted it), and lodging in a company shanty. Lincoln and Johnston, as Chapman notes, "when through working there were paid off in silver Dollars. This is the first silver dollar Lincoln ever had or owned of his own & of it he was very proud." In 1827, while he was working there with his stepbrother, for want of other help and to meet the crushing deadline of completion of the locks by November 1, 1827, the project turned to hiring slave labor from local white masters at ten dollars a month. As usual in such arrangements, none of the money went to the slaves themselves (unless there was an unusual, and unrecorded, special arrangement between a master and his slave). Although Lincoln would not have shared living quarters with the slaves or taken his meals with them and probably didn't actually dig alongside them, it was in the nature of the tasks at hand—poling the waters of the canal, moving barges, hammering nails, cutting boards, and moving construction items— that he worked nearby the slaves and with them on this huge project.[14]

In contrast to that cooperative endeavor in Kentucky, Lincoln's most direct and important early encounter with blacks and slavery, including its loathsome trade, came in the two flatboat trips he took to New Orleans as a young man. The first was in 1828, when he was nineteen years of age, and the second three years later, just after he

left home and before he landed back in New Salem. It was not uncommon for those living near the Ohio River, or indeed along any of the
many tributaries of the Mississippi, to transport their goods to New
Orleans. Thomas Lincoln himself took at least one journey down the
Mississippi on a flatboat, though in his usual ill-fated way he never
came back with any money after selling his goods in New Orleans and
returning on foot to Indiana. Lincoln's trips, long ensconced in legend, have been recently described in a masterful monograph by Richard Campanella, *Lincoln in New Orleans: The 1828–1831 Flatboat Voyages
and Their Place in History*. The details of building the flatboats and the
difficulties in navigating the river systems, first in Kentucky and then
in Illinois on the way to the Mississippi, capture a wonderful era of
travel that was quickly overtaken and wholly replaced by railroads.[15]

It appears from a number of sources that Lincoln was deeply
affected by what he witnessed on his flatboat trips to New Orleans,
though he was curiously cryptic. In his 1860 autobiography he tells a
number of stories about his voyages, but the only consequential one
was his description of being attacked by some blacks during his first
trip. While at rest and tied to the shore at night, they were attacked
by "seven negroes with intent to kill and rob them." In the fight that
ensued, he and his companions were hurt but able to fend off the
attackers, cut the cable, raise the anchor, and escape. The blacks were
English-speaking runaway slaves, and the site of the attack was near a
convent and girl's school some sixty river miles north of New Orleans,
details filled in by Campanella. Lincoln avoided saying anything more
about his experiences in New Orleans in what was, after all, a campaign document. It would not have been politic, for example, to discuss his disgust at the slave trade he witnessed in New Orleans, as that
might have put him in the camp of the abolitionists, something he was
studiously trying to avoid in the election.[16]

After both flatboat trips Lincoln seemed to have spent a couple of
weeks in New Orleans before setting off for home. The city brimmed
with activity, especially the sale of slaves. It was always busy, but
spring was the peak of the commercial season. Lincoln undoubtedly
saw slaves everywhere in all kinds of situations and must have visited
Hewlett's Exchange, which was the busiest slave mart in New Orleans.
There he witnessed what Campanella calls the "degrading banalities"
of the slave trade that so appalled most foreign visitors to the city. It

seemed to have a powerful impact on Lincoln. He later wrote Alexander Stephens of the "slavery and slave market" that he saw there, "as I have never seen them in Kentucky." John Hanks told Herndon that Lincoln saw slaves chained, beaten, and maltreated ("whipt & scourged"), and his "heart bled." He determined to "hit it hard," a line that is hard to evaluate, given its post–Civil War context. Hanks's account is often dismissed because he wasn't in New Orleans with Lincoln, having left the boat in St. Louis, which Lincoln notes parenthetically in his autobiography. But Hanks adds, "I have heard him say [his feelings about slavery from his experiences in New Orleans]—often & often—," suggesting that Hanks heard Lincoln talk later about his experiences, and his feelings about slavery, from his trip, even though Hanks was not actually in the city with him.[17]

Lincoln also encountered quite a number of blacks and even an occasional slave during his early days in Springfield. Billy the Barber is well known, but there was also Hepsey, an orphaned mulatto woman, who was an indentured servant in the home of Ninian and Elizabeth Edwards between 1835 and 1842; James Bell (Speed's uncle) listed a female slave in his possession in the 1840 census; a woman in Mary Todd Lincoln's church was disciplined for using excessive force in whipping her black servant in 1843; and William Butler employed a number of free blacks as servants. Richard Hart, who did the research into this history, estimates there were some twenty-six African Americans in Springfield and the occasional slave until 1848, when the new state constitution specifically banned slavery in Illinois.[18]

Lincoln also dealt with an important slavery case in his practice. A female slave named Nance Legins-Costley (called only "Nance" in the various court cases in which she figured) sued for her freedom several times in Illinois after 1827, consistently losing, until on appeal in the summer of 1841 Lincoln argued before the Supreme Court, meeting in Springfield, that slavery is a status to be proved and that there was a presumption in the state of Illinois that everyone is free. The case lacks moral luster because Lincoln chose to come at it indirectly and only in support of David Bailey's unpaid promissory note for the purchase of Nance; furthermore, some six years later, Lincoln defended a white man, Robert Matson, who sought to recover a runaway slave. Still, in July 1841, just before departing for Farmington, Lincoln argued successfully in court to grant freedom to a black woman. He probably didn't talk much about the case over dinner with the Speeds in Kentucky.[19]

* * *

The *Lebanon*, carrying Lincoln and Speed, arrived in St. Louis on Monday, September 13, at 8:00 pm. They then set off the next day for the two-day stagecoach trip to Springfield, arriving in the late afternoon of September 15. One wonders where the two friends lived that fall. Unfortunately, there is no documentary evidence, no allusion in a letter, and no context to suggest where they stayed. One can only make some educated guesses. One good possibility is they simply returned to the bed in Speed's old store. Charles Hurst, after all, Speed's old clerk doubtless buying on credit, still did not own the inventory or even the store outright. It is entirely possible that Speed reasonably felt some continued ownership of the store and, since he needed temporary quarters, settled back in with Lincoln and continued to take their main meal with the Butlers. It is also possible that Lincoln went to the Butlers, where he had lived from January until his trip to Farmington, and Speed lived in the store. There is good evidence that a year later, up to his marriage in November 1842, Lincoln was living with Butler. Assuming Lincoln and Speed were sleeping in different quarters, they would have been together for their main meal socializing with the Butlers. The least likely possibility is that they lived together at the Butler home. That would have put Speed in overly close and probably uncomfortable proximity to Sarah Rickard in the immediate wake of his engagement to Fanny Henning.[20]

Lincoln experienced some indisposition of his own. A toothache that was treated unsuccessfully in Louisville was "cured" in Illinois by a dentist who Lincoln colorfully says pulled out "a bit of the jawbone" with it. Otherwise, he picked up his law practice with vigor that fall. The very next day after returning to Springfield he went out on the circuit, spending much of his time until mid-November handling cases all over central Illinois. In those days he seldom stayed more than a few days at a time away from home, but the cumulative effect of his busy law practice meant that he was often out of town. Of course, just because Lincoln might try a case in Charleston, for example, as he did on October 25, doesn't preclude the possibility that Speed went with him. Speed had little else to do, and it is well documented that he sometimes traveled with Lincoln on the circuit. Furthermore, Speed seemed to know a lot about Lincoln's law practice, which he wrote his sister was "eminently successful" these days and Lincoln himself in "fine spirits and good health."[21]

Politics played a less important role for Lincoln in this period. After his frantic efforts to win the state for Harrison in 1840 ended ingloriously, Lincoln decided for the moment to exert his influence among Whigs more quietly. Speed joined in those efforts. On October 20, the two, along with Anson G. Henry, Edward Baker, and William May—all members of the "central committee" of the Whig party— issued a call in the *Sangamo Journal* for a "convention" of the party in Illinois to meet on the "third Monday of December next" (December 20) to nominate candidates for governor and lieutenant governor for the upcoming election. There was much politicking going on behind the scenes. It is a mark of Lincoln's stature that his was among those names being bandied about to be nominated as governor. He was not interested, however, though he also may have read the tea leaves after an editorial in the *Sangamo Journal* on October 29 endorsed Joseph Duncan. He announced in the paper on November 12 that he declined to be a candidate. In tandem with his decision not to run again for the legislature and now his lack of interest in executive office, Lincoln was not signaling a lack of interest in office per se. Within himself, he was intent upon national office: he was going to run for Congress. For the moment, however, Lincoln's statement of noninterest in running cleared the way for the unanimous selection of Joseph Duncan as the Whig candidate for governor, and in fact the convention was called off on December 13.[22]

* * *

Speed, meanwhile, seemed to play something of a role supporting a local effort to try to convince Illinois farmers to grow hemp. At least it seems hardly likely that local enthusiasts for hemp would not consult someone as intimately familiar with growing the crop as Speed. In the *Sangamo Journal* on October 15, beneath the screaming headline "Hemp! Hemp! Hemp!" a letter addressed "To the Farmers of Sangamon County" extolled the crop's virtues. In light of the "present low prices of our staple articles" and the "depressed condition" of farming in general, the signers of the letter strongly urge the cultivation of hemp. The Illinois soil and weather seem ideal. It could be very lucrative for all concerned. Early the next year the *Sangamo Journal* ran a story about an article in the *Louisville Journal* reporting on a Navy contract to buy up water-rotted hemp at three hundred dollars a ton. In a larger sense, wheat tied farmers in central Illinois to Chicago and the Northeast; hemp would have connected them deeply with the cotton South. That was not in the cards for central Illinois by the 1840s. To the extent Speed was involved in this hemp-farming project, it was largely quixotic.[23]

Speed stands in the shadows of this aggressive hemp campaign; he also follows Lincoln's custom of writing and lobbying Simeon Francis, the editor of the *Sangamo Journal*. Speed was a man always on the lookout for a good business deal, and perhaps he saw some wise investments to be made in growing hemp in Illinois. It is possible, though a stretch, to imagine he even thought of getting rich in Illinois rather than returning to Louisville, a prospect for his life that would have kept him close to Lincoln. Such a decision, however, at this point would have meant bringing his future wife to Springfield, which had all kinds of things to argue against it, including his attachment to his family and nascent business interests with his prospective brother-in-law, not to mention what seemed to be her firmly placed self in Louisville.

Fanny was at the center of Speed's thoughts this fall, and he curiously believed that his sentiment for her was a great secret between him and Lincoln. Speed thus wrote his sister Mary on October 31 in a humorous way that "There are three subjects Love, Religion, and Politicks upon which any man of common sense bestows a good deal of thought at some time of his life—" Politics he has abandoned as a "mean and beggarly business." Religion he "never had." But love, "gracious heavens!" He is "completely filled" and "thoroughly changed" with "delicate and refined sentiment, high hopes, and firm resolves." He is quite exuberant. "I am something like the rich fruit of the tropicks—that bursts its vine because of its richness and luxuriance," or "like a tea [pot] that is lifting its top and losing its contents by the constant boiling," or like a "china pitcher filled with ice water and oozing through the glass—and standing on the outside of the vesil [*sic*] in heavy drops like perspiration upon the brow of a laborer in a harvest field." Thus, he says, "is your poor and unfortunate brother again changed with love." That "again" suggests he has experienced the infatuation of love before, which he confirms in the next sentence: "You perhaps are anxious to know who now is the object of my admiration unless you conclude it is all a lie as usual that it will finally blow off and amount to nothing." And he adds: "Let time determine that and suspend your judgment till next spring—," that is, when he is planning his marriage. The supposed suspense is despite Lincoln's letter to Mary a little over a month earlier, in which he wonders if she has now met Fanny and found her as wonderful as he and "one of the sweetest girls in the world," clearly indicating that Lincoln talked with Mary about Fanny. Speed concludes his letter to Mary by mentioning that "Lincoln told me that he wrote to you from Bloomington and requested you to write him at Charleston—he was disappointed in not getting a letter from you there."[24]

The contradictions abound. Lincoln knew all about Fanny and shared his thoughts about her with Mary Speed. Joshua, however, must not have told his sister about his engagement with Fanny, apparently wanting for the moment to keep his engagement a secret between him and his beloved—and with Lincoln. Amazingly enough, Lincoln and Speed didn't have a conversation about what Mary Speed knew. That is odd, but both were busy, and Lincoln might well have assumed Mary knew about Fanny without bothering to talk about it with Speed. What is most important, however, is that Speed clearly wanted only Lincoln to know of his love for Fanny and to keep knowledge of his approaching marriage even from Mary, his favorite sister. It was indeed a great secret between Lincoln and Speed that fall, more even than Lincoln knew. Speed wanted to keep Fanny in fantasy for the moment as he clung tenaciously to the presence of Lincoln, whom he would soon lose again, this time for good.

***

An important date was approaching: the anniversary of the "fatal first." It was a weighty moment for Lincoln. The first anniversary of the date he had been scheduled to be married was something guaranteed to revive his intense sense of loss and the confusion. A year before, as 1840 came to an end, the imminent separation from Speed threw him into panic that in turn led him to act in contradictory and ultimately self-defeating ways with Mary Todd. He broke up with her against his better judgment, then felt remorseful and guilty at the pain he caused her. He might well have committed suicide in the aftermath but for the intervention of close friends and the continued support of Speed. Of all his confused feelings at that time, what he was perhaps least clear about—or even consciously aware of—was the significance of the loss of his intimate connection with Speed, a loss that precipitated his broken engagement. The trauma surrounding the events in 1841 threatened to flood him as the anniversary approached. He also faced, once again, the loss of Speed in 1842.

First anniversaries of loss are generally important dates. For individuals and cultures, first anniversaries of deaths, catastrophes, and other traumas have special significance. It is not that one works things through completely after that or that painful memories of momentous loss will not persist for many years after an important event. In certain kinds of traumatic experience around loss, the sadness never ends. But more commonly it ebbs and flows, not linearly but in a circular pattern of returning emotions that gradually move toward working through. Lincoln did eventually recover from the death of Ann Rutledge, just as he got out of his bed in late January 1841 and resumed his work and some of his friendships. But he remained uncertain, tentative about his future, and withdrawn from social life. The experience of renewal with Speed in Farmington and then having him by his side in the fall proved important. Now he needed another favor from his friend, a favor he may not have consciously understood: he needed to see Speed up to the point of the anniversary of the "fatal first" before dispatching him to go marry Fanny Henning.[25]

10

A VICARIOUS ROMANCE

He allways thanked Josh for his Mary.

—Abner Y. Ellis

As 1841 ended, the time at last came for Speed to leave Lincoln in Springfield and return to Kentucky. Speed was eager to marry Fanny Henning and settle for good in his home state. But there was a serious problem. As he explicitly told Herndon, Speed was troubled and anxious about his upcoming marriage in many of the same ways Lincoln had been a year earlier about his engagement with Mary Todd. Speed was filled with self-doubts over his love for Fanny and, it seems, about the sexual consummation of that love.[1]

Lincoln could readily identify with such paralyzing uncertainties and took the guileless step of pressing into Speed's hands a long letter that, together with four more he wrote and posted in February, were the most revealing psychological documents Lincoln ever penned. This most interior of men, "shut-mouthed," as Herndon called him, bared his deepest feelings to his best friend. Speed's real feelings and what he shared with Lincoln from Kentucky have to be inferred, since his letters to Lincoln have not survived, but it is reasonable to guess that Speed was equally open and expressive as Lincoln; in the context of what Lincoln wrote one can also make some very good guesses about much of what Speed wrote.

These Lincoln letters are not newly available, nor have they been ignored by scholars. Lincoln's letters to Speed were published first by Nicolay and Hay in 1894 in their *Complete Works of Abraham Lincoln*, after Speed had earlier made them available for publication. They were then included in a number of collections of Lincoln's writings after that; read and commented on by all of Lincoln's biographers from Herndon, to Albert J. Beveridge, to Carl Sandburg, to Benjamin Thomas, and to more contemporary writers such as David Donald and Douglas Wilson; and of course included in Roy Basler's authoritative version of the *Collected Works*, the first volume of which, published in 1953, included the letters. The issue with the letters to Speed, in other words, has never been their availability. It has been much more in the difficulty in reading them.

***

Lincoln wrote the undated first letter in late December when he and Speed were together, if not a few yards apart, then gave it to him as they parted on January 1, 1842. This first letter from Lincoln to Speed in early 1842 lacks a postmark or a date, which means that Lincoln handed it directly to Speed. It is quite clear from the context of the first paragraph that Speed would not have known of the letter before he opened it after he left town. Lincoln therefore wrote the letter in late December. Roy Basler assigns the letter a date of January 3 (though with a question mark after it), which follows the date given it by Nicolay and Hay in 1894. In choosing to follow Nicolay and Hay, Basler argues in a footnote that they were "presumably" given that date by Speed himself, though there is no evidence for this assertion. In fact, there is contrary evidence from Speed himself, who told Herndon in 1866 that he remained in Springfield "till the 1st of Jany 1842."[2]

It is a curious scenario: Lincoln writing an intense letter full of feeling to his friend while with him, even perhaps in the same room, without telling him what was occupying his thoughts, secretly stashing it away (in his top hat?) until just before Speed got into the stagecoach to leave town. It is telling that Lincoln kept the knowledge of writing the letter a secret so that he could personally press it into the hands of his dear friend. The personal transmission of the letter thus lent it an additional meaning and was itself part of the significance of their friendship.

It was a decisive moment for both men. Speed was leaving Springfield and his best friend to return to Louisville for his scheduled wedding to Fanny Henning, something he both yearned for and dreaded. For Lincoln January 1, 1842, was the auspicious first anniversary of the trauma he had experienced on the "fatal first." That day and the events that had immediately preceded it brought much suffering into Lincoln's life. The first of January offered the danger of a repetition of the agonized courtship rupture but also (but less consciously) the hope that, through Speed's marriage to Fanny, Lincoln could heal his own despair.

The letter, fraught with these meanings, was itself a kind of talisman. In religious practice, a talisman is an object that possesses occult power. It has a special relationship with death and resurrection and magically links the bearer with such a divine connection. Both Lincoln and Speed were prone to be superstitious, and the letter, so tightly bound in the resurrected traumatic feelings about the fatal first, which, once again, reminded Lincoln of losing Speed (this time for good), was imbued with this talismanic quality. The letter magically opposes the loss of Speed by symbolically preserving what they both experienced as a mystical and eternal bond between them. The letter opens:

> Feeling, as you know I do, the deepest solicitude for the success of the enterprize you are engaged in, I adopt this as the last method I can invent to aid you, in case (which God forbid) you shall need any aid. I do not place what I am going to say on paper, because I can say it any better in that way than I could by word of mouth; but because, were I to say it orrally, before we part, most likely you would forget it at the verry time when it might do you some good. As I think it reasonable that you will feel verry badly some time between this and the final consummation of your purpose, it is intended that you shall read this just at such a time.

Lincoln personally hands Speed the letter "as the last method I can invent to aid you, in case (which God forbid) you shall need any aid." It is not that he can't say to Speed what he needs to hear in writing any better than "by word of mouth." The problem is that important spoken communications can be forgotten. "Were I to say it [what Speed needs to hear] orrally, before we part, most likely you would forget it at the verry time when it might do you some good." Lincoln expects Speed will feel "verry badly some time between this and the final consummation of your purpose [his marriage to Fanny]." At those precise moments, the letter "is intended that you shall read this just at such a time." For Speed, Lincoln lives still in those fraught words. For Lincoln, Speed remains in his psychological universe in the knowledge that when full of fear he will pull out the letter and pore over all Lincoln's tortured sentences.

Lincoln's anxiety about the approaching departure of Speed and what his marriage to Fanny possibly foretells comes through in some surprisingly awkward sentence structures. In the first and last sentences of the first paragraph, Lincoln begins with long dangling phrases and a lot of bad spelling ("Feeling, as you know I do, the deepest solicitude for the success of the enterprize you are engaged in" and "As I think it reasonable that you will feel verry badly some time between this and the final consummation of your purpose"). A formal letter, Lincoln argues, allows Speed to return to his words as a healing balm whenever doubt descends. The suggestion is that Lincoln expects Speed to keep the talisman on his person and probably read it repeatedly to ease his anxiety and to link the two men symbolically, binding them as one in a permanent mark of remembrance as marriage approaches, for one actually and the other vicariously.

Lincoln's special knowledge of Speed's feelings pervades the very fabric of this and the other four letters in February. "Feeling, as I know you do," begins the very first sentence of this first letter, and the second paragraph opens: "Why I say it is reasonable that you will feel verry badly." Lincoln inserts himself into Speed's self, which he experiences as an extension of his own. What Speed feels, Lincoln feels. What Speed knows, Lincoln knows. What Speed does, so does Lincoln. Such mirroring of self incorporates the other as an essential dimension of one's very being. The functions of the other become his own. One's arm blends into the beginning of the other. In that union the self is grounded.

Separation in such a psychological universe can be deeply troubling. It is the need for connection, a need that grows out of vulnerabilities in the self, that prompts such linkages in the first place. To sever that bond can throw one into despair. Lincoln knew that experience well, and Speed testified to some of the same anxieties before his marriage. Lincoln sought to soothe his friend from a distance and in the process hold himself together. Lincoln allowed himself to become so fully identified with Speed that he could feel as his own his friend's anxieties about the approaching marriage with Fanny. Lincoln was in and of what Speed felt. For the moment, that deep connection kept them united symbolically, as Lincoln projected himself into his friend's experience and as Speed held on to the talisman he had been given to ward off the evil eye of hopelessness.

Lincoln and Speed, thirty-two and twenty-seven years of age respectively in January 1842, were delayed in their quest for intimacy, and the delay made their struggles more intense and confusing. They were not star-struck adolescents sharing doubts about their first loves. Countless love poems, songs, and ballads have been written about the anxieties—and thrills—of budding young love. In a very broad sense, it is the appropriate developmental task of the young who have just entered history to find their way into meaningful and mutual love with someone else. Lincoln and Speed had stumbled on that path. Both were talented young men, one a rising star in law and politics, the other a shrewd businessman destined for a noted career. Each had a firm grip on reality, a grip that had been harshly tempered and tested. Each man understood his place in life and work. But in the domain of intimacy and love each man felt adrift. A confused heart throws everything into doubt. Lincoln especially was wobbly. No longer young, he suffered self-doubts about his capacity to connect with and marry a woman he loved. Speed had helped Lincoln through years of transition that avoided a resolution of his issues with intimacy. Years of living together, during which they came to share their most intimate feelings (feelings that Lincoln shared with no one else), brought them together as one, each an extension of the other. It was now the moment for Speed to serve as Lincoln's other in a vicarious romance that proved decisive.

Lincoln says in this first letter that he knows why Speed feels "verry badly." There are, he says, one "*general*" and "*three special*" causes, the naming of which he underlines to emphasize his certainty on the matter.

The general cause is, that you are *naturally of a nervous tempera-ment*; and this I say from what I have seen of you personally, and what you have told me concerning your mother at various times, and concerning your brother William at the time his wife died.

The first special cause is, *your exposure to bad weather* on your journey, which my experience clearly proves to be verry severe on defective nerves.

The second is, *the absence of all business and conversation of friends*, which might divert your mind, and give it occasional rest from that *intensity* of thought, which will some times wear the sweetest idea thread-bare and turn it to the bitterness of death.

The third is, the rapid and near approach of that crisis on which all your thoughts and feelings concentrate.

Lincoln begins with the general explanation for his friend's appar-ently paralyzing anxiety. It is because Speed is *"naturally of a nervous temperament,"* again underlined for emphasis. What Lincoln means in this context is Speed's biological predisposition to what we would now tend loosely to call neurotic anxiety or, in the parlance of contempo-rary psychiatry, an anxiety disorder in which someone experiences anxiety as a symptom of depression. Having diagnosed Speed, Lincoln adds immediately that he knows of its truth "from what I have seen of you personally" but also from what Speed has told him "concerning your mother at various times" and an obscure reference to something Speed told him about the emotional reaction of his brother William (born in 1817) to the death of his wife. To have a nervous tempera-ment meant in the nineteenth century that you carried something in your soul that was a given (in our discourse, something of biologi-cal origin), something that could be mitigated but never really cured, a kind of taint. Such was Lincoln's melancholy, as it was called, and Speed's nervous temperament. Cultural attitudes, however, dictated that many factors in one's background and experience could aggravate a nervous temperament. In relation to Speed, Lincoln mentions *"three special causes."*

The first such immediate factor is Speed's exposure to bad weather on his journey home. This peculiar explanation for Speed's nervous temperament, rooted as it is in popular prejudice and bordering on superstition, is doubly odd in this letter, because Lincoln writes it before Speed's journey has even begun. He cannot possibly know yet that his friend's journey back to Louisville will occasion an emotional reaction. In fact, Lincoln cannot even know that the weather will be bad, though it would not have been too far off to guess that the weather might well be terrible on a journey from Springfield to Louisville at the beginning of January, especially if the weather was already bad when he wrote in late December.[3] One has to suspect that Lincoln had occasion in the past to comment on the worsening of Speed's psychological state during bad weather, especially the winter, and that his assumption of what Speed is about to encounter on his trip is based on that prior knowledge. Lincoln's comment anticipates what Speed will experience. He speaks for his feelings before Speed has even had them.

Lincoln's deep knowledge of Speed's reaction to bad weather comes from within himself as he extends his understanding to his friend. Lincoln notes that "my experience" of exposure to bad weather "clearly proves to be verry severe on defective nerves." What Lincoln knows explains his understanding of Speed's feelings and reactions to bad weather. And in fact there is some evidence Lincoln seemed to dread the snow and cold of central Illinois winters. An old New Salem friend, William Greene, later told Herndon, in speaking about Lincoln's reaction to the death of Ann Rutledge in 1835, that "We watched during storms—fogs—damp gloomy weather Mr. Lincoln for fear of an accident. He said, 'I can never be reconciled to have the snow—rains & storms to beat on her grave.'"[4]

The second factor is what Lincoln assumes will be Speed's "*absence of all business and conversation of friends.*" Lincoln seems certain that his friend will be isolated and alone, which, again, must come from a familiarity with how Speed dealt in general with his states of depression but also probably is based on what he observed in his friend when he visited Farmington the previous summer. It is Lincoln's further thought, however, that is most telling. Being isolated from friends, Lincoln asserts knowingly, will turn Speed to "that *intensity* of thought" that will "wear the sweetest idea thread-bare and turn it to the bitterness of death." Intense thought, or, in more psychological language, obsessive rumination, fostered by Speed's isolation, wears even good ideas "thread-bare" and turns them morbid. But whose death? It would not seem from the context of the letter that Lincoln fears suicidal tendencies on the part of Speed (as he had in himself). Speed's thoughts of death are rather about Fanny Henning, about which we learn much more in the letter.

The third factor that concerns Lincoln about Speed's emotional state centers on his approaching marriage, "*that crisis on which all your thoughts and feelings concentrate*," which Lincoln breathlessly underlines. Speed's marriage was scheduled for February 15, a mere forty-five days away. Speed was terrified, and Lincoln fully embraced and identified with his friend's dread.

> If from all these causes you shall escape and go through triumphantly, without another "twinge of the soul," I shall be most happily, but most egregiously deceived.
>
> If, on the contrary, you shall, as I expect you will at some time, be agonized and distressed, let me, who have some reason to speak with judgement on such a subject, beseech you, to ascribe it to the causes I have mentioned; and not to some false and ruinous suggestion of the Devil.

Lincoln's hope is that Speed shall escape from his distress and go through with his marriage "triumphantly" and without another "twinge of the soul." But Lincoln doubts it while he unconsciously mirrors Speed's miseries and makes them his own. If Speed does become "agonized and distressed," as Lincoln suspects he will, he hopes at the very least that Speed will listen to what Lincoln is saying, because "[I] have some reason to speak with judgement on such a subject." Lincoln urges Speed to understand his unhappiness in the terms he has laid out (the one general and three specific causes of his nervous temperament) and beseeches him not to ascribe it to "false and ruinous suggestion of the Devil." This peculiar sentence can have several meanings, none mutually exclusive. It may reflect Lincoln's own superstitious inclinations that often crop up in his writings but equally reflect those of Speed. One also cannot exclude Fanny's beliefs and attitudes in such a specter of the Devil interfering with Speed's marriage. She was a deeply religious woman, something Lincoln affirms in his reference to her in his second letter of February 3: "Her religion, which you once disliked so much, I will venture you now prize most highly."

The letter at this point takes a rhetorical turn as Lincoln imagines Speed objecting to the argument Lincoln is making on the grounds that any man about to be married would be anxious.

> "But" you will say "do not your causes apply to every one engaged in a like undertaking?"
>
> By no means. *The particular causes*, to a greater or less extent, perhaps do apply in all cases; but the *general one*, nervous debility, which is the key and conductor of all the particular ones, and without which *they* would be utterly harmless, though it *does* pertain to you, *does not* pertain to one in a thousand. It is out of this, that the painful difference between you and the mass of the world springs.

Lincoln answers Speed's question that he himself has posed by distinguishing between the *"particular causes"* (bad weather, isolation, imminence of the marriage) and Speed's clear and present "nervous debility," a more ominous, though still somewhat euphemistic, term Lincoln introduces into the letter at this point that has the effect of pathologizing Speed's psychological state. Lincoln's argument distinguishes normal anxiety about marriage from the neurotic misery that afflicts him and Speed. Not "one in a thousand" suffers the more general state of nervous debility that Lincoln evokes in the circumstance of Speed's anticipated marriage. It is that mutual disease of the mind, something Lincoln identifies with, "that the painful difference between you and the mass of the world springs." Lincoln feels that his and Speed's chronic state of depression and anxiety fall well beyond the range of normal, that not one in a thousand fit their psychological mold. One has to grant the probable accuracy of his observation without falling into the trap of indirect diagnosis. It is enough that Lincoln speaks for himself and Speed as suffering from a nervous temperament that distinguishes them from the mass of humanity *and* unites them in their misery on the margins of the normal.

Lincoln then turns to show how Speed's nervous temperament expresses itself in his concerns about the approaching marriage while at the same time attempting to console his friend.

I know what the painful point with you is, at all times when you are unhappy. It is an apprehension that you do not love her as you should. What nonsense!—How came you to court her? Was it because you thought she desired it; and that you had given her reason to expect it? If it was for that, why did not the same reason make you court Ann Todd, and at least twenty others of whom you can think, & to whom it would apply with greater force than to *her*? Did you court her for her wealth? Why, you knew she had none. But you say you *reasoned* yourself *into* it. What do you mean by that? Was it not, that you found yourself unable to *reason* yourself *out of* it? Did you not think, and partly form the purpose, of courting her the first time you ever saw or heard of her? What had reason to do with it, at that early stage? There was nothing *at that time* for reason to work upon. Whether she was moral, aimiable, sensible, or even of good character, you did not, nor could not then know; except perhaps you might infer the last from the company you found her in. All you then did or could know of her, was her *personal appearance and deportment*; and these, if they impress at all, impress the *heart* and not the head.

Lincoln inserts himself into Speed's feelings: "I know what the painful point with you is, at all times when you are unhappy." It is "an apprehension" that you do not love Fanny as you feel you should. But "what nonsense!" Lincoln exclaims. "How came you to court her?" Lincoln asks with some implicit humor in the reversal of the more logical placement of the verb. Was it because you merely responded to what "you thought she desired" and you had given her "reason to expect it?" If that were the case, you could just have easily courted Ann Maria Todd (born 1824, Mary's younger sister, who had followed her two older sisters from Lexington to Springfield), and if not Ann "at least twenty others of whom you can think." Speed by all accounts was more at ease with women in social events than Lincoln, and it seems clear from Lincoln's reference that he had any number of female admirers—including Mary Todd's own younger sister. The linking of both Todd sisters in this way offers up a most tantalizing historical scenario, but it seems Speed had no interest in Ann Todd. So Lincoln moves on.

Did you court Fanny "for her wealth," Lincoln adds? Of course not, he sniffs with disdain. "Why, you knew she had none." But Lincoln is concerned with something Speed had clearly confided in him at some point, namely that he had "reasoned" himself into loving Fanny. After mentioning it, Lincoln exclaims, "What do you mean by that?" Is it not rather that you were unable to "*reason yourself out of it?*" Did you not plan to court her "the first time you ever saw or heard of her?" And Lincoln adds, in a teasing way, that Speed's immediate attraction for Fanny had nothing high minded about it at all. You could not know at the very outset, except perhaps by the good company she kept, whether she was "moral, aimiable, sensible, or even of good character." Lincoln narrows his focus. All you knew about was her "*personal appearance and deportment,*" which "impress the *heart* and not the head."

> Say candidly, were not those heavenly *black eyes*, the whole basis of all your easily *reasoning* on the subject?

This lighthearted sentiment, especially the reference to Fanny Henning's "heavenly *black eyes,*" undoubtedly carried much meaning for Speed about Fanny's beauty, which had so captured Speed's imagination. Lincoln then reminds Speed of how intensely he had courted Fanny.

> After you and I had once been at her residence, did you not go and take me all the way to Lexington and back, for no other purpose but to get to see her again, on our return, [in that] seeming to take a trip for that express object?
>
> What earthly consideration would you take to find her scouting and despising you, and giving herself up to another? But of this you have no apprehension; and therefore you can not bring it home to your feelings.

Lincoln is comforted that Speed is not worried about Fanny leaving him for someone else; all the dread is in Speed's head and lurking indirectly in Lincoln's own. For a man seeking to calm the jittery nerves of his absent friend, Lincoln ends on a disquieting note:

> I shall be so anxious about you, that I want you to write me every mail. Your friend LINCOLN

Speed did not write for nearly three weeks after his return for reasons that are unclear. At this time Fanny was apparently laid low by an illness. Speed described his preoccupation with Fanny's fragile health and an "excessively bad feeling" in the letter he posted on January 25, a letter that only arrived in Lincoln's hands on February 3. Lincoln immediately sat down to reply.

> Your letter of the 25th. Jany. came to hand to-day. You well know that I do not feel my own sorrows much more keenly than I do yours, when I know of them; and yet I assure you I was not much hurt by what you wrote me of your excessively bad feeling at the time you wrote. Not that I am less capable of sympathising with you now than ever; not that I am less your friend than ever, but because I hope and believe, that your present anxiety and distress about *her* health and *her* life, must and will forever banish those horid doubts, which I know you sometimes felt, as to the truth of your affection for her.

Lincoln's tortured discussion of his shared feelings with Speed has the effect of mirroring those feelings in himself as he attempts to console his friend. The language is very personal and intense, and part of the obscurity in some of the phrasing may reflect the intimacy the men shared. They could communicate elliptically. Lincoln assures Speed that "I do not feel my own sorrows much more keenly than I do yours" but was not much hurt by Speed's outpouring of "excessively bad feelings at the time you wrote." This apparent coldness on Lincoln's part, however, is not because "I am less capable of sympathizing with you" and certainly not that "I am less your friend than ever," but since he knows the "truth of your affection for her," Lincoln can put into some perspective Speed's "present anxiety and distress" about Fanny's health and even her life.

Uncertainty brings Lincoln to death images:

> If they [Speed's doubts] can be once and forever removed, (and I almost feel a presentiment that the Almighty has sent your present affliction expressly for that object) surely, nothing can come in their stead, to fill their immeasurable measure of misery. The death scenes of those we love, are surely painful enough; but

these we are prepared to, and expect to see. They happen to all, and all know they must happen. Painful as they are, they are not an unlooked-for-sorrow. Should she, as you fear, be destined to an early grave, it is indeed, a great consolation to know that she is so well prepared to meet it. Her religion, which you once disliked so much, I will venture you now prize most highly.

But I hope your melancholly bodings as to her early death, are not well founded. I even hope, that ere this reaches you, she will have returned with improved and still improving health; and that you will have met her, and forgotten the sorrows of the past, in the enjoyment of the present.

Speed seems to have written Lincoln that he felt Fanny's serious but unspecified health issues resulted from doubts of his affections for her. Lincoln relates to Speed's existential concerns in baffling ways. The somewhat illogical role that Lincoln imagines God playing in Speed's life touches profound thoughts of death in his own. "The death scenes of those we love," Lincoln writes, are painful but expected. "They happen to all, and all know they must happen."

Lincoln then attempts—without a break in the narrative despite the shift in logic—to console his friend. The pained death scenes of loved ones, presumably as a result of God's work and wisdom, may not in fact be an "unlooked-for-sorrow." If Fanny is "destined for an early grave," at least Speed can take comfort that she is "well prepared" by her apparent deep and abiding faith, which he once disparaged. But maybe all Speed's "melancholy bodings as to her early death" are for naught. Certainly, Lincoln hopes that by the time his letter reaches Farmington Fanny will have recovered.

I would say more if I could; but it seems I have said enough. It really appears to me that you yourself ought to rejoice, and not sorrow, at this indubitable evidence of your undying affection for her. Why Speed, if you did not love her, although you might not wish her death, you would most calmly be resigned to it. Perhaps this point is no longer a question with you, and my pertenacious dwelling upon it, is a rude intrusion upon your feelings. If so, you must pardon me. You know the Hell I have suffered on that point, and how tender I am upon it. You know I do not mean wrong.

Whatever happens, Lincoln feels Speed "ought to rejoice, and not sorrow, at this indubitable evidence of your undying affection for her." In other words, though between the lines, Lincoln suggests that the depth of Speed's concerns for Fanny is also the proof of his affections. "Why Speed, if you did not love her, although you might not wish her death, you would most calmly be resigned to it." Because Speed loves her, Lincoln argues by implication, the idea of Fanny dying is horrible for him. Lincoln has subtly shifted Speed's concerns from a fear that his doubts about his love for Fanny may have made her sick to an affirmation of his love because of his concerns that she might die. It is a neat rhetorical trick that comes from a place of concern for his friend; it could also reflect Lincoln's experience as a trial lawyer in which one concedes an adversary's allegations, even embraces them, but then, as the truth teller in court, sinks an opponent with a switch in perspective. Lincoln's discussion of the relationship between death and love, however, confused as it is, evokes his own mostly unconscious guilt and remorse resulting from his experiences of loss.

Lincoln hopes that all his "pertenacious dwelling" on these issues of love and death are not a "rude intrusion upon your feelings." If so, he begs Speed's forgiveness, but bringing the focus back directly on himself, he writes: "You know the Hell I have suffered on that point, and how tender I am upon it." Lincoln offers his solicitude to Speed, but in this sentence reminds him, and perhaps himself, that Speed's fears about love and death mirror Lincoln's own experiences—experiences that he also knows Speed, and only Speed, fully appreciates. Lincoln's identification with Speed's fears about his approaching marriage to Fanny has a projective quality to it in that he imposes on Speed his own characterization of what he feels from within his own experience. Lincoln's legerdemain serves the further purpose of projecting or imagining Speed's feelings and evoking his own. The objective becomes subjective: the lines drawn between the two men so far apart geographically but within one imagined space psychologically begin to blur.

The letter ends on a more upbeat note and includes some local news.

I have been quite clear of hypo since you left,—even better than I was along in the fall.

I have seen Sarah but once. She seemed verry cheerful, and so, I said nothing to her about what we spoke of.

Old uncle Billy Herndon is dead; and it is said this evening that uncle Ben Ferguson will not live. This I believe is all the news, and enough at that unless it were better.

Write me immediately on the receipt of this. Your friend, as ever LINCOLN

Lincoln reports he has been "clear of the hypo" since Speed left and feels even better than he did in the fall, though he gives no explanation for the change in mood. Perhaps the approach of Speed's marriage has lifted him out of his depression in anticipation of a vicarious resolution of his own misery. Lincoln also reports he has seen Sarah Rickard once but "said nothing to her about what we spoke of." Some have read this reference as one piece of evidence for Lincoln's affections for Sarah Rickard. One cannot exclude that as a possibility, but, as argued earlier, everything in the documents suggest Sarah and Lincoln never courted but that Sarah may well have had an interest in Speed. The sentence, of course, is entirely cryptic, for it makes no mention of what Lincoln and Speed agreed not to tell Sarah, but if we assume, as is reasonable, that Sarah had some feelings for Speed, then the most likely news that Lincoln did *not* provide Sarah was that Speed was about to marry Fanny Henning.

Lincoln then reports some local news in Springfield, namely that "old uncle Billy Herndon" died and "uncle Ben Ferguson" may not live, thus keeping to the theme of death. He urges Speed to write "immediately on the receipt of this."

One can feel Lincoln's anxiety mount as Speed's marriage approaches. Anxiety is like that: it tends to spread, like an oil slick. Lincoln in February 1842 works himself into a lather as Speed's wedding approaches.

Speed broke the sequence of writing with every post by penning a letter to Lincoln on February 1 (after writing on January 25). Lincoln replies on February 13.

Yours of the 1st. Inst. came to hand three or four days ago. When this shall reach you, you will have been Fanny's husband several days. You know my desire to befriend you is everlasting—that I will never cease, while I know how to do any thing.

Lincoln's letter in reply was pointedly not immediate, as on February 13 he notes that he received Speed's letter of February 1 "three or four days ago." Speed was to marry on February 15. The knowledge that the dreaded moment of marriage will have already occurred by the time Speed reads the letter he is writing fills Lincoln with excited anticipation and feelings of closeness to his friend. "You know my desire to befriend you is everlasting—that I will never cease, while I know how to do any thing." But the fact of marriage puts Speed on ground "I have never ocupied [sic]," and thus anything Lincoln might advise could be wrong. Such a note of distance is the first and only hint of psychological separation in the letters, as much hinges on the impact of Speed's marriage on Lincoln himself. And it is not marriage per se that concerns Lincoln—or Speed—but the *consummation* of marriage.

But you will always hereafter, be on ground that I have never ocupied [sic], and consequently, if advice were needed, I might advise wrong.

I do fondly hope, however, that you will never again need any comfort from abroad. But should I be mistaken in this—should excessive pleasure still be accompanied with a painful counterpart at times, still let me urge you, as I have ever done, to remember in the dep[t]h and even the agony of despondency, that verry shortly you are to feel well again. I am now fully convinced, that you love her as ardently as you are capable of loving. Your ever being happy in her presence, and your intense anxiety about her health, if there were nothing else, would place this beyond all dispute in my mind. I incline to think it probable, that your nerves will fail you occassionally for a while; but once you get them fairly graded now, that trouble is over forever.

I think if I were you, in case my mind were not exactly right, I would avoid being *idle*; I would immediately engage in some business, or go to making preparations for it, which would be the same thing.

If you went through the ceremony *calmly*, or even with sufficient composure not to excite alarm in any present, you are safe, beyond question, and in two or three months, to say the most, will be the happiest of men.

I hope with tolerable confidence, that this letter is a plaster for a place that is no longer sore. God grant it may be so.

I would desire you to give my particular respects to Fanny, but perhaps you will not wish her to know you have received this, lest she should desire to see it. Make her write me an answer to my last letter to her at any rate. I would set great value upon another letter from her.

Write me whenever you have leisure. Yours forever.

A. LINCOLN

Speaking to himself through Speed, and despite his falsely humble disqualification for giving advice, that is exactly what Lincoln proceeds to do in the February 13 letter. "I do fondly hope," he begins, that you will not ever again need comfort "from abroad." Lincoln frequently used "fond" and especially its adverbial form, "fondly." Lincoln mostly used "fond" to mean "much pleased" and "relishing highly," as Webster's first American dictionary in 1828 defined it, but it was the adverbial use of "fondly" for which he is most remembered, namely toward the end of the long third paragraph of the Second Inaugural, where he writes: "Fondly do we hope—fervently do we pray—that this mighty scourge of war may speedily pass away." As in the Speed letter, what is most striking and memorable about Lincoln's use of "fondly" in the Second Inaugural is that it modifies "hope." Nothing matches hope in human experience. It is primal, simple, eternal. In Christianity the essence of hope is *agape*, or love, on which Jesus centers his entire gospel. To "fondly hope" is Lincoln's subtle embrace of the deepest human yearnings for good things to come. Lincoln's sentence beginning "I do fondly hope" in this letter to Speed is the first time (in what has survived) that he tried out the linkage for a phrase that is forever embedded in our political discourse.

Lincoln wants Speed to hope for the good, even if despair descends on him again. "Should I be mistaken in this"—namely that Speed's "excessive pleasure" will come with its "painful counterpart" at times—remember, "as I have ever done," that even in the "agony of despondency" you will "verry shortly" feel well again. And that is because Lincoln is "fully convinced" that Speed loves Fanny "as ardently as you are capable of loving." That Speed is "ever happy in her presence" and shows "intense anxiety about her health," if nothing else, confirm absolutely for Lincoln the depth of his friend's love for Fanny. Perhaps,

Lincoln adds, your nerves will "fail you occasionally." But once you get them "fairly graded" the trouble will quickly pass and be "over forever."

Lincoln gives Speed some practical advice to keep busy and engage in business. This practical aside, however, quickly brings Lincoln back to the wedding and his imagined terrors. He hopes Speed went through the ceremony "*calmly*," which he underlines, or at the very least with enough composure not to alarm those present. If so, "you are safe, beyond question, and in two or three months, to say the most, will be the happiest of men." Lincoln's image is of his friend risking revelation of his anxiety during the wedding ceremony itself in ways that might have completely derailed the marriage, and he hopes Speed was able to keep it in rein. If so, he is sure marital bliss awaits. Lincoln has no fears that Fanny will be a good wife nor that Speed will not provide for her and love her deeply. He has no concern about their compatibility. There is one and only one concern that fills him with dread: Can Speed successfully consummate the marriage after the wedding? That is equally Lincoln's fear.

Lincoln concludes on a special conspiratorial note that binds him tightly to Speed in the very midst of Speed moving into the arms of Fanny. Lincoln sends his "particular respects" to Fanny but adds that Speed may not want to tell her that, "lest she should desire to see it [this letter]." Lincoln says Speed should perhaps tell Fanny to write an answer to his last letter to her (now lost). This otherwise obscure reference to a letter from Lincoln to Fanny in the context of worrying about Speed showing his letter to her clarifies an important detail in the dynamic of the relationship between Lincoln and Speed. What Lincoln clearly had gone to some pains to set up was a parallel correspondence with Fanny to mask his letters to Speed, so that she would not learn that they were special and "everlasting" friends. The unspoken and probably unconscious fear on Lincoln's part is that once Speed consummates his marriage to Fanny he would forever draw away from him. The bond would break. Lincoln seeks therefore to maintain his special connection with Speed as a secret from Fanny, even as he loses him into marriage. Consciously, Lincoln wants nothing more than for Speed to manage the difficult task of marrying, which has the crucial added advantage, given his mirroring relationship with him, of freeing him in his own life from his fears of intimacy. More unconsciously, Lincoln works to keep Speed separated from Fanny and symbolically at his side and in his heart. There is one suggestion in the letter that could be read differently: "P.S. I have been quite a man ever since you left."

That postscript could, of course, mean he had had sex with a woman, but in the context of this and the other letters it is much more likely a simple statement that he was not feeling so depressed, able to work more efficiently, and even socialize with friends. Given the intense anxiety that he expressed in the letter, Lincoln might have thought on rereading it before he sealed it that Speed would be worried about his state of mind and thus added the postscript. The contrast, in other words, that Lincoln seems to be setting up is that he is feeling like a man and *not* a woman, that is, not depressed (which is itself a curious association). Sex, of course, is a complex process with many meanings. It can, for example, evoke a dreaded fear of disintegration in the merging of selves that accompanies intimacy. It seems Lincoln and Speed felt such dread as a shadow cast on their yearning for love and marriage. Their apparent sexual naïveté and fear of what such intimacy entails, however real, also served as something of a veil for each man's loss of the other, a loss that would happen in the connection with finding a wife.

In the very midst of this romance drama, as Lincoln waited to hear about Speed's marriage, he took the opportunity to speak about temperance to the Springfield Washington Temperance Society on February 22.[5] His remarkable speech, not often noted as most others, especially in its personal context, bristles with self-reference and suppression of appetites.

Lincoln grew up with alcoholics everywhere in his world, had seen William Berry drink himself to death in New Salem, and in the future would more than once have to deal with Herndon blacking out after drinking too much and acting outrageously. Drunkenness was everywhere, and the per-capita consumption of hard liquor was then at its highest in American history. Barrels of whiskey commonly were placed outside "grocery" stores, and for a nickel one simply drank up a ladle's worth—at ten in the morning. During the Lincoln-Douglas debates, Douglas, to applause and laughter, accused Lincoln of having kept just such a "grocery." Lincoln denied it but admitted that he had worked "the better part of one winter" at Isaac Burner's still. During his speech, Lincoln also expounded upon liquor as "every where a respectable article of manufacture and of merchandize." Concerns of many observers about the social costs of an alcohol-soaked economic system sparked the rise of a temperance movement that waxed and waned throughout the nineteenth century but never died out. The Washingtonian Total Abstinence Society, founded in 1840 in Baltimore, joined with others committed to temperance but focused less on public policy and more on the individual and his or her struggle to get free of dependence on alcohol (it is the historical precursor of Alcoholics Anonymous). It was a movement, in other words, focused on personal control of desire, on tamping down unwelcome impulses, and as such was well positioned to appeal to Lincoln in February 1842.[6]

Lincoln himself never drank, except to try it out at some point. He said it made him feel "flabby and undone" (we do not know anything about Speed's experiences with alcohol, but nothing indicates it was a problem for him). Despite his own natural abstinence, in his address, one that Lincoln sends to Speed and Fanny as a clipping once the *Sangamo Journal* printed it, he is at pains not to talk down to alcoholics. In rather high-flown language, Lincoln notes how the temperance movement has been transformed from a "cold abstract theory" to a "living, breathing, active, and powerful chieftain" going forth to conquer. Past attempts to control drinking were mostly led by people without empathy for those who directly suffer from the curse of alcoholism. Fanatical preachers wanted to use the temperance movement as a way to shame the sin of drunkenness. Pompous lawyers (he might have said with a wink and a nod) enjoyed hearing themselves speak. And hired agents sought only a salary. Today, on the contrary, the struggle for liberation from alcohol addiction is in the hands of its very victim, who has burst the "fetters that have bound him," appears before his neighbors "a redeemed specimen of long lost humanity," and stands up "with tears of joy trembling in his eyes" to tell of his "miseries *once* endured, *now* to be endured no more forever." That redeemed man can now feed and care for his "naked and starving children" and comfort his "wife longed weighed down with woe, weeping, and a broken heart."

Lincoln has absolute distaste for the attitude of many reformers that "all habitual drunkards were utterly incorrigible" and must be "turned adrift, and damned without remedy." Such an approach for him is "so repugnant to humanity, so uncharitable, so cold-blooded and feelingless" that it can never serve to enlist the "enthusiasm of a popular cause." The generous man cannot adopt such an approach. It will not "mix with his blood." The Washingtonians, on the other hand, repudiate the idea of "assigning the hopeless drunkard to hopeless ruin." They teach hope to all and despair to none. They turn away from the false Christian notion of "unpardonable sin" and embrace the truer teachings of Jesus about forgiveness and love.

"Habitual drunkards as a class," he continues, often stand apart from the mass of humanity. "There seems ever to have been a proneness in the brilliant, and the warm-blooded, to fall into this vice." The "demon of intemperance" often delights in "sucking the blood of genius and of generosity." Who of us do not know of a friend or relative who has fallen a "sacrifice to his rapacity"? Like the Egyptian angel of death, he has gone forth to "slay if not the first, the fairest born of every family." The Washingtonians are the makers of a great potential revolution. If we measure a revolution by its impact on peoples' lives, this one will be magnificent. In its effects there will be "bondage broken," a vile "slavery manumitted," and a "tyrant deposed." Disease will be healed and sorrow assuaged. Orphans will eat and widows stop weeping. Even dram makers and dram sellers will benefit as they move into other, more productive enterprises and "join all others in the universal song of gladness."

And then the grand peroration, which one can best understand in the context of Lincoln's personal life as it stood in February 1842. Though indirect, it is as passionate a statement about how much he desperately wanted his powers of reason to control his confused feelings about intimacy as he ever made:

> Happy day, when, all appetites controlled, all passions subdued, all matters subjected, *mind*, all conquering *mind*, shall live and move the monarch of the world. Glorious consummation! Hail fall of Fury! Reign of Reason, all hail!

And in that glorious moment, "there shall be neither a slave nor a drunkard on the earth."

In late March 1842, Lincoln sent a copy of his speech to Joshua and Fanny Speed. He asked them, as an "act of charity to me," to read it aloud to each other. One wonders what they felt *after* their marriage, reading the speech aloud, when they came to the peroration and Lincoln's grand celebration of controlling desire and suppressing passions. Was it Speed or his Victorian bride who got to utter "all appetites controlled, all passions subdued" and gush about "glorious consummation" in this minefield of double meanings? But for Lincoln, in that control lies the triumph of reason, its "glorious consummation," a phrasing that in its contradictions reveals Lincoln's own deep confusions.[7]

Three days after delivering his Temperance Address, on February 25, Lincoln opened the anxiously awaited letter from Speed. Lincoln's reply:

> I received yours of the 12th. written the day you went down to William's place, some days since; but delayed answering it, till I should receive the promised one, of the 16th., which came last night. I opened the latter, with intense anxiety and trepidation— so much, that although it turned out better than I expected, I have hardly yet, at the distance of ten hours, become calm.

This was the consummation letter. Speed got married on February 15, and clearly he had promised Lincoln that as soon as he possibly could after consummating his marriage he would write to report on its outcome. Speed, it seems, had barely tumbled out of his wedding bed on the morning of February 16 before he wrote Lincoln, who opened the letter with "intense anxiety and trepidation." In fact, even though "it turned out better than I expected" Lincoln was still not calm "at the distance of ten hours." That is a long time for a man, then thirty-three years of age, to be experiencing such anxiety from the news of how his friend's wedding night turned out.

The relief is palpable for Lincoln: "I tell you, Speed, our *forebodings*, for which you and I are rather peculiar, are all the worst sort of nonsense." Lincoln then recounts the dreaded passing of days for him in his letter of February 25 as he awaited news of the February 15 wedding with an obsessive-compulsive intensity punctuated by gratuitous underlinings.

> I fancied, from the time I received your letter of *saturday*, that the one of *wednesday* was never to come; and yet it *did* come,

and what is more, it is perfectly clear, both from it's [*sic*] *tone* and *handwriting*, that you were much *happier*, or, if you think the term preferable, *less miserable*, when you wrote *it*, than when you wrote the last one before. You had so obviously improved, at the verry time I so much feared, you would have grown worse.

But a shadow remains.

You say that "something indescribably horrible and alarming still haunts you.["] You will not say *that* three months from now, I will venture. When your nerves once get steady now, the whole trouble will be over forever. Nor should you become impatient at their being even verry slow, in becoming steady. Again; you say you much fear that that Elysium of which you have dreamed so much, is never to be realized. Well, if it shall not, I dare swear, it will not be the fault of her who is now your wife. I now have no doubt that it is the peculiar misfortune of both you and me, to dream dreams of Elysium far exceeding all that any thing earthly can realize.

The perplexing line in the letter ("You say that 'something inde-scribably horrible and alarming still haunts you'") suggests Speed felt great relief at his ability to carry out sexual intercourse with Fanny but remained troubled that the sky did not suddenly clear and the heav-ens part. Lincoln at first seems not to be particularly worried about Speed's feelings that something "indescribably horrible" still haunted him. Lincoln says with confidence, "You will not say *that* three months from now." Your nerves will get "steady," and "the whole trouble will be over forever." But Lincoln cannot entirely dismiss Speed's fears that his "dreams of Elysium," that place in the ancient world where the great and heroic live a blessed and happy life after death, would never be realized. Lincoln's argument addressing these concerns in this section of the letter is somewhat elliptical. On the one hand, he is confident that Speed's fears will fade in due time based on the most welcome news that the marriage consummation went well. As long as that is over, things have to improve, and Speed's anxiety will gradually dissipate. It would seem the message from Speed was: "Things went well, but I still feel bad." Lincoln is of course most pleased that things went well. His encouragement for Speed, on the other hand, reflects some ambivalence for Speed's continued doubts that, given his identification with his friend, poses the danger of circling back onto himself. Lincoln gently chastises Speed and tells him his unhappiness lingers from his nervous temperament and "will not be the fault of her who is now your wife." But perhaps feeling bad for this subtle criticism Lincoln immediately returns to his identification with Speed and affirms their common experience with emotional problems. "I now have no doubt that it is the peculiar misfortune of both you and me, to dream dreams of Elysium far exceeding all that any thing earthly can realize."

In that imagined joy lies a contradiction. Speed's marriage to Fanny means he will never again be available in the same total way for Lincoln. Speed is now joined with Fanny, forever apart. The marriage is a moment of fulfillment for Lincoln, one that because he vicariously made it his own frees him from his tormented fears of intimacy. Lincoln had been as much attuned empathically with Speed as with anyone in his life. He was completely immersed in Speed's inner life. Nothing matches in intimacy that kind of empathic connection with another. To lose such a connection leaves one feeling lost and alone, abandoned, despairing. Speed's marriage, for all the joy it brings Lincoln, is simultaneously a moment of dreaded loss, even a kind of symbolic death. In his triumphant experience of love, Speed categorically abandons his friend, though Lincoln tries mightily to relish Speed's new love.

> Far short of your dreams as you may be, no woman could do more to realize them, than that same black eyed Fanny. If you could but contemplate her through my immagination, it would appear ridiculous to you, that any one should for a moment think of being unhappy with her. My old Father used to have a saying that "If you make a bad bargain, *hug* it the tighter"; and it occurs to me, that if the bargain you have just closed can possibly be called a bad one, it is certainly the most *pleasant one* for applying that maxim to, which my fancy can, by any effort, picture.

In this ironic and lighter tone, Lincoln writes Speed that while Fanny may not match Speed's dreams of Elysium, "no woman could do more to realize them, than that same black eyed Fanny." Lincoln imagines his way into Speed's experience: "if you could but contemplate her through my imagination," he would see how "ridiculous" it is even to think of being unhappy with Fanny. "My old Father" used to say, Lincoln adds, "If you make a bad bargain, *hug* it the tighter." Your bargain, Lincoln concludes, if you can possibly call it bad, "is certainly the most *pleasant one* for applying that maxim to, which my fancy can, by any effort, picture." This story from his father about hugging a bad bargain, seemingly told as something of a joke, comes across as inappropriate, even odd. He does not feel at all that Speed has made a bad bargain in marrying Fanny Henning. On the contrary, he feels Fanny is lovely and a perfect match for his friend. What he tries to address are Speed's continued doubts, which he gently mocks while at the same time identifying with them. What comes across, however, in the story from his father is the wrong idea that Speed has settled. The befuddled argument is all part of Lincoln's confusions in dealing with his complex feelings about Speed and Fanny. He wants Speed to be happy in his marriage. At the same time, he hates losing Speed to Fanny and wants to keep him for himself.

This ambivalence carries over to continuing the subterfuge of fooling Fanny about Lincoln's relationship with Speed.

> I write another letter enclosing this, which you can show her, if she desires it. I do this, because, she would think strangely perhaps should you tell her that you receive no letters from me; or, telling her you do, should refuse to let her see them.
>
> I close this, entertaining the confident hope, that every successive letter I shall have from you, (which I here pray may not be few, nor far between,) may show you possessing a more steady hand, and cheerful heart, than the last preceding it. As ever, your friend LINCOLN

Earlier in the month the strategy between the two men was for Lincoln to carry on a parallel exchange of letters with Fanny so as not to alert her to their separate communications. The letters, of course, have no real secrets per se, only Speed's doubts, which they both seemed anxious to shield from Fanny. That kept alive, at least for the moment, Lincoln's special intimacy with Speed while he moved decisively to open up a new love with Fanny. On February 25, when so much is at stake, Lincoln goes to the extraordinary length of enclosing with his real letter to Speed a second decoy letter in the same envelope:

Yours of the 16th. Inst. announcing that Miss Fanny and you "are no more twain, but one flesh," reached me this morning. I have no way of telling how much happiness I wish you both; tho' I believe you both can conceive it. I fell som[e] what jealous of both of you now; you will be so exclusively concerned for one another, that I shall be forgotten entirely. My acquaintance with Miss Fanny (I call her thus, lest you should think I am speaking of your mother) was too short for me to reasonably hope to long be remembered by her; and still, I am sure, I shall not forget her soon. Try if you can not remind her of that debt she owes me; and be sure you do not interfere to prevent her paying it.

I regret to learn that you have resolved to not return to Illinois. I shall be verry lonesome without you. How miserably things seem to be arranged in this world. If we have no friends, we have no pleasure; and if we have them, we are sure to lose them, and be doubly pained by the loss. I did hope she and you would make your home here; but I own I have no right to insist. You owe obligations to her, ten thousand times more sacred than any you can owe to others; and, in that light, let them be respected and observed. It is natural that she should desire to remain with her relatives and friends. As to friends, however, *she* could not need them any where; she would have them in abundance here.

Give my kind rememberance to Mr. Williamson and his family, particularly Miss Elizabeth—also to your Mother, brothers, and sisters. Ask little Eliza Davis if she will ride to town with me if I come there again.

And, finally, give Fanny a double reciprocation of all the love she sent me. Write me often, and believe me Yours forever LINCOLN

P.S. Poor Eastham is gone at last. He died a while before day this morning. They say he was verry loth to die.

No clerk is appointed yet. L.

Lincoln tells Speed he can show Fanny the second and innocuous letter "because, she would think strangely perhaps should you tell her that you receive no letters from me; or, telling her you do, should refuse to let her see them." That second letter is indeed completely different in tone; it is joking and easygoing, lacking any suggestion of the troubled emotional waters that lie beneath the calm surface. In the fake letter, Lincoln sends his greatest happiness to the Speeds, happiness that is greater in fact than "you both can conceive," a curious verb in this context. Lincoln continues by noting that Speed and "Miss Fanny" are now "no more twain, but one flesh," a reference to a passage in Matthew 19:6, which ends with the often-quoted wedding blessing "What, therefore, God hath joined together, let not man put asunder." Lincoln wishes them the best, though he fears the Speeds will now care only for themselves and "I shall be forgotten entirely" (clearly said ironically, even if it carries deeper, less clearly avowed or even understood meanings). He says some nice things about "Miss Fanny," an awkward and wrong term for someone no longer a maiden that he explains he uses to distinguish her from Speed's mother. Lincoln then adds a paragraph about how he misses Speed and their friendship but recognizes his obligations to his wife are now "ten thousand times more sacred than any you can owe to others." The letter concludes with casual comments: Lincoln hopes Speed will give his remembrance to his family and other common friends and acquaintances. Finally, he tells Speed to give Fanny "a double reciprocation of all the love she sent me."

This letter ends with "Write me often, and believe me Yours forever LINCOLN." The first, more honest, letter ends in an expression of his true feelings: "I close this, entertaining the confident hope, that every successive letter I shall have from you, (which I here pray may not be few, nor far between,) may show you possessing a more steady hand, and cheerful heart, than the last preceding it. As ever, your friend LINCOLN."

February 25, 1842, marked the turning point in what had been up to that point the crippled emotional life of Abraham Lincoln. Everything after that changed—and almost entirely for the good.

11

MARY TODD, ONCE AGAIN

How miserably things seem to be arranged in this world! If we
have no friends, we have no pleasure; and if we have them, we
are sure to lose them, and be doubly pained by the loss.

—Abraham Lincoln to Joshua Speed, February 25, 1842

After February 25, the letters between Lincoln and Speed take on a
different character. For one thing, the friends stop writing by every
post. Speed, who last wrote Lincoln the "promised one" of February 16, waited until March 10 to write again. Lincoln waited an extra
week after receiving the letter before replying on March 27. Speed
replied promptly to that letter but only because he wanted Lincoln to
handle an important business matter. Lincoln wrote again on April
13, but Speed then waited until June 16 to write back. Lincoln, in
turn, waited until July 4 to reply to that letter, and he wrote his last
letter in 1842 to Speed on October 5. It is reasonable to assume there
are no missing letters because Speed seemed to be diligent in saving his complete correspondence with Lincoln. After Speed's marriage, in other words, the urgency disappears in the communications
between the two men. It is partly that they are separated but more
significantly that Speed had (mostly) fulfilled the psychological role
assigned to him by Lincoln. Speed was now dispensable. Lincoln no
longer required him as his symbolic other, someone who could act
in love in ways that paralleled Lincoln. The drama of the vicarious
romance was playing itself out.

Lincoln was emotionally freer after February 25 and able to enter public life with more vigor than before. Benjamin Thomas, one of the great Lincoln biographers of the twentieth century, tells the story of when after his presidency Martin Van Buren took a tour of the West in 1842. On June 16 he stopped for a night in Rochester, just to the southeast of Springfield. A large group of Democrats traveled out to visit with Van Buren, and they invited a few Whigs, including Lincoln, to join them. Van Buren related some stories of New York politics, and some local Democrats spun yarns of frontier life. "But all yielded at last to Lincoln, who kept them in an uproar far into the night with a seemingly inexhaustible supply of yarns, until Van Buren insisted that 'his sides were sore with laughing.'"[1]

But there was still a shadow. Lincoln hovered between relief and uncertainty, doubt, and guilt. He felt terrible for the pain he caused Mary, "for even wishing to be happy while she is otherwise." And Lincoln had been keeping track of Mary's life, something surely not difficult in a small town with a tight and tiny cluster of educated middle-class people who all knew one another well. He reports in a letter, for example, that Mary took a train ride to Jacksonville "last Monday" with a large party and on her return, "spoke, so that I heard of it, of having enjoyed the trip exceedingly. God be praised for that." Lincoln watches and waits.[2]

For the first time since the fatal first, Lincoln feels some hope, however, in Speed's reports of his happiness in marriage. "It now thrills me with joy," he writes, "to hear you say you are *far happier than you ever expected to be.*" He says he knows Speed too well not to have believed that at least sometimes his expectations were "extravagant." But to hear now that the reality of his marriage exceeds even those large expectations brings more pleasure to Lincoln than the "sum of all I have enjoyed" since he broke off the engagement with Mary. Lincoln is quite clear about his vicarious emotional involvement in Speed's courtship and marriage. "You know with what sleepless vigilance I have watched you, ever since the commencement of your affair."

Lincoln's "sleepless vigilance" in his watch over Speed brought him relief at the consummation of Speed's marriage, but now the issue was whether that moment has led to continued joy. It was "thrilling" for Lincoln to hear that things continued to go well. But having said that, some anxiety creeps in. "I can not forbear," Lincoln says, "once more to say that I think it is even yet possible for your spirits to flag down and leave you miserable." But if that happens, he counsels Speed, just remember it won't last long.

After a rather lengthy discussion of an annoying business matter, Lincoln ends his note reporting on the "sweet violet" that Fanny had given Speed to enclose in his last letter. It crumbled to dust when he opened the letter, but the "juice that mashed out of it, stained a [place] on the letter, which I mean to preserve and ch[erish] for the sake of her who procured it to be se[nt]." Fanny Speed, it seems, felt close to Lincoln for his role in helping Joshua follow through on the marriage. The violet she sends Lincoln via her new husband is a powerful symbol of the delicate love she feels, and, as she is a deeply religious woman, the violet evokes her Christian association with the Virgin Mary's modesty, wisdom, humility, and faithfulness.

Lincoln's next letter of April 13 deals basically with business matters, though it ends with the hope that the Speeds will visit him in Springfield "during the summer or autumn" (a visit that never occurred). Lincoln's July 4 letter, however, is a different matter altogether. He begins both by apologizing for and explaining why he has not written in so long, in response to Speed's complaint: "You speak of the great time that has elapsed since I wrote you." There seemed to be some delay with the letter itself, and Lincoln had during that time been out on the circuit, but it is striking that such a complaint had surfaced at all between either Speed or Lincoln. It was a mark of their gradually changing relationship.[3]

A dramatic psychological shift has occurred: Speed now has assumed the role of advising Lincoln. The reason for his concern about Lincoln's delay in writing is that Speed was concerned Lincoln was displeased with his advice. What advice? It can only have been that Lincoln should now reach out to Mary Todd and try to resume their relationship. The delay in their communication had made Speed feel that Lincoln resented his new role. In the confusion about the delay in the letter, William Butler had been something of an intermediary, as he had been in Kentucky, clearly seen Speed, and told Lincoln on his return to Springfield that Speed would be writing soon. When Lincoln, who was waiting for Speed to write, didn't reply, Speed felt Lincoln was displeased at Speed's intervention on a very touchy subject. Lincoln assures Speed that is not at all the case, though he remains uncertain what he will do. "True," Lincoln says, "that subject is painful to me; but it is not your silence, or the silence of all the world that can make me forget it." Most importantly, "I acknowledge the correctness of your advice too," suggesting Lincoln recognizes it is high time for him to reach out to Mary Todd.

There is a catch, however. Before "I resolve to do the one thing or the other," Lincoln writes, "I must regain my confidence in my own ability to keep my resolves when they are made." He had already once decided to marry Mary Todd but then backed out of the engagement suddenly and mysteriously, to his own great distress and her anger and hurt. He never wanted to be in that position again. In his ability to "keep my resolves" he once "prided myself as the only, or at least the chief, gem of my character; that gem I lost—how, and when, you too well know." Lincoln has yet to feel he has "regained it; and until I do, I can not trust myself in any matter of much importance." Lincoln, in other words, can't yet adopt Speed's recommended course of action and reach out to Mary because he still doubts himself to be able to follow through on things emotionally. And he adds that had Speed "understood my case at the time"—that is, prior to the fatal first—"as well as I understood yours afterwards," with that aid Speed would have given him, "I should have sailed through clear" and gotten married. But with all that has occurred, the pain and depression, "does not now afford me sufficient confidence, to begin that, or the like of that, again."

Lincoln then acknowledges Speed's deep gratitude for his "present happiness." The truth, however, Lincoln says, is that he felt he (and Speed) were in the hands of a much greater power that made that love possible. "I was drawn to it as by fate," Lincoln says, acknowledging the unconscious dimension of his ceaseless involvement in Speed's courtship and marriage. "I always was superstitious; and as part of my superstition, I believe God made me one of the instruments of bringing your Fanny and you together, which union, I have no doubt He had fore-ordained." Lincoln's greatest hope is that the divine power who brought Speed and Fanny together "will do [the same] for *me* yet." Lincoln even quotes Exodus 14:13 as his text that now captures his reality: "Stand *still* and see the salvation of the Lord."

***

Mary Todd, meanwhile, was probably also tracking the whereabouts of Lincoln, waiting and hoping, having come through the ordeal of the last year and a half with more "poise than he had," as Ruth Painter Randall wisely put it long ago in the 1950s. Just as he was keenly aware of her ride on the new-fangled train to Jacksonville, she surely noticed when he was in town and what he was up to. She did continue to be courted in the swirl of parties at her sister's home. In her June 1841 letter to Mercy Levering, Mary says, "we have an unusual number of agreeable visitors, but in their midst the *winning widower* [Webb] is not." Later in the same letter, Mary seems at least somewhat taken with Lyman Trumbull. "He is the interesting gentleman, whom Mrs Roberts gave you for a beau," but "now that your fortune is made [Mercy is engaged] I feel much disposed in your absence to lay in my claws, as he is talented & agreeable & sometimes countenances me." But the clearer impression in her long and rambling letter to Mercy is that she was waiting for Lincoln. "I have been much alone," she says, and later in the letter adds:

[Lincoln] deems me unworthy of notice, as I have not met *him* in the gay world for months, with the usual comfort of misery, imagine that others were as seldom gladdened by his presence as my humble self, yet I would that the case were different, that he would once more resume his Station in Society, that "Richard should be himself again," much, much happiness would it afford me   4

There is a good deal of disagreement about the sequence of events that brought Lincoln and Mary back together. Douglas Wilson has argued recently that they didn't reunite until late in September and then only because of the role of John J. and Sarah Hardin. John Hardin was a good friend of Lincoln's and a most impressive man, widely regarded as someone with a bright political future that was cut short by his death in the Mexican War. Wilson makes some good guesses based on much later and therefore suspect reports about the role of the Hardins, but he may impose a certainty on the narrative that it otherwise lacks. Wilson's tone is also relevant. He has a decidedly negative view of Mary in general (a theme in recent writing) that reflects his views of the courtship drama, feels Lincoln never really loved her, and argues that Lincoln's decision to go through with the marriage was simply his fulfilling his honorable obligations (an argument that curiously recycles that of Herndon, though with some less than completely convincing additional pieces of evidence).[5]

The old view of how Lincoln and Mary got together, however, is not entirely hokum. Herndon, based on his own experience and interviewing, wrote in his book that at some point in the summer of 1842 and certainly before mid-August Lincoln's friend Simeon Francis and his wife, Eliza Rumsey Francis, knowing the feelings of both, got Lincoln and Mary together in their home; later, in some independent interviewing, Octavia Roberts talked with the niece of Mrs. Francis, who reported the same story. Furthermore, Elizabeth Edwards (Mary's sister) was quite clear about the role of Eliza Francis, who, she says, "shrewdly got them together." This is about as good as it gets in something this remote in time and place. Eliza Francis was apparently the key player in the reconciliation. She was a "great social entertainer," writes Herndon, "and one day arranged a gathering at her house for the express purpose of bringing these two people together." They were at first somewhat embarrassed. She told them, "Be friends again." This and subsequent meetings occurred mostly in the Francis home, which was contiguous with the *Sangamo Journal* (an important detail for some subsequent developments), though others, like Anson G. Henry, might have played a role in their meetings (Elizabeth and Ninian Edwards said, "Doct. Henry who admired and loved Mr. Lincoln had much to do in getting Mary and Lincoln together again"). Since these subsequent meetings were clandestine, it is entirely possible that the reports of the Hardins bringing them together arose from confused memories of those who were there, or who heard from those who were there, and wished decades later to insert themselves as key players in the Lincoln story.[6]

In any event, the most important point is that in the late summer or early fall Lincoln and Mary did reconcile and began meeting secretly. The intrigue was part of the thrill of the reunion. Mary went to some lengths to keep knowledge of the meetings from her sister, but eventually Elizabeth found out and asked why she was so secretive. Mary replied evasively that "after all that had occurred, it was best to keep the courtship from all eyes and ears."[7]

* * *

But something else happened in August and September of great import for Lincoln that was to draw in Mary as well and bring them even closer. It was a drama of bitter words and nearly clashing swords that could have ended as a Shakespearean tragedy but was instead more of an "opera bouffe," as Gustave Koerner put it. The drama involved many of the elite in Springfield, including Whigs and Democrats, key figures from the Coterie, the local editor of the *Sangamo Journal*, doctors, a host of lawyers, and of course Abraham Lincoln. Mary Todd, who wrote some of the script for the play, stood ready to use her sharp wit and tongue as the occasion demanded. Her dear friend, the lovely Julia Jayne, soon to be married to Lincoln's friend, the future U.S. senator Lyman Trumbull, nursed her special grievances. The ebullient William Butler proved himself always ready for a fight. Dr. Elias H. Merryman revealed himself as something of a hothead. General John D. Whiteside showed up early and hung on beyond the end, eager to be in the thick of things. Only the distinguished John J. Hardin remained heroically steady.

The dark prince of the play was James Shields. He was a man of many talents though also erratic, bombastic, narcissistic. Shields was born in 1806 but later gave his birth date as 1810, one of his many affectations. At about twenty years of age, and at some point around 1826, he came to America to make his fortune, though over the years he spun different tales to different audiences about when and why he left Ireland for America. At first he taught, in part because he knew English, French, Latin, Greek, and Irish. In time, however, he decided to become a lawyer, and by the mid-1830s he opened a practice in Kaskaskia, Illinois, then moved to Belleville, where he joined Koerner as his law partner. Like most Irishmen in America, Shields was a Democrat. It didn't take long for Irishmen, once off the boat, to figure out that Whigs were decidedly pro-British, and therefore they nearly universally became Democrats.[8]

Shields was quickly recognized in Illinois as a potent figure in Democratic politics. He was second in importance only to Stephen Douglas, with whom he was close; he would serve as best man at Douglas's wedding. At a party once, when both were probably drunk, Douglas and Shields "encircled each other's waists, and to the time of a rollicking song, pirouetted down the whole length" of a banquet table, shouting, singing, and kicking glasses and dishes. In time Shields would serve as a U.S. senator in three states: Illinois, Minnesota, and Missouri, an accomplishment that will probably never be repeated and all the more remarkable as Shields was a Catholic in an age of rampant nativism. He captivated audiences with his Irish brogue, which gave texture to his voice, and many found him "fluent, witty and eloquent," as one early and decidedly sympathetic biographer, who knew him later in life, put it.[9] In his forties, the flamboyant Shields fought in the Mexican War, in which he was wounded several times, and in his fifties he fought in the Civil War as a major general. He holds the distinction of being the only general to defeat Thomas "Stonewall" Jackson in battle. His subsequent performance was mediocre, however, and he eventually resigned his commission.

The drama that brought these players together centered on some local side effects of the panic that had been waxing and waning throughout the country since 1837. Everybody wanted to blame someone else for the slump, tight credit, and bankrupt banks. In Illinois the State Bank collapsed in February 1842, making the currency it backed of no value. For the state government the collapse raised the issue of how taxes would be paid. The only feasible immediate solution was to require citizens to pay their taxes in silver coins. By August, Democrats, then in control of the state government, were forced to implement this new requirement. Whigs smelled blood in the ludicrous irony of the state not accepting its own currency for payment of taxes. The official in the crosshairs of the crisis was the state auditor, James Shields, who had been elected to the office in March 1841. The unpleasant task of announcing and enforcing the new policy of not accepting the currency of the State Bank for payment of taxes fell to Shields.

James Shields, unfortunately, was not a man well suited for dealing with the intense criticism and ridicule he would face. A man with brittle self-esteem, he was vain and mercurial, eccentric, and somewhat odd. He also fancied himself an attractive bachelor in the eyes of women, with whom he ostentatiously flirted. Herndon said he was "blind to his own defects," defects that set him up as the target for all the complaints surrounding the banking crisis. He was a regular at the Coterie soirees held at the Edwards home and thus a familiar figure for someone like Mary Todd, who said later that "Shields was always, a subject of mirth, his impulsiveness & drolleries were irresistible."[10]

Shields's visibility as the state auditor in 1842, along with his volatile personality, gave Whigs the chance to personalize their political attacks, which made a complicated economic crisis comprehensible for ordinary people. The idea was to blame Shields personally for the absurd situation in which the state government would not accept its own money from its loyal citizens attempting to pay their taxes. Someone, perhaps Simeon Francis, came up with the idea of creating a fictional writer named Rebecca who would write letters to the *Sangamo Journal* expressing her astonishment at the new policy. This idea of a fictional letter writer had already been well tested by Francis, who had employed it in 1838. The first Rebecca letter in 1842, written by Francis and dated August 10, appeared on August 19 and is relatively mild in its attacks. The letter fits well the long tradition in America of political satire.[11]

At this point, however, Lincoln jumped into the fray. He could not resist the opportunity for ripe satire. He wrote a second Rebecca letter "from the lost township," and it differs in tone and form and is much more hard hitting politically and personally. It is dated August 27, shortly after Shields's office formally issued the order for the State Bank not to accept its own currency for payment of taxes, and appeared in the paper on September 2. Written in satiric vernacular, the letter brims with sarcasm and disdain. If in fact Lincoln and Mary were meeting secretly by that point, one can imagine much mirth constructing the letter in the home of Simeon and Eliza Francis and even Mary's presence egging Lincoln on.[12]

The letter specifically calls Shields a "fool and a liar . . . With him truth is out of the question, and as for getting a good bright passable lie out of him, you might as well try to strike fire from a cake of tallow." The letter also makes great fun of Shields bombastically flirting with "all the galls . . . finickin about, trying to look like galls, tied as tight in the middle, and puffed out at both ends like bundles of fodder that hadn't been stacked yet, but wanted stackin pretty bad." In an "exstatic agony of his soul" he tells them, "Dear girls, *it is distressing*, but I cannot marry you all. Too well I know how much you suffer; but do, *do* remember, it is not my fault that I am *so* handsome and *so* interesting."

Shields was not amused by the second Rebecca letter. It was probably not a good idea for Lincoln to humiliate a narcissist, someone prone to react with rage to even a hint of an insult, let alone an outright and public humiliation. Did Lincoln sense he was mocking emotionally wounded prey? Shields had his friend Dr. John D. Whiteside contact Simeon Francis, demanding to know the author. Sending a "second" to make such a demand evoked subtextually the *code duello*. With a long history, dueling was always something between gentlemen, as what was at stake was honor (common folk wrestled and gouged out each other's eyes). In America, dueling was especially important in the South with its exaggerated notions of honor, but it was not infrequent elsewhere.

The point of the code, however, with its rituals and highly elaborate rules involving seconds and who can say what, when, and to whom, was not to encourage fights but to restrict them and to set up the specific ways in which the duel could be avoided yet honor maintained. It was particularly important in 1842 in Illinois to avoid an actual fight if at all possible, since dueling was illegal in the state. As an institution, it was outmoded but hardly banished from the cultural landscape. For two men of stature like Lincoln and Shields, dueling could have meant the end of their political careers—if not the life of one or the other.

Whiteside's demand on behalf of Shields put Simeon Francis in an awkward position as editor of the *Sangamo Journal*. He wanted to stay apparently neutral and certainly not betray his friend Lincoln. He was able to buy some time, however, because Shields had to leave town on business, and when he returned Lincoln went out on the circuit to Tremont.

In this interval another Rebecca letter appeared in the paper on September 9. Julia Jayne, with some help from her dear friend Mary Todd, drafted this letter (as well as some verses that appeared separately). It would seem likely that Lincoln and Mary were in communication as they wrote this letter, but the other back story was Jayne's own longstanding annoyance with Shields. William Butler, in an interview later, said that at a party at the Edwards home sometime earlier in the summer of 1842, Shields "squeezed Miss [Julia Jayne's] hand," presumably meaning that he was forward with this very lovely young woman. Butler, though cryptic in his account, makes clear that Jayne's revenge for Shields's unwanted advances was to write the last "lost township" letter, though Butler had the mistaken idea that Jayne wrote all the letters, "probably with Mary Todd's connivance."[13]

Shields's unwanted advances to Julia Jayne play out in this Rebecca letter. Relentlessly mocking, the letter draws on Jayne's personal experience with Shields to make a complete fool out of him. The letter also additionally taunts him for his threats to force a duel over the contents of the previous letter. Aunt Becca thus reports that she had heard Shields didn't like the previous letter and was "threatnin' to take personal satisfaction of the writer." When she heard this, "I was so skart that I tho't I should quill-wheel right where I was." She is ready to apologize by offering Shields the satisfaction of squeezing her hand. "If that ain't personal satisfaction, I can only say that he is the fust man that was not satisfied with squeezin' my hand." But if he still wants to fight, rather than "get a lickin'," she will marry him. "And I don't think, upon the whole, that I'd be sich a bad match neither— I'm not over sixty, and am just four feet three in my bare feet, and not much more around the girth." If he still insists on fighting, she will only use "broomsticks or hot water or a shovelful of coals or some such thing."[14]

Shields probably assumed this third letter was a prodding by the same person who wrote the second one (though by this point Shields may well have suspected it was Lincoln, given his reputation as a humorist and his close friendship with Simeon Francis), and it naturally fueled Shields's rage. Whiteside now made another demand of Francis to reveal the author of the Rebecca letters. Mary Todd was definitely involved with Jayne in some way in constructing the last letter, had probably been at least aware of Lincoln's second letter, and had herself also published some satiric doggerel making fun of Shields in the paper on September 16 under the name of "Cathleen." Francis could not, of course, reveal the names of the women nor the nature of their involvement, as dueling was strictly a male thing. Polite women did not write publicly, especially satire. The demand by Whiteside gave Lincoln the opportunity not only to come out of the shadows but also in the process become Mary's savior. She liked that. Mary wrote later, in discussing Shields and the letters, that Lincoln thought "he had some right, to assume to be *my* champion, even on frivolous occasions." And in another letter, Mary said that some "silly verses" she wrote "irritated Shields & he demanded the author, of the Editor, the latter, requesting a few days, for reflection repaired to Mr Lincoln, who having heard of it, through me, immediately told the Editor, that

202 MARY TODD, ONCE AGAIN

'he would be responsible.'" That "through me" can only mean that Lincoln and Mary were already in close communication throughout the drama of the Rebecca letters. William Butler corroborated that the "requirement of gallantry" left Lincoln no choice and told Francis that he should be named as the author.[15]

Since Lincoln was in Tremont, Shields and Whiteside made a special trip there on September 17 to hand Lincoln a letter that all knew now was the formal beginnings of the steps that had to be followed in the duel narrative. The letter noted Francis had told Shields that Lincoln was the author of the Rebecca letters. Shields wrote that the letters made him the object of "slander, vituperation and personal abuse" and demanded a "full, positive and absolute retraction of all offensive allusions used by you," along with an apology. And Shields adds: "This may prevent consequences which no one will regret more than myself."[16]

At this point Lincoln could not easily sidestep the challenge with a simple apology, as he had done when he offended William Anderson much less personally two years earlier. Besides, Shields was touchier. But Lincoln also had his dander up, perhaps related to the renewed presence of Mary in his life, for whom he had "gallantly" assumed responsibility for all the Rebecca letters. He had someone now whose honor he needed to protect and to impress with his courage. When Whiteside returned later in the day on September 17, Lincoln handed him a haughty note, acknowledging his authorship of the Rebecca letters but asserting, "I cannot submit to answer that note any farther than I have." That evening Shields wrote another testy note that was delivered two days later. Lincoln didn't deign to reply. Shields issued a challenge to a duel.[17]

Lincoln seemed both furious at Shields's intransigence but eager to find a way out of his dilemma without seeming cowardly or failing to act as a "gentleman." He decided to accept the challenge, perhaps, as Albert Beveridge argued many years ago, encouraged by his combative second, Elias H. Merryman. In the code of dueling, the person challenged chooses the weapon, site, and time of the duel. Lincoln chose "Cavalry broad swords of the largest size" and a ten-foot-long plank as the line between him and Shields; for either to "pass his foot" over the plank is to "forfeit of his life." Some four to five feet back (the length of the sword plus three feet) two lines will be drawn parallel to the plank. If either party steps over that line, he forfeits. The area for fighting was thus tightly circumscribed. The time for the duel was set for Thursday evening, September 22 (he wrote his memorandum about the conditions on Monday), and the place an island opposite Alton on the other side of the river and technically a kind of no-man's land.[18]

The choice of broadswords at close range suggests a touch of humor on Lincoln's part, not to mention a practical way not to get killed. The fiery Shields was five feet, eight inches tall and could not hope to match Lincoln's height of six feet, four inches, his long, strong arms, or his athletic ability. Lincoln, however, unlike Shields, did not possess any special skill in using guns. Furthermore, the terms of the duel were so odd and out of sync with tradition that they in fact mocked Shields. Dueling with swords had gone out of favor by the seventeenth century. Lincoln later told his law friend Usher Linder, "To tell you the truth, Linder, I did not want to kill Shields, and felt sure that I could disarm him, having had about a month to learn the broadsword exercise [presumably in the Blackhawk War]; and furthermore, I didn't want the d—d fellow to kill me, which I rather think he would have done if we had selected pistols."[19]

Quite a few colleagues and friends of both parties—including William Butler and John J. Hardin—got involved to try to prevent the duel. There was much to-ing and fro-ing at the site on "Bloody Island" and many stories, most unlikely, that were told later about what happened that day. At the last moment, however, it is clear that Shields's friends forced a settlement on him by withdrawing his note and accepting as an apology Lincoln's written "explanation" that he never intended to injure "the personal or private character or standing of Mr. Shields as a gentleman or a man." Lincoln did not have to retract anything from the newspaper concerning the Rebecca letters, which had been the demand Shields made initially through Whiteside to Francis. It was an inglorious end, especially for Shields, but a duel was averted. Everybody went home.[20]

Lincoln was ambivalent about his near-duel with Shields. It has been noted by most biographers that he was later ashamed of the affair, didn't talk about it, and was more careful after 1842 never again specifically to write anonymous attacks against anyone and generally to be more careful in his satirical comments about political opponents. Lincoln had a history of mocking political opponents. He was so skilled with language and satire that he sometimes hurt and offended people.

After the Shields affair, he never crossed that line again. Mary said later that after it was over, she and Lincoln were "mutually agreed, never to refer to it & except in an occasional light manner, between us, it was never mentioned." Lincoln wanted to banish discussion of the Shields episode. He wanted it out of public awareness, as any discussion of his involvement in what was after all illegal activity could have negatively affected his career. Once during the Civil War an impertinent army officer referred to the affair. Lincoln, with a flushed face, replied, "I do not deny it, but if you desire my friendship, you will never mention it again." Discretion about the near-duel was politically wise and the better part of valor. A decent man, Lincoln probably did also come to think of the possibility of actually killing Shields with horror. Speed later told Herndon that Lincoln "did not wish to kill Shields—The very thought was agony." Dueling was not in character for Lincoln. He obviously didn't shy away from the challenge, but he also never issued one himself nor baited political opponents with the intention of fighting a duel. He seemed surprised, even if naïvely so, at Shields's challenge.[21]

But in the moment Lincoln was rather pleased with the way things turned out. He had avoided bloodshed but put Shields in his place. His friends regarded him as having acted with gentlemanly courage and honor. The only thing Lincoln ever told Herndon about the near-duel was that "if it had been necessary I could have split him from the crown of his head to the end of his backbone." He also seemed at the time more disdainful of Shields than ashamed of the near-duel. Less than a week later, Lincoln wrote Speed a long letter describing the "dueling business" that "still rages in this city." Shields, it seems, humiliated and out of control, the day after he returned from Alton challenged William Butler, who accepted, but Whiteside, Shields's second, averted it "because of the law." Whiteside then "chose to consider himself insulted by Dr. Merryman," who had been Lincoln's second. Lincoln served as Merryman's second and provides Speed with details, but eventually that challenge, too, fizzled out. "The town," Lincoln notes sarcastically, "is in a ferment and a street fight somewhat anticipated." Street fights are not what gentlemen engage in.[22]

Lincoln had also been manly regarding Mary. In that regard, the following May (1843), Lincoln wrote his friend John J. Hardin, who more than anyone had worked out the final wording of the note that satisfied Shields, to "measure one of the largest of those swords, we took to Alton, and write me the length of it, from tip of the point to tip of the hilt, in feet and inches, I have a dispute about the length." Lincoln was clearly talking with friends about the duel. Was the issue who had the longer sword?[23]

✳✳✳

After Hardin took possession of the broadswords, the would-be duelists returned home. Shields sulked and caused more trouble; Lincoln threw himself enthusiastically back into his relationship with Mary, his covert coauthor. Lincoln wrote Speed anxiously on October 5 about "that subject which you know to be of such infinite solicitude to me." Lincoln notes the "immense suffering" Speed endured from his engagement to his marriage and how Speed never tried to conceal it from Lincoln. Now, "You have been the husband of a lovely woman nearly eight months. That you are happier now than you were the day you married her I well know; for without, you would not be living," which is a curious and oblique reference to Speed's own possible suicide talk at some point in the buildup to his marriage. Lincoln has Speed's word for his happiness now, however, not to mention the "returning elasticity of spirits which is manifested in your letters." Lincoln was a close reader of texts. Just to be absolutely sure, however, Lincoln asks: "Are you now, in *feeling* as well as *judgement*, glad you are married as you are?" He knows that such a question from anybody else would be "impudent" and "not to be tolerated." But Lincoln trusts that Speed will "pardon it in me." He urges Speed to answer quickly, "as I feel impatient to know."[24]

Speed must have answered quickly and favorably that indeed he was happy to be married. The context of Lincoln's letter suggests he had not yet formally proposed to Mary. Assuming Speed wrote back immediately after receiving the October 5 letter, Lincoln probably actually proposed around October 20, and he and Mary proceeded with plans for their marriage.[25] The most difficult challenge for Mary was how to bring her sister along with her decision to marry Lincoln. Mary reasonably feared Elizabeth might object. The last time Mary and Lincoln planned a wedding, it ended in disaster. Besides, Mary may have felt that Elizabeth and especially Ninian remained opposed to her love for and choice of Lincoln, though Elizabeth also undoubtedly worried that Mary could get hurt again. A big wedding like the one Elizabeth arranged for Frances when she married Dr. Wallace seemed out of the question.

They therefore needed another site. Mary had been attending the Episcopal church and knew and respected its minister, Dr. Charles Dresser. While Lincoln was unchurched, he was friendly with Dresser and quite comfortable with having him officiate (and it was Dresser who would later sell the Lincolns their house at Eighth and Jackson Streets). Mary also needed a ring, and at some point they visited Chatterton's jewelry shop, close to Speed's old store on the west side of the square. Lincoln purchased a gold ring and had it inscribed with a phrase he and Mary selected together: "Love is eternal."

The big day came on Friday, November 4, and with it some drama. Lincoln and Mary planned it all in secret and hoped to pull it off quietly with Dresser in the Episcopal church. But when Mary told Elizabeth that morning, a fight ensued that ended with Elizabeth finally accepting the inevitable. Lincoln meanwhile met with Ninian and announced his plans to wed Mary that evening. Ninian may have been upset, but the only thing he insisted on was that, since Mary was his ward, the wedding must be in his home. Dresser would still officiate, but the ceremony was to take place in the parlor of the Edwards home.

The rest of the day was filled with Elizabeth and her servants feverishly scurrying about buying food and drink for the reception. Mary set off to round up bridesmaids in her cousin, Elizabeth Todd, and Julia Jayne and to figure out what to wear, which was a dress of white satin. In passing, Lincoln's law partner, Judge Logan, handed him five dollars from Samuel D. Marshall, an attorney who wanted Lincoln to handle his client's case upon appeal. Without time to reply to Marshall, he went upstairs for a moment to ask the court clerk, James H. Matheny, to be his best man, that literate and sensitive soul serving surely as a stand-in for Speed; got a haircut from William de Fleurville, a Haitian-born black man in town known as "Billy the Barber"; and then remanded himself to the Butlers to get dressed. The nervous groom, in what may well be an apocryphal story, joked with young Speed Butler, who asked where he was going. "To hell I suppose."

Some thirty guests crowded into the parlor for the wedding and reception. One witness said Lincoln looked "as if he was going to the

Slaughter," but Frances Wallace (Mary's sister) said he was "cheerful as he ever had been, for all we could see." When it was over, the Lincolns walked to their temporary new home, the Globe Tavern, on the north side of Adams Street about halfway between Third and Fourth Streets. The Globe was a bit seedy and crowded for Mary's tastes, but it was home—and where Robert Lincoln was conceived almost immediately. Lincoln wrote Speed the following May that he was still boarding at the Globe, "which is very well kept now by a widow lady of the name of Beck." The room, he adds, costs only four dollars a week.[26]

Lincoln was no longer in a room over a store or living in Butler's bustling, crowded mansion but waking up in the mornings with a wife by his side. She was on his mind often during that honeymoon stage. On November 11 at his desk in his law office, Lincoln scribbled the overdue reply to Samuel D. Marshall, agreeing to the suggested contingency arrangement by which he would charge nothing if he lost the case on appeal. He asked Marshall, himself an attorney, to take the necessary steps to procure the underlying court record of the case. Musing over his feelings, he added: "Nothing new here, except my marrying, which to me, is matter of profound wonder."[27]

12

THE CRUCIBLE
OF GREATNESS

You, no doubt, assign the suspension of our correspondence
to the true philosophical cause, though it must be confessed,
by both of us, that this is rather a cold reason for allowing a
friendship, such as ours, to die by degrees.

—Abraham Lincoln to Joshua Speed, October 22, 1846

Lincoln's marriage has often been misunderstood. Historians have far too often drawn battle lines about what they believe Lincoln did feel or should have felt about Mary, and most of all they projected back from her later problems onto what she presented at the outset. But people change in the face of life. Mary Todd was charming in her youth, a spritely and unusually well-educated woman full of life and vitality. As a survivor of the early loss of her mother when she was six, Mary also shared an unconscious connection with Lincoln. Both experienced the sudden and traumatic death of their mothers when it was almost impossible to grasp the meaning of such catastrophic loss in any real sense.

Mary Todd also fell desperately in love with Abraham Lincoln, a man riddled with self-doubt about intimacy. He was drawn to her, pulled back, even deserted her, and then finally returned with enthusiasm to marry her. Lincoln certainly had enough time to ponder his choice. He never mocked his love for her, as he had with Mary Owens. In his letters to Speed, Lincoln is full of regret and self-criticism for hurting Mary, precisely because he cares so deeply for her. The issue was not a want of affection but his own inadequacy to follow through on his commitments. When he finally recovers his resolve via Speed's marriage, Lincoln can risk reaching out again to Mary. Even then he hesitates, and it seems it took some well-meaning friends to nudge him along. But, at last, that fall of 1842 Lincoln overcame his fears and married.

Their children, who followed in just over the next decade, completed the family for which he yearned, though the death of his second son, Eddy, in 1850, while sad for him, proved to be the start of Mary's gradual psychological unraveling. She had two more children, in 1850 and 1853, but that extended family came as Lincoln became absorbed by the issues tearing apart the country. He became a public figure once again after 1854, soon for Illinois and then for the entire country. His expanded law practice and constant politicking took him away from Mary when she most needed him at her side. In the first decade of their marriage he spent significantly less time out on the circuit, for example, and tried to come home on weekends when possible. He was also not campaigning much, except when he successfully ran for Congress in 1846 and then served in Washington for one term. In the second decade or so of the marriage, however, he decisively moved away from Mary. His practice became quite lucrative, and he spent more time on the circuit and seldom returned home on weekends. In the mid- and late 1850s he was also in an almost constant campaign mode. This took a great toll on Mary. She fumed and raged because she desperately needed him with her at all times. He pulled away, and she despaired. They may also have stopped having sex. He tried to soothe her, but he couldn't solve her problems fully and at the same time make a bid for the Senate and then the presidency. The love remained on both sides, but the house divided as he tried to solve for all what he couldn't solve for himself alone.[1]

***

Meanwhile, back in Kentucky Joshua and Fanny Speed moved to the "Pond Settlement," a thousand-acre tract about thirteen miles from Louisville on the Salt River Road. It was a lovely site, "lying at the foot of the knobs," as his nephew put it, with a simple house, although it was a large enough operation to require the regular purchase of slaves (Speed owned sixteen by 1850). It was a happy time for the Speeds.

Like Joshua, whose description of Springfield in his *Reminiscences* begins with a list of flowers, Fanny loved flowers and covered the grounds in roses, something remarked on by neighbors and visitors. As the nephew wrote: "They spent many hours together in the fields and woods, seeing rare species of wild flowers." Joshua had a "vein of sentiment in his nature which made him fond of flowers and poetry."[2]

He and Fanny bonded and remained close for the rest of their life together (she outlived him by twenty years). They never had children and therefore never faced the stresses and fault lines that sometimes come from raising children as did, for example, the Lincolns, but both were indulgently affectionate and close to the many Speed nieces and nephews. Speed's family was uniformly supportive and loving toward Fanny. Brother James Speed, later to serve in Lincoln's cabinet, emphasized how well suited they were for each other. "Every man has not such a brother nor every woman such a man as Joshua," James later wrote his mother. "He [Joshua] is a man whom all men who know him must respect, and women love . . . By the way, I think that Fanny's loveliness of character, has contributed its full share to make him what he is." Speed could be distracted and was noted in Louisville as a man of great reserve, but his devotion to Fanny was complete and enduring. Surviving letters illustrate a lifelong love. When absent from her, his letters were tender, even sentimental.

> I wrote to you yesterday, and to-day, having some leisure, I will write again, upon the principle, I suppose, that where your treasure is there will your heart go. My earthly treasure is in you; not like the treasures only valuable in possession; not like other valuables acquiring increased value from increased quantity; but, satisfied with each other, we will go down the hill of life together, as we have risen.

He endeavored to charm the stars in the sky and clouds of the day for her entertainment and pleasure.

And another time he wrote her:

> Last evening, as I sat upon the porch . . . [and] thought of you and wished for you . . . It seemed as though the clouds had more beautiful phantasms of every shape and form, like bridesmaids and

bridegrooms, waiting in graceful attendance upon the wedding of day and night, than I ever saw before. Night, like the blushing bride, was coy and shy, and gave evidence of her modesty in her blushing cheeks, while day, like a gallant knight, who had won his spurs upon the bloody battle-field in the heady current of the fight, had done his duty, laid aside his helmet and his spear, and approached his bride in the rich and beautiful garb of a lover. The wedding over, the stars came out, like guests invited to the feast, and, I suppose, kept up the carousal till dawn of day. I retired, and give no further report.[3]

Imaginative Joshua and Fanny lived on the Pond Settlement for nine years. He planted corn, managed the slaves, and, unafraid of physical labor, sometimes worked in the fields. As he wrote Butler on April 3, 1842, "I am busy now ploughing for corn—have had hold of the plough handle for about ten days myself. I will have about 170 acres in corn and only seven hands, myself included, to cultivate it."[4] What is not clear from existing sources, however, is Joshua's relation in these years to Farmington. In one letter before he left Springfield, Speed mentions that his family proposed that he run Farmington, but he never seems to have considered it seriously and in fact made clear that was not his desire. He wanted his brother Philip to play that role. What probably happened, given the close ties of all the Speeds, is that he consulted with his mother and siblings on the management of Farmington, may well have been involved with the buying and selling of slaves, and probably shared in its wealth but never again actually lived there.

Speed was also doing more than farming his corn. He had many business interests that were prospering, including collecting on debts from his time in Springfield, which lingered for years. At first Lincoln handled Speed's local legal business. Speed wanted regular updates and reports, if not money. He hounded Lincoln to hound others. He relied on Lincoln to go to court and get judgments and then to get those judgments enforced by the sheriff by seizing property or further court action. Lincoln did so, within limits. A few months after leaving town, for example, Lincoln reports to Speed of a "judgment against Lockridge, as you anticipate," but James Bell, Speed's cousin and former partner, fell for a story by the debtor and directed Lincoln to stay the execution of another judgment for a few months. Other notes are in the works, Lincoln wrote, including one from a Mr. Richards ("the judge I presume will attend to it, but for me I cannot even dun him") and a John Branson, who admitted he owed money to Speed but said he would pay soon and begged Lincoln not to sue him. Collecting on Speed's many overdue notes continued to occupy Lincoln's time well into 1843. Between January and July of that year, Lincoln wrote Speed four long and detailed letters about the dealings with Peter van Bergen, William Walters, a note James Speed put on Bell & Boice that Joshua had assigned to his brother William, a note on Cannan & Harlan and another on B. C. Webster & Co., and on and on. One of the things that enormously complicated the various transactions was the conge-ries of currencies that circulated then. On January 18, 1843, for exam-ple, Charles R. Hurst, who bought Speed's store mostly on credit, paid Lincoln, acting on Speed's behalf, a $72 installment on his debt in the form of banknotes, $42 in "Shawneetown paper," and $2.59 in specie.[5]

Not surprisingly, there were delays in Lincoln's ability to sort all this out with Speed so far away. His mind also didn't warm to the nitty-gritty of these complicated debts, which lingered and which he probably handled either without charge or at a reduced fee. As a result, Lincoln may have pushed some of Speed's affairs to the back burner of his own busy practice at a time when he needed to increase his income to support his new family. Whatever the explanation, after 1843 there was a long break in Lincoln's letters to Speed, who got annoyed. Between July 1843 and October 22, 1846, Lincoln wrote nothing, but in his October letter, clearly responding to an angry letter from Speed, Lincoln tries to justify his handling of the hugely complicated issues around the estate of Speed's uncle James Bell after his death. Lincoln adds his regret that whatever happens with Bell and business it is a "cold reason" to allow their friendship "to die by degrees."[6]

Initially after their marriages, Lincoln and Speed tried to remain personally close. On January 18, 1843, Lincoln reports that Mary is doing well and "continues her old sentiments of friendship for you," and he promises to report on married life when he sees him soon in a visit promised for the fall. On March 24, 1843, when Mary was five months pregnant, he tells Speed, "About the prospect of your having a namesake at our house cant say, exactly yet." And on July 26, 1843, just before Mary delivered, Lincoln says "We are but two, as yet," and he looks forward "with impatience to your visit this fall." But a fault line between Springfield and Louisville was opening up. The planned visit for the fall of 1843 never occurred, and the baby born on August 1 that was to be "Joshua" became "Robert." This naming exposed a widening gap. Mary undoubtedly played a role in choosing to name her first born after her father, but that decision clearly altered Lincoln's earlier intention to name his first-born boy after the best friend in his life. The two friends said nothing to each other after the heated exchange in the fall of 1846, and Lincoln pushed all Speed work off on Herndon (his law partner after 1844). Lincoln and Mary did visit with Speed in Louisville in the Scott's Hotel in late October 1847. Lincoln was traveling to Washington for his one term as a congressman. The report of the visit in the local Louisville paper does not indicate if Fanny was with Speed, but it is unlikely he would have left her out of such a visit. But except for that visit, Lincoln and Speed had no contact and corresponded infrequently. After 1846 until the late 1850s they had only two exchanges, both of which were of a political nature (in 1849 and in 1855, discussed below).[7]

* * *

After he left Springfield, Speed actually remained in closer touch with William Butler than with Lincoln. Butler and Speed shared business minds. Speed, of course, had known Butler before Lincoln arrived in town, and together they took their meals with family (and the Butler baby born in 1837 was named Speed Butler). Butler was a shrewd businessman whose deals sometimes hovered on the cusp of being corrupt. In his position as clerk of the circuit court, he learned about land foreclosures before other investors. This knowledge was invaluable after the panic of 1837. Together with Philip C. Latham of Logan County, between 1838 and 1840 Butler bought almost three thousand acres of land from cash-starved farmers for a total of $86.73. That is less than three cents an acre at a time when public-domain land was selling for $1.25 an acre. Impoverished farmers would take almost anything from unscrupulous investors. Butler also invested in all kinds of other deals that at least in the 1840s involved Speed at times from a distance.[8]

One remarkable letter Speed wrote Butler in 1842 suggests the range of the business interactions between the two men.[9] Speed begins by telling Butler not to worry about a note he holds on Butler. "Do not permit it to harass you," he says, because the money was not transferable. Speed then mentions three deals in cryptic terms that cannot now be explained ("I have the thought that the B—t farm had better be included with the rest," for example). Speed also mocks the business sense of Moseby, the postmaster, whose debt to Speed was communicated to him by Charles Hurst. Speed also reports that Lincoln told him "old Billy Herndon" (an uncle of William Herndon) had died. Old Billy had been taking care of a six-acre lot Speed owned. He offers Butler the use of the land to pasture his cow as payment for protecting the timber on the land.

But most remarkably Speed asks Butler to help in his purchase of a slave. Someone named Mr. Bradford, "a partner of Johnson the Book binder," was in Louisville and asked Speed if he wanted to "purchase his negro," a man about forty-eight years of age, for $250. As part of the deal, Bradford wanted to exchange some property Speed owned in Springfield ("he seemed to like my lots in Edwards addition"). Speed asks Butler to facilitate the exchange of lots as part of the deal in which he would buy the slave. The long hand of slave trading reached its fingers into Springfield as late as the early 1840s.

***

At just the moment Lincoln went to Congress, Speed entered politics himself. He did not take to it. In 1848–1849, Speed served one term in the legislature. Joshua followed his brother James, who served in the legislative term immediately preceding Joshua's. James had found legislative work mostly "frivolous and foolish," as he wrote his mother. Joshua would agree soon enough himself, but when the slavery debate heated up, he got interested. Kentucky had a robust antislavery movement that was not abolitionist but did seek to limit the importation of slaves into the state and to place restrictions on its trade. Various laws, including the Nonimportation Law of 1833, tried to accomplish those goals, even though they were often flaunted. The passage of that bill aroused the even larger and more robust proslavery elements that sought annually to amend it. They were able consistently to pass amendments gutting the bill in the Senate but were never able to get it through the House. By 1847 it seemed the proslavery groups would succeed. The reason was the backlash in the state against the abolitionist movement, which had increasingly gained traction nationally because of the opposition to the Mexican War. That war threatened to bring into the country vast new lands that would be open to slavery. The threat had stirred moderates (like Lincoln, who said he voted repeatedly for the Wilmot Proviso) as well as firebrands like William Lloyd Garrison, who talked ceaselessly about the evils of slavery and the necessity to abolish it, with or mostly without compensation. Many of those in Kentucky who sought to restrict the importation of slaves into the state were themselves slave owners. These were liberals in the tradition of Henry Clay but hardly radicals who wanted abolition. They just didn't want too many slaves in the state and hoped for gradual and compensated emancipation followed by colonization.[10]

During the intense Kentucky parliamentary struggles in 1847, James sided with those seeking to maintain the integrity of the 1833 law and not gut it with amendments or riders. A crucial vote on such an amendment passed in the House but just failed in the Senate, setting up the fight to continue in the next session of the legislature. James decided not to run this time around, but Joshua did run and got elected. Like his brother, Joshua also found most of the work tedious and boring. As he wrote his sister, "My mind has been forced to act upon subjects foreign to my usual habit of thought." Nor did the sensitive Speed like the ungentlemanly ways of some fellow legislators, as he makes a vague reference to men flirting with his attractive wife.[11]

The slavery issue, however, that drew him to the legislature kept him going. After much debate and maneuvering, the House unanimously adopted a resolution stating, "We, the representatives of the People of Kentucky, are opposed to abolition or emancipation of slavery in any form or shape whatever, except as now provided for by law and the Constitution." The qualification was virtually toothless, however, for the constitution of the state expressly forbade the legislature ever to abolish slavery without the express permission of slave owners. Later in the session, the antislavery groups tried, again, to amend the 1833 law and limit the importation of slaves and to restrict the slave trade in the state. The bill was soundly defeated, with Joshua Speed voting with the majority. It was a satisfying outcome but not enough to keep him in office.

Speed determined after that not to play a visible role in politics. He preferred to be a power broker behind the scenes rather than try to lead out front, which was exactly how he operated in Springfield. There Lincoln's presence was much larger. In his years in Springfield, Speed served on many key committees, was one of the young Turks in the local Whig party, and was often consulted on the issues of the day, but Lincoln was the public figure, the one who gave powerful speeches and nurtured great ambitions. Besides, Speed was much too courteous and retiring for the rough-and-tumble atmosphere of the prewar Kentucky legislature. Politics was not his passion the way it was with Lincoln, but he did stay close to the action. His nephew said that Speed was always engaged in public affairs and made sure to have friends across the political spectrum: "His friendships were never affected by political or religious views differing from his own." As Lincoln would find at an urgent moment, Speed stood ready to play a crucial role in the state when the time came for him to come out of the shadows.[12]

* * *

By the late 1840s, the Speeds seemed to tire of the Pond Settlement: it was too long of a trip into Louisville. Joshua also realized he was much better at business than he was at running a plantation. As a result, in 1851 he and Fanny moved into Louisville and bought a house on 413 W. Jefferson, which was not far from his brother James and his mother, Lucy. Joshua and Fanny moved to two other houses in Louisville, one in 1861 and another in 1865, before locating outside of town in 1869. The year 1851 also brought a formal shift in Speed's career. He formed a real-estate partnership with his brother-in-law James W. Henning. This business lasted until his death in 1882 and became very large and lucrative. The two men were a good mix. Henning knew real estate in the city extremely well, and Speed, as his nephew put it, had "no superior as a financier." They became trustees for all kinds of public and private businesses in the city. Everyone attested to Speed's "ability, fidelity, and fairness." Besides his involvement in real estate, Speed took an interest in the burgeoning business of railroads, becoming president in 1853 of the Louisville, Cincinnati, and Lexington line (after 1855 he was vice president and served on the board).[13]

Although Speed had moved into Louisville and was no longer running a medium-sized plantation, he retained ownership of his slaves.
In the tax lists, he owns fifteen slaves in both 1850 and 1851, sixteen
in 1852, down to fourteen in 1853, ten in 1854, and for the next decade
stays with between ten and eleven. In 1864 and 1865—after the passage of the Emancipation Proclamation the first of January 1863,
which technically didn't apply to Kentucky, but before the Thirteenth
Amendment, which made slavery illegal in the United States at the
end of 1865 (though it never actually was ratified by Kentucky until
1976, and then only symbolically)—Joshua Speed owned three and
then two slaves.[14]

Some questions occur immediately from this startling evidence
of Speed's continued ownership of a fairly large number of slaves
throughout the 1850s and even during the war. Where did they live?
During his years at the Pond Settlement in the 1840s (when he came
to own fourteen slaves by 1848), Speed almost certainly had slave
quarters like those he was familiar with as a child at Farmington. But
once he moved to Louisville in 1851, he would not have needed slaves
except as servants to cook, garden, do the washing and other chores,
and drive his carriage. Such slaves generally lived in a basement or in
a room above a kitchen. But it is hard to believe the Speeds needed, or
wanted, anywhere from ten to fifteen slaves living with them in their
house. Those not needed as servants Speed probably held onto as an
investment and hired out for work. In such arrangements, the person
who leased the slave paid taxes on him while Speed remained on the
tax lists as the owner. Speed also regularly, in three different business
partnerships, as Pen Bogert and his colleagues have noted, "engaged in
brokering, selling and hiring enslaved African Americans."[15]

* * *

Joshua Speed, in other words, moved in opposite directions on a number of fronts from Lincoln after their years together in the late 1830s
and early 1840s. He prospered and was deeply happy in his marriage,
but he was inevitably confused by the national debate over slavery in
the years leading up to the war. The issue in Kentucky had never been
about the abolition of slavery (except on the fringes) but whether to
place restrictions on it. After the contentious parliamentary struggles

in 1848 and 1849, a constitutional convention was called in the early 1850s to try to alter the strict limits on any kind of emancipation in Article 9 of the state constitution. It went nowhere. But Kentucky could not escape the national ferment of the 1850s, especially after passage, by the U.S. Congress, of the Kansas-Nebraska bill in 1854, which opened up the possibility of extending slavery into the territories and giving it new life to grow and thrive. It was that bill, engineered by none other than Senator Stephen Douglas, that aroused Lincoln to return to politics and become the main spokesman for a position that came to define the new Republican Party and eventually catapult him into the presidency. This new context for the debate over slavery after 1854 led to the disintegration of the Whig Party and the rise of the Know-Nothing Party, which sidestepped slavery and centered its ideology on nativism and anti-Catholicism. At the same time, the Democratic Party, in an attempt to gain more national power, tried to soften its previously rabid defense of slavery.

This political swirl swept up Speed as it did the nation. After 1854 Joshua was basically without a party, once the Whigs disintegrated. He had always despised Democrats and now distrusted the ugly nativism of the Know-Nothings. He would eventually become a Democrat, however, as did his brother James, at least for a while and perhaps as early as the mid-1850s, but at first after 1854 Speed wasn't sure where he stood as a slave owner and Unionist.[16] It was in that context that he wrote Lincoln on May 22, 1855 (a letter since lost), clearly wanting his advice but also seeking some support from former Whigs for a clear national stance guaranteeing slavery. He must have been surprised at Lincoln's response. This was not the principled but circumspect man Speed had once known so well.

Lincoln's reply to Speed on August 24, 1855, pointedly articulates his position on slavery.[17] It is a stance consistent with his earlier beliefs and attitudes but markedly changed in emphasis and tone. The fact that he takes so much effort to clarify his positions with Speed suggests his continued good feelings toward his old friend, whom he says he disagrees with probably less than Speed believes. Lincoln doesn't want to offend Speed and wants him to remain his ally, but he no longer studiously avoids treating issues that previously lay below the surface between them.

Lincoln thus states, "You know I dislike slavery; and you fully admit the abstract wrong of it," which may grant Speed more moral authority than he deserves. In his letter, Speed apparently claimed he would rather see the Union dissolved than relinquish his constitutional right to own slaves. Lincoln bristled at any talk of dissolving the Union. "I am not aware that *any one* is bidding you to yield that right [to own slaves]; very certainly, *I* am not . . . I acknowledge *your* rights and *my* obligations, under the constitution, in regard to your slaves." Lincoln "hates to see the poor creatures hunted down" and "carried back to their stripes, and unrewarded toils," but—and this is the first time he has ever said as much to Speed—"I bite my lip and keep quiet."

Lincoln, rewriting history a bit, reminds Speed of their trip together on the Ohio River returning to Springfield from Louisville in the fall of 1841, when they witnessed the slaves on board "shackled together with irons . . . precisely like so many fish upon a trot-line." Now in 1855, however, Lincoln breaks through the numbed image to tell Speed that the sight of those slaves is "a continual torment to me." He chastises Speed for not being "fair" to assume he has "no interest" or stake in something (that is, slavery) that has the power to make him "miserable." Like most Northerners, he has to "crucify" his feelings to maintain "loyalty to the constitution and the Union." These are strong words intentionally kept out of his discourse and probably at best only in the back of his mind in 1841.

Seeking to clarify his own position to a friend and former Whig who was drifting toward or already in the Democratic Party, Lincoln then goes into a long discussion of the complicated situation in Kansas, where in a bogus election on March 30, enhanced by "border ruffians" from Missouri, the territory voted in a proslavery legislature. Speed seemed mostly concerned about an unfair election and had written that if he were president he would send in the army and hang the ruffians from Missouri. Lincoln wants to avoid hanging anybody and painstakingly argues that there cannot even be such a thing as a fair election in Kansas because the law of 1854 that made it possible for there to be such a question put before voters was not valid and was "*violence* from the beginning." For Lincoln, that is the crucial question. The Kansas-Nebraska bill "was conceived in violence, passed in violence, is maintained in violence, and is being executed in violence." By every principle of law, he says, "every negroe taken to Kansas is free," a position Speed surely disagreed with, having made arrangements with Butler to consider buying a slave who was then residing in Illinois a decade earlier.

After a discussion of his position that there is no right to slaves as property in the territories, Lincoln turns to what had become for him the sacred status of the Union. The man who had spoken in 1838 about the perpetuation of our political institutions was at the lectern again. He hates all the talk of dissolving the United States into two countries. Even if Kansas were to be admitted as a slave state against everything that is legal and right, for example, he would not seek to destroy the Union to undo it. But people can also be bribed and persuaded to do all kinds of things. In the current turmoil, it is especially difficult to know what is right or how Kansas will turn out.

Speed had apparently written that "as a christian" he would "rejoice" if Kansas votes to become a free state. Lincoln refused to allow his friend into such pious posturing. "All decent slave-holders"—meaning Speed and those in places like Kentucky—"*talk* that way; and I do not doubt their candor. But they never *vote* that way." In private conversation, you express your desire to see Kansas free, he tells Speed, but you would never vote for a candidate who would express such views publicly. "No such man could be elected from any district in any slave-state." That refusal allows the most extreme elements to determine the course of events. "The slave-breeders and slave-traders, are a small, odious and detested class, among you; and yet in politics, they dictate the course of all of you, and are as completely your masters, as you are the masters of your own negroes."

Toward the end of his long letter, Lincoln acknowledges the difficulties of defining where he stood politically at that moment of great confusion in the nation. What is he? He is mostly a Whig, "but others say there are no whigs, and that I am an abolitionist." As a congressman (and a good Whig), he says, he voted "as good as forty times" for the Wilmot Proviso, which sought to exclude slavery from any territory acquired from Mexico in the war. Consistent with his position, then, he does "no more than oppose the *extension* of slavery." One thing he definitely hates is the Know-Nothing Party. "How can any one who abhors the oppression of negroes, be in favor of degrading classes of white people?" We began as a nation declaring all men are created equal. That quickly became all men are equal *"except negroes."* If the Know-Nothings take control, it will read "all men are created equal, except negroes, *and foreigners, and catholics."* If that comes to pass, Lincoln says he would prefer "emigrating to some country where they make no pretence of loving liberty—to Russia, for instance, where despotism can be taken pure, and without the base alloy of hypocracy."

Reverting to his role as a friend, Lincoln ends his intense letter about his new understanding of where he stood on politics, slavery, and Kansas on a warm personal note. "Mary," he says, "will probably pass a day or two in Louisville in October" and presumably visit (though there is no record such a visit occurred). Lincoln sends his "kindest regards" to Mrs. Speed, from whom, Lincoln adds, quite knowingly and accurately, "I have more of her sympathy than I have of yours."

Then there was more silence, as Lincoln appeared not to write Speed again for four more years (at least in what Speed scrupulously saved), but Speed did occasionally write Lincoln in what was clearly an effort to keep the friendship alive. Speed was a prolific correspondent whose letters exist in many archives and libraries. Any odd occasion might stimulate him to renew lapsed contacts. On September 22, 1859, for example, he invited Lincoln to the opening of the new racetrack in Louisville on October 10. Speed expects the races will involve "some of the best horses in America to compete for the purses," and, he adds, "we think we can show the prettiest women." Please come "directly to my house—I think that a few days together would rejuvenate us all."[18]

But the events of the day continued to put pressure on the friendship. As the country hurtled toward war, Lincoln emerged as the best choice of the new Republican Party to secure the presidency. After the raucous Republican convention in May 1860, meeting in Chicago, nominated Lincoln for the presidency, Speed wrote him an enthusiastic letter of congratulations on May 19 and asked him, again, to visit Kentucky. He specifically avoided promising to vote Republican, which he in fact did not do in 1860, but he is also confident Lincoln, if elected, would make a good and honest president (even if his praise is tepid). "Should you be elected," he said, "and I think you have a fair Chance for it—I am satisfied that you will honestly administer the government—

and make a lasting reputation for yourself—" Speed, by then firmly identified as a Democrat (though it is not clear whether he voted for Douglas or Breckinridge), added gratuitously that Lincoln would receive Mrs. Speed's vote (women lacked the right to vote nationally until 1920) but that, while a "warm personal friend," he was also a "political opponent." Speed embodied a country in turmoil. The issues of slavery and potential secession were felt so fiercely that Speed, who once knew and admired Lincoln so closely that they could finish each other's sentences, couldn't vote for him as president. Lincoln, however, replied warmly and personally to Speed on May 22, immediately upon receipt of the letter (as he had before only in the early months of 1842). He thanks Speed for the invitation to visit Kentucky and "you in particular," but it would "scarcely be prudent" for him to make such a trip. In those days, it was regarded as unseemly for presidential candidates to campaign, so a trip to Kentucky in what was now the lead up to the elections in the fall would look bad for Lincoln. He says lightly that of course "Mrs. Speed is for me with her nature and views. She could not well be otherwise." Lincoln implores the Speeds to visit him in Springfield and asks if Speed's "good mother" was still living. Finally, he notes that "Mrs. Lincoln joins in good wishes to both Mrs. Speed and yourself."[19]

Lincoln was in no mood to let anything drive a wedge between him and Speed, even if they had drifted far apart in politics. Lincoln was also undoubtedly thinking ahead to how he would run the country if elected. There was no one better suited than Joshua Speed to help him keep Kentucky loyal if the winds of secession blew too hard in the country. The states in general played a greater role in politics than they do now. Shelby Foote best expressed in 1990 an idea that had been around since 1909: "Before the war, it was said 'the United States are.' Grammatically, it was spoken that way and thought of as a collection of independent states. And after the war, it was always 'the United States is,' as we say today without being self-conscious at all. And that sums up what the war accomplished. It made us an 'is.'" No matter how events unfolded—and certainly Lincoln hoped, indeed expected, that there wouldn't be war—it was clear to him that Kentucky as a slave state that was mostly pro-Union would be crucial for effective governance. Speed was trustworthy and honest, a skilled man in the world of finance, respected across political lines, devoted to the Union, and

as a Democrat and slave owner in the tradition of Henry Clay someone Lincoln would want in his cabinet. And, ironically, given Lincoln's
style of leadership, Speed's political affiliation then as a Democrat was
a distinct advantage. If elected, Lincoln was determined to seek out a
diverse group to make up his cabinet, a group Doris Kearns Goodwin
has called his "team of rivals."[20] One last, immeasurably important factor tipped the scale: Speed was his friend.

By some similar calculation of his own, Speed was shrewd enough
to suspect that, once elected on November 6, 1861, Lincoln might offer
him a position in the new administration. Speed dealt with this touchy
subject directly in his letter of congratulations to Lincoln on November 14. Speed warmly sends his regards despite his assertion, once
again, that he was a "political opponent." He does "tremble" for his
friend at what he faces, but all issues of political difference "sink into
utter insignificance" compared to the necessity to preserve "our glorious Union." Speed bemoans that he knows so many in the country will
be completely closed off to listening to Lincoln's message. Speed feels
that he has some thoughts on dealing with the "combustible material
lying around you without setting fire to the edifice of which we are
all so proud" and offers to share his ideas, but he makes clear that his
views are those of a "private citizen seeking no office for himself nor
for any friend he has."[21]

Lincoln, however, had other plans. He did not shelve the idea of
bringing Speed into the cabinet he was then forming, probably as secretary of the treasury. In fact, Speed was the second person Lincoln
consulted (after asking William Seward, the man he defeated for the
Republican nomination, to be secretary of state). There is no question
Lincoln sought a strong cabinet member from Kentucky, but it has not
been generally appreciated that he especially wanted Speed at his side
leading the country. Lincoln wrote Speed on November 19 inviting him
to meet with him in Chicago, and Herndon suggests in his book that
meeting with Speed was the point of the trip. Lincoln wanted to make
it a family affair. He thus adds in his letter to Speed that "Mary thinks
of going with me, and therefore I suggest that Mrs. S. accompany
you." Joshua and Fanny must have gotten on the train immediately
because it seems Lincoln then met with Speed on either November 21
or 22 at Tremont House, where Lincoln was staying. Speed at first had
some trouble gaining admittance to the hotel, but when he produced

Lincoln's letter he was ushered into his room. In Herndon's notes from his interview, Speed says,

> Lincoln was much worn down & fatigued—After the Compli-
> ments—Lincoln Said—Speed have you got a room—"Yes"—
> Said Speed—"Name your hour Speed and I'll Come & see you,"—
> will bring my wife. Lincoln went—took his wife—Said—"Mary
> & Fanny can Stay her—lets you and I go into your room"—
> Lincoln threw himself on the bed—and Said—"Speed what are
> your pecuniary Conditions—are you rich, or poor" Speed Said—
> "Mr Presdt. I think I Know what you wish. I'll Speak Candidly
> to you—My pecuniary Conditions are good—I do not think you
> have any office within your gift that I can afford to take."[22]

Speed was clearly being honest in his November 14 letter when he stated that he had no interest in an appointment in the new govern-ment. He was by then a very wealthy man with extensive and diverse business interests that would have suffered from his inattention if he served in the government. There is no reason to doubt his word on that score. But other factors might have been unspoken concerns for Speed. First, he may have worried that assuming such a public role in the Lincoln administration would have a disruptive impact within his family's social circle and with business associates. Lincoln was widely viewed in Kentucky by his political opponents as a dangerous radical abolitionist (in the 1860 election in Kentucky he received less than 1 percent of the vote). The mirror side of this issue is that Speed might well have feared that he would be regarded as untrustworthy by the Republicans in the administration and in Congress. He was, after all, a slave owner. Second, Speed was probably reluctant to submit to the fray of government again. He had found his one short term in the Ken-tucky legislature trying. He didn't like political battles, strong words, and hot tempers. He was willing to help, however, build a strong cabi-net. In that regard, since he knew it was important for Lincoln to have someone from Kentucky in the cabinet, Speed offered to serve as an intermediary and approach his colleague James Guthrie to be secre-tary of war (who turned down the offer).[23]

✳ ✳ ✳

Speed would provide more important help in the coming months. In fact, no one played a more significant role than Speed in keeping Kentucky in the Union in the critical year of 1861. He worked behind the scenes, maneuvering, scheming, enlisting the right people to do the right things, and most of all drawing on his friendship with Lincoln to do everything from run guns to shape national policy about slavery. It was the kind of role he embraced, and he was remarkably effective. Surprisingly, after the war, Speed was modest in describing his activities to Herndon. He said he never did "any thing [during the war] except in my own State" and "never much in that" except to advise sometimes about "a healthy Unionist Sentiment." Speed, modest as ever, was probably reluctant to toot his own horn to a man he knew was writing a biography of Lincoln. As a result, he vastly understated things.[24] Speed also might have been reluctant in postwar Kentucky to boast of his significant role helping Lincoln keep the state in the Union. In fact, Speed played a pivotal role mostly underappreciated by historians.

Kentucky was central to Lincoln's strategy at the start of the war, and he focused much attention on it that spring. Lincoln said he hoped to have God on his side, but he must have Kentucky. It was touch and go after the war started in the middle of April. As a slave state, there was in Kentucky a strong impetus to go with the South and secede, but loyalty to what Speed called the "glorious Union" also ran strong. What prevailed was a desire to remain neutral. At an important rally organized by James Speed on April 19 in Louisville, speaker after speaker spoke of the dangers of Kentucky becoming a battleground in the war. At the same time, there was much criticism of Lincoln for talking of peace in his inaugural address and then calling for troops to oppose the South's secession. It was generally agreed that the state would not send troops to Washington as Lincoln requested, to his dismay, but the state determined to stay neutral, which for the moment satisfied Lincoln.[25]

The key tactical issue in Kentucky that spring and summer for those who supported Lincoln's effort to save the Union was how to arm the Unionist forces without creating political mayhem. The man at the center of that project was Joshua Speed. The legislature was mostly Unionist, but Governor Beriah Magoffin was secretly conspiring with Confederates to draw Kentucky into the war on the side of the South.

The governor, however, was not very subtle about arming proslavery elements, and Joshua Speed knew all about his furtive and aborted attempt to purchase guns in New Orleans. Speed wrote Lincoln on May 27 about this attempt at gun running, which turned into a fiasco. [26]

It was not, however, so easy to obtain arms for the Unionist forces. Speed wrote Lincoln a bit later that there were "men plenty but no arms." After April and war, the Kentucky congressmen in Washington pleaded with Lincoln to become more actively involved in the affairs of Kentucky, which might otherwise secede and join the South. Lincoln was persuaded and on May 4 instructed Secretary of War Simon Cameron to issue five thousand muskets to Lieutenant William "Bull" Nelson, who left with them that day on a train for Louisville. Lincoln had specifically instructed Nelson to be in touch with Joshua Speed, who was to be responsible for making sure the guns ended up in the right hands. He only trusted Speed to direct this undercover operation. Joshua enlisted his brother James in the project and went immediately to Frankfort to work out with Unionist state legislators how to distribute the arms most effectively. In the course of the next week, there was much cloak-and-dagger work running these guns, but for the most part the project was remarkably successful. Speed had basically worked directly with Lincoln and sidestepped Secretary of War Cameron. Speed might as well have been in the cabinet.[27]

Speed continued his unflagging work for the Union in Kentucky in the summer and early fall. State elections were held on August 5 in the wake of the Union Army's defeat at Bull Run. Some feared the defeat would diminish support for the North, but the Unionists were overwhelmingly elected in both the Kentucky House and Senate. James Speed, for example, decided to run in this election and was elected by over 90 percent in his district.[28] Now Kentucky Unionists were in a much more secure position both politically and militarily.

But just as it seemed Kentucky was secure for the North, on August 30 General John C. Fremont issued declared martial law in the Missouri district he commanded and further declared that anyone who opposed the federal government would have their property seized and their slaves set free. An uproar ensued in Kentucky. The proclamation threatened to turn a war to save the Union into one to end slavery. No one was more distressed than Joshua Speed—and he had the ear of the president. On September 1, he wrote Lincoln in an apocalyptic tone that since Fremont's declaration had been issued he was "unable to eat or sleep" and that the proclamation could stir a slave insurrection, which would in turn unleash great violence by owners against blacks. Two days later he wrote again that if Lincoln allowed the proclamation to stand, "cruelty & crime would run riot in the land & the poor negroes would be almost exterminated." Speed then adds his deeper fears of the very idea of racial equality: "So fixed is public sentiment in this state against freeing negroes & allowing negroes to be emancipated & remain among us—That you had as well attack the freedom of worship in the north or the right of a parent to teach his child to read—as to wage war in a slave state on such a principle—" Speed followed up those letters by a trip to Washington to consult directly with Lincoln. It is unlikely that Lincoln agreed with Speed on the imminence of an insurrection and certainly not with his views of racial (in)equality, but Lincoln tried to assuage Speed's sense of the politics in Kentucky and, to a lesser degree, in Missouri, even though it is not clear that Lincoln had ordered Fremont to withdraw the proclamation on September 11 before he received Speed's letter.[29]

Joseph Holt of Kentucky also became an important player in the unfolding drama over Fremont's proclamation. Holt had been secretary of war in the cabinet of President Buchanan and, after 1862, would be appointed by Lincoln to serve as judge advocate of the U.S. Army. Holt was also Joshua Speed's personal friend and former neighbor. In May 1861, Speed had specifically asked Holt, as a man of stature, to reassure Kentuckians "that this is no war upon individual property and the institution of slavery." Speed concluded that "the production of no man in the nation would attract more attention" than words by his distinguished friend. Holt's response to Speed became a public document that served the administration's purpose, and thirty thousand copies were printed and distributed. During the uproar over Fremont's proclamation in September, Speed wrote Holt a heated letter arguing against turning the war into one to end slavery (it would be like attempting to "ascend the falls of Niagara in a canoe"). Holt by that point had already written Lincoln twice to express his concerns about Fremont and was in fact then selected by the president as his personal emissary to go to St. Louis bearing orders to revoke the proclamation. Speed was impressed by Holt's effectiveness and grateful that at least at that point ending slavery had not become a goal of the war.[30]

Speed went even further in his robust support of Holt. Toward the end of 1861, it was clear Lincoln intended to replace his first secretary of war, Simon Cameron, a deeply corrupt and inefficient man. Speed, in Washington at the time, was aware of the politicking and later wrote Holt in December urging him to accept if Lincoln were to offer him a cabinet post. Speed added, however, a comment in his letter to Holt that suggests his support for his friend went well beyond the hope that Lincoln would make Holt the secretary of war: "Your chances for the highest position within the gift of the people at the next election are better than those of any other man. . . . No man now has so firm a hold upon the popular heart." David Donald, the distinguished Lincoln biographer and author of a book about Lincoln and his friends, expresses astonishment at Speed's hope that Holt would replace Lincoln himself at the next election, which he chalks up to Speed's exhaustion after several weeks in Washington trying to get the administration to act on a variety of fronts. Donald adds that Speed also may have been keenly aware that no president since Andrew Jackson had been reelected to a second term and was already thinking ahead to the 1864 election.[31]

On other fronts, Speed kept his fingers in the pie. On September 24 he wrote Lincoln in an effort to obtain more guns for Kentucky. On October 9 he telegrammed Lincoln, urging him to arm only the three-year volunteers, as that would serve the needs of the army better. And in the same month he traveled to Washington to lobby Lincoln directly to get more money for General William Sherman, then commander in Kentucky, who had been rebuffed by Secretary of War Cameron. He got Lincoln to authorize $100,000. When Speed returned to Kentucky, Sherman was astonished that a private citizen could get him money that the secretary of war had refused. Speed replied that Sherman's only mistake was in not asking for more.[32]

After the fall of 1861, however, with Kentucky securely in the Union, Speed's role in the war became less consequential. He continued to write Lincoln on various issues and to recommend people for positions and for special favors. Speed's main concern in 1862 was Lincoln's move toward the Emancipation Proclamation. It happened that both Joshua and James Speed were in Washington in July 1862. Lincoln had drafted the proclamation, but before he consulted with the cabinet he read it personally to the Speeds and asked their opinion. James, who was much more liberal than his brother and had long since gotten rid of most of his slaves (though he still owned a house slave as late as 1862), objected to the measure because he thought emancipation should come from the states, not the federal government. Joshua—the owner of between ten and fifteen slaves during the 1850s, most of whom he seemed to lease out, and a few house slaves until 1865—felt that the proclamation was unwise, unjust, and a dangerous thing and was especially concerned that it would alienate many in Kentucky. Lincoln probably sought out the opinions of the Speeds partly out of friendship but also to give them advance notice to bring them along, but he had no intention of actually taking their advice about something he had already decided.[33]

In time, however, like many in the nation over the course of the war, Speed came around to accepting emancipation as a necessity and something that was good for the country. He told Herndon one touching story about a conversation with Lincoln about it in the White House, probably in 1864 (though Speed doesn't say exactly when the conversation occurred). Before becoming personal, Lincoln told his old friend he would accept emancipation once he saw the "ha[r]vest of good which we would erelong glean from it." Setting generalities aside, Lincoln then recalled his depression of 1841, when he "almost committed suicide." Lincoln told Speed during his illness that he had done nothing "to make any human being remember that he had lived." But emancipation will connect his name with something that will "redound to the interest of his fellow man" and have made his life worthwhile. "I believe," he concluded, "that in this measure [meaning his proclamation] my fondest hopes will be realized—"[34]

* * *

Such visits and conversations during the war seemed to bring the two men, after more than two decades, back into close communion with each other, though of course on a completely different level. Joshua continued to write Lincoln about Kentucky affairs and sent many requests for appointments (from May to December 1864, for example, he wrote seven such letters). He also committed himself to absolute support of Lincoln. Having probably voted for Douglas in 1860 (though it is not clear), urged Joseph Holt in December 1861 to think of opposing Lincoln for the presidency, and vigorously opposed the Emancipation Proclamation on January 1, 1863, Speed by 1864 openly supported Lincoln in Kentucky and undoubtedly voted for him for a second term. Joshua now opposed the Peace Democrats and other elements that remained Unionist but were against emancipation of the slaves. In the Kentucky context it was impossible to be a Republican (until after the war, when in fact Joshua did join the party), but both Joshua and his brother James helped shape the Kentucky version of the Unconditional Union Party in the spring of 1864, a party that favored the use of black troops and amending the Constitution to abolish slavery. Joshua Speed was firmly in the ranks of this new party and worked hard for its success, including helping fund a new paper in April 1864, the *Constitutional Union Press*, later shortened to the *Union Press*, which pushed the ideas of the new party (ideas that were, for all intents and purposes, indistinguishable from Republican ones). For a man who continued to own three slaves, Joshua Speed had moved very far in his political ideas. And support of Lincoln became something of a family affair, when at the end of 1864 Lincoln appointed James Speed his attorney general.[35]

In one of Speed's many visits with Lincoln during the war, he was invited to spend some time with him in the Soldier's Home outside Washington, a favorite retreat for Lincoln from the pressures of the White House. It was the summer of 1864: the killing continued, but victory was at least imaginable. Speed felt Lincoln was changed, more profound and spiritual. As he entered Lincoln's room, near night, Lincoln was sitting near a window intently reading his Bible. Approaching him Speed said,

> "I am glad to see you so profitably engaged." "Yes," said he, "I am profitably engaged." "Well," said I, "if you have recovered from your skepticism, I am sorry to say that I have not." Looking me earnestly in the face, and placing his hand on my shoulder, he said, "You are wrong, Speed; take all of this book upon reason that you can, and the balance on faith, and you will live and die a happier and better man."

* * *

The death of Lincoln and the pageantry of his prolonged funeral remains one of the most extraordinary moments in our nation's history. Shot on Good Friday, April 14, he died the next day. The Easter morning sermons and their apocalyptic tone that followed on Sunday gave immediate shape to Lincoln as a martyred, Christ-like figure who died for the nation's fratricidal sins. The war was not quite over, but victory was certain, a war with well over seven hundred thousand dead by recent estimates and several times that number of wounded soldiers and their suffering families. Our wars before that had been sideshows by comparison, and nothing since the Civil War has remotely approached it in destruction and death in American experience. Yet many felt—though not Southern whites—that by saving the Union and ending the blight of human slavery it was all worth it. Lincoln's martyrdom embodied that sense of ennobled suffering.

The extended viewing of his body quickly acquired circus-like features. He lay in state in the White House until Wednesday, with Mary Lincoln in a state of complete collapse, sobbing constantly and at times hysterical in her grief. Robert Lincoln played a crucial role dealing with her, getting her to agree, at first reluctantly, to have him buried in Springfield, and deciding on a viewing of the body in the White House on Tuesday, followed by a public funeral in the Capitol rotunda the next day. Some sixty thousand people converged on Washington for this public ritual and passed by the open casket. Then on Friday the body began a twelve-day journey across the country. Millions lined the railroad tracks as the train, pulling the president's coach draped in black, made its way slowly to Illinois. There were ten more funerals in cities along the way, long processions to the beat of muffled drums, cannon volleys, and pealing church bells. The body was brought out again and again for public viewing. By the time the train arrived in Springfield on May 3, Lincoln's body had begun to rot and his face had turned black. Embalming only lasts so long. Before its final viewing in the state capitol on the square, a local undertaker had to use large quantities of rouge chalk and amber to restore the face to something resembling Lincoln. Finally, on May 4, a procession, led by General Joseph Hooker on horseback, marched with the massive coffin to Oak Ridge Cemetery, and Lincoln was laid to rest.

Speed lived another seventeen years after the end of the war. Always successful, he became one of the most conspicuous businessmen in Louisville. He continued to hold investments in everything from real estate, to banks, to railroads; he even owned a hotel. The important role he played during the war keeping Kentucky in the Union, along with his personal relationship with the martyred Lincoln, brought him respect and recognition. He was sought after to be on boards and to engage in public service as much as his increasingly fragile health allowed. He and Fanny in 1867 purchased a beautiful tract of land near Farmington on the waters of Beargrass Creek. As they had when first married, both Speeds planted all kinds of flowers and landscaped the area around the house.[36]

Joshua remained close to his large extended family but especially to his brother James, who remained as attorney general until July 1866. James was a radical Republican, favoring giving the vote to black men, and he increasingly clashed with President Johnson on this and other issues. While in Washington, Joshua handled James's financial affairs. Joshua probably made his brother better off than when he left for Washington, as James had never been a very good businessman. James was completely devoted to his brother. "Whenever Joshua leaves[,]" James wrote their mother in 1865, "there comes over me a singular feeling of loneliness—Since he left here last that feeling has been triggered with sadness." James in general seemed to suffer from his own depression, which he indicated ran in the family, as in another letter to his mother he refers somewhat euphemistically to his "nervous fits." James was a dutiful son, however, and wrote his mother nearly every week while serving in the government in Washington. He is especially attentive to report on his churchgoing and the details of various sermons he heard, including one by a "colored man, a pure negro, and the pastor of a church here—"[37]

Joshua finally got rid of his last two slaves in December 1865, when the Thirteenth Amendment was ratified by enough states and became the law (even though it was not ratified by Kentucky until 1976). He believed in emancipation, however, and was sympathetic to the plight of freedmen. In the context of postwar racist Louisville, he became quite liberal, if paternalistic. "We who know & feel the deeper prejudices against this race," he wrote James, "how incompetent they are to protect themselves from gross injustice and imposition." In another letter the next year, Joshua reports with disgust how some local "regulators" took a black woman named Jane out and "severely whipped" her for no other reason than that her husband and son fought in the war for the North. Nothing was done to those who whipped poor Jane—and this was in a "respectable neighborhood." The men who whipped her said, "No woman who was the wife of a d—n nigger soldier should remain in that neighborhood."[38]

Speed suffered from diabetes for the last twenty-five years of his life, described as "Diabety" in the mortuary records of Louisville. Since he was sixty-eight years of age when he died in 1882, he therefore first developed the disease at forty-three years of age in 1857 (or thereabouts since such records might have rounded out the years). It was undoubtedly what we now call Type 2 diabetes, or the adult-onset version of the disease. Little understood before the twentieth century, we know now that diabetes occurs when the pancreas fails to produce enough insulin or the cells of the body inadequately respond to the insulin that is produced. Diabetes has both genetic and lifestyle origins and is associated with obesity, imbibing too much sugar, and a lack of exercise. One of its early symptoms is excessive urination, which led the Egyptians to identify diabetes as long ago as 1500 B.C.E. But over the millennia there was not much progress made in treating diabetes until 1922, when a young Canadian at death's door received insulin shots and got better.[39]

Untreated—as with Speed—there are usually severe long-term complications, such as heart disease, stroke, kidney failure, foot ulcers, and damage to one's vision. It cannot be known which, if any, of these common complications affected Speed, but we do know the chronic disease progressively wore him down. In the last few years of his life, he often traveled to spas for treatment and in his last winter went with Fanny to the Caribbean, perhaps hoping the clear air and gentle winters would give him some respite from his symptoms. He returned, however, to Louisville that spring and steadily declined. He moved into the hotel he owned for the last months of his life, presumably because it was easier there to receive regular nursing care. He was forced to use a wheelchair because, one suspects, the doctors had amputated gangrenous appendages or limbs. With his devout and loving wife by his side and probably in great pain, Speed formally converted to Christianity in the month before he died on May 29, 1882.[40]

It took six years to probate the estate of Joshua Speed, undoubtedly because he had such diverse investments. In the end, it was valued at over seven hundred thousand dollars, a vast sum in those days worth about twenty-eight million dollars today. Much of it seems to have been distributed to his siblings and over half to Fanny. She in turn lived quietly until 1902, kept up her gardening, and was very active in her church, of which she was also a major benefactor. When she died at eighty-two years of age, her estate was worth four hundred thousand dollars. Half went to relatives and half to Trinity Church on Third Avenue and Guthrie Street.[41]

Joshua Speed stumbled into history that day in April 1837 when Abraham Lincoln walked into his store on the west side of the square in Springfield, Illinois. That Speed was not a great man, he would be the first to admit. But he was smart, loyal to friends and to his country, and kind, and his devotion to Lincoln proved vital for saving psychologically a man we cherish as America's greatest president. The story of their friendship through the vagaries of their times is one uniquely embedded in the nineteenth century. Such friends don't come easily in any life, and we who remember Lincoln ought not to forget Joshua Speed.

Conclusions

ON FRIENDSHIP

If we have no friends, we have no pleasure.
—Abraham Lincoln to Joshua Speed, February 25, 1842

To understand the general significance of the friendship between Lincoln and Speed, one might turn to Aristotle. In the *Nicomachean Ethics*, Aristotle names friendship as the highest form of relationship, for without it, "no one would choose to live." Money and power are for naught without it, just as prosperity cannot be preserved without friends. Friendship helps the young from straying into error, the old by ministering to their needs, and those in their prime to be noble. Those in communities feel it, which helps bind states, while lawgivers "care more for it than for justice." Friendship is noble, and we justly praise those who love their friends.

For Aristotle two kinds of friendship—those based on utility and those based purely on pleasure—are ephemeral. Those who seek friends based on utility do so for the good of themselves; in pleasure the benefit is useful. In both cases, to express it differently, the gain is narcissistic. "Perfect friendship," on the other hand, is that between men who are good "and alike in virtue." In it there is mutuality and trust. Such friendship brings pleasure and may be useful, but its benefits are much greater. These friendships are "perfect" and permanent. Love and friendship, he says, thrive in their "best form between such men." Bad men may be friends for the sake of utility or pleasure, but only good men can truly be friends "without qualification."

Aristotle also notes that there is nothing like living together to nourish a meaningful friendship between good men.

> And in loving a friend men love what is good for themselves; for the good man in becoming a friend becomes a good to his friend. Each, then, both loves what is good for himself, and makes an equal return in goodwill and in pleasantness; for friendship is said to be equality, and both of these are found most in the friendship of the good.[1]

Lincoln and Speed indeed passed from "utilitarian" mutual admirers to devoted "perfect" friends. The arc of their friendship, as Speed himself recounted, began with an impecunious and sad Lincoln needing simply to find a place to stay. Lincoln joined his friend in that large bed upstairs and in time came to share his deepest thoughts and feelings. The friendship grew in fits and starts, as best as one can tell, but soon grew into a well-documented "friendship of the good."

One later thinker who added substantively to Aristotle's ideas is Michel de Montaigne. For him, friendship mainly differs from the kind of bonds that preexist, and often stifle: for example, between brothers, who just happened to have emerged from the same mother. Even in marriage, there is an element of the contract that is "forced and compulsory." Montaigne in this regard is not kind to women, who he feels are incapable of real friendship. "The ordinary talent of women is not such as is sufficient to maintain the conference and communication required to the support of this sacred tie; nor do they appear to be endued with constancy of mind, to sustain the pinch of so hard and durable a knot." Real friendship in this (sexist) tradition can exist only between two men. Familial relationships matter and may be close, Montaigne argues, but friendship is something between men, higher, exalted.

It is that notion of the exalted in friendship that leads Montaigne to his most important insight. Friendship, for Montaigne, is a spiritual experience, with "the soul growing still more refined by practice." With friends, we become "one piece," and there is "no more sign of the seam by which they [friends] were first conjoined." The union is absolute. "If a man should importune me to give a reason why I loved him, I find it could not otherwise be expressed, than by making answer: because it was he, because it was I." Such friendship is also exclusive. One may admire the beauty of someone, the humor of another, the generosity of yet another, and so on, but genuine friendship "possesses the whole soul, and there rules and sways with an absolute sovereignty, cannot possibly admit of a rival."[2]

Herndon and other contemporaries early recognized the exclusivity that developed between Lincoln and Speed. Elizabeth Edwards's image suggests classic Montaigne soulmates: "Mr. Lincoln and Mr. Speed were frequently at our house—seemed to enjoy themselves in their conversation beneath the dense shade of our forest trees." She recalls these two men, in particular of all men, sitting together in the shade of the grove at the edge of the town, facing woods, unencumbered by schedule, engrossed in animated discussion.[3]

One can add to these observations of Aristotle and Montaigne. The fact that friendship is not a biological given means we enter into it willingly and by choice. It is a relationship with much agency. We cannot choose our families, but we do choose our friends. It is a moral and loving choice, one that, as Aristotle notes, can bring out the good in us and in the other. With wise or lucky choices, for many men, who tend toward the guarded in displays of affection, friendship offers genuine affection without sexual surrender, recognition, support, and mutuality bestowed without ambivalence.

Male friendships can, of course, be sexualized, and it is true that the love of homosexual men is something the culture increasingly accepts. That is for the good in its recognition of the wide range of human desire. Such love, however, introduces some of the very limitations in friendship that Montaigne especially notes exists in marriage between a man and a woman. Committed and sexualized relationships, whether homosexual or heterosexual and whether they are formalized as marriage, introduce binding contracts with legal implications in relation to property, children, and much else. Such obligations change friendships as it has been understood since Aristotle, sometimes deepening it but more often compromising the easy and fluid attachments in friendships that we enter into and can easily leave entirely by choice.

The friendship of Lincoln and Speed, certainly one of the most interesting in the nineteenth century and perhaps a paradigmatic

American male friendship, had all the features discussed by Aristotle and Montaigne. It was loving, noble, and exalted in the truest of senses. In psychological terms, however, the friendship, while not sexual, was something more than Platonic. It came to occupy a kind of third level of friendship, one that was moral and spiritual but in its abiding mutuality skirted close to the physical. In fact, there in that creaking bed together for nearly four years, there had to have been occasional touching, a rolling over in a dream, a tossed arm, a cramped leg jerking about, that introduced a familiar intimacy between them much greater than either man experienced in their wide circle of friends in the store, on the circuit, in politics, or socializing at the Edwards home on "Quality Hill." Skirting close to the physical without crossing the line into the sexual seemed to draw them into a psychological universe of acceptance and trust. They became bonded in ways one sees between men in war—the "bunch of guys" who live and die together—and what exists in many other social and historical contexts.[4]

But the Lincoln-Speed friendship also had its specific context in nineteenth-century America. Such friendships for heterosexual men existed in that liminal space between mother and wife that protected them from the heavily garbed and forbidding world of women, who were newly remote in the "cult of domesticity." Of course, many, if not most, men and women in this social context related easily to each other, fell in love, and had children without doubts or confusion. But there had arisen in the middle class a new kind of suppression of sexuality, in large part to limit the number of children, which had consequences for young people. Within the shelter of male friendship, men could develop trust in each other and give themselves the time to grow and mature, court women without pressure, and become secure in their chosen profession or line of work. These close male friendships, extending from school or just beyond to marriage, for many defined the most significant relationships of their youth. In chapter 2, I mentioned the examples of Daniel Webster and James Hervey Bingham, as well as James Blake and Wyek Vanderhoef, not to mention the literary example of Ishmael and Queequeg in *Moby-Dick*. One might also note the friendships of Nathaniel Hawthorne and Franklin Pierce, James Buchanan and William Rufus King, and, a bit later, Henry Adams and John Hay (Lincoln's secretary) and Edward Thomas and Robert Frost.

We know about these remarkable friendships of famous men because biographical work has been done on them. What is needed now is a more complete social history of male friendships among more ordinary people who formed the fabric of nineteenth-century life.[5]

Women at this time in American history had their own form of intimate friendships. The best historian of this cultural phenomenon is Carroll Smith-Rosenberg. She has described in loving detail how women from about 1820 until well into the nineteenth century made close female friends in their adolescence, and, it seems, those friendships played much of the same role as those of their male counterparts in that segregated gendered world. There were, however, two significant differences in the texture of these female friendships. First, they tended to last throughout the life cycle and were not circumscribed to that narrative space between family of origin and husband. In fact, in many cases, the visit of a friend was the occasion to turn the husband out of bed to sleep on the couch and welcome the friend to sleep in bed together! Second, the effusiveness of the expressions of love in the letters women wrote each other, of the talk of kissing and hugging, of their eternal bond, and so on far exceeded the much more measured expressions of love and connection between (heterosexual) men. Lincoln could tell Speed of his "everlasting friendship," but he didn't talk of kissing him.[6]

For men the world of women seemed forbidding and separate, a scary psychological and sexual space that summoned them but presented huge challenges to enter. Lincoln and Speed felt those contradictory yearnings, though in somewhat different ways, and found solace in each other. When Lincoln met Speed in the spring of 1837, he was still reeling from his breakdown after the death of Ann Rutledge in 1835, he remained in debt, and he wasn't at all sure of his future. Then, as later, he was admired and liked, prized for his stories, his honesty, his humanity, his intelligence, and his ambitions. But he kept his inner turmoil to himself. He shared his feelings with no one. At first after moving in, he and Speed circled each other, becoming friendly without being intimate, as Lincoln entered Speed's orbit without surrendering his privacy to a man who idealized him and whose emotional issues curiously paralleled his own. In time and in the daily, and nightly, communion they shared, the two men drew together. Once in that psychological space, they established a remarkable trust. They could finish each other's sentences, however different their intellectual styles. They also seemed seldom to be apart, except during the hours of actual work. They ate their meals together, whether it was a light breakfast, their main meal with the Butlers, or whatever supper they managed in the store. Evenings were spent in the back room of the store talking with friends. Speed at times wandered into court when it was in session in Springfield (or when the Supreme Court met in the state house, across the street from the store) to watch his friend; he even followed Lincoln on the circuit sometimes.

Lincoln's friendship with Speed served at first as a healing balm for the core self issues that haunted Lincoln and held him back: his lingering depression, deep fears of having those he most loved die suddenly and tragically on him, and confusions about intimacy, sex, and love. The sanctuary of emotional closeness that developed between the two men provided relief for Lincoln from this intertwined web of concerns. The haven of Lincoln's friendship with Speed, while secure and healing to a degree, had the side effect of delaying even further the resolution of his conflicts. His relationship with Speed was a loving but not sexualized one, a merging of selves in which young Lincoln managed to negotiate the terms of intimacy toward which he yearned.

The friendship held Lincoln safely and steadied him during these years of his moratorium. He came to feel more grounded after the angst of his New Salem days, especially the latter part, when Ann Rutledge died and he foundered in his ambivalent courtship of Mary Owens. The safety of the friendship, indeed the love he felt for Speed, proved a healing balm and allowed him to postpone further his inner impulse toward companionship with a woman and ultimately marriage. The delay, however, had a downside, for it extended Lincoln's youthful confusions about sex and marriage into his early thirties.

That delay aggravated the intensity of his doubts. That is in general the contradiction of a moratorium for a young man in his youth. It is a time in the life cycle for a creative, and often disturbed, young man to delay the imperatives of work and love, to experiment and explore options before commitments that focus the self on a life course. Everything remains possible, which is both liberating and terrifying. But the longer the delay extends, the greater the tension, confusion, and possible hopelessness. Lincoln in his moratorium moved on the two tracks of love and work at an unequal pace. By his late twenties he had left behind his erratic involvements in a host of failing activities and was clearly established as a young and promising lawyer with political ambitions (though still with debts to settle). But it was in love that Lincoln felt most distress and was the least successful. Then suddenly at thirty-one Mary Todd came into his line of vision. He was stunned with her appeal. She was lively, attractive, very smart, funny, and instantly liked him, a man who was not always comfortable in social situations and whom some saw as "peculiar." When he broke off his engagement with Mary Todd just prior to his thirty-second birthday, he felt truly lost.[7]

It also made no sense, except in the context of losing Speed, who had grounded him through all those years. Lincoln, faced with the imminent loss of Speed, pushed too hard to marry at a time he was unready. The tangled debate about the importance of Mary Todd in the broken engagement, the questions whether Lincoln had feelings for Matilda Edwards or possibly Sarah Rickard, and several other explanations that have been put forward all miss the point. He may well have flirted with Matilda (though she denied it), and he definitely got cold feet about marrying Mary Todd. She in turn probably did toss him out on his ear because she believed he loved Matilda, or for some other reasons that are obscure. And in his renewed emotional disarray it may be that he sought out young Sarah Rickard. But behind all those mostly mutually exclusive explanations lies the really significant fact that in late 1840 Lincoln faced the imminent separation from his common bed with Speed and his friend's departure for Kentucky. It all came crashing down on his head: he broke his engagement and fell into a suicidal depression in January 1841.

A year of torment followed, mitigated by Lincoln's continued closeness with Speed. For much of 1841 Lincoln managed to keep Speed in his psychological orbit. Though they were not rooming together after the first of the year, Speed only left Springfield in March. They continued to take dinner with the Butlers and share daily interaction and contact. In summer, they corresponded. In August, Lincoln made a visit to Farmington to stay with Speed and then returned with him to Springfield for the rest of the year.

To the world, Lincoln seemed recovered. With Speed, he could share his continued misery. Speed listened to Lincoln's doubts, gave reassurance, and provided solace for his emotional hurts. When Lincoln needed a steady hand, it was Speed who was there. Speed was also the leader in reaching out to women. It was Speed who brought Lincoln to the Edwards home and introduced him to all the young belles of the Coterie and Quality Hill. Speed was handsome and at ease. He undoubtedly encouraged Lincoln's courtship with Mary Todd (though there is no direct evidence for this) and was there to counsel Lincoln to avoid being foolish when he felt he had to break off the engagement. Speed nursed Lincoln through his suicidal depression. Speed experienced Lincoln by then as an extension of himself, someone he had come to need even more than he consciously realized. They were drawn together as if by fate (which is how they indeed experienced it). In August in Louisville, with Lincoln by his side, the tables turned. Speed suddenly and rather dramatically fell in love, proposing to Fanny Henning within days or weeks after their initial courtship. At this point Speed himself unraveled psychologically in ways that were very similar to his friend's unraveling less than a year earlier. They needed each other equally then, and Speed determined to return to Springfield with Lincoln.

What transpired that fall with the two men back together in Springfield is not well documented, but one can reasonably infer they spent as much time together as possible, talking endlessly about their doubts. The focus now was on Speed, however, as his marriage approached in a few months. He struggled with whether to call it off, with Lincoln now urging him to stay the course. Lincoln latched onto his friend's courtship. He vicariously made it his own. It was Lincoln's own indirect courtship, Speed's doubts his own, the hoped-for culmination exactly of what he embraced for himself.

Speed left Lincoln on January 1, 1842, to return for good to Louisville and marry Fanny Henning. He took with him all of Lincoln's hopes and fears. The letters Lincoln wrote to Speed in January and February 1842 are the most revealing of anything he ever wrote in his entire life. Speed became his double, burdened with the task of resolving both of their seemingly intractable uncertainties. The climax came with Speed's actual marriage and, most importantly, the great moment of its consummation. That raised Lincoln into a state of high anxiety. Lincoln involves himself as a shadow self in Speed's bed there with Fanny. Reading of Speed's consummation of the marriage, Lincoln is still filled with anxiety ten hours later ("I have hardly yet, at the distance of ten hours, become calm"). He was thirty-three years old then and well past the moment for him to make his own life with his own partner. He could do that now after his experience of love and intimacy through Speed's successful courtship and consummation of his marriage. Lincoln soon sought out Mary Todd, they danced about each other from a distance that summer, got engaged secretly in the early fall, and married on November 4, something Lincoln found a matter of "profound wonder."

That marriage proved complicated. People like Herndon—and many others over the last century and a half—could never figure out Lincoln's attachment to Mary. She seemed too neurotic and full of rage, though most forget that her emotional disarray only developed over time. Herndon aside, what matters is not whether a given historian likes or dislikes Mary but to recognize that Lincoln found her enormously attractive, smart, and compelling from the very beginning of their relationship and after his marriage seemed to adore her, at least in their first decade, when they produced their four children. Over the years, her depression deepened in the wake of life's challenges, which she proved increasingly unable to meet. His response, subtle and unspoken, as he grappled with the nation's woes, was to withdraw from her as he turned to the issues of slavery and a disintegrating Union. The house divided.

After 1842, Speed, formerly Lincoln's chosen vehicle for resolving core self issues, became psychologically dispensable. Speed, having served Lincoln well, was now of the past and not the future. They moved apart. Lincoln's first son, who was to be Joshua instead was named Robert. Letters became infrequent, and only one of the many ballyhooed visits ever materialized. At times in the 1840s they bickered by letter over business matters. And more significantly, although in 1846 Lincoln discounted Speed's annoyance with the way he was handling his financial matters as a "cold" reason for any abatement in their friendship, by the 1850s, when Lincoln emerged as the most articulate spokesman on the slavery issue for the new Republican party, he and his slave-holding friend moved in radically different worlds.

But Lincoln hardly forgot Speed and continued to respect his friend and treasure their relationship. Ironically, the secession of the South and the coming of the war drew Lincoln and Speed close together once more. Before hostilities, Lincoln had wanted Speed in his cabinet. It was fortunate that Speed declined. As a result, he was in place in early 1861 to serve as Lincoln's man in Kentucky. Daringly risking a disaster, trusting his old friend completely, Lincoln secretly shipped a virtual arsenal for Speed to distribute. They communicated directly and frequently via telegram, and, when Speed could, he made the arduous trip to Washington. In the White House, Speed and Lincoln not only conferred on war matters but discussed the Emancipation Proclamation, a measure that Speed at first opposed but later came to understand as both necessary and wise. During one such conversation, Speed recalled, Lincoln did not argue his point but instead reminisced with his friend about when "he was so much depressed that he almost committed suicide."

> At the time of his deep depression—He said to me that he had done nothing to make any human being remember that he had lived—and that to connect his name with the events transpiring in his day & generation and so impress himself upon them as to link his name with something that would redound to the interest of his fellow man was what he desired to live for—He reminded me of the conversation [in 1841]—and said with earnest emphasis—I believe that in this measure (meaning his proclamation) my fondest hopes will be realized—[8]

Lincoln, one might say, had moved on with life after 1842 in ways that no longer required the emotional presence of Speed for survival, but he never lost his abiding love for the man who in a very real sense saved his life and made it possible for him to realize his potential and make a mark that would live on the pages of history.

The one thing that never returned after Lincoln's friendship with Speed in the late 1830s and early 1840s was his clinical depression and suicidality. Whatever he went through as a child—and there is plenty of evidence in the oral history that he was desperately sad after his mother's death—Lincoln was clearly a troubled young man in his late twenties and early thirties. Within a six-year period he fell into two major depressions (the first in late summer and fall of 1835 and the second in January 1841) and was suicidal during both. In 1835 he talked of not wanting to carry a knife for fear of killing himself and wandered about distraught and distracted. In 1841 friends, including Speed, Butler, and Doc Henry, stood watch over him and removed anything like his razor that he might use to kill himself. He was "crazy as a loon," Herndon said of Lincoln. But the next year, in his experience of a successful quest for love and intimacy indirectly through his friend Speed in early 1842, Lincoln found his emotional compass. With this new sense of self-cohesion, he managed to secure his own relationship that realized his aspirations. He was never again suicidal. He remained moody and was often melancholy but found important emotional strategies in his humor and creativity, not to mention the wealth of acclaim that fed his self-esteem as he, Abraham Lincoln, Joshua Speed's best friend, became the most important public figure in the country.

ABBREVIATIONS

ALPL   Abraham Lincoln Presidential Library, Springfield, Illinois

CW   Abraham Lincoln, *The Collected Works of Abraham Lincoln*, ed. Roy Basler (New Brunswick, N.J.: Rutgers University Press, 1953). These books are available online.

FHS   Filson Historical Society of Louisville, Kentucky.

HI   *Herndon's Informants: Letters, Interviews, and Statements About Abraham Lincoln*, ed. Douglas L. Wilson and Rodney O. Davis (Urbana: University of Illinois Press, 1998).

LoC   Library of Congress, whose holdings of Lincoln documents is also available online.

NOTES

PREFACE

1. "But Wilson may go": Douglas Wilson, "William H. Herndon and Mary Todd Lincoln," *Journal of the Abraham Lincoln Association* 22 (2001): 1–26. "He was, she wrote": Justin G. Turner and Linda Levitt Turner, eds., *Mary Todd Lincoln: Her Life and Letters* (New York: Knopf, 1972), 414, 416, and 568. "Once Herndon and some": David Donald, *Lincoln's Herndon* (1948; New York: Simon and Schuster, 1996), 126; and Butler papers, unsorted as yet in the collection in the ALPL. "She said later": Mary Todd to Stuart Brown, December 15, 1873, ALPL, Box 71. Note the collection of papers, *The Mary Lincoln Enigma: Historians on America's Most Controversial First Lady*, ed. Frank J. Williams and Michael Burkhimer (Carbondale: Southern Illinois University Press, 2012), esp. the papers by Richard Lawrence Miller, "Life at Eighth and Jackson," and Kenneth J. Winkle, "'An Unladylike Profession': Mary Lincoln's Preparation for Greatness."

1. BEGINNINGS

1. "On Saturday morning": It is generally sunny in April in central Illinois, and at least one relatively nearby paper, *The Memphis Daily Appeal*, reported

warm weather on that day. "white-throated sparrow": Chris Young, "Identifying Birds Based on Their Songs," *Springfield Journal-Register* (April 19, 2013).
"goodbye to Bennett and Elizabeth Abell" and "sewn and 'foxed' his pants":
Elizabeth Abell to Herndon, February 15, 1867, *HI*, 556–567, reports her care-
taking of Lincoln, who also lived with them for a good part of his stay in New
Salem and was probably still with them when he left (earlier he boarded with
Henry Onstott [Abner Y. Lewis to Herndon, January 2, 1866, *HI*, 170], slept in
a crowded bed with William G. Greene [William G. Greene to Herndon, May
30, 1865, *HI*, 17–18], and often boarded with other families). "He tossed his
saddlebags": Joshua Speed, "Incidents in the Early Life of A. Lincoln," 1882,
HI, 589. Bowling Green's clothes: Jason Duncan to Herndon, late 1866–early
1867, *HI*, 541. "allmost Second Farther": Abner Y. Lewis to Herndon, December 6, 1866, *HI*, 501. "fourteen-mile trip": Joshua Speed, "Incidents in the
Early Life of A. Lincoln," 1882, *HI*, 589, says Lincoln lived "fourteen miles in
the country," though the actual distance from New Salem to Springfield is just
over seventeen miles. "seven dollars": Douglas L. Wilson, *Honor's Voice: The
Transformation of Abraham Lincoln* (New York: Knopf, 1998), 171–172.

2. "It was seven years": Richard Lawrence Miller, *Lincoln and His World:
Prairie Politician, 1834–1842* (Mechanicsburg, Penn.: Stackpole, 2008), 88,
92–93; Lincoln waded through freezing waters to rescue the dog once, as he
told Herndon years later: "His frantic leaps of joy and other evidences of a
dog's gratitude amply repaid me for all the exposure I had undergone"—see
William H. Herndon and Jesse W. Weik, *Herndon's Lincoln*, ed. Douglas L. Wilson and Rodney O. Davis (Urbana: University of Illinois Press, 2006), 55n.
"As he described later": "Autobiography Written for John L. Scripps," June
1860, *CW*, 4:63. "They were then pioneers": Carl Sandburg, *Abraham Lincoln:
The Prairie Years* (New York: Harcourt, Brace & Co., 1926), 1:65. "This removal":
Lincoln, "Autobiography," *CW*, 1:61–62. "Later, some of the same problems":
Glenna R. Schroeder-Lein, *Lincoln and Medicine* (Carbondale: Southern Illi-
nois University Press, 2012), 2.

3. John Hanks to Herndon, 1865–1866, *HI*, 456. Highly regarded by Lincoln, Hanks later served in the Black Hawk War, joined the California gold
rush for three years and, at age sixty, enlisted in the Twenty-First Illinois
Regiment. "His identification in 1860 of some rails split by Abraham Lincoln
led to the latter's being called 'the railsplitter' in the presidential campaign."
HI, 752 (editor's notes).

4. "deep snows": Olivier Fraysse, *Land, Lincoln, and Labor, 1809–60*
(Urbana: University of Illinois Press, 1994), 9–14; Michael Burlingame,
Abraham Lincoln: A Life (Baltimore, Md.: Johns Hopkins University Press,
2008), 1:48–49; and Ida Tarbell, *The Early Life of Abraham Lincoln* (Amazon
Digital Services, 2008), 1:1–3, 6. "On the long journey": Richard Campanella,

Lincoln in New Orleans: The 1828–1831 Flatboat Voyages and Their Place in History (Lafayette: University of Louisiana Press, 2010), 128. "And so Lincoln arrived": Lincoln, "Autobiography," *CW*, 4:63–64.

5. "In this village": William G. Greene to Herndon, December 3, 1865, *HI*, 14.

6. "impressive athlete": James Short to Herndon, July 7, 1865, *HI*, 73–74 (among the many former New Salem residents who told Herndon about the wrestling match). "Ward Hill Lamon": Ward Hill Lamon to Herndon, 1865–66, *HI*, 466. "Lincoln never killed": Lincoln, "Speed in the U.S. House of Representatives on the Presidential Question," July 27, 1848, *CW*, 1:510. "He was elected": Lincoln, "Autobiography," *CW*, 1:64. "important friends": David Donald, *Lincoln* (New York: Simon and Schuster, 1995), 45–46.

7. I detailed these activities in my *Lincoln's Quest for Union: A Psychological Study*, 2nd ed. (Philadelphia: Paul Dry Books, 2000), 36–40.

8. Lincoln, "Communication to the People of Sangamo County," March 9, 1832, *CW*, 1:5–9.

9. "Lincoln lost that election": Lincoln, "Autobiography," *CW*, 4:64. "Perhaps in Stuart": Lincoln to James T. Thornton, December 2, 1858, *CW*, 3:344. "In any event": Henry McHenry (Herndon interview), 1866, *HI*, 534. "Lincoln, he said later": John T. Stuart to Herndon, December 20, 1866, *HI*, 519; John T. Stuart to Herndon, late June, 1865, *III*, 63.

10. "A good dozen": see *CW*, 1:3–51. "Abner Y. Ellis": Abner Y. Ellis to Herndon, January 23, 1866, *HI*, 170. "Lincoln may have accepted": Jason Duncan to Herndon, late 1866–early 1867, *HI*, 539.

11. "Sitting on a wood pile": Russell Godbey to Herndon, 1865–1866, *HI*, 449. "But his years": Earl Schenck Miers, ed., *Lincoln Day-By-Day: A Chronology, 1809–1865* (Washington: Lincoln Sesquicentennial Commission, 1960), 56, 59, 69. "In anticipation of": Sandburg, *Abraham Lincoln*, 1:216. "thirty-dollar stray horse": Lincoln, "Appraisal of an Estray," December 16, 1830, *CW*, 1:3.

12. "Many in Vandalia": Lincoln to John T. Stuart, February 14, 1839, *CW*, 1:143. "In the next few months": Howard F. Rissler, "The State Capitol, 1837–1876," dig.lib.niu.edu/ISHS/ishs-1968winter/ishs-1968winter-397.pdf, 397–430; Lincoln to Levi Davis, April 19, 1837, *CW*, 1:77–78; Burlingame, *Abraham Lincoln*, 1:50; John Hanks, interview with Herndon, 1865, *HI*, 456; Miers, *Lincoln Day-by-Day*, 105, 147; Lincoln to John T. Stuart, February 14, 1839, *CW*, 1:143.

13. The sources for the Speed's family background and about Farmington include Gary Lee Williams, "James and Joshua Speed: Lincoln's Kentucky Friends," PhD diss., Duke University (1971), 3–9; "Kentucky's Abraham Lincoln," a publication of the Kentucky Historical Society in connection with the Bicentennial Commemoration, February 2008–February 2010; "Farmington-

Kentucky Hemp Farm," Kentucky Historical Society; "Farmington's Beginnings," Kentucky Historical Society; John Speed advertisement for recovered slave, posted by Tim Talbott on his blog "Random Thoughts on History," http://randomthoughtsonhistory.blogspot.com/2010/12/sample-of-kentucky-runaway-slave.html.

14. "Some saw him": James Freeman Clarke, *Autobiography, Diary, and Correspondence*, ed. Edward Everett Hale (New York: Negro Universities Press, 1891), 78.

15. James Speed [grandson], *James Speed: A Personality* (Louisville, Ky.: John P. Morton, 1914), 1.

16. "It took a lot of slave labor": Pen Bogert, formerly of the Filson Historical Society and now retired, has compiled a meticulous list of the slaves owned by all the Speeds, based on the yearly Jefferson County Tax Lists, Southern District, along with any references in the Jefferson County Court Minute Book, no. 4, that mentions when Speed built something on his property or when he was charged with "fraudulent list and fraudulent valuations," as he was in 1817. He left a copy of his records of excellent research in the Filson Historical Society library that I was able to access: Filson Library Historical Files, "Historic Homes—KY—Jefferson Co.—Farmington—African Americans," Filson Historical Society, Louisville, Kentucky. "In less than a decade": The information about the blacksmith is from "Testimony of James Speed for the American Freedmen's Inquiry Commission," National Archives Microfilm Publication, Microcopy no. 619, Washington, 1965. Letters Received by the Office of the Adjunct General (Main Series) 1861–1870, file no. 7, "Testimony taken in Kentucky, Tennessee, and Missouri, November and December 1863," roll 201, 1863. See also the pamphlet "Slavery at Farmington," by Pen Bogert with the Farmington Interpretive Committee, which is distributed at the historic site of Farmington.

17. "As James Speed later told": "Testimony of James Speed for the American Freedmen's Inquiry Commission." In a letter of April 17, 1836, John Speed mentions paying African Americans working on his plantation for breaking more hemp than they were required. Speed Family Papers [Mss. C Sd], FHS.

18. "In one letter": John Speed to Joshua Speed, January 7, 1830, Speed Family Papers [Mss. C Sd], FHS. "James Speed reports": "Testimony of James Speed for the American Freedmen's Inquiry Commission."

19. "I do the best": Clarke, *Autobiography*, 217. "At some level": Clarke, *Autobiography*, 217. "He adds": John Speed to Joshua Speed, April 17, 1836, Speed Family Papers [Mss. C Sd], FHS.

20. "In 1840, just before": Pen Bogert et al., "Slavery at Farmington." "John tells Mary": John Speed to Mary Speed, December 24, 1818, Thomas Speed Papers (uncataloged), FHS. "He once placed an ad": see Historic

Homes Foundation, Farmington, June 10, 2013, http://www.edisonhouse
.org/Farmington/History/Slavery/tabid/1371/Default.aspx.

21. "It is an urban myth": e-mail from Jennifer Cole, December 1, 2014, which also contains a quote from Carolyn Brooks, the former director of Farmington House and Museum. Brooks is categorical that Jefferson had nothing to do with the architectural design of the house at Farmington.

22. "Joshua, who was never": The Methodist Church of Louisville, of which Speed's wife, Fanny Henning Speed, was a main supporter, asked Joshua to give a talk on Lincoln before them in 1874; that date is from John Gilmer Speed's short biography of his uncle Joshua in the *Louisville Courier-Journal* (June 23, 1895), whereas the information about the location of the talk is from a tipped-in typed page entitled "History of Lincoln Pamphlet dictated by Mrs. Gilmer Speed Adams" attached to one of the copies of the pamphlet (published by John P. Morton and Co., Louisville, Kentucky, 1884) that had been owned by an early president of the Filson Historical Society in Louisville, Rogers Clark Ballard Thruston. Joshua Speed's speech at the church led to him giving it in various places throughout the state and elsewhere, generally before congregations of Methodist churches. John Gilmer Speed, the son of Joshua's brother Philip, who also wrote several works of history, later wrote the newspaper article about Joshua and is then almost certainly the anonymous author of the useful introduction to Speed's *Reminiscences*, which were published in 1896 by a local Louisville press, the Bradley and Gilbert Company. I am indebted to Jennifer Cole, associate curator of special collections, FHS, Louisville, Kentucky, for her help in figuring out all this.

23. "Joshua's uncle wrote": James Speed to John Speed, September 6, 1795, Speed Family Papers [Mss. C Sd], FHS. "Among Joshua's siblings": James Speed (grandson), *James Speed: A Personality*. "In a crucial letter": Lincoln to Speed, January 3 (?), 1842, *CW*, 1:265, which also includes the reference to William Speed.

24. "John had once noted": John Speed to Joshua Speed, December 23, 1829, Speed Family Papers [Mss C Sd], FHS. "day before Christmas": John Speed to Joshua Speed, December 24, 1829, Speed Family Papers [Mss C Sd], FHS.

25. Joshua to Lucy Speed, February 5, 1835, Speed Family Papers [Mss C Sd], FHS.

26. "Four years later": December 25, 1839, Speed Family Papers [Mss. C Sd], FHS.

27. "In 1829 he then": John W. Muir, *Bardstown in Retrospect* (Bardstown, Ky., 1965), 8; Mattingly Spalding, *Bardstown: Town of Tradition* (Baltimore, Md., 1942), 37. "wrote cleverly": James Speed (grandson), *James Speed: A Personality*, 9–10, FHS.

28. "John dutifully reports": John Speed to Lucy Speed, November 22, 1829, Speed Family Papers [Mss. C Sd], FHS.

29. "Once Joshua was well": James Speed [grandson], *James Speed: A Personality*, FHS.

30. "Joshua chose to move": the details of William H. Pope's wholesale store can be found in the *Louisville Directory for the Year 1832* (Louisville, Ky.: Richard W. Otis, Publisher, James Virden, Printer, 1832), FHS.

31. "Everyone is well dressed": Quoted in *Louisville: A Guide to the Falls City, Compiled by Workers of the Writers' Program of the Work Projects Administration in the State of Kentucky*, American Guide Series (New York: M. Barrows & Co., 1940), 24. "A Galt House Christmas menu": ibid., 24–25. Charles Dickens stayed": Charles Dickens, "American Notes for General Circulation and Pictures from Italy (London: Chapman & Hall, 1913), chap. 12. "Yet another traveler": Clarke, *Autobiography*, 68–69, 98.

32. "In 2002 Allen": Allen C. Guelzo, "Holland's Informants: The Construction of Josiah Holland's 'Life of Abraham Lincoln,'" *Journal of the Abraham Lincoln Association* 23 (2002): 1–55. "Speed also wrote": Speed "Statement" for Herndon, by 1882, *HI*, 588. "On the other hand": Speed, *Reminiscences*, 1.

33. "The only roads": Speed, *Reminiscences*, 15–16.

34. The material about Springfield in the next few paragraphs is principally from Paul Angle, *Here I Have Lived* (Springfield, Ill.: The Abraham Lincoln Association, 1935); Bruce Alexander Campbell, *200 Years: An Illustrated History of Sangamon County* (Springfield, Ill.: Phillips Brothers, 1976); Robert Mazrim, *The Sangamo Frontier: History and Archeology in the Shadow of Abraham Lincoln* (Chicago: University of Chicago Press, 2006); and Susan Krause, "Abraham Lincoln and Joshua Speed: Attorney and Client," *Illinois History Journal* 89 (1996): 35–50. Other writers have added useful details: Donald, *Lincoln*, 67; Burlingame, *Abraham Lincoln*, 1:128–129; and Wilson, *Honor's Voice*, 171ff. Note James H. Matheny to Herndon, November, 1866, *HI*, 431.

35. "The farm women": Sandburg, *Abraham Lincoln*, 1:215–216. "He said he knew": P. K. McMinn, "Lincoln as Known to His Neighbors," *Saturday Evening Post* (February 13, 1904).

36. "Speed's store fitted": Speed, *Reminiscences*, 21; Susan Krause, "Abraham Lincoln and Joshua Speed," 36–38; Joshua Speed to John Speed, March 23, 1835, Speed Family Papers, 1831–1902 [Mss C S], FHS; Daniel Stowell, "James Bell & Co. v. Hall," in *The Papers of Abraham Lincoln: Legal Documents and Cases*, ed. Daniel Stowell et al. (Charlottesville: University of Virginia Press, 2008), chap. 12. Note for context the excellent recent book: Jessica M. Lepler, *The Many Panics of 1837* (New York: Cambridge University Press, 2013).

2. TWO FRIENDS, ONE BED 255

37. "There were relatively few": Krause, "Abraham Lincoln and Joshua Speed," 40–49. In this long-needed article, requiring rigorous research, Krause covered the business associations between Lincoln and Speed.

38. "Speed was quite aware": Speed, *Reminiscences*, 19–20; cf. his statement to Herndon in 1882, *HI*, 589; and Dr. J. F. Snyder, "Governor Ford and His Family," *Journal of the Illinois Society of Historical Studies* 3, no. 2 (July 1910): 45 (George Forquer was Ford's half brother).

39. "In 1872 John Nicolay": The interview is in Michael Burlingame, ed., *An Oral History of Abraham Lincoln: John G. Nicolay's Interviews and Essays* (Carbondale: Southern Illinois University Press, 1995), 22–23. The chronology, however, is a bit confused in Butler's account (not surprising, as he was recalling events from nearly forty years earlier). He says he told Lincoln to study law, but by the spring of 1837 Lincoln was a fully certified lawyer. Butler also has the party leaving Vandalia for Springfield in April, but the legislative term ended on March 6; see Miers, *Lincoln Day-By-Day*, 1:70. The key points of the story, however, clearly locate it in early April 1837; cf. Wilson, *Honor's Voice*, 346–347, n. 1.

40. Joshua Speed to Herndon, 1882, a handwritten statement that appears in *HI*, 589–590; another version of the same story is in Speed, *Reminiscences*, 17–18. The added details to these accounts of the story are from what Speed wrote to Cassius M. Clay, *Reminiscences of Abraham Lincoln by Distinguished Men of His Time*, ed. Allen Thorndike Rice (1888; New York: Haskell House, 1971), 294–295. Cf. David Donald, *We Are Lincoln Men: Abraham Lincoln and His Friends* (New York: Simon & Schuster, 2003), 30.

2. TWO FRIENDS, ONE BED

1. "Lincoln wore his": Joshua Speed, *Reminiscences* (Louisville, Ky.: Bradley and Gilbert Co., 1896), 34; Speed, "Statement" to Herndon, 1882, *HI*, 588–589. "There was a haunting tension": Lincoln to William Herndon, February 2, 1848, *CW*, 1:448; Lincoln, "Fragment on the Struggle Against Slavery," c. July 1858, *CW*, 2:482.

2. Speed, *Reminiscences*, 34.

3. "He spoke in a Southern": When Herndon interviewed Speed on June 10, 1865? (*HI*, 31), about the books Lincoln read, he wrote down (in his rapid style with dashes and misspellings) as one book, "The Bable," which was clearly what he heard for the "Bible." "Speed's thick eyebrows": John Gilmer Speed, introduction to Speed, *Reminiscences*, 5. "Lord Byron": Ruth Painter Randall, *The Courtship of Mr. Lincoln* (Boston: Little Brown, 1957), 12, seems to be the first to note this resemblance (it is not clear if Speed's contemporaries

saw his resemblance to Byron). "Robert Kincaid": Robert L. Kincaid, "Joshua Fry Speed, 1814–1882, Abraham Lincoln's Most Intimate Friend," *Filson Club History Quarterly* 17 (1943): 13–123.

4. "Speed speaks with awe": Douglas L. Wilson, *Honor's Voice: The Transformation of Abraham Lincoln* (New York: Knopf, 1998), 19ff; Speed, *Reminiscences*, 20. "Speed seemed instinctively": Richard Lawrence Miller, *Lincoln and His World: Prairie Politician, 1834–1842* (Mechanicsburg, Penn.: Stackpole, 2008), 164.

5. "Honest Old Abe": Speed, *Reminiscences*, 20. "The introduction": ibid., 4.

6. "Orville Browning said": Michael Burlingame, ed., *An Oral History of Abraham Lincoln: John G. Nicolay's Interviews and Essays* (Carbondale: Southern Illinois University Press, 1995), 6–7. "His ambition": Herndon to Ward Hill Lamon, February 25, 1870, in Emanuel Hertz, *The Hidden Lincoln: From the Letters and Papers of William H. Herndon* (New York: Viking, 1938), 68; William H. Herndon and Jesse W. Weik, *Herndon's Lincoln*, ed. Douglas L. Wilson and Rodney O. Davis (Urbana: University of Illinois Press, 2006), 304; Edmund Wilson, *Patriotic Gore: Studies in the Literature of the American Civil War* (New York: Oxford University Press, 1962), 118–119. "In a typically ironic": Lincoln to Mrs. Orville H. Browning, April 1, 1838, *CW*, 1:119.

7. "In his many letters": In a fragment of an interview Herndon conducted with Speed "by June 10, 1865," the editors determine, Speed tells Herndon of Lincoln's fondness for Lord Byron's poems "The Bride of Abydos" and "The Devil's Drive." The editors unpack an obscure reference, "Piece Put in was Inez," to indicate Lincoln's familiarity with the 1832 edition of Byron's *Childe Harold's Pilgrimage* (canto 1, following stanza 84). See Speed to Herndon, interview, by June 10, 1865, *HI*, 30. Speed was thus a good reporter of Lincoln's interests, but one would never find such a subtle internal reference to a work of literature in one of Speed's letters.

8. "Lincoln was unchurched": Elton Trueblood, *Abraham Lincoln: Lessons in Spiritual Leadership* (New York: HarperOne, 1973), chap. 3, "Lincoln and the Bible," 55–82, is the most authoritative text on this issue. For example, Trueblood notes that Lincoln's quite secular speech on April 6, 1858, "First Lecture on Discoveries and Inventions" (*CW*, 2: 437–442), contains thirty-four separate references to the Bible (66). Cf. Noah Brooks on this issue, quoted in Michael Burlingame, *Abraham Lincoln: A Life* (Baltimore, Md.: Johns Hopkins University Press, 2008), 1:38; and my *Lincoln's Quest for Union: A Psychological Study*, 2nd ed. (Philadelphia: Paul Dry Books, 2000), 248. "One of Lincoln's uses": Robert Bray, *Reading with Lincoln* (Carbondale: Southern Illinois University Press, 2010), 190–191. In Herndon's oral history, and in his own writing, the issue of whether Lincoln was an atheist and what he felt about religion loomed large.

9. "Lincoln knew most": Lincoln's rhetoric book as a child contained the full text of the soliloquies, which he clearly memorized as a child; see Strozier, *Lincoln's Quest*, 248. "Lincoln came to know": Speed to Herndon, January 12, 1866, *HI*, 156; Abner Ellis to Herndon, February 14, 1866, *HI*, 210. "He honed all": see, for example, "Address Before the Young Men's Lyceum of Springfield, Illinois," January 27, 1838, *CW*, 1:108–115.

10. Speed, *Reminiscences*, 19, 25, 38–39.

11. "Richard Lawrence Miller": Miller, *Lincoln and His World* (Mechanicsburg, Penn.: Stackpole Books, 2008), 153; cf. William G. Greene to Herndon, May 30, 1865, *HI*, 17–18; Henry C. Whitney, *Life on the Circuit with Abraham Lincoln* (Boston: Estes and Lauriat, 1892).

12. "As a young boy": The cabin in which Lincoln may—or may not—have been born was "discovered" in the early twentieth century. It rests now ensconced in a Beaux-Arts marble temple with fifty-six steps leading up to it in Hodgenville, Kentucky, a building that had its cornerstone laid by Theodore Roosevelt in 1909 (the centenary of Lincoln's birth) and was finished and dedicated in 1911. The cabin is at least typical of the *kind* of house in which he was born, which is why the National Park Service has now decided to call it a "representative" cabin.

13. Reported in the *Sangamo Journal*, November 13, 1840. The overall gender difference for the population of the county in 1840 was 7,890 men and 7,158 women.

14. "Lincoln strode across": Leonard Swett, interview with Herndon [ca. 1887–1889], *HI*, 731–732.

15. "as noted by Whitney": Henry C. Whitney to Herndon, June 23, 1887, *HI*, 617.

16. "Larry Kramer": For a good account of the Kramer diary saga, see Carol Lloyd, "Was Lincoln Gay?" *Salon* (April 30, 1999), http://www.salon.com/1999/04/30/lincoln/. Cf. the story of the Hitler hoax, including the way some noted historians got bamboozled, in Robert Harris, *Selling Hitler: The Extraordinary Story of the Con Job of the Century—The Faking of the Hitler Diaries* (New York: Pantheon, 1986). Evidence for the burning of Speed's store is from Paul M. Angle, *Here I Have Lived* (Springfield, Ill.: The Abraham Lincoln Association, 1935), 181, who notes that "more than half the block on the west side of the square burned on the night of May 11, 1855," which led the citizens of Springfield to subscribe for a fire engine. The *Illinois State Register* the next day (p. 3, col. 1) lists the businesses affected, saying that the "southward" tendency of the blaze was stopped by "Clark's bank's brick walls." I am indebted to James Cornelius, the curator of the Lincoln Collection at the Lincoln Presidential Library and Museum, for directing me to these references. "In his long-awaited": Larry Kramer, *The American People: Volume 1:*

Search for My Heart, A Novel (New York: Farrar, Straus & Giroux, 2015), 268–272.

17. Jonathan Ned Katz, *Love Stories: Sex Between Men Before Homosexuality* (Chicago: University of Chicago Press, 2001); Charles Shively, *Loving Comrades: Walt Whitman's Homosexual Loves* (New York: Taylor and Francis, 1995); John Stauffer, *Giants: The Parallel Lives of Frederick Douglass and Abraham Lincoln* (New York: Twelve, 2008); Clarence A. Tripp, *The Intimate World of Abraham Lincoln* (New York: The Free Press, 2005). Tripp makes the most aggressive case for Lincoln's homosexuality, but his only example that is worth serious consideration is his relationship with Speed. Tripp also argues for Lincoln's later homosexual relationship with a Captain Derickson, who was part of the unit that guarded the president after 1862 when he stayed in the Soldier Home just outside Washington. There is almost no serious scholar who accepts this story except Jean Baker, in her introduction to Tripp's book. See the excellent summary of the debate by Martin P. Johnson, "Did Lincoln Sleep with His Bodyguard? Another Look at the Evidence," *Journal of the Abraham Lincoln Association* 27 (Summer 2006): 42–55. My review of Tripp is "Gay Abe?" *Illinoistimes.com* (February 10, 2005).

18. "The best historian": Katz, *Love Stories*. "At the same time": Michael Bronski, *A Queer History of the United States* (Boston: Beacon, 2011); David R. Greenberg, *The Construction of Homosexuality* (Chicago: University of Chicago Press, 1988); Thomas W. Laqueur, *Solitary Sex: A Cultural History of Masturbation* (New York: Zone, 2003).

19. "The broader context": E. Anthony Rotundo, *American Manhood: Transformations in Masculinity from the Revolution to the Modern Era* (New York: Basic Books, 1993), 75–90.

20. Ibid., 80–82.

21. "As with a man and his wife": Somewhat further away, but of interest, Sigmund Freud wrote to his very intimate friend, Wihelm Fliess, "all I can say is that I am looking forward to our congress as to the slaking of hunger and thirst. I bring nothing but two open ears and one temporal lobe lubricated for reception." Jeffrey Moussaieff Masson, ed., *The Complete Letters of Sigmund Freud to Wilhelm Fliess, 1887 to 1904* (Cambridge, Mass.: Belknap Press of Harvard University Press, 1986), 193. There is an important parallel story about female friendships in the nineteenth century. Note especially Carroll Smith-Rosenberg, *Disorderly Conduct: Visions of Gender in Victorian America* (New York: Oxford University Press, 1985).

22. *CW*, 3:5, 16. Note also Albert J. Beveridge, *Abraham Lincoln, 1809–1858*, 2 vols. (New York: Houghton & Mifflin, 1928), 1:127, n. 5, says the goods in the Berry store included whiskey. Compare W. NcNeely to Herndon, November

12, 1866, *HI*, 81; and Glenna R. Schroeder-Lein, *Lincoln and Medicine* (Carbondale: Southern Illinois University Press, 2012), 49.

23. Titian J. Coffey, *Reminiscences of Abraham Lincoln by Distinguished Men of His Time*, ed. Allen Thorndike Rice (1888; New York: Haskell House, 1971), 241.

24. See my *Lincoln's Quest*, 3–88.

25. Carl Sandburg, *Abraham Lincoln: The Prairie Years* (New York: Harcourt, Brace & Co., 1926), 1:264.

26. John Gilmer Speed, introduction to Speed, *Reminiscences*; Speed to Holland, June 22, 1865, in Allen C. Guelzo, "Holland's Informants: The Construction of Josiah Holland's 'Life of Abraham Lincoln,'" *Journal of the Abraham Lincoln Association* 23 (2002): 1–55.

3. FRIENDSHIP

1. "It was to Mary Owens": Lincoln to Mary Owens, May 7, 1837, *CW*, 1:78. "Lincoln also refused": Joshua Speed to Herndon, Louisville, November 30, 1866, *HI*, 431. "Furthermore, a close read": Joshua Speed, *Reminiscences* (Louisville, Ky.: Bradley and Gilbert Co., 1896); for his communications with Herndon, see *HI*, 30–32, 52, 133, 156–158, 196, 212–213, 255, 337–338, 341–342, 430–431, 433, 474–477, 477–478, 498–500, 588–591.

2. "In the early afternoon": It was the custom then in central Illinois to take dinner in the middle of the day and have a light supper in the evening. See, for example, Lincoln's anonymous narrative of "The Trailor Murder Case," April 15, 1846, *CW*, 1:371–376. "Speed, who knew more": Speed to Herndon, May 8, 1866, *HI*, 255. The dates of their sleeping together, while certain between April 1837 and January 1, 1841, are less clear after that. They may have stayed together at Butler's for a few months, and we don't know how they slept when Lincoln visited Farmington in the summer of 1841. They probably stayed again at Butler's in the late summer and fall of 1841, but there is no concrete evidence for it or for their sharing a bed together after 1840.

3. "But, in fact, their relationship": This is what Heinz Kohut called a "self-object." The most relevant among his many writings is *The Analysis of the Self: A Systematic Approach to the Psychoanalytic Treatment of Narcissistic Personality Disorders* (New York: International Universities Press, 1971). Note my biography of Kohut, *Heinz Kohut: The Making of a Psychoanalyst* (New York: Farrar, Straus & Giroux, 2001).

4. "A 'throng of loungers'": William H. Herndon and Jesse W. Weik, *Herndon's Lincoln*, ed. Douglas L. Wilson and Rodney O. Davis (Urbana: University

of Illinois Press, 2006), 125; Speed, *Reminiscences*, 3; James H. Matheny, Herndon interview, 1865–1866, *HI*, 470.

5. Alexis de Tocqueville, *Democracy in America*, vol. 2, §2, chap. 5, www.gutenberg.org/file/816/816-h/816-h/h.htm.

6. "Even New Salem": Fern Nance Pond, ed., "New Salem Community Activities: Documentary," *Journal of the Illinois State Historical Society* 48 (1955): 82–101.

7. "In Springfield, a good": Herndon interview with James H. Matheny, 1865–1866, *HI*, 470. "We were in the habit": Milton Hay (Nicolay interview), July 4, 1875, in Michael Burlingame, ed., *An Oral History of Abraham Lincoln: John G. Nicolay's Interviews and Essays* (Carbondale: Southern Illinois University Press, 1995), 27. "At the cyclically slow": Speed, *Reminiscences*, 3; Herndon and Weik, *Herndon's Lincoln*, 125, 153; Herndon interview with James H. Matheny, 1865–1866, *HI*, 470.

8. "Matheny, Noah Rickard": "Mr. Lincoln's Friends, Edward L. Baker (1855–1874)," mrlincolnandfriends.org/inside.asp?pageID=50. "Not only did Lincoln": Herndon interview with James H. Matheny, March 2, 1870, *HI*, 576–577. "In his old age": Herndon and Weik, *Herndon's Lincoln*, 125.

9. "As Herndon described": Herndon and Weik, *Herndon's Lincoln*, 125.

10. "The group was also": Carl Bode, *The American Lyceum: Town Meeting of the Mind* (New York: Oxford University Press, 1956), 14, 90–91, 186–188; Thomas F. Schwartz, "Springfield Lyceums and Lincoln's 1838 Speech," *Journal of the Illinois History Society* 45 (1990): 46–49.

11. "Speed's admiration": Speed, *Reminiscences*, 125.

12. "In what was likely": Speed, *Reminiscences*, 23–24.

13. "But he also": Joshua Speed to Joseph Gillespie, Louisville, April 29, 1876, Speed Family Papers [Ms A S742 f 45], FHS.

14. "Edward D. Baker, whose": Richard Lawrence Miller, *Lincoln and His World: Prairie Politician, 1834–1842* (Mechanicsburg, Penn.: Stackpole, 2008), 164–165. "David Donald says": David Donald, *Lincoln* (New York: Simon and Schuster, 1995), 84. "One of these men": William H. Herndon, "Analysis of the Character of Abraham Lincoln," *Abraham Lincoln Quarterly* 1, no. 8 (1942), 436. "Lincoln in the 1840s": see Stephen T. Logan to Herndon, 1865–1866, *HI*, 468.

15. "John J. Hardin": Donald, *Lincoln*, 84, 92; Paul Simon, *Lincoln's Preparation for Greatness: The Illinois Legislative Years* (Champaign: University of Illinois Press, 1989), 310; Lincoln to Hardin, May 18, 1843, *CW*, 1:323.

16. "Archer Herndon": Archer G. Herndon to Herndon, September 28, 1866, *HI*, 355–356.

17. "When Lincoln offered": Butler interview with Nicolay Hay in Burlingame, *An Oral History*, 23.

18. "Others dropped by": See Robert Wilson to Herndon, February 10, 1866, *HI*, 202; John B. Weber to Herndon, November 1, 1866, *HI*, 390. Herndon's comments on the loungers is from *Life of Lincoln*, 1930 ed., 153.

19. Herndon and Weik, *Herndon's Lincoln*, 125. The story of tying up the wife beater is in James H. Matheny, Herndon interview, September 12, 1888, *HI*, 667.

20. "Sometimes Speed traveled": Joshua Speed to Mary Speed, February 28, 1838, Speed Family Papers [Mss C Sa], FHS. "Occasionally, members of": John Speed to Lucy F. Speed, November 2, 1839, Speed Family Papers [Mss C Sd], FHS.

21. Joshua Speed to Lucy G. Speed, December 25, 1839. Filson Historical Society.

22. "Lincoln's circuit riding": See Strozier, *Lincoln's Quest for Union*, 139–170, where I show that Lincoln significantly extended his stays away from home in the 1850s as compared with the 1840s.

23. "He said to Herndon": Speed statement for Herndon, 1865–1866, *HI*, 478.

24. "In 1839 Speed": Speed Statement to Herndon, 1882 (a statement apparently dictated by Speed not long before his death and written down in the handwriting of an unknown person, then sent to Herndon), *HI*, 590. Speed tells the same story in *Reminiscences*, 25–26 (though in that account he doesn't name the town). In his statement, Speed calls the town "Christiansburg" but probably meant Taylorville in Christian County. There was no town in central Illinois called Christiansburg (which James Cornelius pointed out to me in an e-mail of December 19, 2014). Speed was probably thinking of the small Kentucky town of Christianburg, not far from Louisville.

4. DEPRESSION

1. J. Rowan Herndon to Herndon, May 28, 1865, *HI*, 7.

2. "At an auction": James Short to Herndon, July 7, 1865, *HI*, 74. Cf. William H. Herndon and Jesse W. Weik, *Herndon's Lincoln*, ed. Douglas L. Wilson and Rodney O. Davis (Urbana: University of Illinois Press, 2006), 86. The most complete account of the details of the complicated transactions surrounding this note and especially Van Bergen's role in it is in Richard Lawrence Miller, *Lincoln and His World: Prairie Politician, 1834–1842* (Mechanicsburg, Penn.: Stackpole, 2008), 1:242–243.

3. "Lincoln sold a lot": See Earl Schenck Miers, ed., *Lincoln Day-By-Day: A Chronology, 1809–1865* (Washington: Lincoln Sesquicentennial Commission, 1960), 1:71–72.

4. "The most noteworthy": Herndon and Weik, *Herndon's Lincoln*, 173–179; Thomas F. Schwartz, "The Lincoln Handbill of 1837: A Rare Document's History," *Illinois Historical Journal* 79 (1986): 274.

5. "John Hanks, his cousin": John Hanks to Herndon, 1865–66, *HI*, 454. "Later, in New Salem": Robert L. Wilson to Herndon, February 10, 1866, *HI*, 205. "Douglas Wilson": Douglas L. Wilson, *Honor's Voice: The Transformation of Abraham Lincoln* (New York: Knopf, 1998), 125–126.

6. "The leading psychiatrist": Norbert Hirschhorn, Robert G. Feldman, and Ian A. Greaves, "Abraham Lincoln's Blue Pills: Did Our Sixteenth President Suffer from Mercury Poisoning?" *Perspectives in Biology and Medicine* 44 (2001): 315–332. The authors point out that blue pills were basically mercury and make a highly dubious argument that Lincoln suffered from mercury poisoning from taking this treatment. "Stuart wrote to Herndon": John T. Stuart to Herndon, late June, 1865, *HI*, 63. "Henry C. Whitney": Henry C. Whitney to Herndon, August 27, 1887, *HI*, 631–632.

7. "Herndon related a story": Herndon, note to himself on February 27, 1891, in Emanuel Hertz, *The Hidden Lincoln: From the Letters and Papers of William H. Herndon* (New York: New York: Viking, 1938), 398–399. "At another time, Herndon": Roy P. Basler, *A Touchstone to Greatness: Essays, Addresses, and Occasional Pieces About Abraham Lincoln* (New York: Praeger, 1973), 21.

8. "Henry C. Whitney wrote": Henry C. Whitney to Herndon, June 23, 1887, *HI*, 617.

9. "His father, Thomas": Joshua Wolf Shenk, *Lincoln's Melancholy: How Depression Challenged a President and Fueled His Greatness* (New York: Mariner, 2005), 12–13; cf. Michael Burlingame, *Abraham Lincoln: A Life* (Baltimore, Md.: Johns Hopkins University Press, 2008), 1:179–180, who sees a parallel family history of mental disturbance in Mary Todd's family, suggesting that was an unconscious source of attraction between them and why their marriage was such a disaster (in his view).

10. "The best witness": Dennis Hanks to Herndon, June 13, 1865, *HI*, 35–43; Joshua Speed, *Reminiscences* (Louisville, Ky.: Bradley and Gilbert Co., 1896), 19; Herndon to Weik, January 19, 1886, *HI*; William Woods to Herndon, September 15, 1865, *HI*, 123–125; John Hanks to Herndon, n.d., *HI*, 43–45, 456; Nathaniel Grigsby to Herndon, September 12, 1865, *HI*, 111–115; Herndon to Weik, January 19, 1886, in Hertz, *Hidden Lincoln*, 139. "God bless my mother": Herndon and Weik, *Herndon's Lincoln*, 16; note also three Herndon letters to Ward Hill Lamon: February 28, 1869; February 25, 1870; and March 6, 1870; in Hertz, *Hidden Lincoln*, 59, 62–69, 69–72. The specific connection between the quality of the infantile empathic environment and the shape of the adult personality in terms of empathy, humor, flexibility, and wisdom was first noted by Heinz Kohut, "Forms and Transformations of Narcissism," in *The*

Search for the Self: Selected Writings of Heinz Kohut: 1950–1978, 2 vols., ed. Paul H. Ornstein (1966; New York: International Universities Press, 1978), 427–460.

11. "After a cold winter": In a letter to Herndon, March 12, 1866, *HI*, 229, Dennis Hanks calls the cabin Thomas erected that first winter in Indiana "that Darne Little half face Camp," and another relative, A. H. Chapman (married to Hanks's daughter, Harriet), in a written statement for Herndon sometime before September 8, 1865 (*HI*, 98), says Thomas built a "cabin or camp of poles one side on the face of it being open." Lincoln in his autobiography says he shot a turkey from the "log-cabin" his father had built a few days before his eighth birthday, or early February 1817, after the family moved to Indiana the following autumn. That reference suggests the family was not living in a "half face Camp," as Dennis described it. See also Charles Coleman, "The Half Faced Camp in Indiana—Fact or Myth," *Abraham Lincoln Quarterly* 7(1952): 138–139. I am indebted to James Cornelius in an e-mail of December 29, 2014, for pointing out to me these contrasting sources about this issue.

12. "Lincoln came to love": Dennis Hanks to Herndon, June 13, 1865, *HI*, 35–43; Speed, *Reminiscences*, 36; Herndon interview with Sarah Bush Lincoln, September 8, 1865, *HI*, 107, 108.

13. "At eighteen years": Samuel E. Kercheval to Weik, December 2, 1887, *HI*, 645; Michael Burlingame, *Lincoln*, 1:45 (notes 157, 159, p. 772), tracked down this information of Lincoln's sadness after Sarah's death from Grigsby relatives. Burlingame also quotes from a Grigsby descendant who said in 1940 that it was family lore that the Grigsbys looked down on Sarah because she had been "hired help." William Herndon, *Life of Lincoln*, 1930 ed., in Herndon and Weik, *Herndon's Lincoln*, 44, notes the Grigsbys were the "leading family" in Gentry.

14. "Herndon gathered": Herndon's notes to himself, n.d., in Hertz, *Hidden Lincoln*, 393; Herndon to Truman H. Bartlett, September 30, 1887, in ibid., 205–207. "Thomas was, in": Nathaniel Grigsby to Herndon, September 12, 1865, *HI*, 111–115.

15. "Thomas Lincoln was in fact": Louis A. Warren, *Lincoln's Parentage and Childhood: A History of the Kentucky Lincolns Supported by Documentary Evidence* (New York: Century, 1926), 47; Harry E. Pratt, *The Personal Finances of Abraham Lincoln* (Springfield, Ill.: Abraham Lincoln Association, 1943), 4; Herndon's notes on his visit to the Lincoln farm in Kentucky, September 14, 1865, in Hertz, *Hidden Lincoln*, 359; Dennis F. Hanks to William Herndon, June 13, 1865, *HI*, 35–43.

16. "As Lincoln told Herndon": Herndon and Weik, *Herndon's Lincoln*, 2–3. Note also three Herndon letters to Ward Hill Lamon on this issue: February 28, 1869; February 25, 1870; and March 6, 1870; Hertz, *Hidden Lincoln*, 59,

62–69, 69–72. Compare my more extended discussion of this theme in my *Lincoln's Quest for Union*, 3–12.

17. "He regarded Thomas": Lincoln's "Autobiography Written for John L. Scripps," June 1860, *CW*, 4:61. "Lincoln seldom visited him": Charles B. Strozier and Stanley H. Cath, "Lincoln and the Fathers: Reflections on Idealization," in *Fathers and Their Families*, ed. Stanley H. Cath, Alan Gurwitt, and Linda Bunsberg (Hillsdale, N.J.: Analytic Press, 1989), 289–290. "Herndon and others": Herndon to Weik, November 24, 1882, in *Hertz, Hidden Lincoln*, 88; Richard Lawrence Miller, *Lincoln and His World*, vol. 3: *The Rise to National Prominence, 1843–1853* (Jefferson, N.C.: McFarland & Co., 2011), 217. "Your letter of": Lincoln to Thomas Lincoln and John D. Johnston, December 24, 1848, *CW*, 2:15.

18. "The next day": Miller, *Lincoln and His World*, 3:236.

19. "Lincoln wrote a letter": Lincoln to John D. Johnston, January 12, 1851, *CW*, 2:96–97. "Lincoln then failed": Charles H. Coleman, *Abraham Lincoln and Coles County* (New Brunswick, N.J.: Scarecrow, 1955), 139; Justin G. Turner and Linda Levitt Turner, *Mary Todd Lincoln: Her Life and Letters* (New York: Knopf, 1972), 464–465; Ward Hill Lamon, *Life of Lincoln from His Birth to His Inauguration as President* (1872; New York: Kessinger, 2010), 463.

20. "Erik Erikson has noted": Erik Erikson, *Gandhi's Truth: On the Origins of Militant Nonviolence* (New York: Norton, 1968), 123.

21. "William Greene, Lincoln's good friend": William G. Greene, Herndon interview, May 30, 1865, *HI*, 21. "Herndon gathered": Hardin Bale, interview with Herndon, May 29, 1865, *HI*, 13; William G. Greene, May 30, 1865, *HI*, 21; James Short to Herndon, July 7, 1865, *HI*, 73; Lynn McNulty Greene to Herndon, July 30, 1865, *HI*, 80; Wilson, *Honor's Voice*, 124. "Mentor Graham said": Mentor Graham to Herndon, April 2, 1866, *HI*, 242–243. Carl Sandburg's poetic enthusiasm for the story of Ann Rutledge (see *Abraham Lincoln: The Prairie Years* [(New York: Harcourt, Brace & Company, 1926], 1:181–190) turned off more sober and seemingly reliable historians in the middle of the century, especially J. G. Randall ("Appendix: Sifting the Ann Rutledge Evidence," in *Lincoln the President: Springfield to Gettysburg*, 2 vols. [New York: Dodd, Mead, 1945], 2:231–242), who influenced biographers of Lincoln for decades. But Sandburg had it basically right, as much recent scholarship has shown, including the groundbreaking paper by John Y. Simon, "Abraham Lincoln and Ann Rutledge," *Journal of the Abraham Lincoln Association* 11 (1990). Note also John Evangelist Walsh, *The Shadows Rise: Abraham Lincoln and the Ann Rutledge Legend* (Urbana: University of Illinois Press, 1993); and Douglas L. Wilson, "Abraham Lincoln, Ann Rutledge, and the Evidence of Herndon's Informants," in *Lincoln Before Washington: New Perspectives on the Illinois Years* (Urbana: University of Illinois Press, 1997), 74–98.

22. "In the spring": Robert B. Rutledge to Herndon, November 21, 1866, *HI*, 408–409.

23. "As her brother": Robert B. Rutledge to Herndon, c. November 1, 1866, *HI*, 383; Mentor Graham, Herndon interview, April 2, 1866, *HI*, 243; Hardin Bale to Herndon, May 29, 1865, *HI*, 13. The count of respondents and their reports is in Wilson, *Honor's Voice*, 119.

24. "Lincoln knew intimately": Lincoln to Speed, February 3, 1842, *CW*, 1:267.

25. "A number of respondents": Mentor Graham, Herndon interview, April 2, 1866, *HI*, 243; Johnson Gaines Greene, Herndon interview, October 5, 1866, *HI*, 364–365. Mary herself in a letter to Herndon (August 6, 1866, *HI*, 265) lowered her height to five feet, five inches and her weight to 150 pounds.

26. "His first surviving letter": Lincoln to Mary Owens, December 13, 1836, *CW*, 1:54–55. "But very shortly": Lincoln to Mary Owens, May 7, 1837, *CW*, 1:78–79.

27. "Three months later": Lincoln to Mary Owens, August 16, 1837, *CW*, 1:94–95.

28. "He especially wanted": Mary Owens to Herndon, May 1, 1866, *HI*, 248. "He then wrote her": Mary Owens to Herndon, May 3, 1866, *HI*, 255–256. "She explained": Elizabeth Abell to Jesse Weik, group 4, reel 12, of the Herndon-Weik Collection, LoC, 364. "Mary added": Mary Owens to Herndon, July 22, 1866, *HI*, 262–263.

29. "Another of his": Theodore Calvin Pease, introduction to the *Diaries of Orville Hickman Browning* (Springfield: Illinois State Historical Society, 1927), xii–xiii. Lincoln's letter to Eliza Browning, April 1, 1838, is in *CW*, 1:117–119.

30. "The historian": Richard Current, *The Lincoln Nobody Knows* (1958; New York: Praeger, 1980), 41.

31. "Despite Lincoln's mental": Henry C. Whitney to Herndon, June 23, 1887, *HI*, 617. Matheny seems both a striking exception and the only evidence for what he felt comes from Whitney's secondhand report half a century later.

32. "He was in a state": For his best explanation of the "moratorium," see Erik H. Erikson, *Young Man Luther: A Study in Psychoanalysis and History* (New York: Norton, 1958), 100–101; Lincoln wrote to Mary Owens, December 13, 1836, *CW*, 1:54–55; William Butler in his interview with Nicolay, in Michael Burlingame, ed., *An Oral History of Abraham Lincoln: John G. Nicolay's Interviews and Essays* (Carbondale: Southern Illinois University Press, 1995), 22; Wilson, *Honor's Voice*, 188–193; see also Erik Erikson, *Identity: Youth and Crisis* (New York: Norton, 2013); Erik Erikson, *Identity and the Life Cycle* (New York: Norton, 2013); Erik Erikson, *Childhood and Society* (New York: Norton, 1950).

33. "He became visibly distracted": Speed, *Reminiscences*, 34; Elizabeth Edwards, interview with Herndon, 1865–1866, *HI*, 443–445; Herndon

and Weik, *Herndon's Lincoln*, 351; Wilson, *Honor's Voice*, 188–193; James H. Matheny, interview with Herndon, 1865–1866, *HI*, 470; Speed, interview with Herndon, January 12, 1866, *HI*, 156 (though cf. Speed's comments to Herndon, June 10, 1865, *HI*, 30). Byron was inspired to write his poem imagining the extinction of the Sun and a lifeless, silent Earth one dark day in 1816. See William K. Klingaman and Nicholas P. Klingaman, *The Year Without Summer: 1816 and the Volcano That Darkened the World and Changed History* (New York: St. Martin's, 2013), 167–168. Lincoln lived through the dark year of 1816 at the impressionable age of seven. It was the Lincoln family's last year in Kentucky. Crops failed all over the country, and Boston had a two-day blizzard in June. Anxious Bible readers thought it was the end of the world. In the fall of 1816, the Lincolns moved to Indiana.

34. "Lincoln did mention": David Davis to Herndon, September 20, 1866, *HI*, 348; Paul Angle, preface to Herndon, *Life of Lincoln*, 1930 ed., xxxix; Speed, *Reminiscences*, 34; Lincoln to Speed, January 3, 1842, *CW*, 1:265; Lincoln to Speed, February 13, 1842, *CW*, 1:269; Speed to Herndon, November 30, 1866, *HI*, 430.

5. SEX AND PROSTITUTION

1. "In the latter part": I am grateful to Erika Holst in a personal communication, November 12, 2014, for reminding me of the cultural context of neurasthenia.

2. "The story as reported": Johnson Gaines Greene, Herndon interview, October 5, 1866, *HI*, 365–366; William G. Greene, Herndon interview, October 9, 1866, *HI*, 367–368; Johnson Gaines Greene, Herndon interview, October 10, 1866.

3. "Possibly, though": It is hard to agree with Douglas Wilson's conclusion from his account of this story that it shows that "[Johnson Gaines] Greene all but says his brother and Lincoln took sexual advantage of Nancy Burner." Douglas L. Wilson, *Honor's Voice: The Transformation of Abraham Lincoln* (New York: Knopf, 1998), 113. Cf. Thomas P. Reep, *Abe Lincoln and the Frontier Folk of New Salem*, ed. Constance Reep Unsworth (1918; Middletown, Conn.: Southfarm, 2002), whose meticulous research on the old settlers of New Salem in the early twentieth century turned up nothing untoward in Lincoln's relations with the young women in town.

4. "A number of law cases": Erika Holst, *Wicked Springfield: Crime, Corruption, and Scandal During the Lincoln Era* (Mt. Pleasant, S.C.: The History Press, 2010).

5. Erika Holst, long a researcher in the Lincoln Legals project, pointed out to me in an e-mail (August 16, 2013) that "In general, when a couple got divorced [in this period in central Illinois] the woman either got the children and no support, or support but no children. Women generally didn't get custody of the children AND child support."

6. Martha Benner and Cullom Davis, eds., *The Law Practice of Abraham Lincoln*, complete documentary ed. (Urbana: University of Illinois Press, 2000), LO 3929, http://www.lawpracticeofabrahamlincoln.org/Search.aspx, which has an adequate, if somewhat confusing, search engine. There was a large context for the sex trade in Springfield at the time. For example, New York just after the Civil War hosted some five hundred brothels, so many that a popular guide, "The Gentleman's Directory," a kind of blue Zagat, was widely sold. Alison Leigh Cowan, "For Houses of Ill Repute, a 19th-Century Guidebook to Their Reputations," *New York Times* (January 27, 2011). Cowan, for her fine article, worked with the New-York Historical Society for this article, which includes a listing of the addresses of many of the brothels and a photograph of the guide itself.

7. John T. Stuart to Herndon, [1865–1866], *HI*, 481. The uncritical Michael Burlingame, in *Abraham Lincoln: A Life* (Baltimore, Md.: Johns Hopkins University Press, 2008), 1:69, quotes the source as definite proof of Lincoln's interest in prostitutes, mainly by compressing and distorting the quote to make it meet the needs of his predetermined view of Lincoln: "Stuart, who came to know Lincoln well in the Black Hawk War, recollected that they 'went to the hoar houses . . .'"

8. "In a widely quoted line": Herndon to Weik, January 23, 1890, in Emanuel Hertz, *The Hidden Lincoln: From the Letters and Papers of William H. Herndon* (New York: Viking, 1938), 247. "David Davis, the judge": David Davis, Herndon interview, September 20, 1866, *HI*, 350.

9. "William Greene told Herndon": Greene to Herndon, November 27, 1865, *HI*, 142. "Another old New Salem character": Abner Ellis, statement for Herndon, January 23, 1866, *HI*, 170.

10. "Fools ridiculed him": Herndon to Weik, December 10, 1885, in Hertz, *Hidden Lincoln*, 111–112. "Things went on right": Herndon interview with Joshua Speed, January 5, 1889, *HI*, 719.

11. "More recent observers": Wilson, *Honor's Voice*, 182–183; Richard Lawrence Miller, *Lincoln and His World: Prairie Politician, 1834–1842* (Mechanicsburg, Penn.: Stackpole, 2008), 1:154–155. "Middle-class mores": Carroll Smith-Rosenberg, *Disorderly Conduct: Visions of Gender in Victorian America* (New York: Oxford, 1985), esp. 109ff.; cf. E. Anthony Rotundo, *American Manhood: Transformations in Masculinity from the Revolution to the Modern Era*

(New York: Basic Books, 1993), 120–121, who notes the contradiction between the strict controls that men were supposed to impose on themselves regarding sexual impulses—including masturbation—and the widespread social fact that fully a third of all women in the nineteenth century were pregnant when they got married.

12. "Herndon tended to take in": For those tales of his past, see Herndon to Weik, January 18, 1886, in Hertz, *Hidden Lincoln*, 138–140; Charles Friend to Herndon, in Hertz, *Hidden Lincoln*, 340–341 and *HI*, 673–374; Dennis F. Hanks to Herndon, June 13, 1865, *HI*, 63; Herndon to Ward Hill Lamon, February 25, 1870, in Hertz, *Hidden Lincoln*, 63; Herndon's notes to himself, n.d., in Hertz, *Hidden Lincoln*, 393–394; Herndon to Weik, January 1, 1886, in Hertz, *Hidden Lincoln*, 118–119; Herndon to Weik, January 1891, in Hertz, *Hidden Lincoln*, 259. Wilson, *Honor's Voice*, 348, n. 36, specifically disagrees with my interpretation of the story as a Lincoln joke that got lost in translation. He argues that visiting prostitutes and having a fear of intimacy are not inconsistent. That is a reasonable point, but it fails to reconcile Herndon's unreliable but imaginable story with the absolutely verifiable evidence of Lincoln's self-doubts about sexuality and consummation. As I argue in chapter 10, Lincoln, as judged from his letter of February 25, 1842, to Speed, also seemed terribly inexperienced in sex, if he was not actually a virgin. His conflicts and confusions, in other words, ran very deep. Indeed, the supposed story of Lincoln leaving the Springfield prostitute because he lacks her full fee, even though she doesn't care and trusts him to pay her later, if taken at face value as a true story, reads as a very strange way for any man to behave.

13. "Lincoln, Herndon says": Herndon to Weik, January 5, 1889, in Hertz, *Hidden Lincoln*, 233–234.

14. "In the circle around Lincoln": Charles Strozier, "The Lives of William Herndon," *Journal of the Abraham Lincoln Association* 14 (1993): esp. 9–11. "He wrote up": Lincoln, "Fragment on Niagara Falls," *CW*, 2:10. "When Herndon asked him": William H. Herndon and Jesse W. Weik, *Herndon's Lincoln*, ed. Douglas L. Wilson and Rodney O. Davis (Urbana: University of Illinois Press, 2006), 187–188.

15. "Herndon also reports": Herndon to Weik, January 1891, in Hertz, *Hidden Lincoln*, 259–260.

16. "He reported to Herndon": Speed to Herndon, November 30, 1866, *HI*, 430. Speed added that Drake wrote back that he could only treat Lincoln in person, not by mail. "Speed assumed": Herndon to Weik, January 1891, in Hertz, *Hidden Lincoln*, 259–260.

17. "This Dr. Daniel Drake": J. Christian Bay, "Dr. Daniel Drake, 1785–1852," *Filson Club Historical Quarterly* 7 (1933); William B. Jensen, "Notes from the Oesper Collections: Elijah Slack," http://digitalprojects.libraries

.uc.edu/oesper/museum-notes/Elijah-Slack.pdf; "Drake's Contribution to Medical Education," http://elane.stanford.edu/wilson/html/chap4/chap4-sect9.html; Richard Rhodes, Scott V. Edwards, and Leslie A. Morris, *Audubon: Early Drawings* (Cambridge, Mass.: Harvard University Press and Houghton Library, 2008).

18. "It is also relevant": Herndon's account of the Drake letter in 1889 makes clear he only learned of it from Speed's 1866 letter to him. Herndon latched onto the detail that Lincoln did not read aloud to Speed one section of the letter to assume that he was keeping from Speed the knowledge of the syphilis, an interpretation that is far removed from any evidence or anything Lincoln told him.

19. "But what about": Milton Shutes, *Lincoln's Emotional Life* (Philadelphia: Dorrance and Company, 1957), 70–71; http://www.ancestry.com.

6. BROKEN ENGAGEMENT

1. "The story": William H. Herndon and Jesse W. Weik, *Herndon's Lincoln*, ed. Douglas L. Wilson and Rodney O. Davis (Urbana: University of Illinois Press, 2006), 145; Herndon first described his version of the story in a letter to Ward Hill Lamon, February 25, 1870, in Emanuel Hertz, *The Hidden Lincoln: From the Letters and Papers of William H. Herndon* (New York: Viking, 1938), 62–69; Ruth Painter Randall, *The Courtship of Mr. Lincoln* (Boston: Little, Brown, 1957); Douglas L. Wilson, *Honor's Voice: The Transformation of Abraham Lincoln* (New York: Knopf, 1998); Michael Burlingame, afterword to Clarence A. Tripp, *The Intimate World of Abraham Lincoln* (New York: The Free Press, 2005), 225ff., and more completely in his *Abraham Lincoln: A Life* (Baltimore, Md.: Johns Hopkins University Press, 2008); Richard Lawrence Miller, *Lincoln and His World: Prairie Politician, 1834–1842* (Mechanicsburg, Penn.: Stackpole, 2008).

2. "Randall's version": Randall, *The Courtship of Mr. Lincoln*, ix–x. "Others, in what": Burlingame, afterword to Tripp, *Intimate World*, 225–226; Miller, *Lincoln and His World*; Wilson, *Honor's Voice*, 307–321. "As Herndon put it": Herndon and Weik, *Herndon's Lincoln*, 145.

3. "Mary Todd's father": William H. Townsend, *Lincoln and the Bluegrass: Slavery and Civil War in Kentucky* (Lexington: University of Kentucky Press, 1955), 26–59; cf. Jean Baker, *Mary Todd Lincoln* (New York: Norton, 1987); and Stephen Berry, "There's Something About Mary: Mary Lincoln and Her Siblings," in *The Mary Lincoln Enigma: Historians on America's Most Controversial First Lady*, ed. Frank J. Williams and Michael Burkhimer (Carbondale: Southern Illinois University Press, 2012), 14–35.

4. "In Springfield, meanwhile": Baker, *Mary Todd Lincoln*, 48–49; Carl Sandburg, *Mary Lincoln: Wife and Widow* (Bedford, Mass.: Applewood, 1995), 38; "Erika Holst has": Erika Holst, " 'The Famile Extended': Abraham Lincoln Kinship Network," unpublished paper presented at the Conference on Illinois History, Springfield, Illinois, 2012.

5. "The house itself": Carl Sandburg, *Abraham Lincoln: The Prairie Years* (New York: Harcourt, Brace & Co., 1926), 1:251–252. "A reporter": *Quincy Whig* (February 1, 1840), ALPL, Box 72. "Those in the Coterie": James C. Conkling to Mercy Levering, January 24, 1841, ALPL.

6. "The Todd sisters": Baker, *Mary Todd Lincoln*, 74ff. The chronology in this paragraph, which reflects current scholarship, could be wrong. Mary might have visited her sister first in 1835, returned in 1837, and actually came for Frances's wedding in May 1839 and simply stayed on after she moved out of the house. New sources might emerge to alter the picture, but for the moment that is conjecture.

7. "She was never seen": Elizabeth Norris to Emilie Todd Helm, January 12, 1895, ALPL; Ruth Painter Randall, "What Was Mrs. Lincoln Like," Club Paper, folder box 70, LoC; Herndon to Jesse Weik, January 16, 1886, in Hertz, *Hidden Lincoln*, 137; Sandburg, *Mary Lincoln*, 30–31; Katherine Helm, *The True Story of Mary, Wife of Lincoln* (New York: Harper and Brothers, 1928), 81.

8. "In the fall of 1840": Justin G. Turner and Linda Levitt Turner, *Mary Todd Lincoln: Her Life and Letters* (New York: Knopf, 1972), 15.

9. "Elizabeth Edwards emphasized": Elizabeth Edwards to Herndon, 1865–1866, *HI*, 443.

10. "Marriage, especially": Baker, *Mary Todd Lincoln*, 88–89; Randall, *Courtship*, 9.

11. "His economic philosophy": Gabor Boritt, *Lincoln and the Economics of the American Dream* (1974; Urbana: University of Illinois Press, 1994); note the critique of the book by Stewart Winger, "Lincoln's Economics of the American Dream: A Reappraisal," *Journal of the Abraham Lincoln Association* 22 (2001): 50–80. "One can also exaggerate": Mary Hedges Hubbard to Ellen S. Hubbard, August 28, 1839, Box 72, ALPL.

12. "When he once": Turner and Turner, *Mary Todd Lincoln*, 11. "As a child": Wilson, *Honor's Voice*, 216; Miller, *Lincoln: Prairie Politician*, 446; Helm, *The True Story of Mary*, 32; Baker, *Mary Todd Lincoln*, 85.

13. "It is unclear": Elizabeth Edwards to Herndon, 1865–1866, *HI*, 443; Joshua Speed, *Reminiscences* (Louisville, Ky.: Bradley and Gilbert Co., 1896); Herndon and Weik, *Herndon's Lincoln*, 137.

14. "There is a counterargument": Wilson, *Honor's Voice*, 219–220. In "That Fatal First . . ." in *Lincoln Before Washington: New Perspectives on the Illinois*

Years (Urbana: University of Illinois Press, 1998), 103–112, Wilson quotes Herndon's interview with Speed to the effect that Lincoln "first wrote" Mary in the summer of 1840 to mean that it was only that summer that Lincoln "first made romantic overtures to Mary," a subtle and misleading extension of what Speed actually said.

15. "In her long and": Mary Todd to Mercy Ann Levering, December 15 (?), 1840, in Turner and Turner, *Mary Todd Lincoln*, 19–22. The reference to the two sweet little objections is in Mary's letter to Mercy, June 21, 1841, in ibid., 26.

16. "Lincoln was cautious": David Donald, *Lincoln* (New York: Simon and Schuster, 1995), 86; Wilson, *Honor's Voice*, 187.

17. "The Illinois Whig": Albert Beveridge, *Abraham Lincoln, 1809–1858* (Boston: Houghton Mifflin, 1928), 1:272; Beveridge speculates that the speech Lincoln used as his text was his "Speed on the Sub-Treasury," December [26], 1839, *CW*, 1:159–179. "For about half the time": Earl Schenck Miers, ed., *Lincoln Day-By-Day: A Chronology, 1809–1865* (Washington: Lincoln Sesquicentennial Commission, 1960), vol. 1. "A myth later": Floyd C. Shoemaker to J. G. Randall, January 17, 1953, Box 72, LoC.

18. W. G. Anderson to Lincoln, October 30, 1840; Lincoln to Anderson, October 31, 1840, *CW*, 1:211.

19. "Within a span": Herndon and Weik, *Herndon's Lincoln*, 137, is where Herndon tells the elaborate (and fantasized) tale of the scene waiting for Lincoln to show up. But Herndon's dating of when the wedding had been planned for, based on the testimony of Elizabeth Edwards, a missing letter of Speed that Herndon refers to, and, as is often forgotten, Herndon's own experience at the edges of the courtship drama, is believable, as Lincoln alludes to the meaning of the date (that he doesn't need to explain to Speed) in his letter of March 27, 1842, *CW*, 1:282. Wilson, in his footnote to Herndon's footnote, refers to Speed's interview with Herndon in 1865–1866 (*HI*, 475) and argues that the drama of the broken engagement played out in early December. That may be true, but it doesn't contradict the other evidence that the wedding had been *planned* for the first of January. Wilson, *Lincoln Before Washington*, 118ff., further develops the (unfortunately unconvincing) argument that the date has no significance, though he concludes that the only possible meaning it could have (quoting me in 1982) is that it was the date of the formal notice of the sale of Speed's store and the state's technical bankruptcy.

20. "One is the": James C. Conckling to Mercy Levering, September 21, 1840, ALPL; Mary Todd to Mercy Levering, December 15 (?), in Turner and Turner, *Mary Todd Lincoln*, 22; Wilson, *Honor's Voice*, 221; and Miller, *Lincoln*, 1:448–449, who goes so far on this flimsy evidence as to say Lincoln may have been "repulsed by Mary's weight gain."

21. "Elizabeth Edwards, who": Elizabeth Edwards, interview with Herndon, 1865–1866, *HI*, 444; Wilson, *Honor's Voice*, 115–116.

22. "In Herndon's shorthand": Ninian Edwards, interview with Herndon, September 22, 1865, *HI*, 133.

23. "The second witness": Michael Burlingame, ed., *An Oral History of Abraham Lincoln: John G. Nicolay's Interviews and Essays* (Carbondale: Southern Illinois University Press, 1995), 1–2 (and quotes in the next paragraph).

24. "The third witness": Speed interview with Herndon, 1865–66, *HI*, 474–475.

25. "Finally, Jane D. Bell": Jane D. Bell to Ann Bell of Danville, Kentucky, January 27, 1841. This text is taken from a copy of the letter supplied to Professor John B. Clark of Lincoln Memorial University by Mary B. E. (Mrs. Henry) Jackson, a relative of Jane D. Bell's, dated August 25, 1948, and in turn copied and supplied to Professor James G. Randall by R. Gerald McMurtry on November 7, 1950 (Randall Papers, Manuscript Division, LoC). This text varies slightly from the extract printed in the *Lincoln Herald* 50, no. 4/51, no. 1 (December 1948–February 1949): 47, which omits the final fragment. The letter thus exists only in copies. The detail she provides about Lincoln and Matilda in her sole surviving letter is either astonishingly prescient or perhaps a forgery of some kind.

26. "After reporting": Ninian Edwards, interview with Herndon, September 22, 1865, *HI*, 133. "Besides, it is worth": Elizabeth Edwards, interview with Herndon, 1865–1866, *HI*, 443–444.

27. "Speed's interview": Herndon interview with Speed, 1865–1866, *HI*, 474–477. Note Wilson, "Fatal First," 102ff., who constructs a broken engagement in two parts, the first of which came during the special session of the state legislature.

28. "Elizabeth Edwards told": Elizabeth Edwards, interview with Herndon, 1865–1866, *HI*, 444; Lincoln to Mary Lincoln, April 16, 1848, *CW*, 1:466.

29. Burlingame, *Lincoln*, 1:181–182, 798–800. Burlingame, in his afterword to Tripp, *Intimate World*, 232–233, lists the same letter.

30. "The main problem": Elizabeth Edwards, interview with Herndon, 1865–1866, *HI*, 444.

31. "Mary wrote Mercy Levering": Mary Todd to Mercy Ann Levering, December [?], 1840, in Turner and Turner, *Mary Todd Lincoln*, 20. "Ninian Edwards, the protector": Ninian Wirt Edwards, Herndon interview, September 22, 1865, *HI*, 133. "Ninian Edwards's wife": Elizabeth Todd Edwards, Herndon interview, 1865–1866, though Herndon and Weik in their biography date this interview on January 10, 1866, *HI*, 443.

32. Speed to Mary Speed, February 2, 1841, SC 1443b, ALPL.

33. Baker, *Mary Todd Lincoln*, 89–90.

34. "A little over a month": Lincoln to John T. Stuart, February 5, 1841, *CW*, 1:233. "James Conkling wrote Mercy Levering": Conkling to Levering, January 24, 1841, ALPL. "Abner Y. Ellis told Herndon": Ellis to Herndon, March 24, 1866, *HI*, 238.

35. "As she later": Sarah Rickard Barret to Herndon, August 12, 1888, *HI*, 665.

36. "According to Sarah": Sarah Rickard Barret to Herndon, August 12, 1888, *HI*, 665. "In the winter": Sarah Rickard Barret to Herndon, August 3, 1888, *HI*, 663. "Whether he was joking": Sarah Rickard Barret to Herndon, August 3, 1888, *HI*, 664; Sarah Rickard Barret to Herndon, August 12, 1888, *HI*, 663. Anna Miles Herndon (a distant relative of Sarah) told Herndon in an interview on September 13, 1887, *HI*, 640, that Sarah "ought to have taken Lincoln because she did so badly with Barrett [sic]." But this source is not very reliable (it is old, odd, and several degrees of separation from Sarah).

37. "Lincoln wrote Speed": Lincoln to Speed, February 3, 1842, *CW*, 1:268.

7. THE WINTER OF DISCONTENT

1. "Despite how he portrayed": Speed to Herndon, November 30, 1866, *HI*, 430.

2. "Lincoln in a letter": Lincoln to Speed, January 3, 1842, *CW*, 1:266; Speed to Eliza Speed, February 2, 1841, and March 12, 1841, ALPL, SC 1443b; Mary Todd to Mercy Ann Levering, December [?], 1840; Justin G. Turner and Linda Levitt Turner, *Mary Todd Lincoln: Her Life and Letters* (New York: Knopf, 1972), 20; William H. Herndon and Jesse W. Weik, *Herndon's Lincoln*, ed. Douglas L. Wilson and Rodney O. Davis (Urbana: University of Illinois Press, 2006), 134; Ninian W. Edwards interview with Herndon, September 22, 1865, *HI*, 133.

3. "It is important": Sarah Rickard Barret to Herndon, August 3, 1888, *HI*, 664. "Lincoln's allusion to Sarah": Lincoln to Speed, February 3, 1842, *CW*, 1:268.

4. "Elizabeth Edwards would say": Elizabeth Edwards, interview with Herndon, 1865–1866, *HI*, 444. Breach of promise as a valid form of lawsuit was accepted in Massachusetts in *Wightman v. Coates*, 15 Mass. 1 (1818). The courts of many other states gradually adopted the same opinion. Technically "gender neutral," it became a remedy for jilted women. See W. J. Brockelbank, "The Nature of the Promise to Marry, A Study in Comparative Law," *Illinois Law Review* 41, 1, no. 199 (1946); "Breach of Promise of Marriage," *Law Quarterly Review* 10, no. 135 (1894); "Action for Breach of Promise of Marriage," *Virginia Law Review* 10, no. 361 (1924); "Breach of Promise Suits," *University of Pennsylvania Law Review* 77, no. 474 (1929).

274 7. THE WINTER OF DISCONTENT

5. "One early employee": Wilson and Davis, *Herndon's Lincoln*, 125.

6. "Speed began": Speed to Herndon, September 17, 1866, *HI*, 342. "The point of the ads": Lincoln to Speed, October 22, 1846, *CW*, 1:389–390, though note the many letters in 1843 about Speed's complicated financial dealings from before he left Springfield that Lincoln was then handling for him. See letters of January 18, 1843; March 24, 1843; May 18, 1843; and July 26, 1843: *CW*, 1:305, 319, 323, 325, 328.

7. "A little over": Lincoln to Speed, March 27, 1842, *CW*, 1:282. "As Paul Simon": Paul Simon, *Lincoln's Preparation for Greatness: The Illinois Legislative Years* (Urbana: University of Illinois Press, 1971), 232–236.

8. "In the winter": Speed to Herndon, November 30, 1866, *HI*, 430–431; two interviews in 1865–1866, *HI*, 474–478. The references in the next paragraph also come from these sources.

9. "The issue of Matilda": Speed is clear that "Lincoln did Love Miss Edwards," which must have been something they talked about, but the next sentence is that "'Mary' Saw it," which implies she interpreted it somehow in Lincoln's actions and not something he specifically told her. See Herndon, interview with Speed, 1865–1866, *HI*, 477.

10. Herndon, interview with Speed, 1865–1866, *HI*, 477.

11. Wilson, *Honor's Voice*, 224–225; David Donald, *Lincoln* (New York: Simon and Schuster, 1995), 85.

12. "Lincoln's friend": Michael Burlingame, ed., *An Oral History of Abraham Lincoln: John G. Nicolay's Interviews and Essays* (Carbondale: Southern Illinois University Press, 1995), 1–2; Browning to Herndon, September 22, 1865, *HI*, 133. "Jane D. Bell": Jane D. Bell to Ann Bell, January 27, 1841 (though, as noted, the Bell letter is a problematic source). Michael Burlingame, *Abraham Lincoln: A Life* (Baltimore, Md.: Johns Hopkins University Press, 2008), 1:182–183, who argues instead for the centrality of Matilda as the crucial factor in the broken engagement with Mary, concludes that Lincoln's depression was caused not because of his love for Mary "but because his tyrannical conscience nagged him unmercifully."

13. "A. Y. Ellis": A. Y. Ellis to Herndon, March 24, 1866, *HI*, 238. "Speed said Lincoln": Herndon, interview with Speed, 1865–1866, *HI*, 475; Joshua Speed, *Reminiscences* (Louisville, Ky.: Bradley and Gilbert Co., 1896), 39; cf. Speed to Herndon, February 7, 1866, *HI*, 197. Wilson, *Honor's Voice*, 236 and n. 13 (356–357), quotes Sarah Rickard Barret's 1907 newspaper interview in the *St. Louis Globe-Democrat* in 1907 (in the Lincoln files of the ALPL). In it, Sarah reports her sister Elizabeth's attempted intervention in Lincoln's depression, which suggests she might have also tended to Lincoln, but the remoteness of the source from the event makes it worth noting only in passing.

14. "As the gloom": Simon, *Lincoln's Preparation for Greatness*, 239, points out that Lincoln stopped attending the legislature, then meeting in the court house, between January 13–19. For evidence of his diminished law practice—even as the Supreme Court was in session in Springfield—a perusal of the online records of the Lincoln Legals project shows that Lincoln had only five cases in January and the same small number the next month. Once he began to recover, he resumed his more regular practice of handling thirty-eight cases in March, eleven in April, seventeen in May, and so on.

15. "In two revealing": Lincoln to John Todd Stuart, January 20 and 23, *CW*, 1:228, 229–230. The reference to the job is in the January 23 letter and is vague: "The matter you speak of on my account, you may attend to as you say, unless you shall hear of my condition forbidding it [that is, his depression]. I say this, because I fear I shall be unable to attend to any business here, and a change of scene might help me."

16. "Freud noted": Sigmund Freud, "Mourning and Melancholia," in *The Standard Edition of the Complete Psychological Works of Sigmund Freud*, ed. James Strachey (London: Hogarth, 1956–1974), 14:251, 244.

17. "Speed, however, played": Speed to Herndon, November 30, 1866, *HI*, 431.

18. "But Lincoln also": Lincoln to Levi Davis, April 19, 1837, *CW*, 1:77–78; Resolution Adopted at a Public Meeting Called by Anson G. Henry, June 24, 1837, *CW*, 1:80; Arbitration Award to the State of Illinois Against Anson G. Henry, July 14, 1843, *CW*, 1:327.

19. "One witness": Richard Lawrence Miller, *Lincoln and His World: Prairie Politician, 1834–1842* (Mechanicsburg, Penn.: Stackpole, 2008), 1:458; A. Y. Ellis to Herndon, March 24, 1866, *HI*, 238. "Joshua Wolf Shenk": Joshua Wolf Shenk, *Lincoln's Melancholy: How Depression Challenged a President and Fueled His Greatness* (New York: Mariner, 2005), 57–62. Note Charles Strozier, "Benjamin Rush, Revolutionary Doctor," *American Scholar* 64 (Summer 1995).

20. "Much later Henry": Henry to his wife, February 18, 1863, ALPL. "On January 20": Lincoln to Stuart, January 20, 1841, *CW*, 1:228.

21. "Speed specifically wrote": Speed to Herndon, September 13, 1866, *HI*, 337.

8. KENTUCKY BLUEGRASS

1. "Speed wrote his sister": Joshua to Mary Speed, February 2, 1841, Speed Family Papers—Farmington Collection [Mss A 742e2], FHS. "He complained": Joshua to Eliza Speed, March 12, 1841, SC 1443B, ALPL.

2. "Not long after": Speed to William Butler, May 18, 1841, ALPL.

3. "In any case": Lincoln to Speed, June 19, 1841, *CW*, 1:258.

4. "Farewell Address at Springfield, Illinois," February 11, 1861, *CW*, 4:191. There are three recognized versions of Lincoln's farewell speech at the depot on February 11, 1861 (and other, more spurious, ones). This quote is from the one that appeared in the paper the next day and that Herndon and others felt most accurately reflected what he actually said that day in the misty rain from the back of the train at the depot. The editor of Lincoln's papers, Roy Basler, however, was unable to find verification of its validity. The version of the speech that is usually quoted is one Lincoln began to write down as the train left the depot (and later finished in the handwriting of Nicolay and thus perhaps dictated). It seems Lincoln revised and improved what he had said spontaneously in writing it down. At the very least one can be sure Lincoln said something like this.

5. "And he adds": Joshua to Mary Speed, February 2, 1841, Speed Family Papers—Farmington Collection [Mss A 742e2], FHS.

6. Lincoln to Speed, March 27, 1842, *CW*, 1:282.

7. "He wrote Butler": Speed to William Butler, April 3, 1842, ALPL.

8. "Mary Todd heard": Mary Todd to Mercy Levering, June, 1841, in Justin G. Turner and Linda Levitt Turner, *Mary Todd Lincoln: Her Life and Letters* (New York: Knopf, 1972), 27. "In the family discussions": Census records and the *Records and Memorials of the Speed Family*, FHS; note also Jennifer Cole, "*Semper Eadem*: An Interpretation of the Life and Career of James Speed," Master's Thesis, University of Louisville, 2003, FHS.

9. "The price of hemp": James F. Hopkins, *A History of the Hemp Industry in Kentucky* (Louisville: University of Kentucky Press, 1951), 97. "The price of slaves": "Testimony of James Speed for the American Freedmen's Inquiry Commission," National Archives Microfilm Publication, Microcopy no. 619, Washington, 1965.

10. "John Speed's will": Jefferson County, KY, Inventory and Settlement Book 11, pp. 155–1549, inventoried by James Speed. Photostat copy in John Speed Papers [Mss. C S], FHS.

11. "In Mary Todd's": Mary Todd to Mercy Levering, in Turner and Turner, *Mary Todd Lincoln*, 27. "It was out of character": Herndon interview with Ninian Edwards, 1865–1866, *HI*, 446.

12. "He may have gotten": Speed to Herndon, November 30, 1866, *HI*, 430, makes clear Speed only began to court Fanny sometime after August 18, when Lincoln arrived in Louisville to visit. "From the moment": Lincoln to Speed, March 27, 1842, *CW*, 1:282.

13. "He believed it was": Lincoln to Speed, February 3, 1842, *CW*, 1:269–270.

14. "Stuart's interviews": Stuart, interview with Herndon, July 21, 1865, *HI*, 77. "So Lincoln turned": Lincoln endorsement letter of September 9, 1861, *CW*, first supplement, 98. Logan and Lincoln pleadings begin March 3, although notices of the new partnership did not appear until mid-April in the *Sangamo Journal*. See Earl Schenck Miers, ed., *Lincoln Day-By-Day: A Chronology, 1809–1865* (Washington: Lincoln Sesquicentennial Commission, 1960), 1:156. "Logan, as David Donald": David Donald, *Lincoln* (New York: Simon and Schuster, 1995), 97–98.

15. "He had not been able": Lincoln wrote Stuart: "The matter you speak of on my account, you may attend to as you say, unless you shall hear of my condition forbidding it." Lincoln to Stuart, January 23, 1841, *CW*, 1:229.

16. "The best-documented case": In Lincoln to Speed, June 19, 1841, *CW*, 1:254–258, Lincoln describes what occurred as an "examining trial before May and Lavely," Springfield's mayor and justice of the peace, respectively. An article generally attributed to Lincoln in the *Quincy Whig* (April 15, 1846), *CW*, 1:371, was itself headlined "The Remarkable Case of Arrest for Murder."

17. "Still no body": The specific process Lincoln called an "examining trial" (*CW*, 1:256), or a hearing held by Justice of the Peace William Lavely and Mayor William L. May to determine whether William and Archibald Trailor would be bound over and tried.

18. "The committee offered": The resolution is described in *Lincoln Legals*, newspaper report 125913.

19. "August 18, 1841": Miers, *Lincoln Day-by-Day*, 1:166, which also acknowledges that one can only estimate when Lincoln probably arrived, as there is no documentary evidence, but he was still handling cases in Springfield as late as August 11, so the editors estimate he left the next day for what required about a six-day trip. "He was 'moody'": Speed to Herndon, January 12, 1866, *HI*, 158. "Speed's mother": Speed to Herndon, September 17, 1866, *HI*, 342. "Most of all": Lincoln to Speed, June 19, 1841, *CW*, 1:258. "Recovered finally": Ninian Edwards to Herndon, September 22, 1865, *HI*, 133.

20. "Lincoln was welcomed": Miers, *Lincoln Day-By-Day*, 1:167. "Lincoln came to see me": Speed to Herndon, September 17, 1866, *HI*, 342. "He was assigned a slave": Bryan S. Bush, *Lincoln and the Speeds* (Morely, Mo.: Acclaim, 2008), 21; Donald, *Lincoln*, 88.

21. "In a letter to her": Lincoln to Mary Speed, September 27, 1841, *CW*, 1:259–261. The editor of the *Collected Works*, Roy Basler, 1:261, explains the quotation marks around "Emma," which he wanted to set off, as she was the wife of Joshua's brother Philip and the daughter of George Keats, the brother of the poet John Keats. That connection probably drew Lincoln's attention, given his interest in poetry. James Cornelius, the curator of the Lincoln

Collection at the ALPL, in a personal communication, December 2014, said he feels we have no direct evidence Lincoln was aware of the Keats connection.

22. "She doted on him": Lincoln to Mary Speed, September 27, 1841, *CW*, 1:260–261. "Lucy also connected": Speed to Herndon, September 17, 1866, *HI*, 342.

23. "1846 handbill": Lincoln's "Handbill Replying to Charges of Infidelity," *CW*, 1:382–383.

24. "Lincoln often borrowed": James Speed, *James Speed: A Personality* (Louisville, Ky.: John P. Morton & Company, 1914), 50. "Sometimes Lincoln walked": William H. Townsend, *Lincoln and the Bluegrass: Slavery and Civil War in Kentucky* (Louisville: University of Kentucky Press, 1955), 138. Townsend interviewed George Blackburn Kinkead, the nephew of one of Lincoln's attorneys who remembered the story in the family's oral history.

25. "Joshua wrote his brother": Joshua Speed to James Speed, September 15, 1865, Speed Family Papers [Mss A 742f 11], FHS. "The brothers nourished": "Joshua F. Speed Dead," *Louisville Courier-Journal* (May 30, 1882), FHS, talks of how local blacks loved "Mars Josh."

26. Lincoln to Mary Speed, September 27, 1841, *CW*, 1:261.

27. "Beautiful Fanny": Lincoln to Speed, January 3, 1842, *CW*, 1:266. "Her father, Samuel Henning": Charles P. Stanton, *The Henning and Duke Families of Louisville, Kentucky* (self-published, 1983). I am indebted to Jennifer Cole for locating this book and summarizing the crucial information in it for me.

28. "The lawyer who probated": James P. Helm, "Speech of James P. Helm in the Case of *Henning vs. Stevenson* (The Speed Will Case)," Louisville, F. C. Nunmacher Press. "In a letter Lincoln wrote": Lincoln to Speed, January 3?, 1842, *CW*, 1:266. "Peyton Hoge": Peyton Hoge, "Lincoln Talked to Uncle and Joshua Made Love," *Louisville Courier-Journal* (February 13, 1938); Robert L. Kincaid, "Joshua Fry Speed, 1814–1882, Abraham Lincoln's Most Intimate Friend," *Filson Club History Quarterly* 17 (1943): 16.

9. HOMEWARD BOUND

1. "Lincoln wrote Speed": Lincoln to Speed, February 3, 1842, *CW*, 1:268.

2. "Speed could, of course": Lincoln to Mary Speed, September 27, 1841, *CW*, 1:161, asks Mary if Henning had yet made her promised visit to Farmington.

3. "Speed's family": Lincoln to Mary Speed, September 27, 1841, *CW*, 1:161. "Speed's crisis": Speed to Herndon, November 30, 1866, *HI*, 430.

4. "Moreover, Lincoln": Lincoln to Speed, February 25, 1842, *CW*, 1:281.

5. "On Tuesday": Earl Schenck Miers, ed., *Lincoln Day-By-Day: A Chronology, 1809–1865* (Washington: Lincoln Sesquicentennial Commission, 1960), 1:167; Lincoln to Mary Speed, September 27, 1841, *CW*, 1:260. "That bustling city": Richard Campanella, *Lincoln in New Orleans: The 1828–1831 Flatboat Voyages and Their Place in History* (Lafayette: University of Louisiana at Lafayette Press, 2010), 113.

6. "Not unexpectedly": All the quotes from the letter are from Lincoln to Mary Speed, September 27, 1841, *CW*, 1:259–261.

7. "To prevent runaways": I am indebted to David Traub, who sent me images of four historical markers in Lexington, Louisville, Cheapside Auction Block, and the Emily Thomas Tubman House about the slave trade in Kentucky. Note also Eric Foner, *The Fiery Trial: Abraham Lincoln and American Slavery* (New York: Norton, 2010); and William H. Townsend, *Lincoln and the Bluegrass: Slavery and Civil War in Kentucky* (Louisville: University of Kentucky Press, 1955).

8. "He said in 1864": Lincoln to Albert G. Hodges, April 4, 1864, *CW*, 7:281. "He said in a debate": Lincoln's fourth debate with Douglas at Charleston, Illinois, September 18, 1858, *CW*, 3:145–146.

9. "In a speech he gave": Lincoln's Temperance Address to the Washingtonians, February 22, 1842, *CW*, 1:279. "Around the same time": Lincoln to Williamson Durley, October 3, 1845, *CW*, 1:348.

10. "The increasing political": The discussion that follows of the "Protest in Illinois Legislature on Slavery," March 3, 1837, signed by Lincoln and Dan Stone (*CW*, 1:74–75), draws on the research of Richard Lawrence Miller, *Lincoln and His World: Prairie Politician, 1834–1842* (Mechanicsburg, Penn.: Stackpole, 2008), 1:137–145; and Brian Dirck, "Lincoln's Kentucky Childhood and Race," *Register of Kentucky Historical Society* 106, no. 3/4 (Summer/Autumn 2008): 307–332.

11. "Of three proposals": James Oakes, *The Scorpion's Sting: Antislavery and the Coming of the Civil War* (New York: Norton, 2014), 13. "Lincoln took a public stand": Lincoln to John Hill, September, 1860, *CW*, 4:104–108. "When Lincoln was": January 10, 1849, *CW*, 2:20–22. "After 1854": Oakes, *Scorpion's Sting*, 85.

12. "On the road": Foner, *Fiery Trial*, 36.

13. "John Locke Scripps": James Riley, *An Authentic Narrative* (New York: Skyhorse, 2007). A good account of the impact of the book is Donald J. Ratcliffe, "Selling Captain Riley, 1816–1859: How Did His 'Narrative' Become So Well Known?" *Proceedings of the American Antiquarian Society* (2007).

14. "A. H. Chapman, a relative": A. H. Chapman to Herndon, September 8, 1865, *HI*, 100. "In 1827, while he was": Leland R. Johnson and Charles E.

Parrish, "Triumph at the Falls: The Louisville and Portland Canal," Louisville District, U.S. Army Corps of Engineers, Louisville, Kentucky, 2007.

15. "Thomas Lincoln himself": A. H. Chapman to Herndon, September 8, 1865, *HI*, 100; and Campanella, *Lincoln in New Orleans*, 32. "Lincoln's trips": Campanella, *Lincoln in New Orleans*.

16. "It appears from": Lincoln, "Autobiography," *CW*, 4:62. "The blacks were": Campanella, *Lincoln in New Orleans*, 78–82.

17. "After both flatboat trips": Campanella, *Lincoln in New Orleans*, 111–112, 113–117, 217–221. "John Hanks told Herndon": Herndon interview with John Hanks, 1865–66, *HI*, 457–458. "Hanks's account": Lincoln, "Autobiography," *CW*, 4:64.

18. "Lincoln also encountered": Richard E. Hart, "Springfield's African Americans as Part of the Lincoln Community," *Journal of the Abraham Lincoln Association* 20 (1999): 35–54.

19. "Lincoln also dealt": Carl Adams, "Lincoln's First Freed Slave: A Review of *Bailey v. Cromwell*, 1841," *Journal of the Illinois State Historical Society* 101 (Fall/Winter 2008): 235–259. The Matson case is covered in any number of books and articles, but see esp. Foner, *Fiery Trial*, 48–50.

20. "The *Lebanon*, carrying": Miers, *Lincoln Day-by-Day*, 1:167. "It is also possible": Octavia Roberts, "We All Knew Abraham," *Abraham Lincoln Quarterly* 4, no. 1 (March 1946): 28.

21. "A toothache": Lincoln to Mary Speed, September 27, 1841, *CW*, 1:260–261. "The very next day": Miers, *Lincoln Day-by-Day*, 1:167–174. For the discussion of the documented case of Speed traveling with Lincoln, see chap. 3, above. "Furthermore, Speed": Joshua to Mary Speed, October 31, 1841, Speed Family Papers [Mss C Sa], FHS.

22. "On October 20, the two": "Call for Whig State Convention" (drafted by Lincoln) October 20, 1841, printed in the *Sangamo Journal* (October 22, 1841), *CW*, 1:261–262. "He was not interested": *Sangamo Journal* (October 29, 1841); announcement in *Sangamo Journal* (November 12, 1841); see also Miers, *Lincoln Day-by-Day*, 1:171. "He announced": Miers, *Lincoln Day-by-Day*, 1:169.

23. "In the *Sangamo Journal*": *Sangamo Journal* (October 15, 1841). "Early the next year": *Sangamo Journal* (January 28, 1842).

24. "Speed thus wrote": Joshua to Mary Speed, October 31, 1841, Speed Family Papers [Mss C Sa], FHS. "The supposed suspense": Lincoln to Mary Speed, September 27, 1841, *CW*, 1:261.

25. The classic statement on the mourning process is Sigmund Freud, "Mourning and Melancholia," in *The Standard Edition of the Complete Psychological Works of Sigmund Freud*, ed. James Strachey (London: Hogarth, 1956–1974), 14:243–258. Note also George H. Pollock, "Anniversary Reactions, Trauma, and Mourning," *Psychoanalytic Quarterly* 39 (1970): 347–371; John

Bowlby, *Attachment and Loss: Volume 3: Loss, Sadness, and Depression* (London: Hogarth, 1980); and many other sources in contemporary psychoanalysis that focus on trauma and recovery.

10. A VICARIOUS ROMANCE

1. "he allways thanked": Abner Y. Ellis to Herndon, January 30, 1866, *HI*, 180. "As 1841 ended": Speed to Herndon, September 17, 1866, *HI*, 342; Joshua Speed, *Reminiscences* (Louisville, Ky.: Bradley and Gilbert Co., 1896), 5. "As he explicitly": Speed to Herndon, November 30, 1866, *HI*, 430.

2. "Lincoln wrote": Lincoln to Speed, January 3?, 1842, *CW*, 1:265–266. "Roy Basler": Basler's footnote, *CW*, 1:266, n. 1. "In fact, there": Joshua Speed to Herndon, September 17, 1866, *HI*, 342.

3. "Lincoln cannot even know": James C. Conkling to Mercy Ann Levering, October 24, 1840, Box 71, ALPL.

4. "An old New Salem": William G. Greene interview with Herndon, May 30, 1865, *HI*, 17.

5. "An Address, Delivered before the Springfield Washington Temperance Society, on the 22nd of February, 1842," *CW*, 1:271–279.

6. "Concerns of many observers": Note the recent study by Charles White, *Lincoln and Prohibition* (CreateSpace Independent Publishing, 2014).

7. "In late March": Lincoln to Speed, March 27, 1842, *CW*, 1:282–283.

11. MARY TODD, ONCE AGAIN

1. "Lincoln was emotionally freer": Benjamin P. Thomas, "Lincoln's Humor: An Analysis," *Journal of the Abraham Lincoln Association* 3 (1981).

2. "But there was": Lincoln to Speed, March 27, 1842, *CW*, 1:282.

3. "Lincoln's next letter": Lincoln to Speed, April 13, 1842, *CW*, 1:284–285. "Lincoln's July 4 letter": Lincoln to Speed, July 4, 1842, *CW*, 1:288–290.

4. "Mary Todd, meanwhile": Ruth Painter Randall, *The Courtship of Mr. Lincoln* (Boston: Little, Brown, 1957), 173. "She did continue": Mary Todd to Mercy Levering, June 1841, in Justin G. Turner and Linda Levitt Turner, *Mary Todd Lincoln: Her Life and Letters* (New York: Knopf, 1972), 25–28.

5. "Douglas Wilson has argued": Douglas L. Wilson, *Honor's Voice: The Transformation of Abraham Lincoln* (New York: Knopf, 1998), 283–286, follows the second- and third-hand reports of Sarah Rickard, another of Christopher Brown, and that of his mother-in-law reporting that John T. Stuart played a significant role in getting Mary and Lincoln together. It is worth noting that

Wilson is more interested in the background to the Rebecca letters than he is in refuting the story of whether the Francises brought Lincoln and Mary together in the summer of 1842; note esp. the crux of his argument, 273–274, 283–286. Wilson's argument about honor trumping love is the point of his book. It recycles Herndon, who said of Lincoln's decision to marry Mary Todd: "At last he stood face to face with the great conflict between honor and domestic peace. He chose the former." William H. Herndon and Jesse W. Weik, *Herndon's Lincoln*, ed. Douglas L. Wilson and Rodney O. Davis (Urbana: University of Illinois Press, 2006), 145.

6. "Herndon, based on": Herndon and Weik, *Herndon's Lincoln*, 143–144. "Octavia Roberts talked": Octavia Roberts, "We All Knew Abraham," *Abraham Lincoln Quarterly* 4, no. 1 (March 1946): 27; note Herndon interview with Elizabeth and Ninian Edwards, July 27, 1887, *HI*, 623, which reports the role of Henry.

7. "Mary replied": Herndon and Weik, *Herndon's Lincoln*, 144.

8. The most recent biography of Shields is J. Sean Callan, *Courage and Country: James Shields, More Than Irish Luck* (Bloomington, Ind.: First Books Library, 2004), which is badly written but well researched and complete. Except where otherwise noted, the facts of Shields's life come from Callan, though Shields enters the Lincoln story in the writings of all biographers.

9. William Henry Condon, *Life of Major-General James Shields: Hero of Three Wars and Senator from Three States* (Chicago: Blakley Printing Co., 1900), 11.

10. "Herndon said": Herndon and Weik, *Herndon's Lincoln*, 184; cf. Wilson, *Honor's Voice*, 267. "He was a regular": Mary Todd Lincoln to Francis Bicknell Carpenter, December 8, 1865, in Turner and Turner, *Mary Todd Lincoln*, 298–299; cf. Mary Todd Lincoln to Josiah G. Holland, Chicago, December 4, 1865, in ibid., 293.

11. "The first Rebecca letter": *CW*, 1:291–292, n. 2.

12. "He wrote": Lincoln's Rebecca letter, August 27, 1842, *CW*, 1:291–297. The circular issued by the state was dated August 20, but it appeared in the paper only on August 26.

13. "In this interval": As Roy Basler points out in *CW*, 1:292, n. 2, two more Rebecca letters appeared on September 9. One was mild in its satire and in the "same vein" as the first letter that appeared. It is the fourth letter in the sequence, however, that is brutal in its taunts of Shields and was written by Jayne, probably with some help from Mary Todd. "Butler, though cryptic": Michael Burlingame, ed., *An Oral History of Abraham Lincoln: John G. Nicolay's Interviews and Essays* (Carbondale: Southern Illinois University Press, 1995), 24.

14. "Shields's unwanted advances": *Sangamo Journal* (September 9, 1842).

15. "Mary wrote later": Mary Todd Lincoln to Josiah G. Holland, Chicago, December 4, 1865, in Turner and Turner, *Mary Todd Lincoln*, 293. "And in another letter": Mary Todd Lincoln to Francis Bicknell Carpenter, December 8, 1865, in Turner and Turner, *Mary Todd Lincoln*, 298–299. "William Butler corroborated": Burlingame, *Oral History*, 24.

16. "Since Lincoln was": The letters of Shields here and below are in footnotes Roy Basler provides in *CW* 1:299–300. They were first published in the *Sangamo Journal* in October 1842 and then appeared in Herndon and Weik, *Herndon's Lincoln*, 193–194.

17. "When Whiteside returned": Lincoln to Shields, September 17, 1842, *CW*, 1:299.

18. "Lincoln seemed both": Lincoln's "Memorandum of Duel Instructions to Elias H. Merryman," September 19, 1842, *CW*, 1:300–302. On Merryman egging on Lincoln, see Albert Beveridge, *Abraham Lincoln, 1809–1858* (Cambridge, Mass.: Riverside, 1928), 334–354. Burlingame found a newspaper story from 1876 (and thus late) in which Lincoln's then friend and colleague Albert Taylor Bledsoe claimed to have suggested the use of broadswords, though, since Bledsoe served during the Civil War as the Confederacy's assistant secretary of war, one can question his credibility. Michael Burlingame, *Abraham Lincoln: A Life* (Baltimore, Md.: Johns Hopkins University Press, 2008), 1:191.

19. "Lincoln later told": Usher F. Linder, *Reminiscences of the Early Bench and Bar of Illinois* (Chicago: Chicago Legal News, 1879), 66–67.

20. "Quite a few colleagues": An excellent account of all these details is Beveridge, *Abraham Lincoln*, 334–354. Note also Wilson, *Honor's Voice*, 272–83, and Burlingame, *Lincoln*, 1:190–94.

21. "It has been noted": Albert Beveridge, *Abraham Lincoln, 1809–1858* (Boston: Houghton Mifflin, 1928), 1:353. "Lincoln had a history": Wilson, *Honor's Voice*, 298–302, summarizes these earlier examples. "Mary said later": Mary Todd Lincoln to Josiah G. Holland, in Turner and Turner, *Mary Todd Lincoln*, 293. "Once during": David Donald, *Lincoln* (New York: Simon and Schuster, 1995), 92. "Speed later told": Herndon interview with Speed, June 10, 1865?, *HI*, 31.

22. "The only thing": Herndon and Weik, *Herndon's Lincoln*, 165. "Less than a week": Lincoln to Speed, October 5, 1842, *CW*, 1:302–303.

23. "Was the issue": Lincoln to John J. Hardin, May 11, 1843, *CW*, 1:323.

24. "Lincoln wrote Speed": Lincoln to Speed, October 5, 1842, *CW*, 1:303.

25. "Assuming Speed": Most of the details in what follows are from Randall, *Courtship*, 202–212; and Wilson, *Honor's Voice*, 291–292. Cf. Mrs. B. T. Edwards to Ida Tarbell, October 8, 1895, Tarbell papers (online); and Elizabeth Edwards interview with Herndon, 1865–1866?, *HI*, 444. For what is by far the most negative description of the wedding and of Mary herself in the

Lincoln literature, including affirming the unlikely theory of Wayne C. Temple that Mary seduced Lincoln on November 3 and forced him to marry her the next day, see Burlingame, *Lincoln*, 1:194–212.

26. "Lincoln wrote Speed": Lincoln to Speed, May 18, 1843, *CW*, 1:325. Note James T. Hickey, "The Lincolns' Globe Tavern: A Study in Tracing the History of a Nineteenth-Century Building," in *Collected Writings of James T. Hickey* (Illinois State Historical Library, 1990). Robert was born August 1, 1843.

27. "Nothing new here": Lincoln to Samuel D. Marshall, November 11, 1842, *CW*, 1:305. Wilson, *Honor's Voice*, 292, says this line of Lincoln's reflected his "numbed astonishment." That is a surprising interpretation. To be numb psychologically is *not* to feel; in fact it is actively to suppress feeling and cut yourself off from them. Lincoln, on the contrary, seemed to be expressing the deepest of feelings—and joy—after a long struggle.

12. THE CRUCIBLE OF GREATNESS

1. This idea of solving for all what he couldn't solve for himself alone is from Erik Erikson, *Young Man Luther: A Study in Psychoanalysis and History* (New York: Norton, 1955), a construct at the heart of my earlier study, *Lincoln's Quest for Union: A Psychological Study*, 2nd ed. (Philadelphia: Paul Dry Books, 2000), esp. 155, but really it is the argument of much of the book.

2. "Meanwhile, back in": John Gilmer Speed, introduction to Joshua Speed, *Reminiscences* (Louisville, Ky.: Bradley and Gilbert Co., 1896), 5–6; and Gary Lee Williams, *James and Joshua Speed: Lincoln's Kentucky Friends*, PhD diss., Duke University (Ann Arbor, Mich.: University Microfilms, 1971), 37. "It was a lovely": The number of slaves Speed owned is listed in the Jefferson County Tax List for the Southern District, compiled by Pen Bogert, "Joshua Speed: Chronology of Slave Ownership," and shared with me on April 25, 2013.

3. "Brother James Speed": James Speed to his mother, Lucy, April 30, 1865, Speed Family Papers [Mss A S 742f 8], FHS. "When absent from her": John Gilmer Speed, introduction to Speed, *Reminiscences*, 12. Note also John Gilmer Speed, "Mr. Lincoln's Closest Friend," *Louisville Courier-Journal* (June 23, 1895).

4. Speed to William Butler, April 3, 1842, ALPL.

5. "A few months": Lincoln to Speed, April 13, 1842, *CW*, 1:284. "Collecting on Speed's": Lincoln to Speed, January 18, March 24, May 18, and July 26, 1843, *CW*, 1:305–306, 319, 323–325, 328. "Shawneetown paper," state bank notes that fluctuated notoriously in value, constituted the original stimulus for Lincoln's 1842 near-duel with State Auditor Shields. Lincoln criticized Shields's refusal to accept these notes for payment of taxes. Payment in

stable-value specie would be greatly preferred. Lincoln was basically reporting payment at a discount in mostly weak money.

6. "Lincoln adds": Lincoln to Speed, October 22, 1846, CW, 1:389–391.

7. "Initially after their marriages": The 1843 letters are Lincoln to Speed,
January 18, March 24, May 18, and July 26, CW, 1:305–306, 319, 323–325, 328.
"The planned visit": Gary Lee Williams, "James and Joshua Speed: Lincoln's
Kentucky Friends," Ph.D. diss., Duke University, 1971, 37. "The two friends":
Speed to Herndon, April 18, 1848; Lincoln Legals Online, document no. 94784,
has Speed writing to Herndon, who was clearly handling all matters relating
to Speed, demanding testily that he be paid a $5 arbitrary rebate for the loss
of a promissory note and an insistence that Lincoln owed him $86.57. Speed
also wrote Lincoln, February 13, 1849, LoC, responding to a request from Lincoln (since lost) in which he enlists Speed to use his influence with Governor
John J. Crittenden regarding an appointment issue with which Lincoln was
concerned as his congressional term ended. "Lincoln and Mary": Earl Schenck
Miers, ed., Lincoln Day-By-Day: A Chronology, 1809–1865 (Washington:
Lincoln Sesquicentennial Commission, 1960), 1:295. Robert L. Kincaid,
"Joshua Fry Speed," Filson Club History Quarterly 17 (1943): 63–123, speculates
the Lincolns went on to Farmington with the Speeds, which is highly unlikely,
since the Speeds weren't living there at the time.

8. "Butler also invested": e.g., Speed to Butler, March 24, April 3, and July
7, 1842, ALPL. I am indebted to James Cornelius for sharing his unpublished
paper about Butler based on a talk to the Sangamon County Historical Society, March 2011. Cornelius is the curator of the Lincoln Collection at the
ALPL, and his talk summarizes a large new trove received recently by the
ALPL of Butler papers—over 1,100 pieces—which includes letters, receipts,
and other documents.

9. Speed to Butler, April 3, 1842, ALPL.

10. "James had found": James to Lucy Speed, January 9, 1848, Speed Family Papers [Mss. C Sa], FHS. For the general discussion of the Kentucky slave
debate in this and the following paragraphs, see Jennifer Cole, "For the Sake
of the Songs of the Men Made Free: James Speed and the Emancipationists'
Dilemma in Nineteenth-Century Kentucky," Ohio Valley History Journal 4, no.
4 (Winter 2004): 27–48; Jennifer Cole, "Semper Eadem: An Interpretation of
the Life and Political Career of James Speed, 1812–1887," master's thesis, University of Louisville, 2003; and Williams, "James and Joshua Speed," 44–53.

11. "As he wrote his sister": Joshua to Mary Speed, February 25, 1849,
Speed Family Papers, 1797–1882 [Mss. C S], FHS.

12. "His nephew said": Introduction to Speed, Reminiscences, 5–6.

13. "As a result": Louisville City Directory for 1852, p. 233, courtesy Jennifer Cole of FHS, and her e-mail to me on May 24, 2013, about the other Speed

residences. Cole conducted research in the available Louisville city directories for 1832–1869 and the United Federal Census for 1850, 1860, 1870, and 1880. "Everyone attested": Introduction to Speed, *Reminiscences*, 5–6. "Besides his involvement": Williams, "James and Joshua Speed," 62. The number of slaves Speed owned is listed in the Jefferson County Tax List for the Southern District, compiled by Pen Bogert, "Joshua Speed: Chronology of Slave Ownership," Filson Historical Files, "Historic Homes—KY—Jefferson Co.—Farmington—African Americans," FHS.

14. "In 1864 and 1865": Pen Bogert, Jefferson County Tax Lists, 1850–1865.

15. "Some questions": I am indebted to Pen Bogert in an e-mail of May 26, 2013, for clarifying the details in this paragraph. "Speed also regularly": Bogert et al., Farmington brochure, 4.

16. "He would eventually": Williams, "James and Joshua Speed," 68, argues that Speed was a Democrat by 1855, but there is no direct evidence for this assertion, and Williams's citation at this point is to E. Merton Coulter, *The Civil War and Readjustment in Kentucky* (Chapel Hill, 1926), 62–63, who makes this claim based on his read of the internal references in Lincoln's 1855 letter to Speed. That seems a stretch.

17. "Lincoln's reply": Lincoln to Speed, August 24, 1855, *CW*, 2:320–323.

18. "On September 22": Speed to Lincoln, May 19, 1860, LoC.

19. "After the raucous Republican convention": Speed to Lincoln, May 19, 1860, LoC. "Lincoln, however, replied": Lincoln to Speed, May 22, 1860, photostat copy, Speed Family Papers [Mss. A S 742e 9], FHS.

20. "Shelby Foote": Quoted in the 1990 PBS series on the Civil War by Ken Burns and also in Geoffrey C. Ward, with Ric Burns and Ken Burns, *The Civil War: An Illustrated History* (New York: Knopf, 1990). It seems, however, that the first to note this change in language was Basil Lanneau Gildersleeve, a classics scholar and former confederate soldier, in a 1909 lecture, quoted in Ward W. Briggs Jr., *Soldier and Scholar: Basil Lanneau Gildersleeve and the Civil War* (Charlottesville: University of Virginia Press, 1998), 22. "If elected, Lincoln": Doris Kearns Goodwin, *Team of Rivals: The Political Genius of Abraham Lincoln* (New York: Simon & Schuster, 2006).

21. "Speed dealt with this": Speed to Lincoln, November 14, 1860, LoC.

22. "Lincoln wrote Speed": Lincoln to Speed, November 19, 1860, *CW*, 4:141. "Herndon suggests": William H. Herndon and Jesse W. Weik, *Herndon's Lincoln*, ed. Douglas L. Wilson and Rodney O. Davis (Urbana: University of Illinois Press, 2006), 284–286. "Joshua and Fanny": Miers, *Lincoln Day-by-Day*, tracks Lincoln's time in Chicago but doesn't specifically mention his meeting with Speed, but it appears from the functions he attended that the meeting with Speed was just after he arrived. "Speed says": Herndon interview with Speed, 1865–1866, *HI*, 475.

23. "In that regard": Herndon interview with Speed, 1865–1866, *HI*, 475. Note also Ward Hill Lamon, *Recollections of Abraham Lincoln, 1847–1865* (1872; Lincoln: University of Nebraska Press, 1994), 286.

24. "Speed, modest as ever": Speed to Herndon, February 7, 1866, *HI*, 197.

25. "Kentucky was central": Lincoln to Orville Browning, *CW*, 4: 531–532. "As a slave state": William C. Harris, *Lincoln and the Border States: Preserving the Union* (Lawrence: University Press of Kansas, 2011), 82–83. Note also William Gienapp, "Abraham Lincoln and the Border States," *Journal of the Abraham Lincoln Association* 13 (1992); and Lincoln to Orville Browning, *CW*, 4:531–552.

26. "The governor, however": Speed to Lincoln, May 27, 1860, ALPL.

27. "Speed wrote Lincoln a bit later": Speed to Lincoln, September 17, 1861, LoC. "Lincoln was persuaded": Williams, "James and Joshua Speed," 84–92; Williams quotes Daniel Stevenson, "General Nelson, Kentucky, and Lincoln Guns," *Magazine of American History* 10 (1883): 119, as someone directly involved in the project; note also Speed to Lincoln, May 29 and August 25, 1861, LoC.

28. "James Speed, for example": Williams, "James and Joshua Speed," 97.

29. "On September 1" and "Two days later": Speed to Lincoln, September 1 and 3, LoC. "It is unlikely": Lincoln to Fremont, September 11, 1861, *CW*, 4:531–532.

30. "In May 1861": Joshua Speed to Joseph Holt, May 24, 1861, container 28, Holt Papers, LC. A good recent book about Holt is Elizabeth D. Leonard, *Lincoln's Forgotten Ally, Judge Advocate General Joseph Holt of Kentucky* (Chapel Hill: University of North Carolina Press, 2011). "During the uproar": Joshua F. Speed to Joseph Holt, September 7, 1861, container 30, Holt Papers, LC. "Speed was impressed": James Speed to Joseph Holt, September 20, 1861, container 30, Holt Papers, LC.

31. "Your chances for": Joshua F. Speed to Joseph Holt, December 8, 1861, container 31, Holt Papers, LC. "David Donald": David Donald, *"We Are Lincoln Men": Abraham Lincoln and His Friends* (New York: Simon and Schuster, 2003), 61.

32. "On September 24": William Anderson to Speed, September 24, 1861, LoC. "On October 9": Speed telegram to Lincoln, October 10, 1861, LoC. "And in the same month": Williams, "James and Joshua Speed," 111, says the story came from Sherman, who after the war told it to G. C. Kniffen. He in turn wrote, with W. H. Perrin and W. H. Battle, *Kentucky: A History of the State* (1888), 382, which reports the story.

33. "He continued to": Speed to Lincoln, October 10, November 5, November 22 (with J. F. Bullitt), 1861, and September 17, 1862, LoC; Williams, "James and Joshua Speed," 126. For Speed's dislike of the Emancipation Proclamation, see his letter to Herndon, February 7, 1866, *HI*, 195.

34. "Lincoln told Speed": Speed to Herndon, February 7, 1866, *HI*, 197.

35. "Joshua continued to write": Speed to Lincoln, February 24, May 1, 3, 6, and 19, June 15, and December 5, 1864, LoC. "He also committed himself": Williams, "James and Joshua Speed," 132–136.

36. "As they had": Introduction to Speed, *Reminiscences*, 11–12.

37. "While in Washington": Joshua to James Speed, December 22, March 21, March 25, March 29, April 2, June 17, June 28, July 1, July 10, September 15, September 26, 1865, Speed Family Papers [Mss. A S742f 12, 14. 15], FHS. "Whenever Joshua leaves": James to Lucy Speed, November 5, 1865, Speed Family Papers [Mss. A S742f 12], FHS. "James in general": James Speed [grandson], *James Speed: A Personality* (Louisville, Ky.: John P. Morton, 1914). "James was a dutiful son": James to Lucy Speed, December 3, 1865, Speed Family Papers [Mss. A S742f 12], FHS.

38. "In the context of": Joshua to James Speed, September 5, 1865, Speed Family Papers [Mss. A S742f 11], FHS. "In another letter": Joshua to James Speed, February 18, 1866, Speed Family Papers [Mss. A S742f 13], FHS.

39. "Speed suffered": Jefferson County Death Records for 1882, p. 230, FHS.

40. "With his devout": "Joshua F. Speed Dead," *Louisville Courier-Journal* (May 30, 1882), FHS.

41. "In the end": "Burial of Mr. Speed," *Louisville Courier-Journal* (June 1, 1882); "Ready for Settlement: Final Report of the Commissioner on the Late Joshua F. Speed's Estate," *Louisville Courier-Journal* (June 22, 1882). "She in turn": Obituary for Fanny Speed, *Louisville Courier-Journal* (August 12, August 18, September 21, 1902), FHS.

CONCLUSIONS: ON FRIENDSHIP

1. Aristotle, *Nicomachean Ethics*, trans. W. D. Ross (New York: World Library Classics, 2009), book 8, 128–145, esp. 128–133.

2. *Essays of Michel de Montaigne*, trans. Michael Cotton, ed. William Carew Hazlitt (online).

3. Elizabeth Edwards and Ninian W. Edwards, interview with Herndon, July 27, 1871, *HI*, 623.

4. I want to thank Robert Jay Lifton, who, in an interview on February 2, 2015, had this idea of a "third level of friendship." Scott Atran, in an interview on February 4, 2015, added for me the rich anthropological context of male friendship, including in war.

5. In chapter 2, I note that the best historian of this subject is E. Anthony Rotundo, *American Manhood: Transformations in Masculinity from the*

Revolution to the Modern Era (New York: Basic Books, 1993). See also Patricia O'Toole, *The Five Hearts: An Intimate Portrait of Henry Adams and His Friends, 1880–1918* (New York: Clarkson Potter, 1990); Brenda Wineapple, *Hawthorne: A Life* (New York: Random House, 2003); Edwin Haviland Miller, *Salem in My Dwelling Place* (Iowa City: University of Iowa Press, 1991); Jean Baker, *James Buchanan* (The American Presidents Series, 2004); and Matthew Hollis, "Edward Thomas, Robert Frost, and the Road to War," *Guardian* (February 18, 2015).

6. Carroll Smith-Rosenberg, "The Female World of Love and Ritual: Relations Between Women in Nineteenth-Century America," *Signs: Journal of Women in Culture and Society* 1, no. 1 (1975): 1–29. Smith-Rosenberg elaborated some of these themes in *Disorderly Conduct: Visions of Gender in Victorian America* (New York: Oxford University Press, 1986).

7. Erik Erikson, *Young Man Luther: A Study in Psychoanalysis and History* (New York: Norton, 1955), first introduced the idea of a moratorium in the delayed struggles of Martin Luther.

8. Speed to Herndon, February 7, 1866, *HI*, 197.

INDEX

Page numbers preceded by "insert" refer to illustrations and photographs from insert pages.

266*n*3; "The Devil's Drive," 256*n*7;
as Abraham Lincoln's favorite, 31,
45, 48, 77, 98, 256*n*7; Joshua Speed's
resemblance to, 28, 255–56*n*3

Calhoun, John, 50, 55, 154
Callan, J. Sean, 282*n*8
Cameron, Simon, 226, 228
Campanella, Richard, 157
Campbell, Ann, 94
Campbell, Antrim, 94
capitalism, 118
Carpenter, William, 38
Chapman, Augustus H., 68, 156, 263*n*11
Chapman, Harriet Hanks, 68, 263*n*11
Chatterton's jewelry shop, Springfield,
206
Civil War, 54, 198, 204, 222, 225–27, 231,
243–44
Clarke, James Freeman, 18, 56
Clarkson, James, 81
Clarkson, Nancy, 81
Clarkson v. Clarkson (1860), 81
Clary Grove Boys, 3
Clay, Henry, 30, 93, 98, 215, 223
clinical depression, xv–xvi, 124, 125
Cogdal, Isaac, 69–70
Conkling, James C., 94, 95, 100, 102–3,
111
Constitutional Union Press, 230
Cook, John, 94
Coulter, E. Merton, 286*n*16
Cowan, Alison Leigh, 267*n*6
crimes against nature, 38
Crittenden, John J., 285*n*7
Cummings, Thomas Seir, miniature
painting of John Speed, insert 2
Current, Richard, 75

Danville, Illinois, 35
Darling, Ephraim, 20
Davis, Cullom, 81
Davis, David, 35, 77, 83
Davis, Eliza, 141–42, 189
Davis, Rodney, xii
Davis, Susan Fry Speed (sister), 13, 134,
142
Davis, William S., 38

de Fleurville, William (Billy the Barber),
158, 206
Democratic Party: and defenestration in
special session, 122; and Archer Herndon, 54; Jacksonians, 24, 138; Peace
Democrats, 230; political battles
over economic crisis, 124; and James
Shields, 197–98; and slavery debate,
218; and Joshua Speed, 218, 219, 222,
223, 230, 286*n*16; and Joshua Speed's
store, 50, 51, 55–56; and John Tyler,
138; and Van Buren, 192
depression: clinical depression, xv–xvi,
124, 125; emasculation associated
with, 128, 182; of Abraham Lincoln,
14, 54, 60–63, 66, 69, 71–72, 76–77,
78, 89–90, 99, 113, 122, 123–27, 128,
129, 130, 133–34, 137, 140, 142–43,
147, 163, 172, 178, 182, 194, 229, 234,
240, 241–42, 244–45, 274*n*13, 275*n*14,
275*n*15; of Mary Todd Lincoln, 243;
and self-esteem, 129–30; of Joshua
Speed, 14, 69, 77, 78, 128–29, 130,
148–49, 169, 170–71, 172; of Fanny
Henning Speed, 145; of James Speed,
14, 232; treatment of, 126
Derickson (captain), 258*n*17
diabetes, 233
Dickens, Charles, 18
divorce: effect on women, 97; settlements in nineteenth century, 82,
267*n*5
Donald, David, 53, 122, 138, 165, 228
Douglas, Stephen A.: debates of 1858,
41, 55, 153, 182, 279*n*8; and Matilda
Edwards, 103; and election of 1860,
222, 229; and Kansas-Nebraska bill,
218; and Mary Todd Lincoln, 91, 98;
portrait of, insert 8; rivalry with
Abraham Lincoln, 21, 51, 55, 59; and
James Shields, 197; and Joshua
Speed's store, 50, 52, 55, 56, 133;
untrue charges against Abraham
Lincoln, 41
Drake, Daniel, 44, 88–90, 125, 126,
268*n*16, 269*n*18
Dresser, Charles, 206
duels, 55, 102, 197, 200, 202–4

271*nn*13, 16, 20, 272*n*21, 274*n*11, 281*n*5, 282*n*10, 283*nn*20, 21, 25, 284*n*27; on Abraham Lincoln and Nancy Burner, 266*n*3; on Abraham Lincoln's broken engagement with Mary Todd Lincoln, 91, 271*n*19, 272*n*27; and Abraham Lincoln's correspondence, 165; on Abraham Lincoln's depression, 61, 122; on Abraham Lincoln's engagement with Mary Todd Lincoln, 100, 271*n*14; on Abraham Lincoln's marriage, 284*n*27; on Abraham Lincoln's reuniting with Mary Todd Lincoln, 195–96, 281–82*n*5; on Abraham Lincoln with prostitutes, 268*n*12; on Mary Todd Lincoln, 195–96; *Lincoln Before Washington*, 271*n*19; "That Fatal First . . ." in *Lincoln Before Washington*, 270–71*n*14, 272*n*27; "William H. Herndon and Mary Todd Lincoln," *Journal of the Abraham Lincoln Association*, 249*n*1

Wilson, Robert, 61, 77

women: breach-of-promise lawsuits, 116, 273*n*4; characteristics of friendship, xiv, 236; and "cult of domesticity," 238; "Cult of True Womanhood," 85; customary age at marriage, 96–97; decision on marriage, 97; and friendship in nineteenth century, 239, 258*n*21; lyceums open to, 49; pregnancies before marriage, 268*n*11